Praise for *The Missing Billionaires*

This is a marvelous book that importantly extends the literature on financial decision-making. The authors creatively weave together the essence of practical considerations with insightful academic theory. One of a small handful of books that is timeless and should be read and reread over a lifetime for enjoyment and substance.

—Gary P. Brinson, CFA, Author, and
Founder of Brinson Partners

The missing billionaires in the book's title allude to the difficulty of keeping already-made fortunes. Believing that nobody should get rich twice, Victor and James arm investors with lessons galore, drawn from their long practitioner careers. Yet the core lessons come from academia, and this wonderful book gives the best shot for Expected Utility and lifecycle models to finally become widely used in real-world investment decision-making. Uniquely, this book puts position sizing in the center, showing through many illustrations how "too much of a good thing" can be just too much.

—Antti Ilmanen, Principal at AQR Capital,
Author of *Expected Returns*

The Missing Billionaires addresses a topic that gets far too little attention in the investment community: how much to invest. The book is a terrific blend of theory, practice, and stories from the front lines. This is must-reading for anyone seeking to invest and spend wisely.

—Michael Mauboussin, Author and Head of
Consilient Research, Morgan Stanley

I enjoyed and learned from Victor and James' book on incorporating uncertainty directly into making better financial decisions. Rightly so, for them, risk is front and center. This book is a great education for all of us, seamlessly marrying sophisticated theory with applications, demonstrating the beauty of a risk architecture that combines specificity with illuminating implementations into the lifetime wealth management problem.

—Myron S. Scholes, Frank E. Buck Professor of Finance,
Emeritus, Stanford Graduate School of Business,
Nobel Laureate in Economic Sciences

THE MISSING BILLIONAIRES

THE MISSING BILLIONAIRES

A GUIDE TO BETTER
FINANCIAL DECISIONS

VICTOR HAGHANI

JAMES WHITE

WILEY

Published by John Wiley & Sons, Inc., Hoboken, New Jersey.
Published simultaneously in Canada.

No part of this publication may be reproduced, stored in a retrieval system, or transmitted in any form or by any means, electronic, mechanical, photocopying, recording, scanning, or otherwise, except as permitted under Section 107 or 108 of the 1976 United States Copyright Act, without either the prior written permission of the Publisher, or authorization through payment of the appropriate per-copy fee to the Copyright Clearance Center, Inc., 222 Rosewood Drive, Danvers, MA 01923, (978) 750-8400, fax (978) 750-4470, or on the web at www.copyright.com. Requests to the Publisher for permission should be addressed to the Permissions Department, John Wiley & Sons, Inc., 111 River Street, Hoboken, NJ 07030, (201) 748-6011, fax (201) 748-6008, or online at http://www.wiley.com/go/permission.

Trademarks: Wiley and the Wiley logo are trademarks or registered trademarks of John Wiley & Sons, Inc. and/or its affiliates in the United States and other countries and may not be used without written permission. All other trademarks are the property of their respective owners. John Wiley & Sons, Inc. is not associated with any product or vendor mentioned in this book.

Limit of Liability/Disclaimer of Warranty: While the publisher and author have used their best efforts in preparing this book, they make no representations or warranties with respect to the accuracy or completeness of the contents of this book and specifically disclaim any implied warranties of merchantability or fitness for a particular purpose. No warranty may be created or extended by sales representatives or written sales materials. The advice and strategies contained herein may not be suitable for your situation. You should consult with a professional where appropriate. Further, readers should be aware that websites listed in this work may have changed or disappeared between when this work was written and when it is read. Neither the publisher nor authors shall be liable for any loss of profit or any other commercial damages, including but not limited to special, incidental, consequential, or other damages.

For general information on our other products and services or for technical support, please contact our Customer Care Department within the United States at (800) 762-2974, outside the United States at (317) 572-3993 or fax (317) 572-4002.

Wiley also publishes its books in a variety of electronic formats. Some content that appears in print may not be available in electronic formats. For more information about Wiley products, visit our web site at www.wiley.com.

Library of Congress Cataloging-in-Publication Data is Available:

ISBN 9781119747918 (Hardback)
ISBN 9781119747932 (ePDF)
ISBN 9781119747925 (ePub)

Cover Design: Wiley
Cover Image: Jeffrey Rosenbluth
Author Photos: Courtesy of the Authors

SKY10073773_042524

To my mother and father, Lucille and Moosa, for their love and for bringing me into the world at the best possible time. To my three children, Josh, Jess, and Mark, for giving meaning to everything I do. And to my wife, Celeste, for your love and boundless understanding.

VJH

Contents

Foreword   *xiii*

Preface   *xvii*

About the Authors   *xxi*

Acknowledgments   *xxiii*

Chapter 1: Introduction: The Puzzle of the Missing Billionaires   **1**

SECTION I: INVESTMENT SIZING   **13**

Chapter 2: Befuddled Betting on a Biased Coin   **15**

Chapter 3: Size Matters When It's for Real   **27**

Chapter 4: A Taste of the Merton Share   **41**

Chapter 5: How Much to Invest in the Stock Market?   **49**

Chapter 6: The Mechanics of Choice   **67**

Chapter 7: Criticisms of Expected Utility Decision-making   **103**

Chapter 8: Reminiscences of a Hedge Fund Operator   **117**

SECTION II: LIFETIME SPENDING AND INVESTING   **127**

Chapter 9: Spending and Investing in Retirement   **129**

Chapter 10: Spending Like You'll Live Forever   **149**

Chapter 11: Spending Like You *Won't* Live Forever   165

SECTION III: WHERE THE RUBBER MEETS
THE ROAD   173

Chapter 12: Measuring the Fabric of Felicity   175

Chapter 13: Human Capital   193

Chapter 14: Into the Weeds: Characteristics of Major
Asset Classes   201

Chapter 15: No Place to Hide: Investing in a World
with No Safe Asset   235

Chapter 16: What About Options?   245

Chapter 17: Tax Matters   265

Chapter 18: Risk Versus Uncertainty   275

SECTION IV: PUZZLES   285

Chapter 19: How Can a Great Lottery Be a Bad Bet?   287

Chapter 20: The Equity Risk Premium Puzzle   291

Chapter 21: The Perpetuity Paradox and Negative
Interest Rates   297

Chapter 22: When Less Is More   303

Chapter 23: The Costanza Trade   309

★ ★ ★ ★ ★ ★

Chapter 24: Conclusion: U and Your Wealth   319

Bonus Chapter: Liar's Poker and Learning to Bet Smart   327

Cheat Sheet   335

A Few Rules of Thumb   340

Endnotes **343**

Suggested Reading *357*
References *359*
Index *373*

Foreword

In the first pages of this excellent new book by Victor Haghani and James White, you are going to meet Cornelius "Commodore" Vanderbilt. The name is of course familiar and a quick search on the internet will tell you that he died in 1877, leaving his eldest son, Billy, more than a hundred million dollars, the largest fortune in the world at that time. The family grew and expected to live luxuriously. Asset returns have been so strong over the past 150 years that Cornelius' heirs today should all be worth more than $1 billion each. It didn't turn out that way for the Vanderbilts. By the 1950s, there was not a single descendant of Cornelius who was a millionaire, let alone a billionaire. The Vanderbilt family tree is a conspicuous, but not unusual, example of the "billionaires manqués" that highlight the importance, and the challenge, of making good financial decisions.

When Victor first told me this story over dinner, I suggested many explanations: war, taxes, divorce, the crash of 1929. But none of them held up to scrutiny. We settled on two: the Vanderbilts did a poor job sizing their investment risk (too much concentration) and failed to connect their spending practices to their risk-taking.

This book is profoundly novel in the personal finance literature in its focus on investment sizing rather than investment selection. Victor and James develop a logical and practical framework for thinking through these important "how much" decisions we face in our financial lives, such as how much to allocate between stocks and bonds, how much to spend, or how much capital gains tax to pay. This is especially important in a time of great uncertainty in asset prices, interest rates, inflation, taxation, and even individual longevity.

I believe this book is destined to become a Wall Street classic, to be passed down by generations of trading floor veterans who are passionate about markets and thoughtful about risk. I hope it will serve as an antidote to the stories of wild risk-taking glorified in *Reminiscences of a Stock Operator*, a dog-eared copy of which was handed down to me when I was just starting out. I also expect *The Missing Billionaires* will become an important gift from parents to their children, and beyond.

Victor and James are skilled at explaining difficult concepts in a down-to-earth, intuitive fashion, providing a practical toolkit that readers can use to organize their financial lives. This book will benefit both financially educated readers and readers for whom all this material is quite new. It's packed with case studies and anecdotes that bring the core concepts to life. The authors combine a deep understanding of the academic finance literature with their own extensive experience as finance professionals, both as arbitrage traders and then as the principals of Elm Wealth, their multi-billion-dollar wealth management practice.

For 20 years, Victor and I hosted a regular dinner where we would discuss analytical finance problems over kebabs and decent red wine. A perfect fuel for such a dinner would have been Chapter 8, where you'll find the first inside account by an LTCM partner of the decisions faced over the short but eventful life of the much-studied hedge fund. The lessons learned apply just as much to a tech start-up deciding how much cash to hold between rounds of financing or to getting into an Uber where the driver does not look one bit like the picture on your phone (likely a bad idea). The discussion will force you to think about how to incorporate low-probability, high-consequence tail events into your decision-making. Its humility is sobering.

Finance took an unexpected turn in 1973 when Fischer Black and Myron Scholes published their now-famous paper on option pricing. For 50 years, academic researchers and practitioners have built upon their work. It is not obvious to me what good it has done for individual investors, although it has helped banks create, and profit from, many complicated derivatives (full disclosure: a long time ago, I worked in equity derivatives at Goldman Sachs).

You will learn about another seminal paper published four years earlier in 1969 by Robert Merton, about how much to put in the stock market and what fraction of your wealth to spend each year as you age. This paper has been largely forgotten outside academia, just like the 1956 paper by John Kelly on how to optimize the growth of wealth. Victor and James place the ideas of these papers at the core of the book. They will give you a framework for thinking about whether you're taking too little or too much risk and how to match your spending to the risks you're taking.

Spending from one's wealth in retirement is an important problem, one that I devote a lot of time to at PIMCO in my day job and also through my involvement with the University of Chicago's Roman Family Center for Decision Research. Taxes matter, longevity matters, spending matters, and drawdowns matter. You will find in Section II a full discussion of these topics, and in Section III some excellent unbiased advice on how to practically use these ideas to keep your financial life in order.

Adventurous readers will be rewarded by taking time to read Section IV. Here you will find a set of fascinating puzzles that can be unlocked with the key concepts of the book. This is a book you'll want on your shelf to think through thorny issues again and again. It is a must-have resource for anyone seeking to make informed and thoughtful financial decisions at any stage of life, whether you're a young investor building wealth, an entrepreneur invested heavily in your own business, or at a stage where your primary focus is investing, spending, and giving.

I started working at Goldman Sachs in New York City in July 1987 and have been lucky to ride a wonderful slow wave of strong equity and fixed income returns. But despite this very favorable backdrop, I have observed near-inexplicable financial decisions by numerous wealthy and highly intelligent people, many of whom would count in Victor and James' tally of "missing billionaires." I have also seen my own approach to financial decision-making evolve with time and experience. I am happy to say my thinking has tended to converge with the ideas of this book, but not as quickly as I wish they had. Victor and James say that they wrote this book with their younger selves in mind. They are not the only ones who would have benefited from reading this book decades ago. It is a gift I intend to give frequently!

Emmanuel Roman
CEO, PIMCO
Newport Beach, CA
April 2023

Preface

There are thousands of books on personal finance.† Unfortunately, by and large, these books do not agree with one another, leaving the seeker of sound financial advice adrift. In contrast, textbooks written for university courses on financial decision-making closely agree.[1] Given this harmony among professors writing textbooks, you'd think that when they turn their attention to writing books for a wider, nonacademic audience, they'd deliver a consistent, unified message. Alas, this is not the case. For example, one distinguished professor writes a book titled *A Random Walk Down Wall Street*, and another gives us *A **Nonrandom** Walk Down Wall Street*. We have one advocating investing heavily in *Stocks for the Long Run*, and another warning us of stock market *Irrational*

---

† 3,537 to be precise, according to the US Library of Congress.

Exuberance. Some tell us to only invest in low-cost index funds, while another, in *The Little Book That Beats the Market,* suggests we invest in a handful of stocks that will deliver exceptional returns. Then there are two MIT-minted professors, one who suggests we should *Risk Less* and mostly invest in safe government bonds, while the other advocates that young adults hold a two times leveraged exposure to stocks. And these are just the books by the professors.

Perhaps it's less surprising that we get diametrically opposed advice from industry titans advocating their own firm's offerings. For example, Vanguard founder John Bogle preached the benefits of index funds in *The Little Book of Common Sense Investing,* while the legendary (retired) manager of Fidelity's stock-picking Magellan Fund, Peter Lynch, encourages investors to try to beat the market by picking stocks that make products they like in his popular *One Up On Wall Street.* The cacophony of advice grows louder still, and its deviation from economic theory becomes more unsettling, when we survey the whole of the popular personal finance literature, including such titles as *Rich Dad, Poor Dad* or *The Millionaire Next Door.*[2]

One reason behind this disturbing divergence of financial advice is that most books on personal finance assume a typical reader, subject to typical circumstances, and then endeavor to tell that reader what to do. Different assumptions about who and what is typical can lead to dramatically different recommendations. In writing this book, we have been motivated by the proverb, "Give a man a fish, and he won't be hungry for a day; teach a man to fish, and he won't be hungry for a lifetime." Our intent is to give you a practical framework, consistent with the consensus of university finance textbooks, for making good financial decisions that are right for you. Good decisions will take account of your personal circumstances, financial preferences, and your considered views on the risks and expected returns of available investments.

Who Is This Book For?

This book is for anyone who feels that making better financial decisions can materially improve their welfare. You will likely get the most out of this book if you have already accumulated a decent amount of financial capital or if you are young with a healthy measure of human capital. A good number of our readers will be finance industry professionals, who we trust will find ideas in this book that they haven't encountered in their day jobs. We focus primarily on individuals and families rather than institutional investors, although many of the concepts we discuss are relevant to all stewards of capital.

We assume the reader is familiar with common investment products (stocks, bonds, mutual funds, index funds, ETFs, options) and concepts (compound return, time value of money, yield-to-maturity, inflation). We acknowledge and respect the intelligence of our readers by refraining from giving blindingly obvious advice, such as the merit of paying off credit card debt accruing at 20% interest with cash sitting in the bank earning 2% interest, or that you should avoid paying higher fees or taxes than necessary. We also recognize that all of us wrestle with a long list of cognitive biases in our decision-making, but we trust that you are like we are in wanting to conquer these foibles and make better decisions. Indeed, there is little else we can do, once we acknowledge that not deciding is itself a decision.

For readers who want to build or refresh their knowledge of finance basics before diving into this book, we recommend taking a short, free online course such as "Financial Markets" by Robert Shiller on Coursera. Basic high school math proficiency, including comfort with ideas expressed using symbols and words, is all that's needed to fully understand every concept in this book. We have used shaded technical sidebars to give more mathematically inclined readers a deeper dive, but these can be skipped over without any loss of understanding. We have also used unshaded sidebars to tell stories from our personal adventures in finance and have included several chapters of puzzles that help illustrate key concepts. We use footnotes at the bottom of each page for interesting but nonessential musings, and we employ endnotes to give credit and references, state further assumptions, deal with technical minutiae, or expand on topics beyond the scope of the core text. Each chapter is headed with a cartoon illustration drawn by the very talented Paul Bloomfield, which we hope will help you remember the main landmarks and path of your reading journey.

The book is written from the perspective of a US individual or family, and many of the examples, particularly involving taxation and retirement products, are set in the US context. We hope this doesn't detract from the value that non-US readers can derive, as the concepts and framework we describe can be adapted to any setting.

Of course, all authors hope their books will be useful to as broad an audience as possible. Regardless of your background, we hope to persuade you through practical examples and applications that the financial decision-making framework we describe herein is sensible and emi-nently practical.

Wishing you tight lines, bent rods, and full nets!

We value your feedback and would love to hear your thoughts, experiences, questions, or suggestions. We'll be keeping a running discussion of our interaction with our readers who are comfortable sharing our dialogue publicly on this page of our website, www .elmwealth.com/MissingBillionaires.

About the Authors

Victor Haghani has spent four decades actively involved in markets and financial innovation. He started his career in 1984 at Salomon Brothers in bond research. He moved to the trading floor in 1986 and shortly after became a managing director in the bond arbitrage group run by John Meriwether. In 1993, Victor was a cofounding partner of Long-Term Capital Management (LTCM). He established and co-ran its London office. His participation in the failure of LTCM was a life-changing experience that led him to question and revise much of the way he thought about the economy, markets, and investing.

Through a careful study of the academic literature on investing and many thought-provoking discussions with friends, colleagues, and investors of all backgrounds, Victor concluded that savers can and should do much better. He founded Elm Wealth in 2011 to help investors, including his own family, manage their savings in a disciplined, research-based, cost-effective manner and to capture the long-term returns they ought to earn.

In his 2013 TEDx talk, *Where Are All the Billionaires and Why Should We Care?*, Victor shared his perspective on the synthesis of active and passive investing, which forms the basis of the Dynamic Index Investing® approach offered by Elm Wealth. Over the years, Victor became fascinated with the challenge of making good decisions on broader questions about wealth and personal finances, including sound spending policies, tax decisions, and retirement choices.

Victor was born in New York City in 1962 and grew up in New York, Pennsylvania, Tehran, and London. As an adult, he has resided in New York City and London and, more recently, has been based in Jackson Hole, Wyoming. Victor graduated from the London School of Economics (LSE) in 1984 with a B.Sc. (economics). He has been a prolific contributor to the academic and practitioner finance literature.

Victor has been involved in a variety of other activities, including research and lecturing at the LSE, where he was a senior research associate in the Financial Markets Group, as well as consulting and board assignments and acting as a "name" in the Lloyd's of London insurance market. He loves the outdoors and is an avid skier, hiker, and fisherman and enjoys taking long walks with his dog Milo. He has always been fascinated by airplanes, flying model ones as a boy and full-size ones as an adult.

James White has spent two decades working in finance, covering the gamut of quantitative research, market-making, hedge fund investing, private equity investing, and wealth management. He has been the chief executive officer (CEO) of Elm Wealth since 2018, working with Victor to help friends, family, and clients sensibly and efficiently invest their wealth. After meeting through a mutual friend, James and Victor began working on research and writing together, sharing ideas, and collaborating regularly. After James built the next generation of Elm's portfolio management systems, he and Victor were talking and working together every day so joining Elm as the CEO just seemed natural.

Since then James has moved to Philadelphia to establish Elm's headquarters and has seen the business grow to serve hundreds of families and manage around $1.5 billion of their assets. He splits his time between working with clients, continuing to develop and improve Elm's systems, and research and writing.

After studying math at the University of Chicago, James lived and worked all over the world, first for Nationsbank/CRT and Bank of America, then for Citadel Investment Group, then as a partner at PAC Partners, a boutique private investment firm. His interest in optimal trade-sizing and risk-taking arose from each of these experiences and has culminated in the way Elm Wealth advises and invests for clients today.

James is an avid rock climber, classical guitarist, cook, and lover of renaissance history and music. When not in Elm's office or visiting clients, he can usually be found out climbing, hiking, eating, or traveling somewhere that nicely incorporates all three.

Acknowledgments

We owe a debt of gratitude to the many people who have contributed to our financial education, in both theory and practice, and to our professional and personal development. We have been blessed to have patient and caring teachers right from the start of our careers, including (for Victor) Bob Kopprasch, Bill Krasker, Robert Merton, Chi-fu Huang, and Myron Scholes, and (for James) Sean Becketti, Nessan Fitzmaurice, and Vladimir Piterbarg. We thank our colleagues and co-travelers who have shared so much of their wisdom and experience with us, in particular John Meriwether, Larry Hilibrand, Rob Stavis, Richard Leahy, Eric Rosenfeld, Samir Bouaoudia, Larry Bernstein, Ephi Gildor, Hans Hufschmid, Hedi Kallal, David Heatley, Lord Jacob Rothschild, and Alan Howard. We have learned so much from each of you.

Hedi Kallal first introduced us and saw that we were both on the same intellectual journey and would benefit from traveling it together. Without his inspired and fortuitous introduction, neither this book nor our friendship would have happened, for which we owe him tremendous thanks.

Our friends' generous contributions to this book have been tremendous and humbling. Thank you to Antti Ilmanen for your boundless encouragement, your introduction to our editors at Wiley, and your many valuable comments and corrections. Jeff Rosenbluth and Larry Hilibrand went far, far beyond the call of friendship in the countless hours they spent reviewing and shaping the manuscript, not to mention contributing many of the core ideas of the book. Others who gave much of their time to the development of the book include Ayman Hindy, Richard Dewey, John Glazer, Vladimir Ragulin, and John Karubian. We also received valuable comments and corrections from Jamil Baz, Bruce Tuckman, Steve Mobbs, José Scheinkman, Peter Hirsch, Saman Majd, Arjun Krishnamachar, Bill Montgomery, Ian Hall, Aneet Chachra,

Adrian Eterovic, and Anna Wroblewska. We thank our colleagues Mike Fothergill and Steven Schneider for their help on numerous aspects of the book. Victor's three children, Josh, Jess, and Mark, all served as sounding boards for the quality of our explanations and offered many other useful suggestions. The positive feedback on our short-form writing that we received from professional finance writers Jason Zweig, Michael Mauboussin, John O'Sullivan, Joe Weisenthal, Spencer Jakob, and John Authers made us believe we had a book in us. The prolific writer and financial impresario Frank Fabozzi was the first to publish our work in his anthologies and in the academic journals for which he has served as editor.

Our understanding has been shaped by many deep thinkers and writers in finance who have generously shared their insights through academic articles, lectures, and books, including John Campbell, Robert Shiller, John Cochrane, Phil Tetlock, Ed Thorp, Cliff Asness, and Howard Marks. We thank our coauthors of previous articles, which provide the foundation of several chapters of the book, including Rich Dewey, Vlad Ragulin, Larry Hilibrand, Jeff Rosenbluth, and Andy Morton. There are many people at Wiley who helped make this book a reality, and we thank them all, but in particular we must sing the praises of our publisher, Bill Falloon, whose wisdom, good nature, and patience are responsible for this book coming to life. We'd be pleased if some readers decide to judge our book by its cover art, generated by our multi-talented friend Jeff Rosenbluth.

We are grateful that our dear friend Manny Roman graciously agreed to write the foreword to the book, carving out time from his day job of running the world's largest bond investor, PIMCO. We hope he will one day write a book himself or perhaps publish a collection of his poetry for all to enjoy. We thank Michael Lewis and Matt Levine for their friendship and their inspiration, showing us that it is possible to write about finance in a manner that makes the heart race while conveying valuable and astute insights.

For those of you who have been readers of our monthly Thought Pieces over the past decade, we heartily thank you and have found your steadfast interest and feedback invaluable in spurring us on to writing this book. We are beholden to our clients at Elm Wealth for their trust and openness in giving us an opportunity to develop and test the practicality of many of the ideas we discuss in this book. Finally, we must thank all those "missing billionaires" who have helped us realize that there was a book that needed to be written about making better financial decisions.

THE MISSING BILLIONAIRES

1

Introduction: The Puzzle of the Missing Billionaires

Any fool can make a fortune; it takes a man of brains to hold onto it.
—Cornelius "Commodore" Vanderbilt

A beautiful statue of Cornelius Vanderbilt, the nineteenth-century rail and shipping tycoon, adorns the outside of Grand Central Station in New York City. It's there because "the Commodore" ordered the station's construction. Although partially obscured today by an eyesore called the Park Avenue Viaduct, the statue sits right at the heart of mid-town Manhattan, the global center of finance, regularly visible to many of today's financial titans.

When Vanderbilt died in 1877, he was the wealthiest man in the world. His eldest son, Billy, received an inheritance of one hundred million dollars—95% of Cornelius' fortune. Unfortunately, it came without even the most basic of instructions on how to invest and spend this wealth over time. Within 70 years of the Commodore's death, the family wealth was largely dissipated. Today, not one Vanderbilt descendant can trace his or her wealth to the vast fortune Cornelius bequeathed.[†] The Vanderbilt clan grew at a higher rate than the average American family, but even so this outcome was far from guaranteed. If the Vanderbilt heirs had invested their wealth in a boring but diversified portfolio of US companies, spent 2% of their wealth each year, and paid their taxes, *each one living today would still have a fortune of more than five billion dollars.*

What went wrong?

The Vanderbilt experience is noteworthy in scale but not in substance. The dissipation of great wealth over just a few generations is a common enough occurrence to warrant its own maxim: "from shirtsleeves to shirtsleeves in three generations." The truth of this dictum can be seen in how remarkably few of the billionaires in the news these days are the scions of old-money wealth. From these observations, we can tease out a valuable insight: the wealthiest families of the past were not equipped to consistently make sensible investing and spending decisions. If they had been, their billionaire descendants would vastly outnumber today's newly minted variety.

To get a rough count of these "missing billionaires," let's turn back the clock to 1900. At that time, the US census recorded about four thousand American millionaires, with the very richest counting their wealth in the hundreds of millions. If a family with five million dollars back then had invested their wealth in the US stock market and spent from it at a reasonable rate, that single family would have generated about 16

[†] Hopefully his descendants had a good time while dissipating their wealth. It brings to mind how George Best, the legendary Manchester United winger in the wild 1960s, answered a reporter's question asking how he went through all his money: "I spent a lot of money on booze, birds, and fast cars. The rest I just squandered."

billionaire households today.† If even a quarter of those millionaires in 1900 started with at least five million dollars, their descendants alone should include close to *16,000* old-money billionaires alive today. If we include the private wealth created throughout the twentieth century as well, rather than just a snapshot in 1900, we believe the tally of potential billionaires is vastly greater.

But as of 2022, *Forbes* estimated there were just over 700 billionaires in the United States, and you'll struggle to find a single one who traces his or her wealth back to a millionaire ancestor from 1900. We needn't go so far back in the past to find this pattern. Fewer than 10% of today's US billionaires are descended from members of the first *Forbes* 400 Rich List published in 1982. Even the least wealthy family on that 1982 list, with "just" $100 million, should have spawned four billionaire families today. We recognize that some wealthy families purposefully chose to give away or consume virtually all of their wealth in their lifetimes, but we believe these cases were relatively rare and do not account for the near-complete absence of "old-money" billionaires we see today.

We're not lamenting a scarcity of billionaires in the world today. Our point is that, collectively, *we all face a really big and pervasive problem when it comes to making good financial decisions*. If even the most financially successful members of our society, at least some of whom were smart and capable, and all of whom could afford the "best" financial advice, consistently made atrocious financial decisions, what can be expected from the rest of us? There's a Persian proverb Victor's father was fond of, which seems improbable at first, but the truth of which has become a main motivation for this book: *"It's more difficult to hold on to wealth than it is to make it."* This book sets forth our framework for addressing the challenge faced by all families—not only potential and actual billionaires—to find a path to better financial decisions.

In the chapters that follow, we're going to explore in detail the most common ways in which these missing billionaire families discarded their enormous head start: taking too much or too little risk, spending more than their wealth could support, and not adjusting their spending as their wealth fluctuated. Above all, they did not have a unified decision-making

---

† We are assuming the families spent and donated 2% of their wealth each year, paid taxes on what they spent, had no other income, and procreated at a typical rate. Full investment in the US stock market as the baseline assumption for these families is meant to be representative of the many attractive ways wealthy families could have invested. We are not suggesting that people could or should have invested that way in the past or should in the future.

framework, which left them susceptible to chasing whatever was hot and dumping it as soon as it was not, anchoring spending decisions on hoped-for portfolio returns, and paying exorbitant fees for poor advice.

Notice that among the primary errors we listed, we did not include choosing bad investments. That's because one thing that did not cause these billionaires to go missing was a poor investment environment. Indeed, it's hard to imagine a better one. The US stock market delivered a 10% pretax annual return over the period, turning one million dollars in 1900 into roughly *one hundred billion* dollars at the end of 2022, a 100,000x return. Instead, perhaps the heart of the problem is one of misplaced attention. In investing, the natural tendency is to focus on the question of *what* to buy or sell. Nearly 100% of the financial press is dedicated to this question, so it's reasonable to suppose that the *"what"* decision is the most important thing we should be thinking about. It isn't.

We'll explain that the most important financial decisions you need to get right are of the *"how much"* variety. How much should you buy of a good investment; how much should you spend today and over time; how much tax should you defer to the future; how much should you spend to insure against low probability, high consequence events. Implicit in these questions is the recognition that risk is present in just about every good thing we come across. So, whenever we're trying to figure out how much of a good but risky thing we should do, we need to weigh the greater expected benefit from doing more versus the cost of taking more risk. We hope to leave you with a practical framework for making these sizing and risk-taking decisions consistently and confidently.

Why do we think sizing is so important? Consider this: if you pick bad investments but do a good job sizing them, you should expect to lose money, but your losses won't be ruinous. You'll be able to regroup and invest another day. On the other hand, if you pick great investments but commit way too much to them, you can easily go broke from normal ups and downs while waiting for things to pan out.

Our own personal experience backs up the proposition that the sizing decision, often an afterthought, is actually the most critical part of investing. We've both experienced first-hand the impact of getting the "how much" decision wrong, losing the majority of our personal wealth in the process. Victor was a founding partner at the hedge fund Long-Term Capital Management (LTCM). In 1998, at age 36, he took a nine-figure hit when LTCM was undone by that decade's second financial crisis. The monetary loss was compounded by the psychological blow of the *business'* failure and its impact on the 153 employees who worked there, as well as the impact on the reputations of all involved. A decade later, James at 28 lost a smaller sum but still a material fraction of his wealth in part through his investments in the hedge fund where he worked.

In each case, we believed we'd selected investments with an attractive risk/reward profile that were highly likely to pay off in the long run. The trades that took down LTCM in 1998 were money-makers over the ensuing years, and the hedge fund that employed James also bounced back to generate strong returns following its precipitous swoon in 2008. Unfortunately, the short run always comes before the long run, and neither of us got to enjoy the rebound of these investments. The lesson: good investments plus bad sizing can result in cataclysmic losses.

The LTCM story has been told countless times—several books, many articles, and even a Harvard Business School case study. It was colorful, involving Wall Street traders straight off the pages of Michael Lewis' *Liar's Poker* together with a band of highly respected professors, including two Nobel Laureates. To the outside world, it appeared that they had built a money machine (one of the books about LTCM was rather hyperbolically titled *Inventing Money*), so it's not surprising that most of the LTCM partners were heavily invested in the fund they managed. The fund had returned more than 40% per year from inception to shortly before its decline, with an annual volatility of about 12%. And prior to founding LTCM, the older partners could look back on their 20 years of very positive experience doing the same kind of investing at Salomon Brothers.

Victor had about 80% of his family's liquid wealth invested in the LTCM hedge fund. With the benefit of hindsight, this level of investment concentration was a mistake. But the more useful question to ask, which hasn't been addressed anywhere in the LTCM literature, is this: what analysis should Victor have done to determine how much to invest in the fund, and what would that analysis have said? We'll provide a detailed answer, and we'll also show why "as much as you can get" is almost never the correct answer to the question "how much of a good thing is right for you?"

Is this poor sizing judgment confined to the likes of your authors when they were young, highly confident bond arbitrage traders, and to wealthy families living in the first half of the twentieth century? Unfortunately, there's quite a bit of evidence that this failing is more widespread and persistent, suggesting that investors are systematically hurt by poor money management skills. For example, individual investors in aggregate severely underperform market returns, in both absolute and risk-adjusted terms. Some of this underperformance comes from paying high fees, but much arises from having too much or too little at risk and usually at just the wrong times. A landmark study of individual broker-age accounts by University of California Professors Brad Barber and Ter-rance Odean, aptly titled, "Trading Can Be Hazardous to Your Wealth," found that individuals who actively traded their portfolios underper-formed market returns by 6% per annum. Other researchers have found that the aggregate returns that investors in mutual funds experience are typically several percentage points per year below the returns that a buy and hold investor in those same funds would have earned.[1]

In an attempt to better understand how people deal with the siz-ing of attractive investment opportunities, Victor and his co-researcher Richard Dewey conducted an experiment in 2013 that was later pub-lished in the *Journal of Portfolio Management*. In a controlled setting, they invited 61 financially and quantitatively trained individuals to play a sim-ple coin-flipping game. The participants were informed that the (virtual) coin was programmed to have a 60% chance of landing on heads. They were each given $25 and allowed to bet any way they wanted. They were told that at the end of 30 minutes—time enough for about 300 flips—they'd be paid however much the $25 had turned into, subject to a maximum payout of $250.

As we'll discuss in more detail throughout the book, there are a range of simple, sensible betting strategies that would result in an expected payout in the vicinity of the $250 cap.† So, how did the players do? More than 30% of them lost money, and incredibly, over 25% went bust! Only 20% made it to $250, a far cry from the more than 90% who should have. Our thesis in this book is that the ideas leading to doing well in our coin-flipping game are equally helpful in making good decisions on the important financial matters in our lives.

Investing isn't the only area where making sound financial decisions under uncertainty is important. Everyone needs a coherent saving and spending plan for all stages of life, especially if they expect to enjoy peri-ods of retirement. Even when it comes to the seemingly simple decision of at what age to start taking Social Security benefits, a recent study

---

†Not a bad return for 30 minutes of quickly pecking at a keyboard, especially for a bunch of university students!

found that Americans are leaving more than a trillion dollars on the table by making suboptimal decisions, primarily by taking the benefits sooner than they should.[2] There's also good evidence that many people spend too much on certain kinds of insurance, from protection on their kitchen appliances to comprehensive car insurance, while spending too little on other types of insurance products, such as annuities. Sadly, personal finance books just don't provide enough good advice either, as documented in a recent easy-to-read survey of the 50 most popular ones by Yale Professor James Choi.[3]

The decision-making problems we focus on have three common features:

1. They require a decision to be made in the face of uncertain outcomes.
2. Some of the outcomes will have a meaningful impact on your happiness or welfare.
3. The impact on your welfare will not exactly mirror the monetary outcomes.

Philosophers, economists, and mathematicians have been thinking about how to systematically evaluate these kinds of decisions for almost 300 years, since Daniel Bernoulli introduced the concept of a "utility function" in order to provisionally solve the St. Petersburg Paradox, which we describe in Chapter 6. It's virtually a law of human nature that we experience a diminishing marginal benefit from further and further increases in spending (or wealth). This is why the utility we derive from spending our wealth doesn't mirror the monetary sums involved. Thinking this way makes it clear that we should make decisions that maximize our utility rather than purely monetary outcomes. These ideas are at the root of economic thought and permeate even through the younger branches of the economics tree, such as behavioral finance.

The utility-based decision framework has at its core three main steps for any given financial decision. First, we need to assess possible monetary outcomes and estimate their associated probabilities. Then we need to map these monetary outcomes into utility outcomes. Finally, we need to search over the range of different possible decisions, to find the one which produces the highest Expected Utility.

The framework of maximizing Expected Utility is the foundation of the field known as "decision-making under uncertainty" as well as most other theories of individual choice and human interaction. Many of the ideas that form the basis of this book are found in the sub-field known as "lifetime consumption and portfolio choice," an area first formulated and explored in the 1960s by Nobel Prize-winning economists Paul Samuelson and Robert C. Merton. The basic problem addressed is to determine the choices that a person should make with regard to investing, saving, and spending that will maximize Expected Lifetime Utility.

Unfortunately, many of the original papers in this field have been too complex or abstract to gain traction in practice, with the result that very few people are using these tools to make better decisions. In the pages that follow, we hope to present these important ideas in a way that will not only resonate, but also change your thinking. It can take a surprisingly long time for a great idea to make the jump from theory to practice; we believe these are great ideas whose time has come.

The framework of making decisions to maximize Expected Utility has been criticized for not being a realistic representation of how people actually behave. Indeed, researchers have documented myriad cognitive biases that result in inconsistent and irrational decision-making. We agree with this evidence wholeheartedly, and that's exactly why we've decided to write this book—in order to help people make better decisions by understanding what happened to all those missing billionaires and overcoming some of those cognitive biases! No framework would be needed if people were *naturally* excellent at making decisions involving a complex web of probabilities, scenarios, and transformations of monetary sums to personal utility. But we know that we aren't.

The fact that the framework and actual behavior don't always agree is a sign that the framework can add value. People will undoubtedly still choose to make seemingly suboptimal decisions in some ways—that's part of being human—but better to do so knowingly and with an ability to estimate the cost rather than out of ignorance or for lack of a better alternative. In this book, we are not going to describe how people *do* make important financial decisions; our goal is to explain how they *should* be making them. We hope to change behavior by convincing our readers to adopt a framework centered on Expected Utility for making the important financial decisions in their lives.

The Expected Utility you get from a particular course of action in an uncertain world is a model—it is a simplified representation of reality. Like any model, it is a framework for organizing and simplifying a complex situation. Sometimes we get so familiar with a model that we don't even realize that's what it is. For example, in the world of government bonds, the concept of yield to maturity is a model that really came into its own when computer power became cheap enough to quickly make the relevant calculations for any bond, on any settlement date, at any price.[4] Without the model of yield to maturity, it would be very hard to compare bond A, with a price of 102.15 maturing in 4 years and 11 months paying a coupon of 3%, to bond B, with a price of 125.67 maturing in 5 years and 2 months paying a coupon of 8%.[†] The "yield model" just converts price and other relevant information into a better metric to compare bonds. Expected Utility, just like yield to maturity, is a model. And it's a good model in that it allows us to compare and evaluate different and complex decisions in a way that is intuitive and has an underlying economic rationale.

One of the first steps on the path to better decision-making will be to understand your own personal utility function. This is not as difficult as you may think. In a 2018 survey we conducted with about 30 of our clients—if you haven't guessed, we run a wealth advisory practice—we found that all of them were able to express a relationship between wealth and utility that helped them weigh different risk/reward trade-offs in a consistent manner. Our goal is to increase your comfort with this framework by working through a wide variety of practical case studies, from deciding how much of your wealth you should invest in your own business to when it makes sense to pay capital gains tax. We'll dive deeply into the primary ways that risk impacts your financial well-being. Our aim is to give you core concepts, without dumbing them down to the point where they become hidden behind vague general guidance. There will be some math involved, but nothing beyond ideas you'd have met in high school—and we'll always try to explain the economic logic behind an idea, not just the math.

We recognize that a big part of your financial decisions still involves figuring out *what* to invest in, so we won't ignore the "what" question altogether. For many investors today, the potential investment universe is daunting: index funds, active funds, individual stocks and bonds, real estate, hedge funds, private equity, venture capital, and the list goes on and on. Plenty of books have been published to help you evaluate each of these types of investments, so we'll only dedicate one chapter to discussing how to assess the expected return and risk of the most common

[†] For readers who tried to figure it out in their heads, the yield to maturity of bonds A and B are 2.53% and 2.65%, respectively.

investments. Most of this book explains how to translate your evaluation of individual investments into a decision on how much risk to take, on each investment and in total, and how to make the connected decision of how to spend your wealth over time.

Most of the methods we discuss will be usable by anyone with a calculator or a simple spreadsheet. Some may require more sophisticated technology to implement them exactly as we do, but with minor simplifications these too can nearly always be worked out on a spreadsheet. We've built a set of modeling tools to help work through some of the most common and important problems that benefit from them, and they're available on our website, www.elmwealth.com. If you find yourself wanting to use a piece of the framework but can't find a good tool for it, please do feel free to engage with us, and we can very likely help or point you in the right direction.

We've broken the book into four main segments:

- Investment Sizing
- Lifetime Spending and Investing
- Where the Rubber Meets the Road
- Puzzles

We know that for most readers, this book won't make for light and relaxing reading. One suggestion we have to make things a bit easier going, if desired, is to begin reading just a subset of chapters that cover core concepts, skipping over those that primarily discuss illustrations and applications of those ideas. We hope you'll find the skipped chapters calling your name later. We think the following 10 chapters are important to read on your first pass through the book: 2–6, 9, 12–14, and 24. In whatever order you get to them, we hope you'll find the other 14 chapters informative and helpful in bringing the core ideas of the book to life.

There are places where we'll describe key concepts with symbols and formulas as well as words. Have no fear; there are only four formulas in the entire book, which you can find for reference in the section "A Few Rules of Thumb" near the end. One of the four formulas, which we call the Merton share, is simple and important enough that we hope you'll finish the book with it indelibly recorded in your mind! We hope that in these few instances, stating ideas both in natural language and the language of mathematics will make these concepts clearer and more memorable.

We've written this book with our younger selves never far from our minds. We hope that, if we had read it early in our careers, it would have helped us to avoid the investment sizing mistakes we made. Indeed, the mission of Elm Wealth, our investment management and wealth advisory business, is to help our clients benefit from our experience in the broad area of financial decision-making under uncertainty. Returning to our coin-flip experiment, our optimism that this book can do good stems in part from the fact that once we explained a more sensible sizing strategy to the participants, they took that on board and would mostly have reached the maximum payout if given another chance to play. If people are exposed to a good framework, they will often readily understand and embrace it.

Making better decisions is not a zero-sum game. Sound financial decision-making, consistent with your individual preferences, will not only increase your and your family's expected happiness, but will dramatically increase the welfare of our entire society.

An investment in knowledge pays the best interest.

—Benjamin Franklin

I

Investment Sizing

We have two related goals for Section I: to acquaint you with the important frameworks and results related to investment sizing and, more importantly, to help you develop your intuition and understanding for thinking through investment sizing questions. We try to accomplish this without resorting to the formal mathematical arguments typically encountered in academia. So throughout Section I, we talk extensively, lovingly almost, about the flipping of biased coins.

This is not because we think our readers are fascinated by flipping coins or because we naively think coin-flipping is a reasonable approximation to the real world of investing. Rather, when we talk about coin-flipping, that's a sign that we're exploring a new concept, and we want to help build intuition for what's going on in a context limited enough that we can really get our heads around it. Then, we can extend results from the artificial coin-flipping to more realistic scenarios by using a framework that naturally encompasses both. So get those coin-flipping thumbs warmed-up and ready!

2

Befuddled Betting on a Biased Coin

Introduction[1]

Imagine you're invited to a talk by a guy who cofounded a hedge fund that famously flopped about 25 years ago. You turn up, hoping to hear some valuable insights—or at least some entertaining tales—but instead, you're offered a stake of $25 to take out your laptop and bet on the flip of an electronic coin for 30 minutes. You're told the coin is biased to come up heads with a 60% probability, and each flip you must decide how much to bet on either heads or tails. It's always an even-money bet, meaning if you bet $1 and win, your bankroll increases by $1, and if you lose, it decreases by $1. You can bet as much as you like up to your current bankroll, and you will be paid out for however much is in your account at the end of the half hour, up to a maximum payout that will be disclosed if you get close.

That's it. Would you feel it's worth your time to play? How would you play the game? What heuristic or mental tool-kit would you employ? These questions led Victor and his colleague Rich Dewey to conduct the exact experiment just described. By having participants engage in an activity as simple as flipping a coin, the betting strategy and its evolution are easily isolated for observation. Also, you'll see that this simple game has properties that are similar to investing in the stock market, as well as implications for finance and economics education.

The Experiment

The coin-flipping experiment was played by 61 subjects, in groups of 2 to 15, in the quiet setting of office conference rooms or university classrooms. The proctor for the game outlined basic principles—such as no talking or cooperation—and that subjects were not to use the internet or other resources while playing the game.

The experiment began when subjects were directed to a purpose-built application for placing bets on the flip of a simulated coin. Prior to starting, participants read a detailed description of the game that included a clear statement, in bold, indicating that the simulated coin had a 60% chance of coming up heads and a 40% chance of coming up tails.

Participants were given $25 of starting capital and were told in text and verbally that they would be paid the amount of their ending balance subject to a maximum payout. The maximum payout would be revealed if and when subjects placed a bet that, if successful, would make their balance greater than or equal to the cap. The cap was set at $250, ten times the initial stake. Participants were told that they could play the game for 30 minutes, and if they accepted the $25 stake, they had to remain in the room for that amount of time—regardless of whether they hit the cap, went bust, or chose not to play at all. Participants could place a wager of any amount up to their account value, in increments of one cent, on heads or tails. They were asked a series of questions about their background before playing, and about their experience when they finished.

The sample consisted of 49 males and 12 females, mostly college-age students in economics and finance, as well as young professionals at finance firms, including 14 analysts and associates at two leading asset management firms. It seems reasonable to expect that these participants should have been well-prepared to play a simple game with a defined positive expected value.

Optimal Strategy

Before continuing with a description of what an optimal strategy might look like, perhaps you'd like to take a few moments to consider what you would do if given the opportunity to play this game. Even better, you can go to our website and play the game for yourself here: www. elmwealth.com/coin-flip/.

Once you read on you'll be afflicted with the "curse of knowledge," making it difficult for you to appreciate the perspective of the subjects encountering this game for the first time. So if you want to take a moment to think about your strategy, this is the time to do it.

To figure out the optimal strategy, first we need to define the objective we want to maximize. Given the setup of this game, and in particular that the stakes involved aren't material to the long-term financial well-being of the players, it seems like a reasonable objective would be to finish with the most money at the end of the 30 minutes of play. With this objective in hand, in principle we could look at a wide range of betting strategies to find which one gives the highest average payoff.

Let's look at three basic betting strategies and see how well they do, always assuming the player bets on heads for every flip:

- Constant fractional betting, which requires betting the same percentage of the player's current bankroll on each flip.
- Constant absolute betting, which calls for betting the same dollar amount on each flip.
- Doubling down betting, originally called the "Martingale system" following its development in eighteenth century France, which doubles the bet size after every loss. The idea is that the first winning bet will recoup all previous losses plus pay out a profit equal to the original stake.

We'll assume that a player could make 300 bets over the 30 minutes. In Table 2.1, we show statistics calculated over 10,000 simulated sets of 300 flips of the biased coin for the three strategies. We explore four different bet sizes for the constant fractional betting strategy, and for the other two strategies we've presented, the bet size parameter resulting in the highest expected outcome for each strategy.

The constant fractional betting with bet percentages between 10% and 20% yields an expected payout very close to the cap, so in the context of this game, these are near-optimal strategies. Even if a player had only been able to place 150 bets, these strategies still would have delivered

Table 2.1

Betting Strategy	Bet Size	Expected Outcome	Probability of Hitting Max Payout	Probability of Going Bust
Constant Fractional	5%	$218	70%	0%
Constant Fractional	10%	$241	94%	0%
Constant Fractional	20%	$237	94%	0%
Constant Fractional	40%	$176	70%	0%
Constant Absolute	$4	$213	59%	7%
Doubling Down	$2.5	$72	29%	40%

roughly a $200 expected payout. Also, it's not so surprising that neither the constant absolute nor the doubling down strategies do very well. In the constant absolute betting strategy, if exactly 60% of the flips come up heads you just barely hit $250, but any more than one fewer heads and you won't, which is why the probability of hitting the cap is about 50%.[†]

With the doubling down strategy, our player goes bust about 40% of the time from hitting streaks of tails that are too long to survive. That's the main problem with this system: bet sizes will increase exponentially over time—doubling, then doubling again, and again—so eventually the bet size will become equal or greater to your total bankroll. If you play long enough, you're near certain to lose your entire bankroll and have only a microscopic chance of turning a profit, which is why this type of betting is collectively referred to as "Gambler's Ruin." Some gamblers— and stock market day-traders too—have argued this strategy can generate a sure profit from a game in which the odds are against the player because a winning bet is sure to be made eventually. It turns out the financial alchemy by which this strategy can transform a losing game into a winning system only applies if the player has both an infinite amount of money and time. For mere mortals like us, it's almost certain we'll wind up broke instead.

For now, we'll take the strategy of betting 10% on each flip as the optimal strategy for this coin-flip game, although technically there is a slightly better strategy that involves making bigger bets as the 30 minute time limit winds down if the cap hasn't yet been hit. But the simple 10% strategy captures 96% of the maximum possible winnings—that sure seems good enough and a lot better than other simple alternatives. We'll discuss in the next chapter a simple rule of thumb for sizing bets like this, which our subjects could have used to get well within the ballpark of a nearly optimal strategy.

Findings: How Well Did Our Players Play?

"How did you go bankrupt?" "Gradually, and then suddenly."
—Ernest Hemingway, *The Sun Also Rises*

[†]A bit higher than 50% because of the cases where you reached the max before the end of the flipping.

Our players did not do very well. The average payout across all subjects was $91, saving your intrepid researchers from the roughly $240 per person they expected to pay out if participants used any of the near-optimal strategies.

While we expected to observe some suboptimal play, we were surprised by its pervasiveness. Suboptimal betting came in all shapes and sizes: overbetting, underbetting, erratic betting, and betting on tails were just some of the ways a majority of players squandered their chance to take home $250 for 30 minutes of play.

We defined "maxing out" as players who reached at least $200 by the end, and "going bust" as those finishing the game with less than $2 in their account at the end. Only 21% of participants reached the maximum payout of $250, dramatically below the 95% that should have reached it through a good betting strategy. One of our many surprises was that one-third of the participants wound up with less money in their account than they started with. More astounding still is the fact that 28% of participants went bust. That a repeated game with a sizable built-in 60/40 advantage produced so many subjects that lost everything is startling.

The average ending bankroll of those who didn't reach the maximum or go bust, which represented 51% of the sample, was $75. While this was a tripling of their initial $25 stake, it still represents a very suboptimal outcome given the opportunity presented. Exhibit 2.1 summarizes the performance of the 61 subjects, who in aggregate wagered on 7,253 coin flips, 59.6% of which came up heads.

Only 5 of our 61 financially sophisticated students and young investment professionals reported they had ever heard of constant fractional betting or related strategies.[†] Interestingly, this did not seem to help two of them: one barely managed to double his stake, and the other only broke even after about 100 flips. In post-experiment interviews, we found that the notion of betting a constant fraction of current bankroll seemed to be a surprisingly nonintuitive approach to playing this game. Our results do not offer any indication that participants were converging to optimal play over time, as evidenced by suboptimal betting of similar magnitude throughout the game.

[†] The actual question we asked them was whether they had ever heard of the Kelly criterion, which is one form of constant fractional betting, which we'll discuss later in the book.

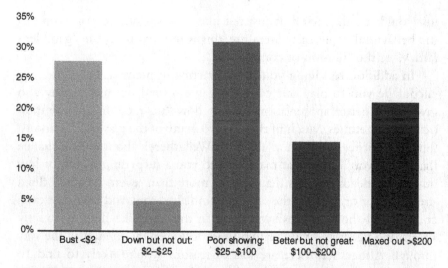

Exhibit 2.1 Summary of Coin Flipper Performance: Betting on a Coin with Disclosed Bias Toward Heads of 60%, $25 Starting Stake, $250 Maximum Payout

Of the 61 subjects, 18 subjects bet their entire bankroll on one flip at least once, which increased the probability of ruin from close to 0% using a constant fractional strategy to 40% if their all-in bet was on heads, or 60% if they bet it all on tails, which, amazingly, some of them did. The average bet size across all subjects was 15% of their bankroll at each flip, but the betting patterns were generally very erratic, with individuals betting too small and then too big, or vice versa. Betting patterns and post-experiment interviews revealed that quite a few participants felt that some sort of doubling down betting strategy was optimal. Another approach followed by a number of subjects was to bet small and constant wagers, apparently trying to reduce the probability of ruin and maximize the probability of ending up a winner.

We observed 67% of the subjects betting on tails at some point during the experiment. Betting on tails once or twice could potentially be attributed to curiosity about the game, but 48% of the players bet on tails more than five times in the game. It is possible that some of these subjects questioned whether the coin truly had a 60% bias toward heads—but that hypothesis is not supported by the fact that, within the subset of 13 subjects who bet on tails more than 25% of the time, we found they were more likely to make that bet right after the arrival of a string of heads. Victor's mom played the game just for fun and when asked why she bet on tails on a few occasions, she said, "I knew I shouldn't, but I just couldn't help myself. It just felt like tails was due to come up." In the behavioral economics literature, this is referred to as the "gambler's fallacy" or the "illusion of control bias."

In addition to giving you some practice in practical bet-sizing, we encourage you to play our coin-flip game several times as it may also give you a better appreciation for just how "un-random" randomness can feel sometimes. Much of the time, to many of the players, the first 10 flips will not feel random at all. Why? Well, there's about a 60% chance that either you'll flip what may seem to you a surprisingly high or low number of heads (say less than five, or more than seven) or you'll flip a streak of four or more of the same outcome in a row. And that's not even counting all the "patterns" you'll see in the flips, like flipping exactly alternating heads and tails, or two heads followed by one tail all the way through. Altogether, there are lots of reasons[†] you're likely to find 10 flips of the coin "un-random," and we invite you to play the game a few times to see if you agree.

It is widely believed that both Apple's iTunes and Spotify have made their algorithm for "shuffling" songs from a playlist somewhat nonrandom because in early versions when it was truly randomly generated, they got so many complaints from users that the play order just didn't seem random to them. In this spirit, we conducted a survey in 2017,[2] asking respondents to guess how many flips they'd want to see in order to discern, with 95% confidence, a fair coin from a coin biased 60% to land on heads. About 30% of the people thought 10 or fewer flips would do the trick, and roughly half thought that fewer than 30 flips would be enough. Most people, your authors included, are surprised at first that the correct answer is 143 flips, which we think is another indication of just how hard-wired humans are to draw conclusions from sample sizes that are too small, a behavioral bias termed the "law of small numbers bias."

Uncapped

If Victor and Rich had allowed the subjects to play the game without a maximum payout, and assuming the players bet 20% of their bankroll each flip, this would have been the most expensive social science

---

[†]None of them good reasons of course.

experiment of all time! For example, they'd have faced a one-in-four chance of having to pay out more than $100 million and a small but real chance of being on the hook for more than $1 billion! Besides being an amusing what-if feature of the experiment to contemplate, it also gives an idea for just how unbelievably great it would be to get a similar opportunity in real life.

Coin Flipping and the Stock Market

If you gave an investor the next day's news 24 hours in advance, he would go bust in less than a year.

—Nassim Nicholas Taleb

There are plenty of differences between flipping a coin and investing in the stock market, but we can draw some parallels too. Over the last 50 years, US equities had an excess annual return over T-Bills of about 7.5%, and returns had about 18% annual variability.[†] We can summarize the overall quality of returns over that period by looking at the ratio of excess returns to variability, which is about 0.4. A 70/30 biased coin has a similar ratio, so in broad strokes we can view the last half-century of equity returns as being similar to 50 flips of a 70/30 coin. It was a very good 50 years for US equities!

Probably the most significant difference to flipping coins is that with stock market investing, no one knows a priori the true distribution of returns. Maybe the last 50 years were just an extremely favorable series of draws. Indeed, looking to the future, we believe the prospective return/risk ratio of the stock market is much lower, closer to 0.3, which is more like flipping a 65/35 coin.

Most investors believe the stock market is not a successive set of independent flips of a coin, but that there are elements of mean reversion and trending in stock market behavior. Outlier events also happen with much higher frequency than with a series of coin flips. There's also a question of time scale: most people we discussed this with felt there is a fundamental difference between flipping a coin 300 times in 30 minutes and investing in the stock market where we have to patiently wait 30 years to get just 30 annual "flips."

[†] Measured by the standard deviation of returns, a statistical concept we'll return to later.

Investing in the stock market is much more nuanced and complex than betting on a biased coin, and no doubt it's easier to stick to a sound, albeit boring strategy for 30 minutes than to maintain that self-control for 30 years. But despite all the extra complexity, we'll be seeing soon that there's a good deal of overlap between the optimal strategy for coin-flipping games and for stock-market investing. We hope that by showing you the value of an optimal approach to this experiment, you'll be better equipped to follow a similar approach to risk-taking with your life-savings over the long term, where it really matters.

Connecting the Dots

This [coin-flip experiment] is a great experiment for many reasons. It ought to become part of the basic education of anyone interested in finance or gambling.
　　　　　　　　　　　　　　　　　　　　　　—Edward O. Thorp

While we did expect to observe some poorly conceived betting strategies from our subjects, we were surprised by the fact that so many players went bust betting on such a favorable opportunity. Before this experiment, we did not appreciate just how ill-equipped so many people are to appreciate or take advantage of a simple advantageous opportunity in the presence of uncertainty. The straightforward notion of taking a constant and moderate amount of risk and letting the odds work in one's favor just doesn't seem obvious to most people. We wondered whether these ideas were being taught in university finance and economics courses, and so we reviewed the syllabi of introductory courses focused on trading and asset pricing at five leading business schools in the United States. Constant fractional betting was not mentioned in any of them, either explicitly or through the topic of optimal betting strategies in the presence of favorable odds.

Given that many of our subjects received formal training in finance, we were surprised that the idea of constant proportional betting, or other approaches to investment sizing, was virtually unknown, and that they didn't seem to possess the analytical tool kit to lead them to constant fractional betting as an intuitively appealing heuristic. Without a framework to rely upon, we found that our subjects exhibited a menu of widely documented behavioral biases such as illusion of control, anchoring, overbetting, sunk-cost bias, and gambler's fallacy.

These results raise important questions. If a high fraction of quantitatively sophisticated, financially trained individuals have so much difficulty in playing a simple game with a biased coin, what should we expect when it comes to the more complex and long-term task of investing one's savings? Is it any surprise that people will pay for patently useless advice, as documented in studies like the aptly titled "Why Do People Pay for Useless Advice?"[3] Our research suggests there is a significant gap in the education of young finance and economics students when it comes to the central topic of this book—how much of a good thing is best for you. The $5,574 in winnings we paid out to our 61 subjects will be money very well spent if it helps encourage educators to fill the void, either through direct instruction, trial-and-error exercises like our game, or assigning this book!

3

Size Matters When It's for Real

There is a precipice on either side of you: a precipice of caution and a precipice of over-daring.

—Winston Churchill

In Chapter 2 we learned a great deal by focusing on a simple coin-flipping experiment, but it was still just a game played in the classroom. Now let's move toward exploring sizing decisions in the world of investing by allowing you to start off with not just $25 but with all your wealth, say one million dollars of hard-earned savings, and removing the cap on upside outcomes. The coin still has a 60% chance of coming up heads, you can bet any fraction of your wealth on each flip, and you have 25 flips. This may still not sound especially like real-world investing! But imagine in this setup betting 10% of your wealth each round. Now there's a 60% chance of making 10% each go, and a 40% chance of losing 10%. In a stylized way, that pattern of returns from each of those 25 flips is actually not so far off from investing in the stock market for about 6 months.[1] It's a crude representation of stock market investing, but looking at what's going on in this simple way is going to let us build up to something more sophisticated down the road.

In this chapter, we will continue to focus on the constant fractional betting approach and our goal will be to explore what's the best fraction of wealth our investor should bet on each flip. Sounds pretty similar to the previous chapter, but there are two critical differences that merit a new look at the whole question: there's no cap, and large fractions of wealth can potentially be on the line. These changes may sound subtle, but as we'll see these nudges in the direction of greater realism make a dramatic difference in how we need to approach the whole problem.

While constant fractional betting is just one of many possible betting strategies, under some fairly reasonable assumptions we'll see that it is the best overall strategy for situations involving a series of independent favorable gambles, like the example at hand. But what do we mean by "best"? In the experiment from Chapter 2, we said the "best" strategy is the one with the highest expected payout, and we found that betting 10% to 20% of current bankroll was in the ballpark of optimal in giving the player an expected payout of about $240, very close to the maximum. In this more realistic situation though, shooting for the same notion of "best" would be disastrous! To see why we need to dig into what we mean by "expected" a bit more.

Defining "Expected Value"

We want to be precise about what we mean by the "expected" payout of a given strategy. For every possible combination of 25 flips, it's the weighted average of each resulting payout using the strategy, weighted by the probability of that payout occurring. In Table 3.1, we show the calculation for the expected payout that would result from betting 10% of wealth on *five* consecutive flips of a 60/40 biased coin.

Table 3.1 Calculating Expected Payout

Number of "Heads" Flips	Number of "Tails" Flips	Probability	Ending Wealth	Probability × Wealth
0	5	1.0%	$590,490	$6,047
1	4	7.7%	$721,710	$55,427
2	3	23.0%	$882,090	$203,234
3	2	34.6%	$1,078,110	$372,595
4	1	25.9%	$1,317,690	$341,565
5	0	7.8%	$1,610,510	$125,233
Expected Payout		100.0%		$1,104,081

Maximizing Expected Wealth?

Now that we've defined what we mean by "expected," let's come back to whether it makes sense to try and maximize your expected wealth using a fractional betting strategy. It seems like a reasonable starting point, so let's take a look at the results in Table 3.2.

The last row in Table 3.2, giving an expected payout of $95 million sounds pretty good! If the objective is to maximize expected wealth, you should bet 100% of wealth on each flip of the coin. Now you don't need to read a book like this to know that's a crazy choice to make, because you'll lose all your money if the coin lands on tails just

Table 3.2 Expected Wealth Over a Range of Betting Fractions

Betting Fraction	Expected Wealth After 25 flips
1%	$1,051,219
5%	$1,282,432
10%	$1,640,606
20%	$2,665,836
30%	$4,291,871
40%	$6,848,745
50%	$10,834,706
75%	$32,918,953
100%	$95,396,217

once during the 25 flips. The probability of getting wiped out at some point is 99.9997%! But the expected payout calculation is nonetheless correct—the reason it's so high is because there's a 0.0003% probability of flipping 25 heads in a row and winding up with a cool $34 trillion (showing why removing the cap was such an important change). We have found this result often surprises people, because they intuitively feel that the strategy that maximizes expected wealth has to be one that avoids ruin and keeps you in the game. But the math says otherwise: betting it all on each flip is the strategy that gives you the highest expected wealth at the end.

What about a strategy designed to maximize expected wealth subject to keeping the probability of a large loss below a given threshold? The reasoning here might be that if individual bets have a positive edge, and you minimize the chance of being "knocked out" and forced to stop betting, the rest will take care of itself. To make it more concrete, say you want to maximize expected wealth subject to keeping the probability of losing more than 80% below a 5% probability. One way to achieve this would be to put 20% of your wealth to the side, and then bet all remaining wealth on each flip of the coin. This achieves the goal of maximizing expected wealth subject to the loss constraint, but the trouble is that now you are nearly certain to lose 80% of wealth. It's pretty clear that defining the "best" strategy using expected wealth in this way isn't getting us very far.

Maximize "Middle" Wealth?

So, onward! Instead of trying to maximize expected wealth, how about choosing the betting fraction that maximizes the "median" payout, which is the middle-most outcome where there's a 50% chance of doing better or worse. With 25 flips of our biased coin, the median outcome is 15 heads and 10 tails. Table 3.3 shows this median outcome over a range of bet fractions.

This is looking more promising. Unlike with the expected payout objective, here we have a clear peak at the 20% bet size, so there's a natural "best" betting fraction from the standpoint of median profit.

Table 3.3   Most Likely Wealth Over a Range of Betting Fractions

Betting Fraction	Most Likely (Median) Wealth After 25 flips
1%	$1,049,960
5%	$1,244,731
10%	$1,456,516
20%	**$1,654,316**
30%	$1,445,875
40%	$940,661
50%	$427,631
75%	$4,217
100%	$0

Size Increases Lift and Drag

But there's something curious at work here too: How can it be that for a series of good bets, each with a 60% chance of winning, betting 50% of wealth each time can lead to a median wealth quite a lot lower than it was initially (see the 50% row in Table 3.3)? That sounds strange, but this is one of those interesting cases where digging a little deeper yields a valuable insight. The following diagram shows what's going on, based on starting with $100 and betting 50% on two consecutive flips that come up heads and then tails:

With fractional betting strategies like we're considering, winning and losing (or losing and winning) a pair of bets doesn't leave us back where

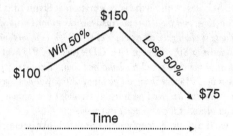

we started—we're down slightly, and this "drag" gets bigger quickly as the bet size increases.[†] Two effects are at work over a series of bets:

1. There's a "lift" from winning more bets than we're losing.
2. There's a "drag" from having lots of win/lose and lose/win pairs.

As bet size increases, both lift and drag increase, but the drag increases faster. This naturally creates the peaked profile we see in median profit from Table 3.3 and explains why even for a great series of bets with a positive edge, betting too big can still most likely be a losing strategy. We'll refer to this drag arising from the variability of outcomes as, not surprisingly, "volatility drag."

This example perfectly illustrates what we mean when we say that bet-sizing is just as important as identifying good bets. By overbetting, it can be highly likely that we'll lose money, even when betting on events where the odds are in our favor. Most people would see it as a cruel joke to lose 99.6% of their wealth after being given an attractive repeated opportunity and then getting exactly the expected series of outcomes—but that's exactly what would happen if we bet 75% of wealth on heads on each flip (see second-to-last row of Table 3.3).[‡]

In *The Biggest Bluff*, Maria Konnikova's book about learning to play professional poker, elite player Erik Seidel explains that even among top poker players, most go broke after a while because of poor bankroll management. We think what Seidel meant is that these highly skilled players could expect to have a positive average return from their play,

---

[†] MIT Economics Professor Andy Lo brought some humor to the topic of volatility drag in a talk he gave at Myron Scholes' 80th birthday celebration at Stanford (October 2022): *I was at Queens College in New York, and there was an economics class that I decided to sit in on. And the instructor who was a graduate student gave an example of GDP. It's 100, and imagine that GDP goes down by 20%, so it goes down to 80. And then later, GDP goes up 20% from 80, and it goes up to 96. And a puzzled student in the class raised his hand and said, "Excuse me, professor, but why is it the case when you go down by 20% and then you go up by 20%, you don't get back to a hundred." And the graduate student scratched her head for a while, she did a few calculations on the board, and said, "Well, economics is an inexact science, so don't worry about it."*

[‡] Later, in Chapter 23, we'll dig more deeply into this cruel joke, seeing how it's possible to lose money on an investment, and on the opposite of that investment too! The example of overbetting on coin flips gives us an insight into this; strategies of betting 75% of wealth on heads every flip will lose money under most possible outcomes of flips, such as the most likely case of flipping 15 heads and 10 tails.

unlike poor and mediocre players, but they play using an overly aggressive level of sizing. So their skill gives them some "lift" from winning more than they lose, but they still go broke in the end because of the high volatility drag at the extreme sizing level they choose.

Goldilocks Bet-Sizing

Returning to betting on 25 flips of a 60/40 coin with no profit cap, we've found that a 20% bet size is what maximizes your median profit. Much smaller and there's very little variance drag but not much profit either; much bigger and the drag is just overwhelming. So this maximizing of the median profit certainly seems like something important to care about, but is that it, are we done? We're getting closer, but need to keep investigating just a little further. Table 3.4 shows all the measures we've been discussing across bet sizes ranging from 1% to 40% of capital. We also show a few more numbers that are focused on the downside: the probabilities of losing 50% and 80% of starting wealth for the different bet sizes, and end wealth if heads come up only 13 instead of 15 times. We encourage you to spend a few minutes looking at the table and thinking about which bet size most appeals to you.

Table 3.4 Betting "Heads" on 25 Flips of a 60/40 Biased Coin, $1mm Starting Wealth

Bet Size (% of Wealth)	1%	5%	10%	20%	40%
Probability of losing 80% or more of starting wealth	Impossible	Impossible	0.005%	1%	27%
Probability of losing 50% or more of starting wealth	Impossible	0.01%	1%	15%	41%
End wealth from winning 13/25 flips	$1,008,789	$1,018,930	$975,023	$732,252	$172,774
End wealth from winning 15/25 flips (median outcome)	$1,049,960	$1,244,731	$1,456,516	$1,654,316	$940,661
Expected final wealth	$1,051,219	$1,282,432	$1,640,606	$2,665,836	$6,848,475

Which of these bet sizes looks best to you? From our own experience, surveys we've conducted, and academic studies, we would guess that of the five choices presented in Table 3.4, almost all readers would narrow the choice down to the 5%, 10%, or 20% bet sizes, and that the most popular bet size would be 10%. The 20% bet size has the distinction of producing the highest median profit, but it entails a material chance of serious loss too. Notice that if we bet 20% and end up getting 13 heads, still pretty close to the median and winning more than we've lost, we lose 26% of starting wealth—ouch! By contrast, the 10% bet size still produces a healthy profit in the median case, but with much lower risk of loss. The 5% bet size is also in the running, as it completely eliminates the chance of losing 80% or more of wealth. The 1% and 40% bet sizes just don't pass the smell test: the 1% is just too small to be worthwhile, while at 40% there's a high chance of large loss, and it loses money even in the median case of flipping 15 heads. So a 10% bet size seems pretty good. We're not claiming it's exactly optimal, for anyone or everyone, but we think for many people it's a reasoned and reasonable choice for a good bet size in this particular situation.

Standard Deviation as a Measure of Risk

Expected profit allows us to compare coin flip bets based on how much they will . . . well . . . profit. We are also going to need a measure to compare their risks. Far and away the most common measure of risk is standard deviation, a measure of statistical variability. It's not the only useful measure of risk, and it does not fully represent the risk of many investments. Later in the book, we'll discuss how to evaluate risk more generally beyond standard deviation, but for the purposes of developing a simple rule of thumb for bet-sizing, it does the job as well or better than any of the alternatives. The standard deviation of a $1 bet on the result of flipping a fair coin is $1.

The two most important characteristics of standard deviation for us here are the way that standard deviation scales with bet size and how it grows for a series of bets. Standard deviation scales one-to-one with bet size, so a bet of $2 on a fair coin would have a standard deviation of $2. The part that may not be as intuitive at first is that the standard deviation for a series of four independent $1 coin-flipping bets is $2. For nine flips it would be $3, etc. So for an arbitrary number of N bets of $1, the standard deviation of outcomes would be $\sqrt{N}$ dollars. A moment's reflection can give us some intuition for why the standard deviation of two $1 bets for example is $\sqrt{2}$ = $1.41 and not $2. When a coin is flipped twice, we wind up with cancellations in the case of heads followed by tails, or tails followed by heads, which reduce the spread of possible outcomes.

In Search of a General Rule of Thumb

In our discussion of Goldilocks bet-sizing, to get to our "feel good" bet size of 10% we analyzed a table of statistics for different bet-sizing strategies applied to twenty-five flips of a 60/40 biased coin. The only thing needed to generate Table 3.4 was the probability of heads, p. It would be nice if we had a rule of thumb that told us what fraction of wealth to invest based on p. It seems natural to want to bet a larger fraction of wealth the more attractive the bet is—that is, the bigger p is. And in fact in this limited case we could come up with a useful rule based solely on p. But it turns out that if we generalize slightly, our rule will be useful in more realistic scenarios like how much we should invest in the stock market. So instead, let's try to derive our rule based on the two most important statistics for any probability distribution, expected value (or mean) and standard deviation.[†]

Let's assume you went through the effort to generate Table 3.4 and concluded that 10% is your optimal bet size for a 60/40 biased coin. How attractive would the coin-flip have to be to double the optimal bet size to 20%? We can simplify the discussion and avoid constantly saying "10% of your wealth," by just talking about doubling the optimal bet size from $100 to $200. So let's think about making the $100 bet on a 60/40 coin four times in a row. The expected profit on each individual bet is $20 (60% probability of a $100 gain minus 40% probability of a $100 loss), so the expected profit on the series of four $100 bets is $80. And each of the four $100 bets has a standard deviation of $100, so the series together has a standard deviation of $200, *the same as one $200 bet*.[‡]

[†] Our treatment here is meant to give intuition and a more general feel for why this bet-sizing rule of thumb makes sense, under the stylized assumptions on which it's based. More rigorous derivations are provided in Rosenbluth and White (2023), "The Merton Share" on www.elmwealth.com/research. For the original derivation, see Merton, 1969. Also see Campbell & Viceira, 2002, Chapter 2.

[‡] More precisely, the standard deviation of both one $200 bet or four $100 bets is $196 for a 60/40 coin. We've done some rounding of the numbers here and through the rest of this chapter for clarity of exposition.

Since betting $200 on one flip has the same risk, i.e. standard deviation, as the series of four flips, it seems sensible to want the same expected profit. So for $200 to be the optimal size to bet on just one flip, you'd want $80 of expected profit on the $200 bet. This implies that you'd need the coin to have a 70/30 bias in order to bet $200 on just one flip ($80 = 70% probability of a $200 gain minus 30% probability of a $200 loss).

Zooming out a little, what we're finding is that if standard deviation *doubles*, you'll need to get *four times* the expected gain. If it triples, you'll need to get nine times the expected gain; if it halves you'll need only one quarter of the expected gain, etc. This suggests a relation between expected gain and the *square* of standard deviation, which is called variance. Thus, for a given level of risk preference and an optimal investment size, the ratio of expected gain to variance is going to be **constant**.

Let's call that personal risk preference constant γ (the Greek letter "gamma"), and the optimal wealth-fraction to bet we'll call k.[†] This is going to be the only time we do any algebra in this book, but it'll be very helpful to put these words into symbols. If you've bet the fraction $\hat{k}$ on a gamble with expected return μ and standard deviation σ, then the expected return of your bet is $\hat{k}\mu$, the standard deviation is $\hat{k}\sigma$, and the variance is $\left(\hat{k}\sigma\right)^2$. We can write:

$$\gamma = \frac{\hat{k}\mu}{\left(\hat{k}\sigma\right)^2},$$ which we can simplify and rearrange as:

$$\hat{k} = \frac{\mu}{\gamma\sigma^2}$$

Putting the symbols back into words, our rule of thumb for bet-sizing says:

The optimal bet size, expressed as a fraction of wealth, is directly proportional to the gamble's expected return, and inversely proportional to its variance and to your personal degree of risk-aversion.

If you would optimally bet 10% of wealth on a coin-flip that had $0.20 of expected gain and $1 of standard deviation, that means that your personal risk preference constant, γ, would be equal to 2. And we

---

[†] If it helps, you can think of "k" as the fraction of "kapital" to invest in the risky asset.

see that the rule of thumb does produce your chosen 10% optimal bet size for a 60/40 coin:[†]

$$10\% = \frac{0.20}{2(1)^2}$$

We've shown that this general rule of thumb for bet-sizing is sensible, but we haven't proven that it's absolutely optimal. A somewhat more complex endeavor was Robert Merton's proof that, given normally distributed returns, continuous rebalancing, and a few other assumptions, $\hat{k} = \frac{\mu}{\gamma\sigma^2}$ is indeed the optimal bet size, nicely marrying theory and intuition.[2] One of the most influential finance theorists of the twentieth century, Merton was instrumental in developing the mathematics used to answer many questions like this in finance, and the formula is often known as the "Merton share." His focus extended beyond discrete, binary gambles and into more continuous investment opportunities like stocks. He went on to link optimal investment strategies and optimal spending strategies. This isn't the last time we'll encounter his work and influence in these pages.

The Kelly Criterion

There's another path we could have taken in finding a general rule, a path first marked out by the Bell Labs physicist John Kelly in a now-classic 1956 paper on information theory.[3] Kelly was thinking about the optimal amount of wealth to bet on a binary gamble and concluded, as we did at the beginning of this chapter, that optimizing expected wealth makes no sense. Instead, he proposed optimizing the rate of growth of wealth. He wrote a mathematical expression for the wealth growth rate as a function of the terms of the bet and from that derived a formula for the optimal bet size that maximizes it, which has since become known as the Kelly criterion:

$$\hat{k} = \frac{edge}{odds}$$

[†]This is an approximation, as the exact variance of a 60/40 coin is 0.96. The rule of thumb is also implicitly assuming a continuous distribution of returns while the coin-flip outcomes are discrete, so it won't in general perfectly reproduce the long-form method for finding the preferred bet size, though it will typically be close.

where "edge" is the ratio of expected gain to potential loss, and "odds" is the ratio of potential gain to potential loss.[†] For example, risking $10 to make $30 represents "odds" of 3. Our coin-flipping game has an edge of 20% and odds of 1, so the Kelly criterion yields an optimal bet size of 20%. For symmetric, binary gambles like our coin flip, the formula simplifies to an easy-to-remember formula of:

$$\hat{k} = p - q$$

where p and q are the probabilities of winning and losing, respectively.

But we had decided that 10% was in fact our preferred bet size. How do we reconcile this discrepancy? In getting to the 10%, we had taken our personal risk-aversion into account, and the Merton share formalized this in the parameter γ. But the Kelly criterion has no explicit notion of risk-aversion; it's just maximizing the rate of growth of wealth, period. It turns out that for continuous-time investments, this is exactly equivalent to the Merton Share with $\gamma = 1$, though we won't see exactly why until Chapter 6. Many professional gamblers in practice use a variant of the Kelly criterion called "fractional Kelly," in which they incorporate a personal risk preference by betting a fraction, most frequently one half, of the "full Kelly" bet, according to their taste. We can see that "half Kelly" agrees with our preferred sizing of 10% for a 60/40 coin flip, and 20% for a 70/30 flip. In the case of coin flips, half Kelly and the Merton share with risk-aversion of 2 will agree pretty closely, especially when the optimal bet size is small, though they won't agree exactly save in the case of continuous and normally distributed returns.

Connecting the Dots

What we've discussed in this chapter is not in the curriculum of finance programs or bank training programs. At several talks Victor has given at university business schools and investment bank training programs, he

---

[†]The Kelly criterion is often expressed as $\hat{k} = p - q/b$, where p and q are the probabilities of winning and losing, and b is the "odds," or ratio of winning payout to losing payout. This can be rearranged to $\hat{k} = (pb - q)/b$, where the numerator is the "edge," the expected gain of the bet, and b is the "odds."

would display the Merton share and ask for a show of hands for those who had seen it before:

$$\hat{k} = \frac{\mu}{\gamma\sigma^2}$$

Hardly a hand in the audience would go up. By contrast, the majority of the audience consistently raised their hands when shown the much more complex Black-Scholes option pricing formula:

$$C = N(d_1)S_t - N(d_2)Ke^{-rt}$$

$$d_1 = \frac{\ln\dfrac{S_t}{K} + \left(r + \dfrac{\sigma^2}{2}\right)t}{\sigma\sqrt{t}}$$

$$d_2 = d_1 - \sigma\sqrt{t}$$

We know that banks and universities are not generally interested in teaching people to bet on sports, cards, or coin-flipping games, but they should be preparing people to think sensibly about markets, risk, and investing. As we develop increasingly realistic portraits of markets and our financial lives in further chapters, we'll eventually need to move beyond this coin-flipping paradigm and the simple Merton share. But there are actually some important personal financial decisions we can get started answering just with the work we've done so far.

4

A Taste of the Merton Share

In the previous chapter, we arrived at a very useful rule of thumb for investment sizing decisions, the Merton share:

$\hat{k} = \dfrac{\mu}{\gamma\sigma^2}$ *where μ is the expected excess return of the risky investment*

you're considering, σ is the riskiness of that investment expressed as standard deviation of returns, and γ is your personal degree of risk-aversion.

Let's get a taste for the Merton share by seeing what light it can shed on some practical investing questions.

Should You Have a Static or Dynamic Allocation to Equities?

If you believe that the expected return and risk of the equity market change over time in a way that can be estimated, then your optimal allocation to equities should also change. In the next chapter, we'll explore this topic in considerably more depth.

What Expected Return and Risk for the Stock Market Underlie the Traditional 60%/40% Portfolio?

Using the Merton share, we can draw Exhibit 4.1, which shows, for three different levels of risk-aversion, what combination of stock market expected excess return and risk would justify wanting to allocate your wealth 60%/40% between stocks and bonds. We measure excess returns relative to bonds, which we take to be risk-free. For our typical coefficient of risk-aversion (γ) of 2 and 20% annual standard deviation of stock returns,[†] the required excess return for stocks relative to bonds is about 5% per annum. Perhaps the 60/40 recommended stock/

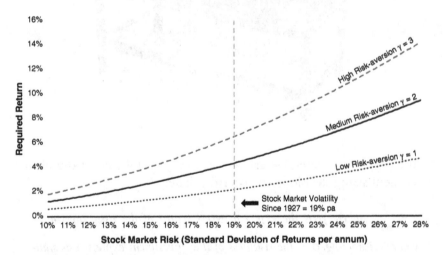

Exhibit 4.1   Return Versus Risk Trade-offs to Justify 60/40 Stock/Bond Allocation Using Merton Share Formula

---

[†] Taking a round number, a bit higher than the 19.2% annualized volatility of S&P 500 daily returns from 1928 to the end of 2022.

bond allocation isn't quite as arbitrary as it may seem, considering that since 1900, the realized return of US stocks in excess of US government bonds was roughly 6% per annum.[1]

Many of the examples we use to illustrate core concepts will assume that we live in a two-asset world in which there is one risky asset and one risk-free asset. Toward the end of Chapter 14, we'll devote more discussion to how to build a multi-asset portfolio, but we hope a few words here will make you more comfortable staying with us in a two-asset world for a while. The reason we can focus on the investment sizing decision on its own without worrying about how every possible investment or strategy interacts with every other one, is that, in an ideal world where asset prices are well behaved, it is possible to approach portfolio construction in two steps:[2]

1. Taking as inputs expected returns and covariances, find the combination of risky assets that produces the highest ratio of expected excess return versus risk, measuring excess return against the risk-free asset. This is your optimal risky portfolio.
2. Decide how much of that optimal risky portfolio you want to own, based on its attractiveness and your risk preferences. Then put the rest of your capital into the risk-free asset, or borrow if you want to put more than 100% of capital into the risky portfolio.

What Would It Take to Be an All-in Tesla Investor?

On social media, we find many self-confessed "All-in Tesla" investors who have virtually all their wealth invested in the stock. Indeed, Elon Musk has borrowed money to be close to all-in on Tesla, while also holding big stakes in SpaceX and Twitter. Many of these investors have increased their wealth spectacularly in the process.[†] It's often the case that the path to great riches involves taking a lot of risk, and so it's not surprising that such investors often find it difficult to make the transition to more reasoned investment sizing.

[†] And many of them are not shy about letting the rest of the world know.

It's interesting to consider how bullish you would need to be to justify such a position, given Tesla's stock volatility has been around 60% per annum since it became a public company. Using the Merton share formula, and assuming our Base-Case risk-aversion of 2, we find that you needed to believe the expected return of Tesla stock was 72% per annum.[†] And, in fact, Tesla returned 60% per annum since its initial public offering in June 2010 through November 2021, not so far from the required expectation. If you believed Tesla was going to return 12% per annum above the risk-free rate, which was still a very bullish outlook at about twice the expectation for the broad US stock market, the Merton share would have suggested putting 17% of your wealth in Tesla.

We should note that in both previous applications of the Merton share, we're making the unrealistic assumption that Tesla was the only risky asset available, or that it would have zero correlation with the broad stock market. More realistic assumptions would require even greater optimism on Tesla to justify high allocations to this highly volatile stock.

What About Really Small Investments?

Human felicity is produced not so much by great pieces of good fortune that seldom happen, as by little advantages that occur every day.

—Benjamin Franklin

If your net worth is $1,000,000, what expected gain is needed to optimally bet $100 on a coin flip? Using the Merton share the answer is we need just 2 cents of advantage on a $100 bet. Expressed in terms of a biased coin, this is saying that with $1,000,000 of wealth you should gladly bet $100 on a coin biased only 50.01% toward heads. Talk about a tiny edge! If that seems too small, consider this: if you have 60% in the stock market and the rest in a riskless asset, in just 15 seconds your wealth will fluctuate by about $100, just like with the coin flip.[3] Using a 3% return for your portfolio of stocks and bonds, the expected gain in those 15 seconds is about 2 cents, just as with the coin flip.

While this exploration of how much to wager on small bets may seem irrelevant to most real-world investors, in fact it sits at the foundation of many successful market-makers, high-frequency trading firms,

---

[†] $\dfrac{72\%}{2 \times 60\%^2} = 100\%$. This is in excess of the safe asset return, but at 72%, that hardly matters.

and professional book-making operations. A Wall Street trading desk with $10 billion in capital would be happy taking $10 million of risk on a trade for an expected gain of just $20,000, *as long as* the many individual trades they're making have a low correlation with one another. Finding a high volume of low-correlation trades is difficult, so for competitive reasons these firms tend to be quite secretive about their edge. But Robert Mercer, former co-CEO at Renaissance Technologies, has stated that historically their trades have been successful only about 50.75% of the time.[4] By being able to find lots of these opportunities that are ever-so-slightly in their favor, *and sizing them sensibly*, they've generated a compound return of more than 60% from 1988 to 2021.

Many of the bets that professional gamblers face also have just a tiny bit more than a 50% chance of winning. For instance, gamblers proficient at card-counting in casino six-deck blackjack games have about a 51% chance of winning each hand when the deck evolves in their favor. Correct bet-sizing is critical to success and has been written about extensively by a number of professional gamblers. One of the most well-known and prolific of these is Ed Thorp, a mathematics professor, professional gambler, and hedge fund manager who in 1962 penned *Beat the Dealer: A Winning Strategy for the Game of Twenty-one*.

A good rule of thumb for people with a normal amount of risk-aversion is that if you are offered a gamble that is independent from existing risks you bear, and the downside represents less than 0.1% of your wealth, you should accept it if it has a positive expected value, because the edge you need to accept such a gamble is so small.

Does Time Horizon Matter?

In the Merton share formula, you may have noticed that time is not one of the inputs, suggesting that horizon may not matter. And indeed with coin flips, for a given edge the optimal amount to bet on one flip or a series of one hundred flips is the same. To the extent investments are like a series of biased coin flips and follow a random walk, then whether we choose a month, a year, or a decade as the horizon for our investment won't affect the optimal amount to invest.

Most observers reasonably feel that things are more complicated when it comes to real-world investing. Financial asset prices are not as well behaved as coin flips, and also our personal circumstances, including taxation of capital gains, can make investment time horizon a very relevant input to sizing decisions. However, it is a useful starting point to realize that under a simple set of assumptions, horizon does not impact the sizing decision. We'll spend more time on this issue in Chapter 9, when we address multi-period frameworks for lifetime investment, saving, and spending decisions.

$1,000,000, No Tears

It seems fitting to finish this chapter with an example bringing us back to a situation that is essentially a single coin flip. The opening pages of *Liar's Poker*, Michael Lewis' classic take on Wall Street in the 1980s, describes an unconsummated and, according to the protagonists, apocryphal mano-a-mano hand between two senior Salomon Brothers executives. One of them, John Meriwether, was Victor's boss at the time:

> One hand, one million dollars, no tears. Meriwether grabbed the meaning instantly. The King of Wall Street, as Businessweek had dubbed Gutfreund, wanted to play a single hand of a game called Liar's Poker for a million dollars. . .
>
> The peculiar feature of Gutfreund's challenge this time was the size of the stake. Normally his bets didn't exceed a few hundred dollars. A million was unheard of. . . . But why?. . . Meriwether was the King of the Game, the Liar's Poker champion of the Salomon Brothers trading floor. . . .
>
> The code of Liar's Poker. . . required a trader to accept all challenges. . . . Because of the code—which was his code—John Meriwether felt obliged to play. But he knew it was stupid. For him, there was no upside. If he won, he upset Gutfreund. . . . But if he lost, he was out of pocket a million bucks. . . .Although Meriwether was by far the better player of the game, in a single hand anything could happen. . . . Meriwether spent his entire day avoiding dumb bets, and he wasn't about to accept this one. "No, John," he said, "if we're going to play for those kind of numbers, I'd rather play for real money. Ten million dollars. No tears. ". . .
>
> Gutfreund declined. . .he smiled his own brand of forced smile and said, "You're crazy."
>
> No, thought Meriwether, just very, very good.

Connecting the Dots

What we've seen is that the expected profit required from a gamble increases not with the size of the risk, but rather with the size of the risk *squared*. A single hand of Liar's Poker is random enough that there's essentially no expected profit, so when John Meriwether proposed upping the risk 10-fold, he was actually raising the "cost" of the game to both of them a hundredfold (remember, it's the standard deviation of the gamble *squared* that matters). As Meriwether guessed, that kind of increase in the cost of the risk was too much for Gutfreund to accept on a lark. And, as Michael Lewis rightly surmised, it was a calculated decision from a person who had a sound understanding of the price of risk.

5

How Much to Invest in the Stock Market?

I was in front of an ambulance the other day, and I noticed that the word "ambulance" was spelled in reverse print on the hood of the ambulance. And I thought, "Well, isn't that clever. I look in the rear-view mirror; I can read the word ambulance behind me. Of course while you're reading, you don't see where you're going, you crash. You need an ambulance. I think they're trying to drum up some business on the way back from lunch."
—Jerry Seinfeld, Comedian

In the previous chapter, we started to discuss using a personalized formula, in the form of the Merton share, to decide how much to invest in a risky investment like the stock market. The rule encodes the idea that we should own more of a risky investment when its expected return is higher or when its riskiness is lower. It only seems natural that we should want to use this formula as part of a dynamic asset allocation strategy, where we vary the fraction of our portfolio we keep in the stock market.

Believing that the expected return of the stock market changes over time is not at odds with a belief in market efficiency. Just like the price of milk and eggs, the expected aggregate real returns available in the market are a function of supply and demand—in particular, the supply of investments and the demand from savers. As this supply/demand dynamic changes over time, so too do expected market returns, even in the perfectly efficient markets imagined by finance theorists. As an example, consider the market for US Treasury bonds. The market is highly efficient, the expected returns to maturity are known at each point in time, and they change every day as well.

It's not enough to believe that expected returns change over time—in order to sensibly act, we also must be able to reasonably estimate just how they're changing. Happily, there is good reason to believe there are major asset classes for which this can be done. The most popular metric for estimating the expected return of a broad stock market is known as Shiller's cyclically adjusted price-to-earnings ratio (CAPE).[†] When the CAPE ratio is high, investors are paying a high price for a normalized stream of earnings, and the prospective return of the stock market is low. This finding makes logical and intuitive sense and is borne out in historical data over a long horizon. However, we caution that this relationship holds only for broad stock markets, not for individual stocks or sectors.

We can say something still more specific and powerful: $\frac{1}{CAPE}$ is a pretty good, though imperfect, predictor of the inflation-adjusted (i.e., *real*) return of the stock market over a long horizon. The measure $\frac{1}{CAPE}$ is known as the cyclically adjusted earnings yield (we'll often

---

[†] While the CAPE ratio has become most closely associated with Yale Professor Robert Shiller, it was first suggested by Benjamin Graham and David Dodd in their classic text, *Security Analysis* (1934). It might also have been called the Campbell-Shiller CAPE ratio, as John Campbell coauthored the 1988 paper, *Stock Prices, Earnings and Expected Dividends* in which they observed that "a long moving average of real earnings helps to forecast future real dividends."

shorten to "earnings yield") because it's calculated as earnings divided by price. If you invest in the stock market when the earnings yield is 6%, your best expectation is that you'll earn a long-term return (after inflation) of 6%.[1] This is telling us that, contrary to some popular views, when earnings yield is low, we shouldn't expect to lose money in the long term from the earnings yield reverting to some average higher level. In other words, the predictive power of earnings yield over a long horizon is *not* improved by assuming that it is mean-reverting. What's important is the starting earnings yield of the market, much as the yield to maturity of a 10-year fixed rate bond at time of purchase almost entirely predicts its 10-year return.[2] Exhibit 5.1 illustrates the relationship between earnings yield and prospective realized real return, using a horizon of 10 years.

Does this seem reasonable? Ask yourself if you would have expected the US stock market to deliver the same long-term real return starting in 1965 when the earnings yield was 4.3%, versus what it would deliver from 1985 when the earnings yield was 10%.[3] If you answered no, you'd be correct. Since we're looking at just two data points, we'll evaluate them over a long horizon of 30 years. What we find is that over the subsequent 30 years, the real return of the US stock market was only 4.2% from 1965, but a hefty 8.2% from 1985, neither outcome too far

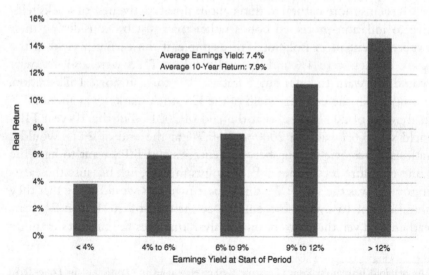

Exhibit 5.1 Next 10-year Realized Real Return Versus Earnings Yield at Start: US Equities 1900–2022

from the earnings yield at the start of the period. Also, while expected returns were very different from the starting points of 1965 and 1985, the realized market risk over the two ensuing 30-year periods was virtually the same. It is important to realize that the bars in Exhibit 5.1 represent returns averaged over many 10 year periods, and they do not show the sometimes quite large difference between forecast and realized return for any one particular 10-year window. For example, a large miss occurred in the 10 years starting in 2012, with a forecast real return of about 5% and a realized return of 14%.

If we want to use earnings yield and expected real returns to decide how much to invest in the stock market, to be consistent we also need to evaluate alternatives to stocks in terms of their expected long-term real return. It seems natural to turn to US Treasury inflation-protected securities (TIPS) as the relevant low-risk alternative to stocks, since the yield on TIPS is a measure of their expected *real* return, and so provides a directly comparable measurement to the earnings yield of equities.[4] Indeed, there are strong arguments that "the [inflation] indexed perpetuity is the riskless asset for a long-term investor, since it finances a constant consumption stream over time," as suggested by Harvard professors Campbell and Viceira in "Who Should Buy Long-Term Bonds" (2001).[†] For practical purposes, long-term TIPS are pretty close to the inflation-indexed perpetuity they suggest.

It seems more natural to think about the attractiveness of stocks relative to inflation-protected bonds rather than just by considering their expected returns in isolation. For example, if the earnings yield of the stock market were 4% and the real yield on TIPS were also 4%, why would we want to own any equities?[5] Or for a historical illustration, consider that the earnings yield of the US stock market was about 2.7% at the end of 2000 and also at the end of 2021—but the 10-year TIPS yield was 3.6% back in 2000 and −0.7% at the end of 2021. Would a rational investor choosing between equities and TIPS want to have the same exposure to equities at both points in time, just because the earnings yield was the same? We think most investors would agree that they should want to own more equities at the end of 2021 than 21 years earlier. And yet, the conventional analysis that uses the market's earnings

---

[†] As Stanford economist John Cochrane further elaborates in "Portfolios for Long-Term Investors" (2021), *"Their [Campbell and Viceira's] proposition is obvious if you look at the payoffs. An (inflation) indexed perpetuity gives a perfectly steady stream of real income, which can finance a steady risk-free stream of consumption. It is the risk-free payoff stream."*

yield by itself without reference to the real return offered by safe assets suggests owning the same amount of equities in both cases.

So far we've only focused on returns, the top half of the Merton share formula. To use it to guide our allocation to equities we also need an estimate of the risk of the market, the bottom half of the formula. Unfortunately, we cannot directly observe expectations of long-term market risk. Even if there were liquid, long-term markets in options that we could look to, it would be difficult to disentangle the true expectation from the insurance premium built into those prices. It's also not possible to derive expectations of risk from expected cash flows in the way we do when determining long-term expected returns for equities or bonds. What we can do is build up an estimate for market risk using a blend of long- and short-horizon realized volatility.[6] This is the approach that options trading desks at most banks use to forecast market volatility.[7]

With all the inputs to the Merton share formula in hand, and assuming as before a risk-aversion level of 2, we can see in Exhibit 5.2 what your desired allocation to US equities would have been since the end of 1997, which is the earliest time that we have good TIPS data.

Notice that from the end of 1997 until the middle of 2001, the Merton share would have suggested no US equity market exposure at all, assuming that we don't allow short positions. This is because throughout this period, US equity expected returns were *below* the real yield

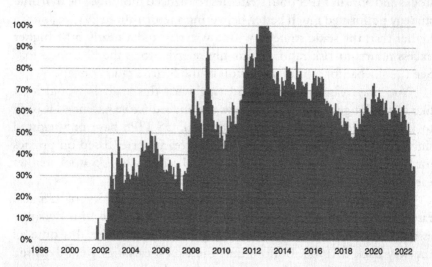

Exhibit 5.2   Allocation to US Equities Based on Merton Share Using Excess Earnings Yield 1997–2022

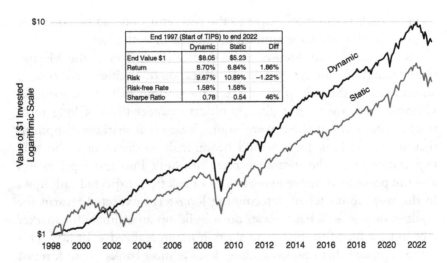

End 1997 (Start of TIPS) to end 2022			
	Dynamic	Static	Diff
End Value $1	$8.05	$5.23	
Return	8.70%	6.84%	1.86%
Risk	9.67%	10.89%	−1.22%
Risk-free Rate	1.58%	1.58%	
Sharpe Ratio	0.78	0.54	46%

Exhibit 5.3   Excess Earnings Yield Dynamic Versus Static Asset Allocation, US Equities and 10-Year TIPS 1998–2022

available from 10-year TIPS.[8] By contrast, the highest allocation to equities was called for in the second half of 2012 when the earnings yield was around 4.7%, 10-year TIPS were yielding −0.7%, and we estimated stock market volatility at just over 16% per annum.[9]

Exhibit 5.3 shows the performance that this dynamic allocation strategy would have produced, compared to a static allocation of 65% in stocks and 35% in TIPS, both strategies rebalanced monthly. The dynamic strategy performed much better, delivering a return about 2% per annum higher than the static strategy, with lower risk and a nearly 50% higher excess return-to-risk ratio, commonly referred to as the Sharpe ratio.[10] See the sidebar for a brief discussion of the Sharpe ratio concept.

You may reasonably be wondering what this analysis would look like over a longer historical window, and indeed we've extended it back to the year 1900. As we already indicated, US TIPS have only existed since 1997, and so we had to create a historical series based on proxies for US TIPS, which is shown in Exhibit 5.4, along with US stock market earnings yield in excess of US TIPS back to 1900.[11]

Using this combined hypothetical and actual history of US real rates, we get Exhibit 5.5, showing the performance of the same dynamic asset allocation strategy based on using the Merton share, this time all the way back to 1900. Bottom line: the excess earnings yield dynamic strategy did a lot better than a static strategy. Not only did the dynamic strategy do much better in terms of absolute return and quality of return,

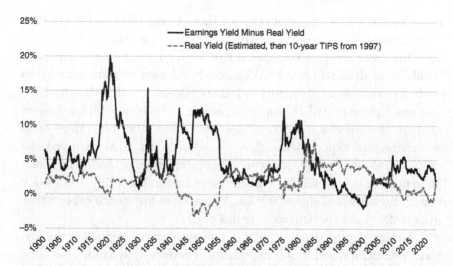

Exhibit 5.4 US Equities: Earnings Yield Minus Real Yield and Real Yield 1900–2022

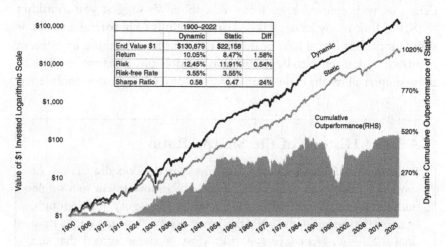

Exhibit 5.5 Excess Earnings Yield Dynamic Versus Static Asset Allocation: US Equities and 10-year TIPS 1900–2022

but even more remarkable, it outperformed being 100% in US equities, which produced a lower total return with 40% more risk.

One more thing to consider is that it's hard to say how an investor would have decided on a 65/35 stock/bond asset allocation to begin with, without use of some sort of framework, such as the Merton share, that put a price on risk. If you were sitting in 1900 and thinking about how much to invest in equities based on some other objective—such as maximizing expected wealth—you would have tried to invest the most you could in equities with maximum leverage. Following such an approach, you would have likely gone bust in the 1929–1933 stock market meltdown of almost 90%, and possibly in the several other 50%+ market declines experienced over this period.

We have explored a range of different assumptions applied to the historical simulation and found the historical benefit of dynamic asset allocation held across all we tested. The dynamic asset allocation provided a higher Sharpe ratio over ten of twelve 10-year subperiods too.[12]

The time period of this analysis is just over 24 years for the case with actual TIPS yields, and 120 years with our estimated TIPS yields. Both of these periods are relatively short from a statistical standpoint. So the evidence we've presented is far from rock solid. We suggest you shouldn't decide to follow any strategy based on the results of historical analysis or simulations. But if you have reason to believe that a dynamic investment approach makes sense to begin with, as we do from first principles, then these empirical results can reasonably give somewhat greater confidence.

A Brief History of the Sharpe Ratio

Early in the 1950s, academics and investors developed a variety of summary statistics to capture the quality of an investment in a single number. It was recognized that expected return wasn't quite enough, because two investments with the same expected return could have dramatically different levels of risk. Most everyone agreed that the quality statistic should be something like "expected return/risk," but the devil was in the details, and especially in the definition of risk. In the 1960s, William Sharpe was a graduate student working with Harry Markowitz on modern portfolio theory and the capital asset pricing model, work for which they'd later share a Nobel Prize along with Merton Miller. In "Mutual Fund Performance" (1966), Sharpe proposed a risk/reward ratio that he called the "reward-to-variability ratio," or "R/V Ratio" defined as follows:

$$\frac{Expected\ Return - Risk\ Free\ Rate}{Standard\ Deviation\ of\ Return}$$

The name didn't quite stick. Thirty years later, in a 1994 paper cheekily titled "The Sharpe Ratio," Bill Sharpe himself conceded that his original term never gained popularity and gave his tacit approval to the term "Sharpe ratio," which we still use today.

Though the original name wasn't a hit, the concept was: a measure originally coined in the very specific context of a theoretical model came to be the de facto standard amongst academics and investors for measuring the risk/reward quality of a wide variety of real-world investments.[†]

Today, use of the Sharpe ratio in both language and practice is ubiquitous—and naturally, critiques of its use are nearly as abundant. Here are some of the core critiques:

- Standard deviation captures risk relative to an expected return, not risk of loss, which some believe is the main type of risk investors should care about.
- Standard deviation does not directly measure the degree to which return distributions are asymmetric or fat-tailed. Most real investments, from individual equities to broad stock market indexes to corporate bonds, have return profiles that exhibit these characteristics, resulting in the Sharpe ratio misstating the true riskiness of the investment. Over longer periods, this non-normal behavior tends to lessen, though there's still disagreement over whether the normal distribution is a sufficiently good model for long-term returns.
- Limited historical data can result in a Sharpe ratio estimate that is significantly biased, due to sampling error, survivorship bias, or fat tails.

These critiques aren't wrong, but like any tool, the Sharpe ratio has its uses and abuses and must be handled with some care and with a knowledge of its limitations. While there are certainly situations where the Sharpe ratio can be a misleading metric, we find it still a useful shorthand for investment quality in the case of many mainstream investment questions, although not a substitute for a more complete and robust framework, which we'll be discussing in Chapter 6.

[†] The three inputs to the Sharpe Ratio are typically expressed as per annum quantities.

For the rest of this chapter, we're going to take a deeper dive into details, extensions, and an assortment of critiques of the dynamic asset allocation approach we've been discussing.

Remember, It's Not All About Returns

When we look back to assess whether dynamic asset allocation has served us well, we must be careful to view outcomes not solely based on return, but also to take account of how much risk we took along the way. To illustrate what we mean, imagine you are presented with the opportunity to bet on a coin that has a 70% chance of landing heads. You determine you want to bet 20% of your wealth on each flip. Then you are told that this coin is being replaced with a coin that has a 60% chance of heads. You now change your betting fraction to only bet 10% of your wealth on each flip, which is the consistent thing to do because a 60/40 coin has half the edge of a 70/30 coin. In the next 100 flips, 60 come up heads, and 40 come up tails, the most likely outcome. You calculate that, if you had still been betting 20% of your wealth on each bet, you'd have more wealth. Did you make the wrong decision to reduce your betting size from 20% to 10% of your wealth? We hope you'll agree that you did not, because with the 60/40 coin there was a higher chance of a worse outcome, and you rightly accounted for that risk by lowering bet size accordingly. In the next chapter we'll explain how to quantify the cost of risk, which will allow us to calculate Risk-adjusted Returns.

Just a Good Draw?

It's possible that the past 120 years were just a favorable period for dynamic asset allocation. Even so, we can determine how much better we'd expect dynamic asset allocation to perform *in the future* given the range of expected excess returns equities have offered historically. To do this, we ran a simulation in which half the time the expected excess return of equities was 1% and the other half it was 9%, which roughly matches the spread of expected excess returns experienced in the past 120 years.[13] We found that dynamically scaling the exposure to equities over many simulated histories delivers a roughly 30% average improvement in the Sharpe ratio versus a static strategy. Against this backdrop, the historical experience of the past 120 years appears to be just a little bit worse than we'd expect. The simulation also suggests that over a shorter horizon of 40 years, the dynamic asset allocation has an 85% probability of generating a higher return and a 65% chance of resulting in a higher Sharpe ratio than a static weight strategy.

Improvement in Sharpe Ratio Is a Twofer

Since 1900, the dynamic strategy has generated a Sharpe ratio about 30% higher than that of the static strategy. Just how big a deal is that kind of increase in Sharpe ratio?[14] A *very big* deal indeed! A 30% increase, whether it comes from a higher expected excess return or lower risk, delivers a compound benefit to an investor for the following reasons:

1. It provides 30% more return per unit of risk.
2. You'll optimally want a 30% larger risk allocation to a strategy with a Sharpe ratio that is 30% higher.

So, a 30% increase in the Sharpe ratio generates roughly double that improvement (a 69% improvement, to be exact) in the optimal port-folio's excess return. An improvement of this magnitude, compounded over the long horizons typical of investing for retirement, can offer a truly life-changing enhancement to investor outcomes.

Alternatives to Earnings Yield

Many other popular metrics are used in dynamic asset allocation strat-egies, such as Tobin's Q, equity market value to GDP, and aggregate investor allocation to equities (AIAE), to name a few. We prefer earn-ings yield because it directly gives an estimate for the long-term real return of the equity market, whereas all the other metrics need to be regressed against their historical averages in order to provide a return estimate. There is consensus that the basic cyclically adjusted earnings metric can be made more predictive by incorporating the effect of retained earnings and stock buybacks, at the cost of some added com-plexity. A survey-based forecast of future earnings may be useful as an alternative or complement to using historical earnings, but it is hard to assess the value of this metric as such survey data don't go back very far into the past, nor do they forecast earnings far into the future. Another metric, cyclically adjusted dividend yield plus dividend growth, closely relates to earnings yield and might be effectively used in conjunction with it, but this metric suffers from requiring an estimate of growth and being more sensitive to changes over time in corporate earnings payout policies.

Momentum

Time series momentum[†] of equity markets can be considered as an indicator of prospective risk or expected return. Momentum is typically calculated by comparing the current level of a market to the average level over the past year. When the market is higher than it has been, momentum is said to be positive, and the near-term expected risk of equities is generally lower than normal, and vice versa when it is negative. As the saying goes, the stock market tends to grind higher and plummet lower.

Momentum can be effectively used in combination with earnings yield by increasing the equity allocation when momentum is positive and reducing it when momentum is negative. There is considerable academic literature on the use of long-term valuation metrics together with time series momentum to drive asset allocation decisions, such as "Value and Momentum Everywhere" by Asness et al. (2013), "A Case Study for Using Value and Momentum at the Asset Class Level" by Haghani and Dewey (2016), and "Time Series Momentum" by Moskowitz et al. (2012).

In Exhibit 5.6 we compare the historical simulated performance of a static asset allocation strategy to that of a strategy that changes its equity allocation based on excess earnings yield and momentum.[15] The dynamic strategy generates a substantially higher return and Sharpe ratio over the 120-year period than the static allocation. It also generated a markedly higher return, particularly over the past 50 years, than the dynamic strategy we analyzed in Exhibit 5.5 based on estimating risk from historical realized volatility.

A number of cousins of momentum produce similar or even better historical results, but at the cost of increased complexity and more parameters to pin down. Another close relation, more like a sibling than

---

[†]As distinct from cross-sectional momentum, which is used to build portfolios of individual stocks based on their relative momentum.

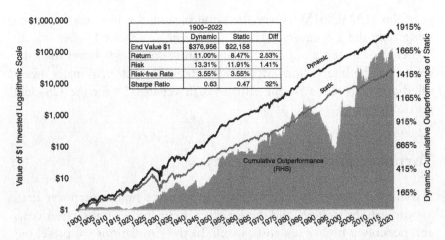

1900–2022	Dynamic	Static	Diff
End Value $1	$376,956	$22,158	
Return	11.00%	8.47%	2.53%
Risk	13.31%	11.91%	1.41%
Risk-free Rate	3.55%	3.55%	
Sharpe Ratio	0.63	0.47	32%

Exhibit 5.6 Excess Earnings Yield Dynamic Versus Static Asset Allocation Using Momentum as Risk Proxy: US Equities and 10-year TIPS 1900–2022

a cousin, that produces similar historical results and shares the simplicity of momentum is the "stop-loss" approach to investing. It is almost universally endorsed by successful macro hedge fund traders, including George Soros, Paul Tudor Jones, Louis Bacon, and Alan Howard. In Jack Schwager's series of Market Wizard books, he finishes each interview with the question:"What advice would you give someone aspiring to be a successful trader?" More than three-quarters of his subjects answered with the dictum:"Cut your losses early; let your profits run."

International Diversification

We've used the US stock and bond markets as the only two assets in our analysis of dynamic asset allocation. As you would expect if the ideas we've been discussing so far are sound, adding non-US equities to the asset allocation menu does make the dynamic approach even more attractive versus a static asset allocation on a historical basis. Good data on international equity market returns, risk, and earnings start around 1975. In Haghani and Dewey (2016), we found that dynamic asset allocation applied to a portfolio including US and non-US equity markets had a simulated return 2.5% per annum higher than the relevant static portfolio (1975–2015).[†] Over the same period, the dynamic approach using only the US equity market had a return of about 1% per annum higher than its static portfolio baseline, and about 1.5% lower than the return on the international dynamic strategy. The internationally diversified portfolio had a Sharpe ratio of 0.78 versus 0.58 for the US-only portfolio.

Turnover and Tax Efficiency

A dynamic strategy is very likely to experience higher turnover than a static weight strategy and, hence, may incur higher transaction costs and possibly a higher tax cost as well. In the simulations we presented in Exhibits 5.5 and 5.6 with monthly rebalancing, the average turnover of the dynamic strategies were 30% and 65% per annum, respectively, versus 10% for the static weight strategy. The strategies can be much more tax efficient than one might guess based on these turnover figures. This is because the buying and selling is usually limited to the most recently traded segment of the portfolio. This allows long-term tax deferral to build up in the oldest and lowest basis tax lot holdings. The strategies can be made even more tax efficient through a tax loss harvesting overlay and through rebalancing less frequently and less fully to targets.

Merton Share Modification: Hedging Demand and Volatility Skew

By construction, when the market drops over a short period of time, the cyclically adjusted earnings yield will go up, because it's based on the past 10 years of earnings, which hardly change from day to day. If the expected return of the stock market consistently goes up when the market falls (and vice versa), then you should want a higher allocation to equities than suggested by the basic Merton share, which assumes a constant expected return. This extra amount of equities was called "hedging demand" by Merton (1971) because it represents a hedge against the investment opportunity set you face. When the market goes down, your portfolio value goes down, but the

---

[†]Note that the details of the dynamic asset allocation simulation in Haghani and Dewey (2016) were not identical to those discussed in this chapter, but we believe the results are not materially impacted by those differences.

increased expected return offsets some of that loss in value, and so your risk is less than it appears.

Pushing in the opposite direction of this hedging demand is the tendency for equity markets to be more volatile when they fall. This is reflected in options markets and called "skew," which we'll discuss more in Chapter 16 on options. You would optimally invest less than the Merton share in a market exhibiting this feature. Because hedging demand and volatility skew tend to offset each other, for equity markets we still view the Merton share as an excellent starting point for thinking about asset allocation.

Can Everyone Be a Dynamic Asset Allocator?

Economists would say that a strategy that cannot be pursued by all investors at the same time is not "macro-consistent." This is a pretty stringent test of an investment approach, as any strategy that requires you to trade with other market participants would not meet this condition. For example, even a static asset allocation strategy that aims to keep a fixed fraction of wealth in equities would not be macro-consistent. Whenever an investor is considering pursuing a strategy that not everyone can follow at the same time, he needs to have confidence that what he's doing makes sense for him.[16] A dynamic asset allocation strategy is probably a good fit for long-term investors who expect their risk-aversion to remain steady through time and who are willing and able to estimate expected real returns and risk offered by their investments.

Not All Dynamic Asset Allocation Is "Market Timing"

Any investment approach that varies exposures based on some set of rules or views can be called "market timing." Unfortunately, this term has acquired a bad reputation and with some reason—investors in general haven't done too well by "trading the market." Most personal trading is ad hoc, sometimes chasing returns based on an extrapolation of recent returns or patterns, at other times following aggressive contrarian strategies that depend on a rapid reversion to an average level or some subjective assessment of fair value. One thing most commonly practiced forms of "market timing" strategies have in common is that they rely on some amount of market inefficiency to generate short- or medium-term profits. Betting that a certain pattern will repeat itself, or that one sector will go from being "hot" to "not," all fall into this category, relying on the investor knowing more than the market.

In contrast, following a dynamic asset allocation using the Merton share doesn't rely on market inefficiency. Market expected returns naturally change over time as the supply and demand for capital changes, even in highly efficient markets, nor is it necessarily inefficient for long-term returns to be somewhat predictable.

Connecting the Dots

We agree with investor advocates such as Vanguard founder Jack Bogle and Burton Malkiel that it's better to be a buy-and-hold investor maintaining a fixed exposure to the market than to follow a misguided approach to dynamic asset allocation. Many financial advisers—human and robo—follow this line, recommending that investors choose a level of equity exposure they are comfortable with and stick to it for the long term. Target Date funds, which now allocate $2 trillion of investor savings, abide by a similar dictum that asset allocation should simply follow a smooth glidepath to lower equity exposure as investors age.

Investing in the stock market has usually been a good thing, but to a varying degree relative to safe assets. It is useful to have a logical, simple framework, such as the Merton share, to decide *how much* to own as conditions change rather than the more seat-of-the-pants, subjective approach that is evoked by market timing.

When the stock market offers lower expected *excess* returns, all else equal, it's both good theory and good sense to own less of it. We think there's a fundamental flaw in the prevailing conventional advice given to individuals, in which the investor decides how much risk to take based solely on whether they have a "high" or "low" risk tolerance, without factoring in how much they're being "paid" to take that risk. It would be like deciding to bet the same amount on a biased coin regardless of whether it's 70/30 in your favor or fair at 50/50.

An even more perverse approach would be to bet more when the coin toss is less in your favor, thinking that you need to make up for the low expected returns by taking extra risk. In the Merton share formula, the best amount of the risky asset to own is a function of its expected excess return relative to the safe asset. For a given level of expected excess return, the allocation shouldn't change whether the absolute returns are high or low. Yet some investors do actually act in this perverse way—there's even a name for the behavior: "reaching for yield."[17]

No doubt, implementing a dynamic strategy is more complex and takes more attention than following a static-weight policy. On the other hand, a rules-based dynamic approach may be easier for an investor to stick with because it can satisfy the investor's desire to feel responsive in the face of a changing world.

The improvement in welfare that is available to investors who vary their exposure to equities as excess return and risk change over time is too big to be left on the table. Of course, real-world investments are very different from the biased coin-flips that have driven much of our analysis so far. But don't worry. In the next chapter, we're going to develop a much more versatile and powerful set of tools than the Merton share. Still, it's good to have this simple, easy to remember heuristic in your back pocket.

6

The Mechanics of Choice

It is our choices, Harry, that show what we truly are, far more than our abilities.

—J.K. Rowling

In Chapter 3, we developed intuition for sizing simple risks and worked out some useful rules of thumb:

- Bet size is a function of individual risk attitudes (γ), but should be made consistently across bets with differing attractiveness.
- Bet size should be proportional to expected gain (μ).
- Bet size should be inversely proportional to the square of risk (σ^2): if risk halves, bet size should quadruple.

We saw how these three characteristics come together to give us an optimal betting rule, the Merton share:

$$\hat{k} = \frac{\mu}{\gamma\sigma^2}$$

This rule of thumb can take us pretty far beyond simple bets too, as we saw by extending the same ideas to thinking about sizing exposure to the stock market.

But now we're ready for something a bit more industrial strength, not just a rule of thumb, but a full framework for sizing financial risks that are more realistic and relevant than we've seen so far.

This framework is compatible with the rules and intuition we've already worked on. Indeed, we'll see they agree extremely well, but this more general framework will allow us to make sizing decisions and many other financial decisions more directly, robustly, and for a much broader range of financial risks. Before we get there though, we'll detour into the foundations of risk-taking and the relationship between our wants and needs and the risks we're willing to take.

Desire 101

Why then, can one desire too much of a good thing?

—Shakespeare (*As You Like It*)

We all have different tastes and desires, but one remarkable similarity we share is that for most of us our desires are naturally self-regulating. A good rule of thumb for human desires is that the more we have of something, the less we want still more of it. This isn't just a foible of a particular culture or a quirk of human psychology, but a deep requirement for normal functioning. Your authors both have an improbable passion for gummy bears,[†] yet have managed to live normal, successful lives because, after the first few treats, we generally find ourselves sated and not wanting any more. Imagine though if that weren't the case, if after eating a dozen gummies we want the next dozen even more, and the third dozen more still, and so on. It would require an inhuman strength of will to rein in such desires. Happily, thanks to nature, we mostly don't have to. There are some major

---

[†]The variety you buy at a candy store, not a dispensary.

exceptions of course, addiction being one of the most prominent. But addiction is rightly regarded as a *disorder,* a departure from the normal way of things, rather than the rule. The "rule" is that the more we have, the more sated we feel. Economists lovingly call this *"diminishing marginal utility of consumption,"* which just means that each incremental item brings us somewhat less happiness than the one before it. It's such a simple idea, but it's central to essentially everything in this book.

You may now be wondering why we're talking about this in a book primarily about risk-taking. It turns out there's a deep connection between the structure of our desires and risk-taking: how quickly we become sated determines our *risk-aversion*. In a game of chance where we start with one dozen gummies, winning an extra dozen isn't the opposite of losing one dozen, because we enjoy the second dozen meaningfully less than the first. This means that wagering a dozen gummies on a fair coin-toss is a bad bet, since if we lose, it's going to feel worse than winning will feel good. Instead, we might need to win something like two dozen gummies to offset the risk of losing a dozen. How many extra gummies we need for each one at risk is a measure of our risk-aversion.

Very few people have gone through the process of explicitly calibrating their personal level of risk-aversion, even though all of us are regularly making decisions about how much risk to take. When we decide how much of our savings to put at risk in the stock market or in a business that we're trying to build, or whether to rent versus buy a home with or without a mortgage, we are making decisions that are related to our personal risk-aversion, even if we're not consciously aware of it.

Everyone has different desire profiles and levels of risk-aversion under different circumstances and with different objects, and there's no right amount. One of us, James, fills up very quickly on pizza but can eat a virtually unlimited amount of challah bread, so he's much more risk-averse about pizza than challah: extra pizza isn't worth much, so there's less incentive for taking a risk to get it. In this book we'll primarily be talking about risk-taking and risk-aversion relative to *money*. Of course we all value money and strongly prefer having more than less, but nearly everyone also experiences diminishing returns to wealth. The first million is life-changing, the second less so, and the third less still. This naturally produces risk-aversion to material changes in wealth. In Chapter 12 we discuss in greater detail the process we recommend for uncovering and calibrating your own personal level of risk-aversion.

A Silly Game Gives Birth to a Sensible Idea

The desire to quantify risk-averse behavior isn't new. In the early eighteenth century, Daniel Bernoulli was thinking about a now-classic problem called the St. Petersburg paradox. Here's how the game works: Imagine a casino offers you a game of chance in which a fair coin is repeatedly tossed until it lands on tails. The payoff starts at $2 and is doubled every time heads appears, until the coin lands on tails. So, if tails appears on the first toss, you receive $2. If you flip heads once, followed by tails, the casino pays you $4. You are paid $8 if you get two heads in a row followed by the game-stopping tails toss. In general the casino will pay you 2^{h+1} dollars, where h is the number of consecutive tosses of heads that occur before a tails is tossed.[†]

The question Bernoulli tried to answer was: How much should you pay to play this game? It turns out that the expected value of the game is infinite, but Bernoulli perceived that it would be crazy to put up all of your wealth, or even a good fraction of it, for the privilege of playing—doing so creates a near-certain chance of catastrophic loss, with only a microscopic chance of gain. We've seen this before with our coin-flip bettor: sizing each bet to optimize the expected outcome led to near-certain disaster. Bernoulli wanted to formalize exactly why this is the case, and he wanted to do it with a summary measure, rather than requiring that the player look at the full distribution of outcomes and subjectively assess the best balance of return and risk, as our coin-flipper did in Chapter 3. Bernoulli posited that it's correct to compute a mathematical expectation, just not an expected value of the monetary outcome of the game. Instead, he proposed we should be taking the expectation of the happiness or benefit we gain or lose in each outcome, and he called his index of benefit *utility*.

The determination of the value of an item must not be based on the price, but rather on the Utility it yields.

—Daniel Bernoulli, Swiss mathematician
and gambler (1738)

[†]Admittedly this is a very unusual casino, since, as we'll see, they're offering a game that will always have a negative expected value for the house!

The Happiness Curve

Thus he proposed that, for risk-taking purposes, instead of keeping track of monetary wealth directly, we instead track utility, an index of how much benefit is imparted by a given amount of wealth. He also proposed a starting point for the relationship between wealth and utility, now typically called the log-utility function.[†] Exhibit 6.1 shows how utility goes up with wealth according to Bernoulli and log-utility.

We can see that this more-or-less captures the important features of how we value different amounts of wealth. Utility goes down faster and faster as wealth gets close to 0, as it should: when you have very little wealth, each extra little bit is very valuable to you. In the other direction, utility keeps going up as wealth increases, but at a slower and slower rate. Once you've become fabulously wealthy, extra wealth just doesn't move the needle like it used to. Of course this isn't yet a *personalized* picture of utility—it's hard to say if log-utility gets your personal preferences quite right, but it's a place to start and in general the shape looks pretty good.

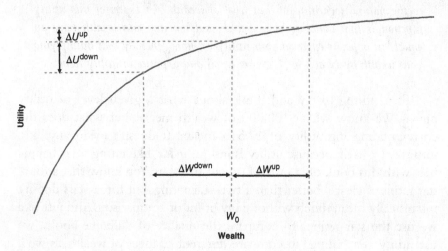

Exhibit 6.1 Concave Utility Curve and Decreasing Marginal Utility of Wealth

---

[†]The natural logarithm, or log for short, of x, written $\ln(x)$, is the power to which the mathematical constant e would have to be raised to equal x. For example, $\ln(2)$ is 0.693 because $e^{0.693}=2$. The value of e is approximately 2.718.

Pain, I have already had occasion to observe, is, in almost all cases, a more pungent sensation than the opposite and correspondent pleasure. The one, almost always, depresses us much more below the ordinary, or what may be called the natural state of our happiness, than the other ever raises us above it.

—Adam Smith, *The Theory of Moral Sentiments*

If you've taken an Introduction to Economics class, you probably remember discussions of utility, and if you do, you probably recall how abstract and impractical it felt then. In the context of building highly general economic models blending all kinds of goods and services, utility can indeed feel highly abstract. But for our purposes in this book, we're only interested in the utility of wealth, and in the context we're going to use it, we'll see it's actually quite concrete and intuitive.

The formal relationship between wealth and utility under log-utility is simply:

$$U(W) = \ln(W)$$

which says that your utility (U), at a given level of wealth (W) is equal to the natural logarithm of that level of wealth. An aspect of this utility function is that doubling your wealth and halving your wealth have an equal but opposite effect on your utility, or more generally that multiplying your wealth by N and by 1/N are equal and opposite in utility terms.

It's tempting to try and think about what a given level of utility means. We know what $100,000 of wealth means, but what does the corresponding log-utility of 11.513 mean? It doesn't mean anything intuitive by itself, because utility is just an *index*, like rating your happiness with this book on a scale of one to five stars. You know that a four-star rating is clearly better than a two-star rating, but three-stars doesn't intrinsically mean much without any point of comparison. And just like we use the star-ratings to compare the quality of different books, we use utility as a "rating" to compare different changes of wealth, as we'll see below.

Introducing the concept of utility allowed Bernoulli to provisionally resolve the St. Petersburg paradox. A gambler seeking to maximize Expected Utility would pay only a tiny sum to play the game, as our intuition would expect, in contrast to maximizing expected wealth and paying away all his wealth to play the game despite being nearly certain to lose everything. Table 6.1 makes clear what's going on, for the case of a person with log-utility playing the St. Petersburg game, with starting wealth of $100,000.

Table 6.1 Expected Utility of St. Petersburg Game

Num Heads in a Row	Probability	Payoff	Prob × Payoff	Wealth	Util(W) = ln(W)	Prob × Utility
0	50%	$2	$1	$100,002	11.5129	5.75647
4	3.125%	$32	$1	$100,032	11.5132	0.35979
10	0.049%	$2,048	$1	$102,048	11.5332	0.00563
20	0.000048%	$2.1 mm	$1	$2.2 mm	14.6027	0.00001
40	0.00000000005%	$2.2 tn	$1	$2.2 tn	28.4190	0.00000000001

Sum of Probability × Payoff	Infinity
Sum of Probability × Utility	11.51310
Wealth Equivalent to Expected Utility: $e^{11.51310}$	$100,018
Starting Wealth	$100,000
Utility of Starting Wealth: ln(100,000)	11.51293
Increase in Utility from Playing	0.00018
Maximum Amount Willing to Pay to Play	$18

His expected wealth from playing the game is infinite, because the payout of lasting for one more flip doubles while the probability halves, resulting in an infinite stream of constant increments to expected wealth. Hence, by the metric of expected wealth he should happily pay any amount of his wealth to play. But, thinking in Expected Utility, the utility gain of lasting one more flip is less than double, resulting in an infinite stream of decreasing increments to Expected Utility. For reasonable utility functions, including log-utility, this results in a finite total.

As seen in Table 6.1, the incremental Expected Utility from playing is tiny, just 0.00018 compared to a starting utility of 11.51. This is what we'd expect and what good sense demands. We can translate that increase in utility back into dollar terms by calculating how much extra wealth is equivalent to the extra Expected Utility that comes from playing the game. It turns out that in utility-equivalent wealth, he's only $18 better off from playing the game! So he should not be willing to pay more than $18 to play, resolving the "paradox."[†] The reverberations from this change in perspective from expected wealth to Expected Utility are still being felt nearly 300 years later.

[†] Exactly how much he should be willing to pay to play will be a function of his starting wealth. If his starting wealth is just $1,000, the maximum he'd be willing to pay would be $11, and if he's a trillionaire, the most he'd be willing to pay would be $41.

Expected Utility and Choice Theory

If people do not believe that mathematics is simple, it is only because they do not realize how complicated life is.

—John von Neumann

Bernoulli's ruminations on the St. Petersburg paradox, utility and Expected Utility took place in the early 1700s. For the next two centuries, economists and philosophers appropriated and expanded Bernoulli's concept of utility, applying it in wide-ranging economic, political, and moral models, sometimes far removed from the original application to individual financial decision-making. The embers of Bernoulli's original idea were kept burning by a handful of economists and mathematicians throughout the years. The flame burned brightly again in 1944 with the publication of *The Theory of Games and Economic Behavior* by polymath John von Neumann and economist Oskar Morgenstern, a work which gave birth to two new fields of study: choice theory and game theory. They took Bernoulli's concept of subjective utility and extended it into a logical, axiomatic framework for rational decision-making under uncertainty. In a nutshell, they proved that any individual whose preferences satisfy four "axioms of rational choice" would prefer actions that maximize Expected Utility.

Axioms of Rational Choice[1]

1. Completeness: An individual has well-defined preferences. If A and B are two outcomes, then the individual can always specify exactly one of three possibilities: A is preferred to B, B is preferred to A, or A and B are equally attractive.
2. Transitivity: Preferences are internally consistent across any three options. If A is preferred to B, and B is preferred to C, then A is preferred to C.
3. Continuity: If A is preferred to B, then outcomes almost the same as A must also be preferred to B.
4. Independence: A preference holds independently of the existence of an unrelated third outcome C. If A is preferred to B, then a third, "irrelevant" option C does not cause the individual to switch to preferring B to A.

Maximizing Expected Utility may seem like a good thing to do, as it gives us a general way of weighing the benefits of positive outcomes against the risks inherent in an uncertain future. But von Neumann and Morgenstern provided the context in which it can be proved to be the *best* thing to do, among all possible alternatives. So far in this book we've talked about why maximizing expected wealth isn't a good objective, but we certainly can't explore *every other* possible objective for making good decisions. By proving the optimality of Expected Utility—subject to their assumptions—von Neumann and Morgenstern saved us from the impossible task of searching over this infinite number of alternative decision rules. It is hard to overstate the impact their work has had on modern economics, finance and game theory.

The One-shape-fits-all Suite of Utility Functions

I've been rich and I've been poor. Believe me, rich is better.

—Mae West

You might be wondering, what if the log-utility function we've been using as an example so far doesn't correctly represent the relative value of different wealth levels *for you*? It is a problem: log-utility might appear reasonable and resolve the St. Petersburg paradox, but it's not customizable. Happily, the log-utility function is a member of a larger *family* of utility functions, called the constant relative risk-aversion (CRRA) family. This family has a special property, which is that it implies the same level of risk-aversion to percentage changes of wealth, regardless of your absolute level of wealth. For example, if you have CRRA utility and losing 10% of your wealth is equivalent to making 15% given a starting wealth of $1 million, that ratio will be equivalent in utility terms at every other wealth level too. Economists have been attracted to the CRRA family for many reasons. An important one is its independence of wealth levels, which is required to explain the stability of interest rates and asset returns through two centuries of economic growth.

In *Stumbling on Happiness*, the Harvard psychologist Daniel Gilbert explains that the most effective way to predict your experience in a different circumstance is *not* to imagine how you'll feel, but rather to find out how others that are actually experiencing it feel. In general, we are not as individually different as we like to think we are. It might be

difficult to imagine how risk-averse you'd be if you had a lot more or a
lot less wealth than you have right now, but you can get some indication
of how you might feel by exploring the risk-aversion of other people
with much higher or lower wealth. The empirical finding that we see
similar levels of risk-aversion for people at quite different wealth levels
supports the use of CRRA utility as a reasonable fit for most people.

Each CRRA family member represents a different level of relative
risk-aversion, and there's one for every possible choice of required profit
versus risk (within reason). CRRA utility is formally written as follows:

$$U(W) = \frac{1 - W^{1-\gamma}}{\gamma - 1}$$

*where γ is the parameter that dials the level of risk-aversion and W is your
wealth.*[†]

Exhibit 6.2 shows CRRA utility curves representing different levels
of risk-aversion. We usually normalize wealth, setting starting wealth

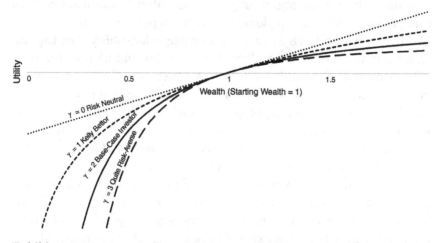

Exhibit 6.2 Constant Relative Risk-aversion Utility With Different Levels of
Individual Risk-aversion

[†]Also known as isoelastic utility or power utility, it's written in other equivalent forms as
well, with the main requirement being that $-\dfrac{WU''(W)}{U'(W)}$, known as the coefficient of relative
risk-aversion, is a constant. Our choice of expression is our preferred form to work with. For
$\gamma = 1$, $U(W) = \ln(W)$.

equal to 1, which does not affect results but does make for easier computations. Each curve with positive risk-aversion goes up more slowly as wealth increases, and this effect is more dramatic for higher levels of risk-aversion.

Higher γ produces a more highly curved, *concave* utility function, which implies a higher degree of risk-aversion. An investor with $\gamma = 0$ is considered "risk-neutral." His utility function is a straight line, so that maximizing Expected Utility will be the same as maximizing expected wealth. An individual with γ less than zero would be risk-seeking and has a convex utility curve that increases faster and faster with increasing wealth. We do not think it makes sense for investors with substantial wealth to be even close to risk-neutral, let alone risk-seeking.

Many experts are concerned that most people are not capable of determining their own level of risk-aversion—that the concept is either too abstract and difficult or that people give such inconsistent responses to different framing of risk questions that their answers aren't useful in decision-making. We disagree with this view, at least as applied to a relatively financially literate investor. There is simply no escaping the need to somehow choose a risk stance, and ideally one that can be consistently applied. If your goal is to make decisions that improve your expected welfare across the many issues you will face in your financial life, then you've got to take a stance on how much you value different levels of wealth and thus how much risk you should take.

Using a family of utility functions like the CRRA family imposes an intrinsically sensible structure on your choices and boils down your calibration to just one number you have to pick. And researchers (including your authors) have some suggestions for a range of risk-aversion that most individuals fall into, so there's a relatively narrow range of reasonable values within which you're likely to find a fit with your preferences. These features make it easier to do a good job calibrating to a risk-aversion level that will work for you, without getting tripped up by the variety of cognitive biases that can creep in. We also don't think this is an area where it makes sense—or is even possible—to be overly precise. The primary goal is to choose a level of risk-aversion that feels "about right" for you and that you can apply consistently.

In theory, an infinite number of possible forms of utility function exist, and a wide range of commonly studied functional families are available to academics.[†] But we focus on CRRA utility because we've found that it's intuitive, useful, and usable in practice. There are few, if any, real-world situations where we think the advantages of using something more complex outweigh the drawbacks.

It is comforting to note that for small to moderate sized risks, most reasonable utility functions will agree pretty well with CRRA. Specifically, given a utility function with smoothly decreasing marginal utility, if you calibrate it to agree with CRRA on a given bet at a given wealth level, it will also approximate CRRA on other moderately sized bets around the same starting wealth. This means that the Merton share, and the constant return-versus-variance trade-off it embodies, can be seen as a pretty good guideline across a wide range of utility functional forms, not just CRRA utility.

We and other researchers have found direct evidence that at least some people are capable and comfortable calibrating their personal risk-aversion, and that CRRA utility described their preferences pretty well. Over a 6-week period in late 2018, we conducted a survey of 31 friends, clients, and former colleagues from the finance industry to test whether a group of financially sophisticated investors could comfortably communicate their preferences in a way that we could then translate into a useful measure of personal risk-aversion. We found that this group—not representative of the general public but perhaps representative of the readers of this book—was comfortable thinking about risk-aversion in a direct manner, and that their answers to multiple question framings were for the most part consistent with one another and with CRRA utility in general. The other very positive finding was that the respondents' answers were clustered around a level of risk-aversion we found intrinsically reasonable and that should provide some confidence and guidance to others.

Utility User's Guide

My pencil and I are more clever than I.

—Albert Einstein

[†] Constant absolute risk-aversion and quadratic utility are both commonly used in academic portfolio theory, but they are generally considered unrealistic for modeling the preferences of most individuals.

You're probably ready to see this utility idea in action. For the rest of this book, we'll be assuming our Base-Case individual has CRRA utility with risk-aversion of 2, which is a nice round number and within the range of risk-aversion expressed by respondents to our survey. In all our previous examples, we've assumed this level of risk-aversion. It's useful to pick a Base-Case reference point, but everything we'll be talking about from now on will work with pretty much any form of utility function and any degree of risk-aversion.

Before moving on to more real-world examples, let's see the mechanics of using Expected Utility by revisiting some coin-flipping. The underlying mechanics will be the same no matter how complex our examples get down the road. But for now, let's say you have wealth of $1 million and risk-aversion of 2; you get to "invest" in 25 flips of a 60/40 coin, and you have to decide what fraction of your wealth to bet on each flip. We know the probabilities for each bet, and we know they're independent, so we can work out the probability of each potential outcome, from flipping 25 tails in a row to flipping 25 heads in a row.

Table 6.2 shows the expected wealth and Expected Utility calculation, in the case where you put 10% of wealth on heads for every flip. To make the numbers in the table easier to work with, we have expressed them in millions of dollars.

Using the calculation procedure in Table 6.2, we can look at Expected Return and Expected Utility over a range of bet sizes, from betting 0% of wealth on each flip to betting 25% on each flip, as shown in Exhibit 6.3. We'll express the expected return on a per flip basis, in the spirit of eventually expressing a multi-year market return on a per annum basis.

We can immediately see one reason we like using Expected Utility—it is directly telling us something about trade sizing. Expected Utility has a peak, in this case at 10%. We call this the *optimal* bet size because it is the bet size that maximizes Expected Utility. By contrast, expected return just keeps going up and up as the bet size gets bigger; it looks best at 100% bet size even when there's a virtual certainty of losing everything after just a few bets.

Table 6.2

Probability of heads	60%
Number of Bets	25
Starting Wealth ($mm)	1
Bet Size	10%
Risk-aversion (CRRA)	2

Number of Winning Bets (Heads)	Probability	Profit ($mm)	End Wealth ($mm)	Utility of End Wealth
0	0.00000001%	(0.93)	0.07	−12.930
1	0.0000004%	(0.91)	0.09	−10.397
2	0.00001%	(0.89)	0.11	−8.325
3	0.0001%	(0.87)	0.13	−6.629
4	0.0007%	(0.84)	0.16	−5.242
5	0.005%	(0.80)	0.20	−4.107
6	0.023%	(0.76)	0.24	−3.179
7	0.092%	(0.71)	0.29	−2.419
8	0.312%	(0.64)	0.36	−1.797
9	0.884%	(0.56)	0.44	−1.289
10	2.122%	(0.47)	0.53	−0.873
11	4.341%	(0.35)	0.65	−0.532
12	7.597%	(0.20)	0.80	−0.254
13	11.395%	(0.02)	0.98	−0.026
14	14.651%	0.19	1.19	0.161
15	16.116%	0.46	1.46	0.313
16	15.109%	0.78	1.78	0.438
17	11.998%	1.18	2.18	0.540
18	7.999%	1.66	2.66	0.624
19	4.420%	2.25	3.25	0.692
20	1.989%	2.97	3.97	0.748
21	0.710%	3.86	4.86	0.794
22	0.194%	4.93	5.93	0.831
23	0.038%	6.25	7.25	0.862
24	0.005%	7.86	8.86	0.887
25	0.0003%	9.83	10.83	0.908
Expectation		0.64	1.64	0.224

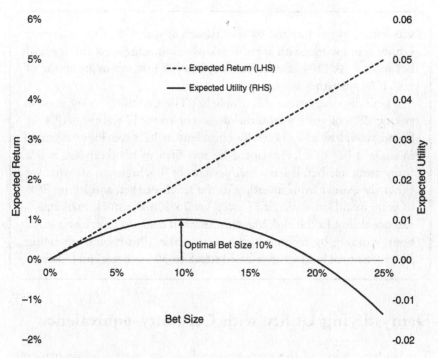

Exhibit 6.3 Expected Return and Utility over a Range of Bet Sizes For a Single Toss

Case Study: Floyd "Money" Mayweather Versus Conor McGregor

The 2017 professional boxing match, billed as "The Biggest Fight in Combat Sports History," pitted undefeated (49–0) 11-time boxing world champion Floyd Mayweather against mixed martial arts world champion Conor McGregor, who had never fought in a professional boxing match. We have a professional gambler friend who before the fight told us that this was one of the most lopsided, big-money sporting matchups he had ever seen. He thought the prospects of McGregor winning were similar to those of the world's best squash player taking on Roger Federer—at tennis! Indeed, Vegas odds started out putting a 95% probability on Mayweather to win, but media hype and love of the underdog eventually moved the odds to a 74% chance of Mayweather to win. Our gambling friend disagreed with the market's odds, feeling that the chance of Mayweather losing was half as big as implied by the market, at just 13%. Our Expected Utility framework, with typical risk-aversion, suggested the optimal bet was to risk 28% of wealth if Mayweather lost, versus an upside of 10% if Mayweather won.

Let's dig deeper into this simple bet. The first thing to say is: wow, risking 28% of your wealth on one event seems like a big bet![†] Our friend would need to be really confident in his probability estimate to make a bet that large. But if he was firm in his estimates, it is a really attractive bet. It has a Sharpe ratio of 0.4, higher than what we generally expect from investing in the stock market, and losing 28% of your wealth in a year, if invested say 75% in the stock market, is a real possibility. In the end, Mayweather won easily in a very one-sided bout, winning by technical knockout in the 10th round, extending his professional boxing undefeated streak to 50 victories and 0 defeats.

Demystifying Utility with Certainty-equivalence

The underpinning of the certainty-equivalence metric is the principle that we should be indifferent between two investments that produce the same Expected Utility. This is the magical property of Expected Utility: it is the single summary metric that combines our preferences with the entire distribution of possible outcomes.

The Certainty-equivalent Return (CER) of a risky investment is the return of a risk-free, *certain* investment that generates utility identical to the Expected Utility of the risky investment. In other words, it's the certain return that makes you indifferent to taking on the risky investment. If we know the Expected Utility of a risky investment, we also know its CER, and this allows us to use CER and Expected Utility *interchangeably*. This is an important concept that allows us to translate the abstract metric of utility into real-world dollars and returns.

We can phrase our goal as "find the bet size that delivers the highest CER" instead of "find the bet size with the highest Expected Utility," and we'll get to the same place. Different utility functions can have different scales, which can make it hard to think about Expected Utility

---

[†] Perhaps more remarkably, a Kelly bettor would optimally risk 50% of wealth on this wager, which we believe most people would find absurd, and more like the kind of bet that would form part of the plot in a Tarantino movie.

directly, but CER always has the same intuitive percentage scale. We suggest always converting from Expected Utility to CER; it doesn't change the conclusions, and it's much easier to talk about an investment with an expected return of 6% and CER of 3%, than an Expected Utility of 0.0289. We're still relying on the *mechanics* of Expected Utility—remember the definition of CER involves Expected Utility—we're just using CER as a tool for translating Utility into a metric that is more concrete and intuitive.

Risk-adjusted Return and the Price of Risk

Investment professionals often talk about "Risk-adjusted Return." In particular, active investment managers of various stripes tend to state their goal as something like "to achieve superior Risk-adjusted Return." This concept intuitively makes sense. The level of risk involved in delivering a given level of return is clearly something we should care about. But what exactly is meant by Risk-adjusted Return is often left a bit fuzzy. We now have a good way of thinking clearly and precisely about this. CER has the two qualities we want in a Risk-adjusted Return metric:

1. Given two investments with very different risk-and-return profiles, and which are independent of each other and the rest of your holdings, we'd be indifferent between them if they had the same impact on the CER of our total wealth.
2. The absolute return and the CER are identical for a risk-free investment.

CER takes in all the information known about the investment's return distribution, and in combination with the investor's utility function, transforms it into one number that can be used to compare across very different investments. Going forward we'll use CER and Risk-Adjusted Return (RAR) interchangeably.

For any risky investment at a given size, we can think of the "price of risk" as the difference between the expected return and Risk-adjusted Return, i.e., how much *extra* return we need to bear the risks involved.

Price of Risk = Expected Return − Risk-Adjusted Return

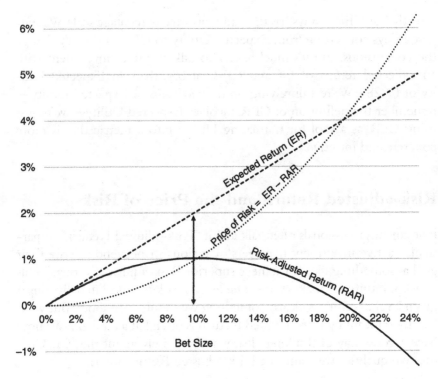

Exhibit 6.4   Expected Return, RAR and Price of Risk Over Range of Bet Sizes For One Toss

Exhibit 6.4 lets us see the relationship between the expected return, RAR, and price of risk for our 60/40 biased coin flip risky investment.

Four useful observations arise from the math of Expected Utility and apply to this particular investment case, which can be seen in the Exhibit 6.4:[†]

1. Expected return goes up linearly with bet size, but the price of risk increases quadratically, that is, with the square of bet size.
2. At double the optimal bet size, 20%, the RAR is 0, meaning that you'd be just as well not flipping the coin at all. Beware the perils of swinging for the fences! If you bet 30%, three times your optimal bet size, your RAR would be −3.2% per flip, more than three times the absolute size of the positive RAR from optimal betting.

[†]These insights only strictly hold with CRRA utility and specific investment setups, but they can prove useful elsewhere as well.

3. At the optimal bet size, the RAR is one half the expected return, and the price of risk is equal to the RAR.

4. The RAR curve is quite flat around its optimal point. This means that if you're a little to the left or the right of the optimal point, your RAR is going to be very close to optimal. Even going just half-way to the optimal sizing gets you three-quarters of the optimal RAR. So for example, if your savings are in cash and you feel that the long-term optimal place to be is 70% in equities, going half-way to just a 35% equity allocation gives you three-quarters of the potential benefit.[2] It's one of those few times that $\frac{1}{2} = \frac{3}{4}$!

What's the Best Way to Get Invested in the Market?

Investors thinking about putting more of their savings into the stock market are faced with many options for how to make that happen. Is it better to jump in all at once, to average-in over time, or to wait for a market correction? Does the Expected Utility framework offer fresh perspectives, beyond the useful axiom that "time in the market" is more valuable than "timing the market"?

First you need to have some idea of how much you'd ideally like to have in the market, given current conditions, and we've already seen that the Expected Utility framework can help with that decision. From there cold logic dictates that we should immediately move our allocation to the optimal point, minimizing the amount of time spent at a suboptimal allocation. An incremental adjustment over time, i.e., "averaging-in," is not strictly optimal. However, averaging-in does provide a benefit to those who simply can't or won't make big changes all at once. If you're below your target allocation then averaging in, while suboptimal, is much better than never investing at all.

There are other benefits along these lines. We've already seen that RAR is relatively flat near the optimal allocation, so taking a little while to get to optimal is unlikely to cost very much in risk-adjusted terms, and if it makes the investing experience more palatable or more sustainable for the long run, that's probably a win for the investor. For those of us who are predisposed to seeing the glass as half full when it comes to our past decisions, we'll be glad we got some of our savings invested at the beginning if the markets go up over the period that

(Continued)

we're averaging-in, and we'll also be comforted that we didn't invest
the full amount right at the start if the markets go down.

The averaging-in we've been discussing is a disciplined program
of investing a fraction of your savings into the market regularly, over a
predefined period. What about other approaches to getting invested?
Some investors are attracted to the idea of contingent averaging-in,
where they plan to increase their allocation to equities only if they fall
below some target price level. The problem here is that you're taking
the risk of the market going up and never coming back down again to
the target level and thereby incurring a very significant opportunity
cost. Because equities tend to have excess return, this is a very real risk.

Choosing a plan is ultimately a matter of personal preference, as
any approach other than moving straight to your optimal allocation is
financially suboptimal. However, some plans are less suboptimal than
others, and the Expected Utility prism is very useful in deciding what
is best for you. In the end, any plan is a good one if it overcomes
the inertia and anxiety that hold us back from our chosen investment destination. And once we're in for a while, forgetfulness will
make us wonder why we spent as much time as we did contemplating
the plunge.

These relationships are exact for small and independent gambles, like
coin flips, and they are useful approximations in many other situations.

A related rule of thumb that is illustrated in Exhibit 6.4 is that the
optimal bet size is one half the bet size at which you become ambivalent
about the opportunity. Here's how Victor and his friend and coauthor
Andrew Morton[†] stated it in a 2016 article on risk-taking:

> You can get an immediate intuition for the problem and its solution by
> asking...: how much ketchup on your fries would be so much that you'd
> be indifferent between no ketchup and that much ketchup?[‡] . . . Then
> ask: How much ketchup is your **optimal amount?** Our first question
> was calibrating your risk-aversion via indifference points, and the follow-
> up question involved choosing an optimal point anywhere in between. The
> halfway point is a pretty good estimate, and exact in some investing models.

[†] Besides being global co-head of markets at Citigroup, Andy is known in academic circles
for being the "M" in the HJM term structure model of interest rates (1987).
[‡] Sorry, but we're assuming you're North American and do like ketchup on your fries.

Putting together the linearly increasing expected return and the quadratically increasing price of risk gives us a simple statement of the risk-adjusted excess return of a portfolio with fraction k allocated to the risky asset:

$$Risk\text{-}adjusted\ Excess\ Return = k\mu - \frac{\gamma(k\sigma)^2}{2}$$

where μ is the excess expected return of the risky asset, σ is its risk measured in standard deviation, and γ is the CRRA coefficient of risk-aversion of the investor. Note that the RAR on your portfolio is the risk-adjusted excess return *plus* the risk-free rate.[†]

The optimal bet size, $\hat{k}$, which maximizes risk-adjusted excess return, occurs when:

$$\hat{k} = \frac{\mu}{\gamma\sigma^2}$$

And here we are, back at the Merton share again! In Chapter 3, we derived this rule with a logical argument, but we didn't prove it was optimal. Using the math of Expected Utility, Robert Merton proved that this is indeed the optimal amount to own of a single risky asset, assuming it has normally distributed short-horizon returns and the investor has CRRA utility.

And here's one final really useful insight we can get from the Merton share, which confirms the third observation we drew from Exhibit 6.4: by substituting the optimal bet size, $\frac{\mu}{\gamma\sigma^2}$, for k in the equation for risk-adjusted excess return, we find that the risk-adjusted excess return at the optimal bet size is equal to half the expected excess return times the optimal bet size, or in symbols:

$$Risk\text{-}adjusted\ Excess\ Return\ at\ the\ Optimal\ Bet\ Size = \frac{\hat{k}\mu}{2}$$

[†] If you happen to have risk-aversion of 2, then the "price of risk," $\frac{\gamma(k\sigma)^2}{2}$, simplifies to $(k\sigma)^2$, which is the standard deviation of your portfolio, squared. So if your portfolio risk is 20% per annum, then the cost of that risk to you is 4% per annum. But halve the portfolio risk to 10%, and now the cost of risk is only 1%.

A Penny Saved Is Two Pennies Earned

Most of us associate the maxim *"A penny saved is a penny earned"* with Benjamin Franklin, but what he actually said is far more insightful: *"A penny saved is two pence clear."* By the time he penned this, in "Hints for Those That Would Be Rich" of the 1737 *Poor Richard's Almanac*, Franklin was an experienced businessman who understood the nature of risk and uncertainty. Although he didn't elaborate on this pithy bit of advice, perhaps he was trying to convey an idea much more profound than the simple identity expressed in the misquote. We believe he was getting at the notion that one risk-free penny saved is worth two pennies of expected, but uncertain, business income. Or as we hear in a saying that he didn't coin, "a bird in the hand is worth two in the bush."

Ben Franklin was a man well ahead of his time: it wasn't until about 230 years later that academics arrived at the same conclusion using the tools of mathematical finance. Starting with the standard set of assumptions of a risk-averse investor and a single risky gamble, they showed that if the risk is "perfectly" sized, the investor should be equally happy choosing between an expected but risky gain equal to *twice* as much as a certain, risk-less payment.

One intriguing implication of this idea is that 1% more in investment management fees requires more than 1% in extra expected return, if getting the extra expected return increases the risk the investor is bearing. Just how much extra expected return is needed to offset the certain cost of higher fees depends on how much extra risk the manager takes and its correlation with other risks. That the active manager is typically taking more risk is a natural consequence of the fact that he must hold a less diversified portfolio than the market portfolio, taking more risk to cover the higher fees and deliver an attractive after-fee return.[3]

What this means is that *even if* you believe an active manager will cover the higher fee that he charges and deliver an extra 1% return, on a *risk-adjusted basis*, you still may be no better off than owning the index fund with its lower fee *and its lower risk*.

Philadelphia's most famous resident tirelessly promoted the virtues of efficiency and rational thought that contributed so much to America's economic success, and it's inspiring to realize that some of his ideas wound up being proven correct using mathematical techniques developed more than 200 years later.

Restating the Merton Share in Terms of Sharpe Ratio

In all the formulas for investment sizing in this chapter, we keep seeing the expected excess return, μ, in the numerator, and risk, σ, down below. We know that the ratio of excess return to risk, $(\frac{\mu}{\sigma})$, is equal to the Sharpe ratio (SR), and so we can make a few of these formulas simpler by replacing the ratio of return to risk by the SR. For our case of a risky and a safe asset, with assumptions of well-behaved asset prices and an investor with CRRA Utility, we get:

$$\hat{k} = \frac{SR}{\gamma\sigma}$$ where $\hat{k}$ is the optimal fraction of wealth to invest in the

risky asset, SR is the Sharpe ratio, σ is the risk measured in standard deviation and γ is the investor's coefficient of risk-aversion.

And for the risk-adjusted excess return of the optimal portfolio, we get:

$$Risk\text{-}adjusted\ Excess\ Return = \frac{SR^2}{2\gamma}$$

So, for our Base-Case investor in a two-asset world where the Sharpe ratio of the risky asset is 0.3, the risk-adjusted excess return on his optimal portfolio will be 2.25%.

This formula conveys the message that, with the idealized assumptions under which it holds, an investment with a higher Sharpe ratio generates a higher RAR, and the relationship is turbo-charged in that *doubling* the Sharpe ratio *quadruples* the portfolio's risk-adjusted excess return. But as we'll see in a moment, in real-world situations, we'll need to know more than the Sharpe ratio of different investments to properly rank their attractiveness.

Although we first arrived at the Merton share as a sensible risk-taking rule within the context of a simple coin-flipping thought experiment, it's reassuring to see that it is consistent with the more fundamental principles of decision-making under uncertainty. But as we stated at the start of this chapter, our purpose in introducing Expected Utility was to give you a more flexible and powerful tool to use in making better financial decisions in real-world situations. Let's try applying it to a few interesting questions that go beyond figuring out the optimal fraction of wealth to invest in assets whose prices move around over small intervals of time like they're generated by a series of coin flips.

A Sharper Lens Than the Sharpe Ratio

As soon as we move away from idealized asset price behavior—in particular, normally distributed returns—we need to know more about the investment than just its expected return and standard deviation. These are the two investment inputs into both Sharpe ratio and the Merton share, so both may misfire when used for investments with materially non-normal distributions.

For example, consider the three investments in Table 6.3. They are set up to all have the same expected return, risk, and Sharpe ratio, but they have different degrees of asymmetry in their payoffs and probabilities.

Using Expected Utility to evaluate the different investments, our Base-Case investor would calculate the RAR produced by each investment as a function of investment size, as shown in Exhibit 6.5. At the optimal investment size for each, the positively asymmetric investment generates about 50% more RAR than the negatively asymmetric investment, a very significant pickup between two investments that have the same expected return, risk, and Sharpe ratio. The preference for positively skewed payoffs that is built into the CRRA utility function is an attractive, and often under-appreciated feature of this family of utility preferences.

Table 6.3 Three Investments with Same Expected Gain and Risk but Varying Symmetry of Payoffs

	Positively Asymmetric	Symmetric	Negatively Asymmetric
Probability of Profit	20%	50%	80%
Probability of Loss	80%	50%	20%
Profit	45%	25%	15%
Loss	−5%	−15%	−35%
Expected Gain	5%	5%	5%
Risk	20%	20%	20%
Sharpe Ratio	0.25	0.25	0.25

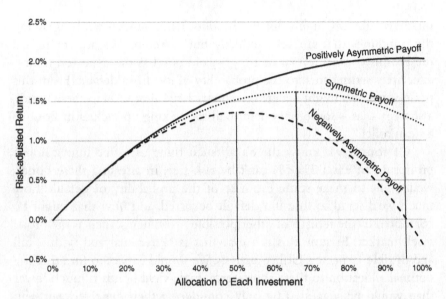

Exhibit 6.5   Impact of Investment Symmetry on Risk-adjusted Return

Many investments have return patterns that are significantly different from the normal return distributions that we have been focused on so far. For example, short-term, high-yielding bonds may seem appealing to investors if they don't look beyond summary metrics of return and risk. These bonds are often viewed as unlikely to default, don't come with a lot of daily market risk, and in normal times offer a yield 3% to 5% above safe assets such as Treasuries with similar maturities.[†] For investors who feel that equities will generate relatively meager returns, these bonds may appear to provide a lower-risk alternative with ample excess return.

One way you might think about this investment is to focus on the most likely outcome. We've seen that focusing on the median of a distribution is useful in deciding how much to bet on a coin flip, but the return pattern of these bonds is very negatively asymmetric as compared to the coin flip situations we've been discussing. When thinking fast and intuitively, we all have a well-documented tendency to put too

---

[†] Bonds from banks and other financial companies make up much of this asset class. These bonds are usually subordinated or issued at the holding company level or may even be preferred stock.

much weight on highly likely "headline" outcomes—while ignoring the outcomes that are very unlikely but extreme.[4] We are apt to see the promised extra return of a high-yield bond as the expected return, effectively setting to zero the probability of loss from default. From this perspective, you might decide on a pretty large allocation to these bonds, a strategy that is sometimes described as "picking up nickels in front of a steamroller."

Of course, we know there's no such thing as a free lunch; bonds promising an extra 3%–5% can't be risk-free. In assessing these bonds, we'll want to make some estimate of the probability of default, how much we'd stand to lose if a default occurred, and how that might be correlated to the returns of other possible investments, such as the broad stock market. In sum, this is a case that is better analyzed with a full and flexible Expected Utility analysis. We should expect to find that the optimal allocation to these short-term, high-yield bonds is much lower than would be suggested by only considering their expected gain and standard deviation of returns.

Some Clarity on Risk Parity

Staying with the high-yield bond example, let's assume that the stock market has twice the excess expected return as the high-yield bonds, and also twice the standard deviation, so they both have the same Sharpe ratio. We've seen that just because high-yield bonds and stocks have a similar Sharpe ratio doesn't mean a whole lot when it comes to our optimal allocations because the shape of their return patterns is so different. However the foundational idea of Risk Parity, a much-discussed modern investment strategy, is to take the same amount of risk in a range of different asset classes, which are assumed to have the same Sharpe ratio. Risk Parity strategies generally use leverage to achieve equal risk contributions from all asset buckets, which calls for frequent rebalancing of positions to maintain constant leverage and equal risk weighting.

Maximizing Expected Utility, which explicitly weighs the differing return distributions, will suggest taking much less risk in high-yield bonds compared to the risk taken in stocks because of the bonds' negatively asymmetric returns. This might surprise an advocate of Risk Parity, who would have argued it's optimal to hold the same amount of risk in both assets, since both assets have the same Sharpe ratio. The Expected Utility framework will find Risk Parity optimal only if all asset returns are normal, have equal pairwise correlations, have equal Sharpe ratios, and there's no constraint on leverage.

To a greater or lesser degree, many popular investment strategies— such as selling puts on the stock market, buying investment grade bonds, or investing in leveraged hedge fund strategies that don't or can't employ tight stop-loss limits—have asymmetric return patterns that are more accurately assessed with the Expected Utility framework than with the Sharpe ratio alone.

Case Study: Navigating an IPO Lockup

We have a friend Iggy who invested $100,000 in a social media startup that turned out to be a huge success. The company was about to IPO at a price that valued Iggy's stake at $20,000,000, which represented 90% of his total net worth. He was being advised that the stock would "pop" by about 25% right after the IPO, but that he'd be forced to hold for 1 year however much of his stake he didn't sell at the time of the IPO. Between the IPO pop and being generally optimistic about the company, he expected the stock to return 20% over the next year, and he expected the volatility of the stock to be about 50%. He asked us for advice on how to think about what he should do. Naturally, we turned to Expected Utility for guidance.

We spent some time exploring Iggy's personal level of risk-aversion and determined it was close to our Base-Case assumption. We also discussed his view of the risk and return of investing in the stock market, if he weren't so heavily invested in this single stock. Using an Expected Utility analysis, we suggested that his optimal portfolio would be about 35% in the social media stock and 25% in the stock market. We recommended selling just over half of his shares in the IPO.

A little while later, Iggy came back to us and explained that the underwriters would only let him sell all or none of his holding. Again we turned to calculating his Expected Utility from the two choices and found that he had a higher Risk-adjusted Return by selling his entire stake and investing about 60% of his capital in the broad stock market rather than being forced to hold on to his concentrated position in the one stock for another year. In fact, we found that he had a *negative* expected Risk-adjusted Return of more than 2% per annum from being 90% invested in the social media stock.

This was a very significant decision for him, and the Expected Utility framework gave him comfort that he was making a well-reasoned decision, whatever might happen with that stock over the next year. It turned out that if he had stayed fully invested in the stock, he'd have been in for a white-knuckle roller coaster ride, as the stock rallied about 40% right after the IPO but then sank about 20% over the rest of the year, for a total return of just 12%. He would have made more money keeping 90% invested in the stock over the year, but Iggy appreciated that at the time he made the decision he had to factor in the risks he was taking and felt good about his decision.

In late 2007 the billionaire investor Carl Icahn faced a similar decision with an investment he made in a start-up, Sandridge Energy, which specialized in fracking technology. Icahn was advised that the IPO was going to go very well, but that if he didn't sell in the IPO, he'd have to hold for 6 months. He decided the risk of 6 months holding a very volatile stock outweighed the probable benefit of the IPO pop, and he sold at the IPO price of $18 per share. The stock did jump right after the IPO to $26 per share, but by late 2008, the stock was trading at $6.15. Icahn might have done better if he sold the stock right after the 6-month lockup period ended, but the collapse of the company within a year of the IPO lends support to his decision to accept a lower expected return for a lower amount of risk. The CEO of Sandridge Energy, Tom Ward, had virtually all of his wealth invested in the company, and he suffered a roughly 90% loss in wealth as the company's stock collapsed.[5]

When an Economist Calls You Irrational

Well, so what? Some economist called you irrational. Why should you care?
—Steven Landsburg, professor of economics and author of
Can You Outsmart an Economist?

The economist Steven Landsburg provides a colorful thought experiment highlighting the potential costs of what he terms "irrational" decision-making.[6] "Irrational" is a loaded word, so we'll back off it a little and just use the term "inconsistent" instead. Landsburg poses a set of three questions:[†]

1. Would you pay $10 for a lottery ticket that gives you a one-in-a-million chance of winning a $10 million jackpot?
2. Would you pay $10 for insurance that protects you against a one-in-a-million chance of losing 99% of your wealth?
3. Would you accept a fair coin flip: heads you win a $10 million jackpot, tails you lose 99% of your wealth?

A "yes" or "no" answer to any of these questions individually can be reasonable, depending on your personal preferences. Probably not many wealthy people would answer "yes" to question 3, but some might very well do so. However there are patterns of answers that are logically inconsistent.

We're going to focus on the pattern: "yes" to question 1, "no" to question 2, and "no" to question 3. This is formally inconsistent, because you've said that a remote chance of winning the lottery has more utility to you than does $10, and avoiding a remote chance of losing 99% of your wealth has less utility than does $10. Putting your two preferences together says that the fair coin flip from question 3 is a positive-utility proposition for you, which you should take.

How might this be a problem for you? Landsburg goes on to propose a game: there's a large urn with a million balls in it—one is red, one is black, and the rest are white. He asks if you'd pay him $10 to draw a ball, and you'll get $10 million if the ball is red. And indeed you would, per your answer to question 1. He then asks if you'd accept $10 from him, such that if the ball is black he gets to keep 99% of your wealth. And again indeed you would, per question 2. Then you start playing the game. Eventually he draws a colored ball, but before revealing its color he asks if you'd like to pay him another $10 to throw the ball back in and draw again? And again you would, because per question 3 you wouldn't take a 50/50 chance of the $10 million payout versus losing 99% of your wealth. Play for long enough, and you can see that what happens is Landsburg gets occasional payments from you, and you never get anything!

[†]We've amended the questions slightly while preserving their spirit.

This game is an example of a "money pump," a process that extracts money from you over time and gives it to your counterparty in a risk-less way for him. No one in their right mind would want to play this game, yet you find yourself playing it through making decisions which *individually* matched your preferences, but collectively were *inconsistent*. If you played long enough, you'd be guaranteed to lose all your money, while at each decision point making a decision you're quite happy with.

Obviously this is an extreme and contrived example. Neither we nor Landsburg imagine that games such as these are being intentionally concocted by evil economists or played by their hapless victims. Yet as in all fantastical fables, there's a valuable message here about the real world. In our financial (and nonfinancial) lives we're often forced to make rela-tively narrow, individual decisions, without knowing or being able to see all the other related decisions we'll be called to make in the future. We can see the question in front of us, but not the entire game. This can make us susceptible to the same kind of problem we see in Landsburg's game, where we're happy with each individual decision we made, but because our preferences are inconsistent, the overall result is something we never would have chosen.

As Landsburg concludes:

When an economist calls you irrational, it almost always means that if you follow through on your stated preferences, a sufficiently clever opponent can take all your money, leaving you smiling along the way. It's worth being alert to such things.

The Fallacy of Large Numbers

In a playfully written 1963 article titled "Risk and Uncertainty: A Fallacy of Large Numbers," MIT economist Paul Samuelson tells the story of offering "some lunch colleagues to bet each $200 to $100 that the side of a coin they specified would not appear at the first toss. One distinguished scholar—who lays no claim to advanced mathe-matical skill—gave the following answer: 'I won't bet because I would feel the $100 loss more than the $200 gain. But I'll take you on if you promise to let me make 100 such bets.'"

He continues, "What was behind this interesting answer? . . . 'One toss is not enough to make it reasonably sure that the law of averages will turn out in my favor. But in a hundred tosses of a coin, the law of large numbers will make it a darn good bet. I am, so to speak, virtually sure to come out ahead in such a sequence, and that is why I accept the sequence while rejecting the single toss.'"

In assessing the logic of this position, Samuelson makes the reasonable assumption (which he could have verified by asking) that his colleague would also turn down a single bet at any level of wealth that he could conceivably reach from taking 100 of these bets.

Samuelson then states: "If a person is concerned with maximizing the expected or average value of the utility of all possible outcomes, and my colleague assures me that he wants to. . ., it is simply not sufficient to look at the probability of a gain or loss. *Each outcome must have its utility reckoned at the appropriate probability; and when this is done it will be found that no sequence is acceptable if each of its single plays is not acceptable.* This is a basic theorem. . . .. If at each income or wealth level within a range, the Expected Utility of a certain investment or bet is worse than abstention, then no sequence of such independent ventures (that leaves one within the specified range of income) can have a favorable Expected Utility. Thus, if you would always refuse to take favorable odds on a single toss, you must rationally refuse to participate in any (finite) sequence of such tosses."

He goes on to give a proof of the theorem,[†] which can be summarized as "repeated (identical and independent) fair games yield a fair game; and repeated unfair games yield an unfair game."

Since Samuelson's colleague has stated *a priori* that his preferences are such that any single gamble is a negative Expected Utility, "unfair" game, then repeating it 100 times leaves the sequence as negative Expected Utility too.[‡]

[†] If you will not accept one toss, you cannot accept two—since the latter could be thought of as consisting of the (unwise) decision to accept one plus the open decision to accept a second. Even if you were stuck with the first outcome, you would cut your further (utility) losses and refuse the terminal throw. By extending the reasoning from 2 to 3 = 2 + 1, . . ., and from $n - 1$ to n, we rule out any sequence at all.

[‡] Samuelson warns the reader "against undue extrapolation of my theorem. It does not say one must always refuse a sequence if one refuses a single venture: if at higher income levels the single tosses become acceptable, and at lower levels the penalty of losses does not become infinite, there might well be a long sequence that is optional."

Samuelson really hit a nerve with this article, and much has been written since then to show circumstances under which his colleague's position would be rational.[7] Perhaps what makes Samuelson's argument in this example so hard to agree with is that the opportunity to make 100 of these bets is just so incredibly attractive that how could he argue that his colleague was "irrational" to accept it? After all, 100 of these gambles has an expected gain of $5,000, with less than a 1 in 2,000 chance of loss, and a one in a million chance of losing more than $2,000! Indeed, any normal person should and would take one hundred flips, *but he should also take* just one flip, if that's all that's on offer. As we discussed earlier in Chapter 4 in "What About Really Small Investments?" the expected gain needed for a bet on a small fraction of one's wealth is tiny, and so the really strange thing in this example is that Samuelson's colleague's risk-aversion could be high enough to cause him to reject that single bet. Samuelson's colleague would need to be 250 times more risk averse than what we assume is typical (i.e., $\gamma = 500$) to rationally reject the single bet with starting wealth of $100,000, and 2,500 times more risk averse with starting wealth of $1,000,000. With that degree of risk-aversion, it is hard to imagine such a person ever leaving home.

Baby Needs a New Pair of Shoes, or Investing to Reach a Goal

The goal-based approach to wealth management emphasizes investing with the objective of attaining specific life goals. It is a recent addition to the set of techniques used by financial advisors to help people organize their lifetime investing and spending decisions. We'll define the approach as determining an investment plan that maximizes the probability of reaching a pre-set wealth goal over a chosen horizon. Some advocates of the goal-based system may dispute our simple definition and point out other important aspects of the method, but we think this is its core feature. Let's use our Expected Utility framework to explore how it works and its efficacy.

We've argued that constant fractional sizing is the way to go when faced with a series of independent, attractive investment opportunities. If for example these investments have characteristics similar to betting on a 60/40 coin, then risking 10% of your wealth on each one would be a good, even optimal, choice. But we haven't specifically looked at goal-based investing yet, and perhaps it provides a better overall set of outcomes compared to constant fractional sizing, or maybe it's just about as good but more comfortable and intuitively appealing. Let's see.

We'll use a Monte Carlo simulation to figure out the optimal betting strategy for an investor who is trying to maximize the *probability* of reaching a modest goal of increasing wealth by 50% given the opportunity to bet 25 times on a 60/40 biased coin. The general form of the optimal betting rule is to bet more aggressively the further away the goal is from the current level of wealth, adjusted for the number of flips remaining.[8]

In Exhibit 6.6, we show what the distribution of outcomes looks like for the goal-based strategy with a goal of growing wealth by 50%, and for the strategy of risking a constant 10% on each flip. Notice that the goal-based strategy doesn't generate any outcomes above the goal,

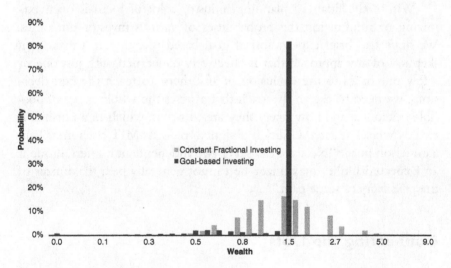

Exhibit 6.6 Comparing Wealth Outcomes for Goal-based Investing Versus Constant Risk Investing, Starting Wealth = 1

because once you reach it, you don't take any more risk, as such risk would only serve to decrease the probability of finishing at your goal. Also, with the goal-based approach, there is a small but real probability of very bad outcomes—about a 7% chance of losing more than 50% of starting wealth. The constant fractional sizing strategy entails only about a 1% probability of such large losses.

We recognize that utility functions can be imagined that would support goal-based investing, such as if you felt that if you don't increase your wealth by 50%, life just wouldn't be worth living, or that your spouse would leave you. Yale finance professor James Choi has called these "get rich or die trying utility functions." However, acting like you do have these preferences, when in fact you don't, can be very destructive to your welfare. While this coin-flipping case study is a fairly unrealistic characterization, it is noteworthy that your Certainty-equivalent Wealth from the constant fractional sizing strategy is about 75% higher than that from the goal-based approach. In fact, your Certainty-equivalent Wealth from following the goal-based approach here would be a loss of 26% from your starting wealth, more than eliminating the value of the opportunity to make attractive investments.

Within the financial planning industry, a lot of focus is on maximizing or minimizing the probabilities of various investor outcomes. We hope this brief exploration of goal-based investing will make you skeptical of any approach that is effectively concerned with just one or a few outcomes to the exclusion of all others. To reach the best decisions, we need to use an approach that assesses the whole range of possible outcomes and how likely they are to occur, which in a nutshell is exactly what Expected Utility is designed to do. As MIT economist Paul Samuelson put it: "No slave can serve two independent masters. If one is an Expected Utility maximizer, he cannot generally be a maximizer of the *probability* of some gain."[9]

Connecting the Dots

We covered a lot of ground in this chapter, from Bernouilli's recognition that maximizing expected wealth is not a great objective for making financial decisions to von Neumann and Morgenstern's conditions under which maximizing your Expected Utility is the optimal course of action. But most of all, we have tried to show how the Expected Utility framework can be applied to practical, real-world situations, with no more than a spreadsheet to calculate probability-weighted sums. In the next chapter, before we move on to other case studies and extensions, we consider the range of criticisms that have been made of Expected Utility as a decision-making framework.

7

Criticisms of Expected Utility Decision-making

COGNITIVE BIASES MAKE US POOR INVESTORS

Control Illusion
Hindsight bias
I knew it all along
Over Confidence
Over Optimism
10% chance of dying
90% chance of surviving
Halo Effect
Money Illusion
Herding
"We prefer Stories over randomness"
framing
Narrative bias
Normalcy bias
Anchoring
Gamblers fallacy
Disaster Myopia
Selective Perception

He who knows only his own side of the case knows little of that.

—John Stuart Mill

This Isn't How Ordinary People Make Decisions

Maximizing Expected Utility was put forward by modern economists such as Milton Friedman and Paul Samuelson as both a descriptive and normative model of decision-making. It was hoped that many micro- and macroeconomic phenomena could be modeled using Expected Utility methods if individuals or groups in an economy behaved *as if* they were utility maximizers. While there is still some debate about this proposition, the preponderance of evidence leans against it. Indeed, if people did reliably make decisions that maximize their Expected Utility, we would not have felt a need to write this book!

However, the arguments against Expected Utility as a valid descriptive model should not be used to discredit it as a normative, prescriptive model of how people *should* make decisions. Rational, consistent decision-making is a valuable goal worth striving for, even if it can never be fully realized. We recognize it often makes sense to act as satisficers[†] when it comes to the low-impact decisions we face day to day, but when we make financial decisions of high consequence, it pays to carefully weigh our decisions and behave as rationally as possible.

The field of behavioral economics pioneered by Kahneman and Tversky provides an extensive catalog of all the ways we make strange and often inconsistent decisions. These are cognitive foibles. It has been the hope of economists and psychologists to help people make better decisions by making them aware of their biases. Far from denigrating Expected Utility as an old-fashioned idea disproven by his work, in 2011 Kahneman declared von Neuman's Expected Utility hypothesis as: "To this day the most important theory in the social sciences."[1]

It's no surprise that even exceptionally smart people need help with good decision-making. At a conference in Paris in 1953, Nobel laureate economist Maurice Allais asked the mathematician and decision theorist Jimmy Savage to choose between a relatively complex set of gambles, a thought experiment that came to be called Allais' paradox. Savage made his choice, and Allais notoriously gloated that in doing so he had violated one of the axioms of rational choice underlying the valid use of Expected Utility, of which Savage was a leading proponent. But Savage, back in his office with some time to reflect, concluded he had just answered wrongly in the heat of the moment and would instead want to make the choice that strictly maximized his Expected Utility. The lesson we take from this is simply that even very smart people need some good tools for consistent decision-making, which doesn't always come naturally. In our view, one of the benefits of having a solid, rational framework is that you don't *need* to rely on intuition and gut feelings, which behavioral economists have convincingly shown to be biased and inconsistent.

[†] Satisficing is an approach to decision-making that involves searching through available alternatives until an acceptability threshold is met.

What Happens in Vegas. . .

It's easy to identify plenty of instances in which people act like they're not risk averse, or with improbably low or high levels of risk-aversion. We stress though that these examples are generally exceptions, not the rule. They tend to involve at least one of these common features:

1. Small amounts at risk relative to wealth
2. A significant element of nonmonetary reward (e.g., the "thrill" of gambling)
3. Systematic mis-estimation or ignorance of the true odds

Playing the lottery or going to Vegas are common examples of people willingly taking gambles they know to be unfair. In addition, it has been widely observed that people systematically require way too much of an advantage in tiny gambles, exhibiting a level of risk-aversion that would imply rejecting larger bets that "a good lawyer could have you declared legally insane for turning down."[2] This inconsistency between attitudes to small risks versus large risks is known as Rabin's calibration paradox and has been viewed as a criticism of the usefulness of Expected Utility. We agree that most people, left to their natural instincts, don't make decisions on small gambles in line with the risk-aversion they exhibit with respect to large, important risks, but this is not a valid critique of how people *should* make decisions. In any case, it shouldn't hurt us too much to turn down a few small bets, as long as we make sound decisions on risks that involve high financial stakes, which are primarily monetary in nature, and where we can estimate the odds reasonably well.

Let's consider people who frequent craps or blackjack tables, where it's known that the odds are stacked in the favor of the casino.[†] In many cases, this behavior can be explained by the existence of some added benefit that is external to the betting on the table, such as being "comped" pricey show tickets and expensive wines at dinner or a pleasurable adrenaline rush from rolling the dice and invoking Lady Luck. Sometimes the player is simply deluding himself that he has a winning strategy. At a talk that Victor was giving at an investment bank about

---

[†]We're excluding professional gamblers who can move the odds slightly in their favor through card-counting or other aids that will get you thrown out of casinos.

investment-sizing, a young trader asked, "How does Expected Utility tell us to size a bet in a casino where the odds are against us?"

Victor had been talking at length about sizing strategies for attractive bets, so perhaps he shouldn't have found the question so surprising. The answer of course is that for risks with a negative edge, there's a very simple precept: the optimal size is zero. You may choose to play anyway for nonmonetary reasons, but if your only goal is increasing your bankroll, such risks are best avoided.

In our days on Wall Street we occasionally came across traders who claimed to be purely risk-neutral. They claimed to have no aversion to risk at all. A truly risk-neutral person would be willing to take any risk as long as it had some positive edge, no matter how scant. Invariably, when we dug deeper by asking if they'd be willing to accept some big risk with small compensation, we always found that in fact they wouldn't. These traders may have had a low level of risk-aversion relative to their peers, but they were still risk-averse, and their claims to the contrary were typically grounded in a misunderstanding. A truly risk-neutral investor would appear to third-party observers as being "on tilt." Such a person would happily bet *all* their wealth on a coin-flip if he or she had just a 50.1% chance of winning. We believe virtually no normally functioning person would actually do that.[†]

A slight variant we've also heard is the proposition that a risk-taker puts aside say 20% of their wealth and is then risk-neutral—or even risk-seeking—with the other 80%. We have not found anyone who actually behaves in this way for long—if they did, they would quickly lose the 80% of wealth that they managed as if they were risk-neutral. For people whose financial decisions are risk-seeking, there's no end to counterparties lining up to bet against them. This is the business of casinos in their purest form, stripped of the shows and steak dinners, and casinos tend to be tremendously profitable.[‡] When evaluated on a purely financial basis, being the risk-seeking punter—at a casino or elsewhere—is a poor business indeed.

[†] We do know of one individual who publicly said he would make decisions in that way, and who seems to have done so. In our November 2022 article, "A Missing Piece of the SBF Puzzle," we explored Sam Bankman-Fried's professed risk-neutrality and how it may have contributed to the collapse of his businesses and wealth.

[‡] So profitable that many countries impose strong regulations on allowable odds to limit their profitability.

Individuals Are Incapable of Specifying Their Personal Utility Functions

In *Pioneering Portfolio Management: An Unconventional Approach to Institutional Investment* (2000), David Swensen argues that the concept of utility is unusable in practice:

> Economists might suggest that a Utility function be employed to identify the appropriate asset allocation. Since few market participants would have any idea how to specify such a function, this technique proves remarkably unhelpful.

To the contrary, we have found that the concept of utility is usable in practice, for ourselves, for many of our clients, and for many others we have discussed the question with over the years. In a more formal survey of finance professionals, which we'll describe in more detail in Chapter 12, all respondents were comfortable answering questions to calibrate their personal utility functions. Furthermore, their preferences were generally consistent with CRRA utility—the most common form of utility function. For the vast majority, their coefficient of risk-aversion fell within a fairly tight range of 2–3. Interactions with our clients confirm the survey findings that CRRA utility is a reasonable and tractable model of utility for most wealthy individuals and families.

Swensen is likely correct that few market participants today *know* how to calibrate their own utility function, but this is an issue of education rather than possibility. Reasonable calibration procedures are both possible and straightforward, and we explore them in detail in Chapter 12.

Prospect Theory and "Loss Aversion"

Prospect theory was developed by psychologists Daniel Kahneman and Amos Tversky to explain how people behave when facing risky decisions. They observed that behavior systematically disagrees with the predictions of classical economics driven by maximizing Expected Utility.

In particular, they observed, over and over again, three noteworthy patterns of behavior:

1. People weigh the pain of small losses a lot more than the pleasure of small gains.
2. They weigh large losses only modestly more than small losses.
3. These preferences don't seem to depend on the level of wealth, but only on changes in wealth relative to the most recent "reference" point.

One of the best known of their experiments involved asking people whether they'd prefer

1. a $3,000 gain for sure, or
2. an 80% chance of a $4,000 gain and a 20% chance of no gain.

Most respondents preferred the $3,000 certain gain, to the risky expected gain of $3,200. Then the same people were asked to again choose which they'd prefer

1. a $3,000 loss for sure, or
2. an 80% chance of a $4,000 loss and a 20% chance of no loss.

Most respondents answered they'd rather the second option, taking the risk of the larger loss, even though the expected loss was $3,200, higher than the certain loss.[†]

Individually either of these observations can be consistent with Expected Utility theory. But taken together, these observations are inconsistent with the classical theory—investors seem to have path-dependent and different risk preferences when the risks involve potential losses than when they involve potential gains. If you have our Base-Case CRRA utility preferences, you would make the opposite choices except for extremely low levels of wealth, in which case you'd decline the risk in both cases.

[†]The certainty-equivalent gain of the 80/20 gamble to win $4,000 or $0 is $3,175, so $175 better than the $3,000 certain payoff, and the certainty-equivalent loss of the 80/20 gamble to lose $4,000 or $0 is a loss of $3,226, so $226 worse than the certain loss of $3,000, for an individual with $100,000 of wealth, and CRRA utility with risk-aversion of 2. As starting wealth increases, the certainty-equivalent values of both gambles converge to their expected values of $3,200.

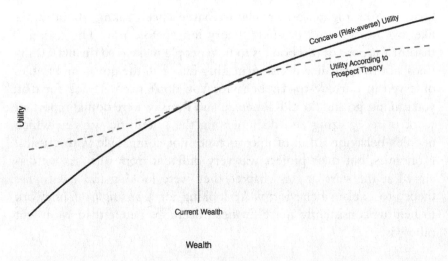

Exhibit 7.1 Prospect Theory Versus Classical Utility Preferences

Prospect theory proposes that people act as if their "happiness" function looks quite different from the classic utility function suggested by Bernoulli and other economists.

Prospect theory describes as "loss aversion" the behavior consistent with the "kinked" utility function displayed in Exhibit 7.1, as distinct from the "risk-aversion" behavior implied by classical Expected Utility. Both theories agree that individuals are averse to losses relative to gains, and the choice of the term "loss aversion" for the specific observed preferences described by Kahneman and Tversky is unfortunate and leads to much confusion. The implication of the kink, and of the convexity in the region of losses, is that people behave as if they have *negative* risk-aversion over lower levels of wealth. This implies they are very sensitive to small losses and only slightly more sensitive to large losses.

We are big fans of Kahneman and Tversky and their work in behavioral economics, for which Kahneman won the 2002 Nobel Prize in Economics.[†] They made enormous contributions to formalizing our understanding of how people actually behave, and convincingly demonstrated that prospect theory is a much better predictor of behavior in many circumstances than classical utility theory. But where does this all

---

[†]Tversky would certainly have shared the Prize if he had been alive.

leave us? You might wonder why we haven't been talking about things like loss aversion and prospect theory long before now. The reason is that the purpose of this book is to help people make *good* financial decisions, not to formalize decision-making full of all the quirks and foibles observed in our day-to-day behavior. You don't need a book for that; you can just go and do it! Kahneman and Tversky were doing important work in recognizing and documenting the systematic ways in which people's behavior is full of idiosyncrasies not compatible with classical economics, but their project was very different from ours. As we discussed at the start of this chapter, they were looking for a *descriptive* theory to explain behavior; we're looking for a *prescriptive* framework to help us consistently make financial decisions better than we might otherwise.

Criticisms of the Axioms of Rational Choice

In the previous chapter we laid out the four axioms of rational choice. Von Neumann and Morgenstern showed that as long as these hold true, it can be proved that maximizing Expected Utility is the best way to make decisions under uncertainty. However there have been a number of criticisms of the axioms and their applicability. Most relate to a concern that violations of the independence axiom can be observed relatively often in the wild. The axiom states: "A preference holds independently of the existence of an unrelated third outcome C. If A is preferred to B, then a third, 'irrelevant' option C does not cause the individual to switch to preferring B to A."

An example that has been used to illustrate an apparent violation of this axiom involves a diner who is offered chicken or steak tartare by the waiter. The diner chooses the chicken. Then the waiter says, "Wait! We also have frog legs on the menu." The diner then changes his choice to steak tartare, seeming to violate the independence axiom. In this tasty example though, the presence of frog legs on the menu might not actually be irrelevant, as they may suggest it's more likely the chef is an expert in French cuisine and so the steak tartare is going to be better than the chicken.[3]

Most instances where violations of the independence axiom are observed involve nonmonetary goods and can often be explained by additional context. However, when real violations do occur, we don't find this a cause for concern. Even if behavioral foibles sometimes lure us into strange decision-making, when consequential financial matters are involved, we should want our choices to be consistent with all four axioms, which form a solid foundation for consistent and rational decision-making.

Wicked Games

One intriguing objection to the use of utility is that it doesn't *really* solve the St. Petersburg paradox. While using Expected Utility resolves the paradox as narrowly stated, it's easy to restate the game in a way that still causes trouble. If the payout after tossing heads n times in a row is e^{2^n} instead of 2^n, now a decision-maker trying to maximize log-utility will be willing to pay almost all of their wealth to play the game. More generally, for any stylized utility function we suspect a sufficiently outlandish game payout can be found where optimizing Expected Utility would lead to an unreasonable outcome.

We don't think this is a problem. This result tends to arise from a combination of using a generic utility function that doesn't quite match a person's true utility at extremes of wealth, with setups that tend to exploit those extremes, such as having an infinitesimal probability of making more than all the money in the world or losing everything. What we're really concerned about in practice is whether our rule results in sensible decisions when applied to the kinds of financial questions we encounter in real-life situations.

Probabilities of Future Outcomes Are Unknowable

[Most of our decisions] to do something positive. . .can only be taken as a result of animal spirits. . .and not as the outcome of a weighted average of quantitative benefits multiplied by quantitative probabilities.

—J.M. Keynes, *The General Theory of Employment, Interest, and Money*

Human knowledge is distressingly limited. Particularly in realms outside the natural sciences, universal laws, robust experimental evidence, and sharp probability estimates are in short supply. Finance is no exception. Financial data are famously thorny: there's often not enough, it's subject to regime shifts so that going back in history may not be helpful, stable relationships are rare and fleeting, and competitive forces have powerful impact. Markets are ever in flux rather than a timeless clockwork we can count on.

How is it possible to use a quantitative framework for investing in the midst of such uncertainty? Our view is that there are differing degrees of essential uncertainty, and we can focus on those areas and markets in which we have reasonable, if only partial, confidence while avoiding those areas in which we have little or none. For example, in the case of broad equity markets, a combination of history and theory can give us reasonable ranges for expected returns, variability, and imperfect but still useful techniques for forecasting. We'll never know the precise shape of the return distribution of the US equity market over any given period, but we can get in the ballpark enough to extract good value out of a quantitative framework. In contrast, the uncertainty around a single, new company in a new industry is of quite a different character.

The non-stationarity and uncertainty that are intrinsic to financial markets mean we must approach our methods with humility, aware they can be abused out of context and be careful not to overreach or rely on extreme results highly tuned to precise inputs. But we cannot avoid making financial decisions, and so we believe that approaching a framework in this spirit is a better response than simply abandoning all decisions to our "animal spirits."

The Kelly Criterion Is Good; Expected Utility Is Bad

Proponents of the Kelly criterion can be a passionate lot, and it's not difficult to find a variety of odes to Kelly that disparage the usefulness of Expected Utility, often trying to paint Kelly and utility as not just distinct but opposing viewpoints. We think this portrayal is wide of the mark in that the "full" Kelly criterion and decision rules arising from maximizing Expected Utility are entirely consistent with each other.

Optimizing the geometric rate of growth of wealth, as with the Kelly criterion, and optimizing log-utility, as suggested by Bernoulli, lead to exactly the same equations and the same decision rules. For binary bets, optimizing expected CRRA utility with $\gamma = 1$ exactly reproduces the classic "full" Kelly criterion. Doing the same with $\gamma = 2$ is a good approximation of "half-Kelly." We find it a bit odd to say that in practice one method is fantastic while the other is fatally flawed, when both arrive at very similar results given the same assumptions. Fractional Kelly strategies seek to mitigate the riskiness of full Kelly, while using CRRA utility provides the flexibility to account for investors being more risk-averse than is implied by log-utility. These two methods of calibrating risk-aversion are not exactly identical, but we suggest they're extremely similar in spirit, and also in outcome over small changes in wealth. Readers shouldn't feel like they have to pick a side in the somewhat unfortunate "Kelly versus Utility" debate—for the kinds of problems where the original Kelly criterion is readily applied, Kelly and utility are more like close siblings than unrelated brawling adversaries.

Some advocates of the Kelly criterion argue that maximizing the expected growth rate of wealth is the only rational approach to sizing risk exposure. However, we have found that strict Kelly betting is far too risk-tolerant for most individuals. For example, a person with this low level of risk-aversion would be just willing to accept a 50/50 coin toss to double or halve her wealth. We don't know many people, especially those near the end of their working careers, who would be willing to take such a high chance of losing half of their entire wealth.

Proponents of Kelly also sometimes argue that as the number of gambles you take gets arbitrarily large, sizing risk according to the Kelly criterion will result in the highest amount of wealth. This is true, but not relevant in practice: this result requires there be such a large number of available favorable gambles that you'd be a trillionaire whether you followed Kelly or more risk-averse sizing strategies too. This rebuttal was presented in "Why we should not make mean log of wealth big though years to act are long" by Paul Samuelson (1979), which he famously wrote using only words of one syllable.

The Long Run Is Very Long

One of the statements put forward by advocates of the Kelly criterion for risk-taking is that in the long run it becomes nearly certain
you will have more money by betting according to Kelly than betting any other way. To explore this a bit, let's go back to our trusty
coin that has a 60% chance of landing heads. We'll compare Kelly
betting, which will call for putting 20% of our wealth on each flip, to
betting half that amount, 10% on each flip, which would be consistent with CRRA utility with a coefficient of risk-aversion of 2.

   After 10, 100, and 1,000 flips, the probabilities that you will have
more money betting Kelly are 63%, 70%, and 94%. Boy would it be
nice to get 1,000 opportunities to bet on a 60/40 coin! If you were
betting just 10% of your wealth on each flip (half-Kelly), you'd have
a 99% chance of turning $100,000 into $200 million or more. And if
you got the median outcome of 600 heads, you'd turn $100,000 into
$340 billion! We think it's kind of silly to be focused on strict opti-
mality in these fantastic cases, which are nearly certain to produce
tremendous outcomes whether you are a full Kelly bettor or are using
the Merton share with a commonly exhibited degree of risk-aversion.

The thread of the Kelly criterion criticism of Expected Utility has
been picked up by the new field of ergodicity economics, put forward by
a group of physicists, which argues that Expected Utility theory is flawed
because in general utility is not ergodic. Ergodicity is an important concept in statistical mechanics. An ergodic variable is one for which the
average of many trials over one period (the ensemble average) converges
to the average over many sequential trials (the time average) as the number of trials becomes infinitely large.

Proponents of this school of thought criticize Expected Utility both
as a descriptive and prescriptive framework. They argue that the only
rational approach to investing is to maximize the growth rate of wealth,
which is equivalent to the Kelly criterion. We have just discussed the
"Kelly is better" argument, and the same analysis applies here too.

The Expected Utility toolkit encompasses the Kelly criterion rather
than being distinct from it. Ergodicity arguments in their strictest form
prohibit even strategies like half-Kelly, which many proponents of
the Kelly criterion gravitate to in practice. Also, while we agree that

ergodicity is an attractive property for a time series to possess, the divergence from perfect ergodicity, which can be experienced in real-world examples over real-world time frames, is relatively small.

Expected Utility for Life and Death Choices

Man with a gun: "This is a stickup. Your money or your life!"
[pregnant pause]
"I said, THIS IS A STICKUP—YOUR MONEY OR YOUR LIFE—what's it going to be mister?"
Man without a gun: "I'm thinking it over."

—Comedian Jack Benny (1930s)

The Expected Utility framework is sometimes criticized for not working well in situations such as a highly likely enjoyable experience, say skiing an untracked mountain snowfield in deep powder, which carries with it a very small probability of a very, very bad outcome—death or severe injury. There are a number of challenges with using Expected Utility to make such choices. Quantifying small probabilities is challenging, but the central difficulty is assigning a utility value to death. It's always possible to assign a sufficiently negative value to death such that the Expected Utility calculation will tell you to never do anything fun. And yet, even in the ordinary course of our lives, we're constantly taking these small risks of meeting an early end, and it's hard to imagine living a productive and meaningful life without taking these risks. There is a broad literature on how as individuals and as society at large we should assess small life-and-death risks. For our purposes, let us acknowledge that this is a reasonable criticism and limitation of the Expected Utility framework for making life-and-death choices, but we do not think it is a compelling argument against using Expected Utility for financial decision-making.

So Why Isn't Everyone Using Expected Utility Already?

In the 1950s and 1960s, when much of the ground-breaking work on choice theory was taking place, the computing power necessary for a mass-market practical application of the approach was not available.

Even with today's much-augmented capabilities, building user-friendly models that can handle a range of real-world complexities is not trivial. We suspect this stalled the transition of Expected Utility methods out of academia, especially because many of the same researchers went on to develop breakthrough derivative-pricing models—such as the Black-Scholes option pricing model—which could be immediately applied to markets. Many of the people with technical skills who subsequently flooded finance focused primarily on "arbitrage" theories and derivatives pricing, and Expected Utility methods were left on the shelf. It also hasn't helped that "utility theory" as a framework for decision-making under uncertainty is often mistakenly associated with a set of out-of-favor political and ethical doctrines known as "Utilitarianism," advocated by the nineteenth-century moral philosophers Jeremy Bentham and John Stuart Mill, in which society should make decisions that maximize the sum of the Expected Utility of its members. Not only is such a political ideology effectively impossible to implement, but it also suggests decisions that would trample individuals' freedoms, rights, and pursuit of happiness. The fact that utility cannot be added across individuals does not reduce its value as a guide to good decisions for each individual.

Connecting the Dots

The criticisms discussed in this chapter are not the only ones lodged against the use of Expected Utility, but they cover the majority of objections with which we are familiar. Making good financial decisions isn't easy, but as the legendary investor Seth Klarman says, "Don't think you can avoid making a choice; inertia is also a decision."[4]

8

Reminiscences of a Hedge Fund Operator

There are certain things that cannot be adequately explained to a virgin either by words or pictures. Nor can any description that I might offer here even approximate what it feels like to lose a real chunk of money that you used to own.

—Fred Schwed Jr, *Where Are the Customers' Yachts?* (1940)

This chapter is about a personal lesson Victor learned from his experience as a partner of the hedge fund Long-Term Capital Management (LTCM), where he had a large fraction of his personal wealth invested. The question of "how much skin in the game is right for you?" is important in many situations: start-up founders, family businesses, actors, athletes, and corporate executives, to name just a few. Of course, third parties who are thinking about betting on you feel better when they see you "eating your own cooking." As Nassim Taleb states in his book, *Skin in the Game* (2018), "There is something respectable about losing a billion dollars, provided it is your own money." However, it's dangerous to allow the desire to send a signal to third-party investors to distract you from first answering the question of what's best for you. We suspect that it will usually be the case, as it was for Victor, that what's right for you will be more than enough to convince backers that they have your full and undivided attention.

The story of LTCM's trading decisions, its rise and fall, and the personalities involved have been amply discussed elsewhere, most notably in the books *When Genius Failed* and *Inventing Money*, and in numerous articles, including a long-form *New York Times* article published in January 1999 by Michael Lewis, titled "How the Eggheads Cracked."[†] In contrast, our focus here will be on a largely untold part of the story, which we think has relevance beyond just hedge fund investors and managers. Perhaps because none of the books and articles written at the time had the cooperation of former LTCM partners, one of the most salient, useful, and incontrovertible lessons from LTCM has been overlooked, namely: how much "skin in the game" made sense for a partner of LTCM? Or more specifically, how should Victor have decided on how much of his personal wealth to invest in the LTCM fund?

Background

LTCM was a hedge fund that had a brief and rather spectacular life from 1994 to 1999. Its partnership was made up of a band of bond traders from the investment bank Salomon Brothers and several distinguished academics, two of whom would go on to receive the Nobel prize in economics. The lead partner was John Meriwether, a preeminent bond trader, who founded Salomon's bond arbitrage business in the mid-1970s. The investment approach employed by LTCM was the same one

---

[†]There is also a Harvard Business School Case Study, filled with meticulously collected figures and details, prepared in November 1999 by Professor André Perold, simply titled "Long-Term Capital Management LP."

that contributed significant and consistent profits to Salomon Brothers for roughly 20 years.[1]

No wonder there was a lot of excitement in the markets and among hedge fund investors when LTCM started operations in early 1994. Initial capital was $1.0 billion, including more than $100 million of investment by the partners, which at the time made it the largest hedge fund launch ever. Believers in the story were not disappointed, as LTCM showed solid—some might say spectacular—profitability in its first 4 years of operation. The return after fees delivered to initial investors through the end of 1997 was 31.2% per annum. Winning months outnumbered losing ones four-to-one, and the fund never lost money 2 months in a row. In just under 4 years, the fund grew to be one of the largest hedge funds in the world, with $7.5 billion in capital, despite being effectively closed to new investors from mid-1995.

Then, in 1998, LTCM suffered losses of more than 90%. At the urging of the New York Federal Reserve, a consortium of 14 large commercial and investment banks—all of whom were LTCM trading counterparties exposed to steep losses from a disorderly unwind—invested $3.6 billion in the fund for a roughly 90% ownership interest. The fund was liquidated by the end of 1999, with the consortium of banks making a positive return on their investment of about 10%.

One year earlier, at the end of 1997, the partners had made a fateful decision to return about 35% of the fund's capital to investors. This was a highly controversial decision, both within the LTCM partnership and among its investors. The return of capital to the fund's roughly 100 outside investors did have a silver lining for the redeemed investors, in that it resulted in the investors earning a positive median life-to-date return of 19% per annum, including the losses in 1998. In fact, over the full life of LTCM, the fund made a small aggregate net profit, with most investors earning a good return due to the return of capital. However, a few investors, notably the Swiss bank UBS, took a large loss on their untimely, late involvement with the fund. Unfortunately for the partners of LTCM, the losses in 1998 wiped out virtually all of their personal investments in the fund.

The Big Decision

Victor was a founding partner of LTCM, and here is how he remembers thinking about it. Afterward, we'll discuss how he would think about it today through the lens of the Expected Utility framework we've been discussing throughout this book. We emphasize that this is Victor's personal recollection, and it is not necessarily representative of any other partner of LTCM.

At the inception of LTCM, our investors expected us to invest a high fraction of our wealth in the fund to show that we had "skin in the game," signaling we really believed in what we were doing. By 1997, this was no longer a consideration, and if anything, our investors would have preferred us to have less invested in the fund so that they could invest more. By this time, I felt free to have as much or as little invested in the fund as I wanted. The fund seemed like an incredibly attractive investment. Partners like me weren't required to pay the incentive fee, so returns on my investments in the fund had compounded at over 40% per annum for 4 years, and the realized risk was running at 10%–15% per annum based on the standard deviation of monthly returns. Prior to LTCM, the partners had been investing the capital of Salomon Brothers for close to 20 years with similar, high-quality realized returns.

It seemed that everybody wanted to invest more in our fund, and we were hearing that some investors were buying out other investors' holdings at a large premium to net asset value. I was 35 years old at the time, the youngest of the LTCM partners. I saw that all my partners, many of whom were like family to me, also thought the fund was a very attractive investment. On top of all this, the fund was far from a black box to me. In fact, it was the investment that I understood the best of all things I could possibly invest in. After all, I was a senior trading partner and had a full picture of everything the fund was investing in, and the rationale behind each decision.

So I think it's pretty understandable that I wanted to invest most of my wealth in the fund. But just how much made sense? I realized at the time that I didn't have any organized, logical framework for thinking about this question. I was very quantitatively oriented, what others might call a "numbers-guy," yet here I was, faced with an attractive investment but without a satisfying way to figure out the right amount to invest in it. I wish someone else had written this book—or pointed me to the research on which this book is based—and put it in my hands with an admonition to read it and take it to heart.

In the end, I had to decide on something. I felt that no matter how attractive an investment opportunity might be, I'd want to keep an amount on the side, invested in the safest asset possible, that would support about

40–50 years of what my family was spending at the time. In this way, I felt that no matter what happened with that attractive investment, including a 100% loss, I'd still have enough left to support a comfortable life for me and my family. This amount that I wanted to keep on the side amounted to about 20% of my investable net worth. I considered my liquid savings to exclude my home, which my wife and I owned free and clear, and also my private, illiquid ownership interest in the LTCM management company, which was earning fees from managing the fund. You could say that what I was doing was maximizing my expected wealth, subject to keeping a minimal acceptable amount of wealth for a disaster scenario.[2] There was no comprehensive assessment of risk in this approach; I was almost exclusively focused on return. Stated another way, I was behaving as though I were completely risk-neutral with regard to investing any wealth above the amount I was putting to the side, which upon reflection wasn't true at all.

I guess it's not surprising I approached the problem in this way. Until that time, I was involved in making sizing decisions for attractive investments for Salomon and then for LTCM, and in both cases, the approach we took was to maximize expected profit subject to a number of constraints, such as balance sheet, working capital, trading volume, liquidity, and risk. In practice, risk was rarely the binding constraint. So, I guess it was natural that I was comfortable trying to maximize my expected wealth with the constraint of keeping a safe amount of wealth on the side, rather than maximizing Risk-adjusted Return as the primary objective for my personal investing. On reflection, it's surprising to me that despite having a pretty thorough training in financial theory from my time at the London School of Economics, and all the time I spent with finance practitioners and academics in the workplace, the topic of the theory of gambling and optimal risk-taking never came up. I never heard of the bet-sizing formulas known as the Kelly criterion or the Merton share, even though Bob Merton was my friend and partner at Salomon and LTCM.

Would've, Should've, Could've

No man steps in the same river twice—different river, different man.

—Heraclitus

Of course, if Victor knew that the LTCM fund would suffer such a huge loss in 1998, he'd have chosen to invest none of his family's wealth in the fund. But what we're interested in here is how he *should* have approached the problem, given what he knew in 1997. As usual when dealing with the trade-offs between risk and return, we think he should have found the amount of wealth to invest in LTCM that maximized his personal Expected Utility. Table 8.1 shows the assumptions he might plausibly have made at the time if he were doing an Expected Utility analysis.

We assume Victor would have had a normal level of risk-aversion, similar to what is typical of investors like him that we have surveyed over the past few years. It's completely reasonable that he'd have viewed the fund investment as very attractive, with a Sharpe ratio of 1, about three times more attractive than what would reasonably be expected of the stock market. Critically, he would have included in his wealth his ownership interest in the LTCM management company, which represented about half of his total net worth. This management company asset, like any single stock, would have been a lot riskier than a diversified portfolio of stocks, and it would have had a very high correlation to the performance of the fund.[†]

Table 8.1 Assumptions Needed for Expected Utility Analysis

Assumptions	
Risk-free rate	5%
Expected fund return with no incentive fee	20%
Standard deviation of fund return in normal times	15%
Annual probability of 90% fund loss	0.5%
Management company expected return	15%
Standard deviation of management company in normal times	25%
Loss in value of management company if fund loses 90%	100%
Fraction of total net worth in the management company	50%
Victor's personal degree of CRRA risk-aversion	2

[†]We've left out an accounting of Victor's primary residence, as it represented a lifetime purchase of a place to live and not part of his risk capital.

One key assumption would be the probability of a really large loss in the fund, which would have had the knock-on effect of wiping out the value of the management company. Victor doesn't recall ever thinking specifically about the probability of a 90% loss, but the LTCM partners routinely discussed probabilities of large losses, and there was a unanimous agreement that fund returns exhibited fat tails. In October 1994, the partners wrote a letter to investors that specifically explained that the probability of large losses was much greater than predicted from the normal distribution.[3] We think it's reasonable, although certainly debatable, to imagine the partners agreeing there was a 0.5% per annum probability of a 90% loss. We're confident that if they had been trying to come up with that probability, the one number they would not have settled on was zero. They had been investing through half a dozen profound market crises over the prior two decades, sometimes experiencing very large mark-to-market losses. They were well aware that the US stock market had declined by about 90% once in the past 100 years, from September 3, 1929, to July 8, 1932. While they may not have settled on exactly 0.5%, we think they would have found it plausible that the sort of crisis which would take the fund down 90% could arrive at least *once every two centuries*. This assumption doesn't have much effect at all on the fund's expected return, dropping it by only 0.5%, nor does it change the standard deviation of fund returns substantially either, moving the standard deviation from 15%, ignoring the 90% loss case, to 16.7% taking it into account. So, the fund would still have been a very attractive investment in terms of normal measures, still sporting a Sharpe ratio of 0.9.

As can be seen in Exhibit 8.1, generated with an in-house calculator we've used for our Elm clients, the optimal amount Victor should have wanted to invest in the fund, from an Expected Utility perspective, was a bit more than 50% of his liquid net worth (excluding the value of his ownership of the management company). This is much lower than the 80% that he actually did invest, based on trying to maximize his expected wealth. That he was overinvested in LTCM becomes obvious as soon as we recognize what a large fraction of Victor's total net worth was represented by his ownership in the LTCM Management Company. Accounted for properly, he effectively had 90% of his wealth exposed to LTCM.

Furthermore, as is generally the case with searching for optimal sizing decisions, getting in the general vicinity of the best choice is much more important than getting it precisely right. For example, anywhere within 10% of the optimal fraction of wealth to invest in the fund would

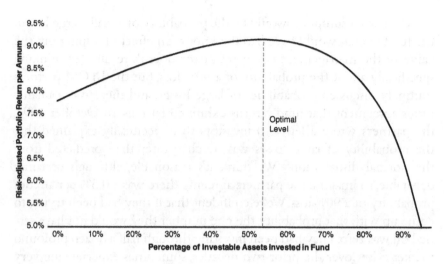

Exhibit 8.1   Risk-adjusted Return as Function of Percentage of Liquid Wealth Invested in Fund

have impacted his Certainty-equivalent Wealth by less than 0.2% per annum.[4] However, being far away, at 80% to 90% invested in the fund, would have caused a really meaningful reduction in his expected—and as it happened, realized—welfare. The result that he should have invested substantially less than 80% of investable assets in the fund is quite robust to a reasonable range of changes to the assumptions, and the recommended allocation would likely have been even lower if modeled more realistically. For example, we could have recognized that Victor's human capital[†] was another large asset that would be highly correlated to a sharp loss at the hedge fund, that there were other assets he could have invested in besides T-bills, that the asymmetric impact of taxes would have hurt the fund's after-tax return versus alternatives, and that he would likely have exhibited higher relative risk-aversion at much reduced levels of wealth.

Of course, this is all a very rough and oversimplified modeling of the situation, but the general result makes intuitive sense once we embrace the Expected Utility maximization paradigm. The small but nonzero probability of a disaster, which would wipe out 90% of his fund investment and 100% of the value of his partnership interest in the management company, is a critical driver of the smaller suggested allocation to

---

[†]The concept of human capital will get a fuller discussion in Chapter 13.

the fund. And taking explicit account of the large fraction of net worth already invested in the risky management company, which was so highly correlated with how the fund performed, beyond doubt also has a significant impact on lowering the desired amount of fund investment.

(Un)common Sense

This may seem like just good old common sense, but common sense doesn't provide us with a specific suggestion. Commenting on LTCM in October 1998, Warren Buffett said, *"But to make money they didn't have and didn't need, they risked what they did have and did need."*[5] Buffett tells us we should never risk everything—and in Victor's personal case he did not—but Buffett doesn't give us a framework for thinking about exactly how much we should put at risk when faced with an attractive opportunity. The Expected Utility framework provides this missing guidance, and while it can only be an approximation, we find its internal consistency much more attractive than the alternative of wetting a finger and holding it up to the wind.

We could make this analysis fuller and more realistic in a number of ways, such as specifying other extreme tail outcomes in addition to the 90% loss case, incorporating other potential investments besides the fund and U.S. Treasuries, examining different time horizons and incorporating the availability of nonrecourse borrowing, which did in fact materialize from UBS in the form of long-dated warrants on the fund in 1997. We could also use this framework to analyze the hotly contested decision the LTCM partners made at the end of 1997 to return capital to third-party investors, which forms the basis of a Harvard Business School case study. Would the Expected Utility of the partners have been higher if they took the alternative course of making the fund very large by raising more third-party capital, with lower expected returns and lower risk, and possibly a different fee structure, or the raising of "contingent capital" that could be drawn in special circumstances? We can't be sure what decisions would have been made and what their outcomes would have been, but we are confident that the Expected Utility framework would have been a useful way to organize the partners' thoughts around these questions.

The questions faced by the LTCM partners are ones that come up in a wide range of situations beyond the world of investment management. Entrepreneurs with most of their wealth tied up in their businesses, investors with concentrated and highly appreciated stockholdings, and managers facing attractive but non-scalable business opportunities are just some examples of cases where Expected Utility can help us reach the best decisions under uncertainty. The following sidebar gives one short case study, in which Victor's son applies some valuable (and expensive) lessons from his father.

In the end, the LTCM experience is a poignant reminder that *getting the sizing of one's investments right can be more critical than identifying investments that will produce good returns.* Most of the trades that LTCM identified and invested in were ultimately profitable. Unfortunately for the LTCM investors and partners, as a result of the fund not getting the "how much" question right, they did not reap the benefits of those profitable investments.

One of Victor's sons recently launched a business and asked for some advice regarding raising equity capital for it. Let's assume that his business has two outcomes: failure or becoming worth a lot, say $50 million. He's trying to decide whether to raise an extra $1 million, which will reduce his ownership stake from 75% to 55%, but will increase the probability of success from 20% to 25%. From an expected value perspective, raising the extra capital is a bad idea, with a negative expected value to him of $625,000. But on an Expected Utility basis, as long as his starting wealth is typical of a 25-year-old founder, including an evaluation of his human capital, he should raise that extra capital because it will increase his Expected Utility. And that's just what he did.

II

Lifetime Spending and Investing

Mr. Darcy soon drew the attention of the room by his fine, tall person, handsome features, noble mien, and the report which was in general circulation within five minutes after his entrance, of his having ten thousand a year.

—Jane Austen, *Pride and Prejudice* (1813)

These days, we tend to assess our net worth by tallying up the market value of our financial assets, but this wasn't always the case. Up until the mid-twentieth century, "wealth" was instead measured primarily in terms of how much you could spend. Perhaps this fixation on lump sum wealth is induced by the media—you won't find Oprah Winfrey on any rich list appraised at $125 million per year, even though that's about what her $2.6 billion of wealth would generate in the form of a lifetime annuity. But if you see your financial assets as a means to the end of future spending and bequests, an annual spending measure seems a more appropriate perspective for assessing your financial well-being. Accordingly, in Section II we focus on the utility of lifetime spending, inclusive of philanthropy and bequests, as the primary lodestar for evaluating core financial decisions.

9

Spending and Investing in Retirement

We steer our financial course through life choosing how much to spend and how to invest what's left, periodically updating our choices as circumstances evolve. The essence of financial planning is deciding, in advance, a desired spending and investment policy conditional on relevant aspects of our life, varying investment opportunities, and our personal preferences. It's a pretty simple problem to put into words, but finding an optimal solution has occupied some very bright minds for the past 60 years, since Harry Markowitz got the ball rolling with his brilliant but highly-stylized one-period, static portfolio selection paradigm.[1] Since then, academic researchers have made tremendous progress in both specifying and solving increasingly realistic and relevant formulations, with the goal of maximizing Expected *Lifetime* Utility at the core of most assaults on the problem. In fact, academic research in this area has been so rich that it's given birth to an entire academic discipline with dedicated university courses and textbooks.[2]

Our focus so far has been on how much risk to take, which we've shown depends on the quality of the investment opportunities available and your personal level of risk-aversion. We have explored the investment decision in the context of a one-period decision, wherein we're trying to maximize the Expected Utility of our wealth at the end of a given time horizon. We hope at this point you are familiar and comfortable with the proposition that maximizing Expected Utility is a good paradigm for making investment sizing decisions across a pretty broad range of real-world situations.

Now it's time to focus on how we should plan to spend our wealth over the course of our lives, on ourselves and as bequests to others. We'll start with a look at spending decisions in a highly simplified world where there are no investment decisions to make, and there's just one risk-free asset to invest in. We will move to a multi-period framework, where our decisions today will incorporate planned decisions for the future— economists call this an *inter-temporal* framework. Once we're comfortable in this highly stripped-down world, we'll introduce an attractive but risky asset into the mix and see how our spending and investing decisions are intimately connected.

The big question we're trying to answer is, *"What is the optimal joint spending and investing rule to follow over the rest of your life?"* You won't be surprised that the solution we will propose involves maximizing Expected Utility. But instead of maximizing the Expected Utility of your wealth at some horizon, here we'll be maximizing the Expected Utility you derive from spending your wealth over your lifetime. To calculate Lifetime Utility, we'll divide your life into units of time, such as years, and then for each year calculate the utility you get from that year's spending. Then we'll add up each year's utility of spending, and that's your Lifetime Utility.† Then it's just a matter of searching over all possible investing and spending rules to find the joint rule that results in your highest Expected Lifetime Utility.

To be clear, we're not suggesting that, without a formal model based on maximizing Expected Utility, you can't make good decisions. Indeed, most successful and financially sophisticated investors and business people—Buffett and Bezos come to mind—have been doing quite nicely, probably without ever explicitly calculating the Expected Utility of different choices they face. However, many people make their decisions either without a framework or based on a framework that often doesn't give reasonable or consistent answers. In fact, some pretty spectacular financial train wrecks could be largely attributed to decision-makers focusing on maximizing wealth rather than the utility we get from spending our wealth.

With the proliferation of defined-contribution savings plans such as 401ks and IRAs over the past 40 years, today more than ever individuals are responsible for creating their own financial security in retirement. Individuals now need to answer questions they mostly didn't need to think about in the days of employer-provided lifetime pensions. Now you have to decide how much to save, how long to work, what to invest in, how much risk to take, how much to annuitize, and how to spend your wealth while you're working and in retirement so you don't go broke before you die. These are complex, interrelated decisions, whose difficulty is compounded by uncertainty and risk in the economy, financial markets, taxation, and in our own personal circumstances. We'll see that the Lifetime Utility paradigm provides an organized framework for thinking about all these questions in a consistent and integrated manner.

It has been widely reported that many families are struggling to save enough in their working years to warrant much attention for how to spend their savings in retirement. We see things differently: getting the most out of one's financial resources in retirement is critical for

---

†We'll also discount each year's utility using your personal rate of preference for enjoying things sooner rather than later (or vice versa). We'll discuss time preference in more detail later in Chapter 12. Whenever we refer to Lifetime Utility, we implicitly mean Discounted Lifetime Utility.

everyone, but especially for families whose retirement savings most need to be used efficiently and intelligently. Also, making better decisions about how to invest and spend should be seen as the low-hanging fruit that everyone should pick and enjoy.

What Do Good Solutions Look Like?

The following are some of the desirable characteristics we should want from any potentially optimal spending and investment policy:

1. Spending more is better than spending less.
2. There are decreasing marginal benefits to spending more.
3. Spending should be as smooth as possible over time.
4. Spending should react to changes in the value and quality of our investments, after tax and inflation-adjusted.
5. Spending and investing should depend on our expected but uncertain personal longevity.

The Merton–Samuelson "Lifetime Consumption and Portfolio Choice" Framework

In 1969, twenty-five-year-old Robert C. Merton and his mentor Paul Samuelson separately published the first solutions to the lifetime spending and investing policy problem that met the five desirable characteristics we just listed. Remarkably, this was the first of Merton's economics papers to be published and also the first in which he used continuous-time calculus to solve a hitherto intractable problem.[3] At the core of Merton and Samuelson's formulation is the assumption of a utility function that maps dollar spending into utility, and the problem they solve is finding the spending and investing rule over the life of the individual that maximizes the lifetime discounted Expected Utility of consumption. This is simply the sum of the utility from each period's spending, all discounted back to the present. From now on we'll refer to this as Expected Lifetime Utility.

The Merton-Samuelson formulation made a number of simplifying assumptions that allowed them to find a simple formula for an individual's optimal spending and investing policy. Their main assumptions were well-behaved asset prices, no taxes, no earned income, constant-relative risk-aversion utility, and lastly that the individual knows the date he'll meet his Maker.[4] Their framework can be implemented numerically with a more realistic set of assumptions, but their solution still provides a wealth of valuable insights. First, it explicitly recognizes the linkage between spending and investment performance by finding that the optimal spending rule must be proportional to portfolio value (though the optimal proportion will change over time). Hence, a 10% increase in portfolio value leads to 10% higher spending. Another intuitive feature is that increases in the expected return on the investment portfolio call for spending less in early years in order for compounding to allow even more spending in later years. Conversely, greater investment risk leads to more front-loading of spending, all else equal.

In addition to capturing a person's risk-aversion, a concave utility function applied to spending also has the attractive feature of encouraging the smooth spreading out of consumption over time.[5] For example, an individual facing two years to spend the rest of their wealth would derive higher total Lifetime Utility by spending half each year rather than spending all of it one year and having none to spend in the other. In fact, the optimal split will tend to be close to 50/50, but not quite, once we take account of the opportunity to earn a return on unspent savings and also the individual's time preference for near-term spending.

To illustrate the mechanics of calculating Expected Lifetime Utility, Table 9.1 explores the case of Sam, a 65-year-old woman, retired with savings of $1,000,000. For now we'll make the simplifying assumptions that Sam has a certain, known lifespan of 20 years and can only invest in a risk-free asset, thereby removing investment risk from the problem. The spending pattern shown in the table is the plan that results in the highest total amount of Expected Lifetime Utility over her remaining 20 years, chosen from among all possible ways she could spend her savings.

Table 9.1 Sam Case Study: 65 Years Old, Retired, $1mm of Savings, 20 Years to Live, Can Only Invest in a Risk-Free Asset Paying 3% After-tax and Above Inflation, Discounts Future Utility of Consumption by 2% per Year, Has CRRA Utility with $\gamma = 2$ Risk-aversion

Age	Wealth ($)	Risk-Free Income ($)	Spending (%)	Spending ($)	Utility of Spending	Discounted Utility of Spending
65	1,000,000					
66	965,547	30,000	6.3%	64,453	0.8448	0.8283
67	929,744	28,966	6.5%	64,769	0.8456	0.8128
68	892,551	27,892	6.8%	65,084	0.8464	0.7975
69	853,925	26,777	7.1%	65,403	0.8471	0.7826
70	813,820	25,618	7.5%	65,723	0.8478	0.7679
71	772,189	24,415	7.9%	66,045	0.8486	0.7535
72	728,986	23,166	8.3%	66,369	0.8493	0.7394
73	684,163	21,870	8.9%	66,693	0.8501	0.7255
74	637,669	20,525	9.5%	67,019	0.8508	0.7119
75	589,453	19,130	10.3%	67,346	0.8515	0.6985
76	539,462	17,684	11.1%	67,675	0.8522	0.6854
77	487,641	16,184	12.2%	68,005	0.8530	0.6725
78	433,932	14,629	13.6%	68,338	0.8537	0.6599
79	378,278	13,018	15.4%	68,672	0.8544	0.6475
80	320,617	11,348	17.7%	69,009	0.8551	0.6353
81	260,888	9,619	21.0%	69,347	0.8558	0.6234
82	199,028	7,827	25.9%	69,687	0.8565	0.6117
83	134,972	5,971	34.2%	70,028	0.8572	0.6002
84	68,652	4,049	50.6%	70,369	0.8579	0.5889
85	0	2,060	100.0%	70,711	0.8586	0.5778

Total Lifetime Spending	$1,350,745	
Sum of Discounted Annual Utility of Spending		13.9207

For those who like to see things expressed mathematically, to generate Table 9.1 we searched for each year's spending c_t as a fraction of wealth W_t which maximizes the sum of each year's discounted utility of spending, assuming wealth grows at risk-adjusted rate r_{ra} and utility is discounted at a personal rate of time preference, r_{tp}.

$$\text{Choose } c_t \text{ for all years that maximizes} \sum_{t=1}^{T} \frac{U\left(c_t W_t\right)}{\left(1+r_{tp}\right)^t}$$

$$\text{where } W_t = W_{t-1}\left(1-c_{t-1}\right)\left(1+r_{ra}\right)$$

Sam's 2% rate of time preference means she gets 2% more utility from spending a given amount now versus a year from now. Notice that optimal spending is rising over time because the Risk-adjusted Return is higher than the rate of time preference, and so it makes sense to forgo some consumption today to invest and spend even more in the future. An obvious alternative to this spending pattern would be to spend the same amount each year, which would result in annual spending of $67,216, on average about $300 less per annum than the optimal spending plan.

A nice feature of this framework is that we can compare how much better the optimal spending pattern is versus an alternative such as the fixed annual spending pattern. Over this horizon and with these assumptions, there's not much difference (less than 1%) in total Lifetime Utility between the two patterns of spending. In fact, the constant annual spending plan is optimal when the investment rate of return and the individual's rate of time preference are equal. As we'll see shortly, these effects are quite small compared to the impact of introducing a more realistic treatment of investment risk and uncertain longevity.

Introducing a risky asset, such as the stock market, into the analysis and then finding the optimal joint spending and investing rules is conceptually easy. If tackled numerically, what we must do is search over all possible combinations of spending and investing rules over all possible movements of the risky asset to find the joint plan that results in the highest Expected Lifetime Utility. Merton and Samuelson short-circuited the brute force numerical calculations, however, using a technique called dynamic programming, to find the optimal solution as a formula. Perhaps the biggest surprise from their solution is that under their simplifying assumptions, the optimal rule for how much to invest in the risky asset is independent of both age and spending. We've already met the formula for the optimal investment rule; it turns out it's just the Merton share:

$$\hat{k} = \frac{\mu}{\gamma\sigma^2}$$

where $\hat{k}$ is the optimal fraction of wealth to invest in the risky asset, μ is the expected excess return of the risky asset, σ is its standard deviation, and γ represents the investor's degree of risk-aversion.

This finding runs counter to the commonly used guideline that investors should reduce their allocation to equities and increase their bond holdings as they age. More complex and realistic models can find decreasing equity holdings with age to be optimal, but it is useful to know that the starting point in the most basic case is that the allocation to risky assets stays constant with age.

The formula for the optimal spending rate to a very long horizon is:[†]

$$\hat{c}_\infty = r_{ra} - \frac{r_{ra} - r_{tp}}{\gamma}$$

where

$\hat{c}_\infty$ is the long (infinite) horizon optimal spending rate,
r_{ra} is the Risk-Adjusted Return of the optimal portfolio,
r_{tp} is the investor's rate of time preference, and
γ is the investor's level of constant relative risk-aversion.

As Risk-adjusted Return rises you can optimally spend more, but an extra 1% higher Risk-adjusted Return doesn't increase your current spending by 1%. This is because your preference for smooth and

---

[†]Technically, this is for an infinitely long time horizon and for $\hat{c}_\infty > 0$, but we'll soon bring this back to more realistic assumptions. Also, we'll see that $\hat{c}_\infty < 0$ gives a sensible result for any finite horizon.

constant spending over time has to be weighed against the prospect of spending more in the future by deferring spending today to invest at the higher rate.

The higher your time preference, the higher your current spending rate, as you want to spend more of your wealth sooner. For circumstances when the Risk-adjusted Return is close to your rate of time preference, the optimal spending rate is simply the Risk-adjusted Return on your portfolio.

Of course, no one has an infinite time horizon. For any finite horizon the optimal spending policy, $\hat{c}_t$, at time t is found by annuitizing your wealth over your remaining horizon, T, using the long-horizon optimal spending rate, $\hat{c}_\infty$, as the annuitization rate, using this formula:[†]

$$\hat{c}_t = \frac{\hat{c}_\infty}{1 - \left(1 + \hat{c}_\infty\right)^{-T}}$$

The optimal spending rule is expressed as a fraction of *current* wealth to spend each year. This is a central feature of this framework, which explicitly recognizes that spending is inexorably tied to investment performance. *If you cannot abide changing your total spending, including gifts, as your wealth changes through time, then it is inconsistent for you to take investment risk in your portfolio.*

Let's put the formula through its paces, assuming $\gamma = 2$, $r_{ra} = 3\%$, and $r_{tp} = 2\%$. This gives us $\hat{c}_\infty = 2.5\%$, which we can plug into the formula for $\hat{c}_t$ to get optimal spending of 6.4% of your current wealth if you have 20 years to live. Notice that this is consistent with the $64,453, which is roughly 6.4% of her starting $1 million of savings, that we found was optimal for Sam to spend in the first year of her spending plan, with 20 years to live, as shown previously in Table 9.1.

Applying the Model to a Real-life Situation

Over the years, economists have extended the Merton-Samuelson model to make it more realistic and flexible. The version of the model we'll use here for our more real-world example incorporates investment risk, longevity uncertainty, taxes, inflation, social security income, and a recognition that legacy bequests can increase the gift-giver's Lifetime Utility.

[†] For $\hat{c}_\infty \neq 0$. For $\hat{c}_\infty = 0$, $\hat{c}_t = \dfrac{1}{T}$.

Using Expected Lifetime Utility to guide family investment and spending decisions in the presence of all these real-world complications involves three main steps:

1. Simulate asset prices, wealth, and spending based on a given investment and spending policy over time.
2. Calculate the Expected Lifetime Utility of the spending that arises from each policy choice, including that from the wealth left over for legacy bequests.
3. Search over many investing and spending rules to find that which gives the best result.

To see what the model needs and what it can tell us, we'll stick with the case of Sam, but we'll increase the realism of her circumstances. She still has $1 million of starting wealth, but she also has just started receiving social security after-tax income of $30,000 per year. We'll assume the absolute minimum she needs to live on, her "subsistence consumption," is also $30,000 per year.

She has two adult children and five grandchildren. She is comforted to know—that is, she derives utility from knowing—that when she dies, her remaining estate will go to her family. We need to calibrate the "utility from bequest" function we'll use to measure the utility she derives from bequeathing wealth. One way to do this is to ask her how much she'd want to leave to her family if she knew for sure that she'd live exactly 20 years, and if her only investment option would generate a real, after-tax rate of return of 0%. For this example, we'll assume in that case she would want to leave one-third of her final wealth to her family.[†] The rest of the information we need to figure out a spending and investment plan for Sam is in Table 9.2.[6]

[†]The bequest function we like to use is the same form as what we use for measuring her

utility from spending on herself, but with an extra parameter $U(Bequest) = \dfrac{b\left(1-\left(\dfrac{w}{b}\right)^{(1-\gamma)}\right)}{\gamma - 1}$.

We solve for b to match her answer in the simplified case. The parameter b can be thought of as the number of years of spending, at the rate of her last year of optimal spending, that she wants to leave to her family under the assumptions of the calibration question. For this specific case, we find $b = 10$. Notice that $\dfrac{b}{(20+b)} = \dfrac{1}{3}$, the fraction of her wealth she would like to bequeath in the calibration question.

Table 9.2 Assumptions Behind Sam's Optimal Investment and Spending Policy

Starting wealth	$1,000,000
Fraction in Roth IRA	40%
Risk-aversion level	2
Rate of time preference	2%
Average tax rate	20%
Safe asset return	4%
Stock market expected return	9%
Stock market risk	20%
Inflation Rate	2%

In the three charts in Exhibit 9.1, we show what we found for Sam's optimal investing and spending rules, and their consequences in terms of her annual spending and end-of-life bequests (all numbers inflation-adjusted to dollars at the start).

The spending rule is expressed as a percentage of Sam's wealth at the start of each year. The optimal spending percentage goes up over time and is high enough that her median wealth is expected to decrease over time. The proportional spending policy has the attractive feature that she can't "run out" of money. The really important thing to understand with this spending plan is that her spending will go up and down as her investment portfolio experiences good or poor performance. If she isn't willing to gradually adjust her discretionary spending above subsistence, then it doesn't make sense for her to take any investment risk.

Under a wide range of individual circumstances, the equity allocation would not remain constant through time, but under the assumptions we've made for Sam, we find that the optimal allocation does remain roughly constant at about 62%. The main reason is that her expected social security income exactly offsets her most basic, subsistence needs.

We can get more understanding of how this all works by exploring how changes in different assumptions alter the recommendations from the model. There are no surprises:

- Higher expected equity returns ⇨ higher desired allocation to equities, higher spending and bequests, and more back-loaded spending
- Higher expected equity riskiness ⇨ lower desired allocation to equities and lower expected spending

- Longer life expectancy ⇨ lower spending each year, lower expected bequests
- A lower subsistence spending requirement ⇨ more risk-taking and higher total expected spending

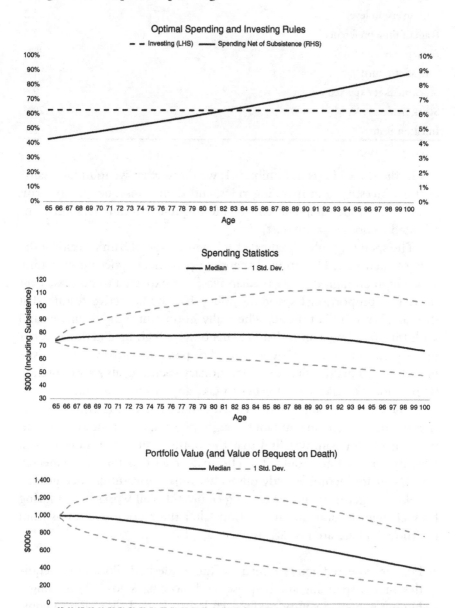

Exhibit 9.1   Spending and Investing Rules and Spending and Portfolio Value Statistics

We can also get a better appreciation of the relative importance of different risks to Sam's lifetime financial situation. All of the following changes would be equivalent to Sam starting off with 10% more wealth:

- 1.5% increase in the risk-free real rate
- 1% increase in the expected return of equities
- decrease in equity risk from 20% to 16% annual standard deviation

A lowering of her tax rate from 20% to 0% would be equivalent to an increase in starting wealth of just 3%, in part because she has a significant amount of wealth in a Roth IRA.

What if Sam didn't want to have as much in the equity market as her preferences suggest she should? As we've discussed earlier, relatively small deviations from optimality tend to have a very small impact on Expected Utility because the curve is quite flat near optimality, more like the top of a hill than a jagged mountain peak. So, if Sam decided to have 5% less in equities than strictly optimal, it would have virtually no effect on her Expected Lifetime Utility. However, if she decided to have no equity allocation at all, she would be significantly worse off. In Sam's case the ability to invest in equities is equivalent in Expected Utility terms to having 25% more initial wealth.

Another issue to think about is that while higher investment returns will naturally lead to higher Expected Lifetime Utility for Sam, the sequence of returns is also important to her outcome. There are lots of ways she could earn a 5% return on her portfolio over 40 years. Earning high returns in early years of retirement, when her wealth is greater, and lower returns in later years would be better for her than the other way around. Unfortunately, there is just no escaping this sequence of returns risk, but the approach we are suggesting recognizes the heightened risk of the early years and takes into account the many possible outcomes, including outcomes with the same average return but experienced in different sequences.

How Does This Compare to Other Popular Rules?

One frequently used method for thinking about spending in retirement is the "4% rule." It's relatively simple: take the value of all of your investments at retirement, calculate 4% of that, and spend that dollar amount every year, adjusted for inflation. . .and hope you don't run out of money before you reach the end of your days. The genesis of this rule was a 1994 article by Bill Bengen, a financial adviser in southern California.[7] The rule was created using historical data on stock and bond returns over the 50-year period from 1926 to 1976. The rule has evolved over time in different directions. Bengen himself, in late 2020, stated that with the benefit of an extra 25 years of data, he now recommends a 5% "SafeMax" initial withdrawal rate.[8]

As we'll shortly see, the major problem with any rule that calls for a constant amount of spending regardless of how wealth evolves over time is that it can lead to an unacceptably high chance of running out of money. The model we are suggesting for Sam based on maximizing her Lifetime Utility calls for reducing spending when her portfolio declines in value and vice versa.[9] Table 9.3 compares how Sam would have fared if she retired at the beginning of 2000 and kept a portfolio of 60% US equities and 40% US T-bills, following a fixed real spending rule of 5% of initial wealth at retirement (Bengen's update to the 4% rule) versus following an optimal spending plan designed to give her the highest Expected Lifetime Utility. We use the spending plan displayed previously in Exhibit 9.1 for this example.[10]

Despite an average annual return on the portfolio of 5.25% per annum, if Sam followed a rule of spending an inflation-adjusted constant amount over time, she'd have run out of money sometime in early 2019! This disappointing situation of earning high average returns on your portfolio, but getting a bad outcome on your strategy, is the same "sequence of returns" problem we discussed earlier.

In contrast, if Sam followed a spending strategy that tracked the value of her portfolio, she'd have wound up with about $900,000 at the end of 2022, which hopefully would be more than enough to sustain her up to the age of 100 and beyond and satisfy her bequest desires as well. She is over 50% better off in purely monetary terms, adding up spending over the 23 years plus her wealth at the end of the period, but in terms of her utility, you could say that she is *infinitely* better off.

This wasn't an especially bad roll of the "equity return" dice either (although pretty bad for the "timing" dice); a Monte Carlo simulation suggests that following a 5% fixed spending rule would result in running out of money about two-thirds of the time over 30 years, even assuming good average investment returns (and over one-third of the time with the 4% fixed spending rule).[11]

Table 9.3   Sam: Fixed Spending vs Utility Optimal Variable Spending (60% in US Stocks, 40% in T-Bills)

	S&P 500 Return	Wealth 5% Spending Rule	Fixed Real Spend per 5% Rule	Wealth Utility Opt Plan	Utility Opt Spend	Utility Opt Spend
1999		$1,000,000		$1,000,000		
2000	-9.7%	$916,247	$50,000	$923,019	4.3%	$42,979
2001	-11.8%	$809,334	$51,693	$826,041	4.4%	$40,618
2002	-21.6%	$662,400	$52,496	$690,400	4.5%	$37,211
2003	28.2%	$713,782	$53,743	$772,316	4.6%	$31,831
2004	10.7%	$707,082	$54,753	$789,537	4.7%	$36,436
2005	4.8%	$679,762	$56,536	$785,175	4.8%	$38,108
2006	15.8%	$692,503	$58,467	$831,956	4.9%	$38,765
2007	5.1%	$660,027	$59,952	$824,263	5.0%	$42,007
2008	-36.8%	$465,904	$62,399	$609,412	5.2%	$42,555
2009	26.4%	$467,423	$62,456	$668,782	5.3%	$32,164
2010	15.1%	$439,705	$64,156	$689,873	5.4%	$36,078
2011	1.9%	$378,901	$65,116	$659,343	5.5%	$38,032
2012	16.0%	$341,855	$67,045	$682,056	5.6%	$37,139
2013	32.3%	$326,729	$68,212	$767,510	5.8%	$39,247
2014	13.5%	$278,446	$69,236	$781,187	5.9%	$45,108
2015	1.2%	$210,632	$69,760	$741,150	6.0%	$46,885
2016	12.0%	$151,759	$70,269	$752,218	6.1%	$45,417
2017	21.7%	$90,889	$71,727	$800,819	6.3%	$47,056
2018	-4.6%	$17,272	$73,239	$733,649	6.4%	$51,131
2019	31.2%	$0	$17,272	$814,514	6.5%	$47,802
2020	18.3%	$0	$0	$844,134	6.6%	$54,149
2021	28.7%	$0	$0	$922,212	6.8%	$57,249
2022	-18.2%	$0	$0	**$884,418**	6.9%	$56,344
Avg Equity Return	7.84%					
Avg T-Bill Return	1.36%					
Avg Inflation	2.51%					
Total Spending			$1,198,528			$984,314
Total Spending + Wealth at End			$1,198,528			$1,868,733

Another bit of conventional advice to retirees is to reduce their exposure to the equity market according to the formula:

$$Allocation \ to \ Equities = 100 - Age \ of \ Investor$$

Recently, with the expectation that people are living longer, some advisers have bumped up the 100 to 110. As we have discussed already, one's allocation to equities should be based primarily on expected excess returns, risk, and on the risk-aversion of the investor. Taking the assumptions we've set up for Sam in Table 9.2, we have found that if she followed the "100 – age" approach to asset allocation, she would need to have starting wealth about \$100,000 (10%) higher in order to generate the same Expected Lifetime Utility she gets from a personally optimized strategy. We can't think of an easier way for a person to increase their effective wealth than by making better joint investment and spending decisions.

We have evaluated other approaches to the investing side of the lifetime spending and portfolio choice problem, such as maximizing wealth subject to a maximum "acceptable" probability of a pre-specified large loss. Another similar approach is sometimes referred to as "goals-based" investing, whereby an investor follows a strategy trying to maximize the probability of reaching a certain amount of wealth, again with a limit on the probability of losing more than a certain amount. As we discussed toward the end of Chapter 6 under the heading "Baby Needs a New Pair of Shoes," these approaches tend to fall far below the approach of expressly trying to maximize Expected Lifetime Utility. We hope the examples in this chapter have helped to illustrate the power and flexibility of this approach.

Updating Your Investment and Spending Plans

While the lifetime spending and investing model can produce an optimal plan, it is important to realize that as circumstances evolve with the passage of time, a new plan should be created to reflect updated conditions. Conditions such as interest rates, expected returns, tax rates, and inflation will generally change over time, calling for a re-run of the model to create a new plan. It's even possible that the individual might want to make changes to longevity assumptions over time, as the aging process can take different trajectories. Ideally the model should build in uncertainty around all these parameters that we know will change over time, but in practice we have found that adding the extra computational complexity of doing so is not worth the further refinement of the optimal plan. Also, see Chapter 18 for a deeper discussion of the impact of modeling parameter uncertainty directly.

To the extent some of the parameters are likely to change in a predictable way, this can be worthwhile to model explicitly. For example, it tends to be the case that when the stock market goes down, its expected excess return goes up. This can have a material impact on the optimal investment and spending plan. As we discussed in Chapter 5, the impact of this effect, known as "hedging demand," is to increase investors' optimal risk levels, which will in turn increase their expected lifetime spending.

Why Don't More Advisors Use This Approach?

Despite more than 50 years of progress in studying the lifetime consumption and portfolio choice problem through a prism of Expected Lifetime Utility of spending, the financial planning and wealth management communities resist putting this framework into practice. While textbooks teaching financial decision-making all start with a discussion of utility theory, financial planners may fear that their clients will be confused by a process grounded in an unfamiliar abstract formalism. It is our belief that these reservations are unjustified, and in any case, there is no escaping the need to take account of an individual's preferences in arriving at a sound lifetime financial plan.

Extensions

In general, the investment and spending problems can't be disentangled, especially for families likely to consume most of their wealth. But under circumstances typically faced by wealthy families—having long horizons and consumption levels relatively low as a fraction of total wealth—the portfolio choice problem can be attacked first, and then used as an input for the lifetime consumption problem. Computational complexity goes up sharply as we account for taxes, uncertain longevity, differential utility arising from personal consumption, philanthropy and inter-generational transfers, and other real-world considerations—but so does the improved welfare offered by doing the analysis versus trying to make these decisions on the back of an envelope.

Free to Choose

How fortunate are we that we can freely invest in risky assets like the stock market? This is not a completely hypothetical question, as pension regulations have sometimes effectively forced retirement savers to only earn the risk-free rate. We can use the framework we've been discussing to answer this question. The answer will be a function of your view of the expected return and expected risk of the best combination of risky assets you could buy, measured relative to the risk-free asset, and it will also depend on your level of risk-aversion, your time preference, and your horizon.

With the assumptions in the following table, we find that your welfare would be roughly 50% higher from having access to risky assets, measured in Certainty-equivalent Wealth. How lucky we are to live in a world in which we are free to invest!

Risk-free rate	2%
Risky asset excess expected return	6%
Risky asset volatility	20%
CRRA risk-aversion	2
Time preference	2%
Horizon (years)	50
Tax rate	0%

The framework can be expanded to incorporate annuities and other asset classes. It's also relatively straightforward to require smooth optimal spending policies, which take account of habit formation, and to add other dynamics, such as inflation, real rate, and expected return variability. For most investors, however, we feel that these extensions are unlikely to produce decisions that differ materially from those suggested by a more basic setup.

Connecting the Dots

Why use crude approximation when you can apply a comprehensive framework that can give you results equivalent to having meaningfully more wealth, without needing to save more or take more risk?

The only cost to this almost-free lunch is the time and mental energy needed to understand, embrace, and use this framework, which has been freely available in the public domain since Merton and Samuelson put it there in 1969.

10

Spending Like You'll Live Forever

A physicist is giving a lecture to a group of university endowment managers, explaining that in 4.5 billion years the sun will exhaust itself of fuel, burn out, and all life as we know it will end. Upset, one of the managers yells out, "Is there anything we can do, professor?" The physicist responds, "Sir, why are you so upset? This won't happen for 4.5 billion years!" "Oh, thank goodness," says the manager. "I thought you said 4.5 million years."

There is much to learn from exploring how endowments and foundations should and actually do determine how to spend their resources over time, and it gives us a setting in which to get more familiar with the concepts introduced in the previous chapter. Families with wealth in excess of what they expect to spend in their lifetimes face similar issues as they may think of that surplus as an endowment to benefit future generations. And for the rest of us, there are valuable lessons to be learned from the question of how you should invest and spend your resources when freed from the complications of taxes and uncertain longevity.

Harvard Professor John Campbell defined an endowment as *"a promise of vigorous immortality."* We think he means an endowment should be able to fulfill its mission indefinitely into the future: spending shouldn't be so profligate that the capital will be exhausted in one generation, nor so miserly that nothing is accomplished and capital accumulation becomes an end in itself. We'll expand on this description of an endowment's mission and explain the important and fascinating result that, under most reasonable sets of assumptions, it is optimal to spend substantially less than the expected real return of the endowment's investment portfolio.

The challenges of choosing the best investment and spending policies are clearly connected. The conventional approach many endowments, especially large ones, have adopted is to invest like the Yale endowment and spend about 4% of the value of the endowment each year. This spending rate is chosen so that there's an arbitrarily low probability of spending falling below a floor usually related to the operating expenses of the university.[1] There are two problems with this orthodoxy, besides the arbitrary nature of the choice of probability of shortfall:

1. The investing and spending choices are not part of a unified framework, even though in reality they are inexorably connected.
2. Neither policy is explicitly responsive to changes in the investing landscape.

It's been more than 20 years since the Yale investment model was introduced in David Swensen's book, *Pioneering Portfolio Management: An Unconventional Approach to Institutional Investment,* which instantly became the de facto endowment operating manual. It was undoubtedly both pioneering and unconventional when Swensen implemented it at Yale in the late 1980s. However, over the past 20 years, there has been a profound decline in interest rates and expected returns on risky assets. From 1999 to late 2022, low-risk real interest rates have plummeted from 4% to levels near 1%. Alternative asset classes can't make up for the decline in the expected returns offered by public markets, as they are no longer the high-return niche they used to be. Unfortunately, there is little in Swensen's book that addresses how an endowment's investing and spending policies should react to such dramatic changes in investment opportunities.

Ironically, nestled right inside the universities with some of the largest endowments, finance professors such as Robert Merton (MIT/Harvard) and John Campbell (Yale/Harvard) have developed valuable insights and tools that explicitly take changing environments and opportunities into account. Sadly, these ideas seem not to have made it into the mainstream of endowment practice.

Three Spending Policy Options

It's helpful to get an appreciation for the problem of choosing an endowment spending policy by taking the investment policy as given. Let's consider three possible annual spending policies, given an investment environment and endowment asset allocation as described in Table 10.1. We'll put to the side for now the role future contributions play on both spending and investment policy, which we'll discuss a little later. As usual, we'll work in inflation-adjusted terms.

The expected real return on the endowment's portfolio, as per Table 10.1, is 5.4% per annum. So let's consider a policy of spending a fixed $5.40 each year (inflation adjusted), assuming a starting portfolio of $100. If the endowment experiences excellent returns, the portfolio will get very big, and the $5.40 of spending will seem too meager. Conversely, if portfolio values decline significantly while spending stays at $5.40, the

Table 10.1 Investment Environment and Policy Assumptions

Long-term risk-free real rate	0%
Expected real return on a well-chosen mix of public and private market risky assets	6%
Risky assets annual variability of returns	18%
Endowment asset allocation	90% in risky assets 10% in risk-free assets
Endowment expected return	5.4%

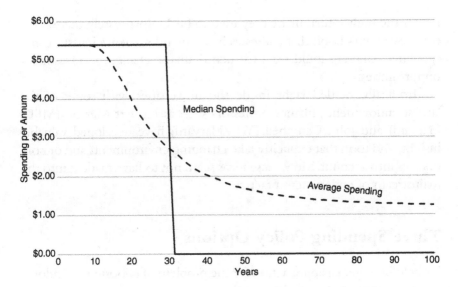

Exhibit 10.1   Policy 1: Spend a Fixed Annual Amount Equal to the Expected
Simple Return of the Portfolio

endowment will run out of money sooner than later. Exhibit 10.1 shows
the median and expected spending over time.

As we discussed earlier in Chapter 3 the median is the outcome that
defines the "middle" of the distribution, and it's often useful to think
about the median separately from the expected, or "average," outcome,
as the median is less influenced by extreme outliers.

In the early years, it's very likely the endowment will have enough
assets to meet the $5.40 spending policy. But in about 35 years, there's
just over a 50% chance that the endowment will have run out of money,
and so median spending drops to zero. The expected spend also drops
over time, although not as dramatically as the median spending amount.

It's unlikely any endowment is intentionally following this kind of
fixed dollar spending policy. However, in personal financial planning,
the most prominent spending rule does take exactly this form. It is the
"4% rule" we just met in Chapter 9, and it advises retirees to calculate
4% of their savings at retirement, and spend that inflation-adjusted dollar
amount every year.[†] We include this as our first rule because it so clearly
illustrates the close connection between spending risk and investment
risk in the long term.

[†]And hope they won't go broke before they die.

The second policy we'll consider is to spend the expected real return of the portfolio each year. From Table 10.2, that means spending 5.4% per year, close to Yale's actual spending target of 5.25% over the past decade.[†]

Exhibit 10.2 shows the median and expected spending over time for this constant percentage spending policy. Under this policy, it may come as an unpleasant surprise that median real spending falls by about 40% over 50 years, and by two-thirds over 100 years. The median endowment value also falls by these amounts, since the spending rule is a fixed percentage of endowment value. We suspect most endowments, or individuals, would find this profile unattractive. The cause of the problem is often referred to as "volatility drag," a phenomenon we met in Chapter 3. It's the effect whereby volatility in returns makes the median return always lower than the expected, or average, return.

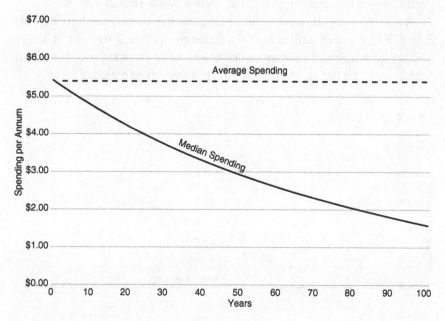

Exhibit 10.2 Policy 2: Spend a Fixed Annual Percentage of the Endowment Value Equal to the Expected Return of the Portfolio

---

[†]Yale's spending policy makes use of smoothing and also collars of 6.5% and 4%, which effectively makes its spending rule something of a hybrid between a percentage rule and fixed dollar rule.

Following a spending policy equal to the expected portfolio return will keep the *average* spending and the *average* portfolio value constant, but this average is heavily influenced by a very small probability of extremely good outcomes. The median outcome will always be lower, and if the average outcome is constant over time, the median will be falling, as we see here.

This brings us to the third spending policy, which is to spend the expected *compound* real return of the portfolio, also known as the geometric average return. With the assumptions from Table 10.1, it is 4.1% per annum.[†]

We can see in Exhibit 10.3 that median spending now stays constant over time, while average spending drifts higher. Early thinking about endowment spending, such as that of Nobel laureate and Yale professor James Tobin, viewed Policy 2—spending the expected return of the portfolio—as the spending rate that endowments should adopt.[2]

More recently, however, the consensus has shifted to viewing this Policy 3 as a better definition of sustainable spending because it keeps median spending and median endowment value constant over time, and medians accord better with what we are likely to experience.[3]

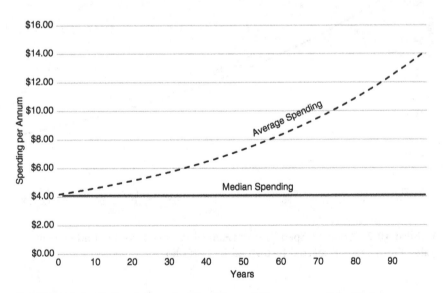

Exhibit 10.3 Policy 3: Spend a Fixed Annual Percentage of the Endowment Value Equal to the Expected Compound Return of the Portfolio

---

[†]We chose the assumptions in Table 10.1 so that Policy 3 would roughly match the 4.2% average spending rate across all US college and university endowments in 2021.

How to Compare Different Spending Policies

For many endowment trustees, they may find the third policy more attractive than the first two, but is it the optimal choice? We can see from the charts that Policy 3 produces the highest total median and average dollar spending over the horizon, because spending less in early years allows more growth to fund higher spending later on, but does that make it the best policy? It would be a pretty tall order to identify the best spending policy just by eyeballing the differences. Focusing on medians rather than averages seems reasonable, but we know we can do much better by using Expected Utility as our summary statistic for comparing spending policies.

In order to use this metric, we need to uncover the endowment's utility function. This is not as difficult an undertaking as it may seem. First, it has been observed that the amount of risk endowments take does not seem to vary much over a wide range of endowment sizes, which suggests constant relative risk-aversion (CRRA) utility might be a reasonable fit. For a particular endowment, its risk-aversion is suggested by the investment policy it has chosen, if we know the estimates of expected return and risk on which it based its portfolio choice.[4] Given the investment environment and chosen portfolio as described in Table 10.1, our model endowment's level of risk-aversion is in line with our Base Case for wealthy, financially sophisticated individuals.

Time Preference: Weighing a Better Present Against a Better Future

With the endowment's utility function and the distribution of portfolio returns in hand, we can calculate the Expected Lifetime Utility of spending for any spending policy. But in order to calculate the discounted Expected Utility, we need to know how the endowment discounts current versus future benefits of spending, or the endowment's time preference. In Chapter 9, we introduced the concept of time preference, "the price of time." Economists and philosophers have long observed the general human preference for good things to happen to us sooner rather than later. But does that apply to an endowment too? James Tobin thought that endowments should have zero time preference, stating:

The trustees of an endowed institution are the guardians of the future against the claims of the present. Their task is to preserve equity among generations. . . . In formal terms, the trustees are supposed to have a zero subjective rate of time preference.

With respect to Professor Tobin's view, we wonder if it is plausible or advisable for any social entity—endowment, foundation, family or individual—to exhibit zero time preference. Is it reasonable that an endowment would put an equal value on the social welfare arising from $1 today as it would on the same amount of welfare generated in 1,000 years? Indeed, there are good reasons why it would be rational for endowments to express some degree of time preference, such as a belief that making the world better today will pay dividends in making the world even better in the future—and acknowledging the truth that, while endowments expect to exist for a very long time, that's not the same as forever.

Another argument against an endowment having zero time preference is to note that in a world in which the only investment available to an endowment was a risk-free asset that paid a 0% real return above inflation, it would be optimal for the endowment to spend *nothing* each year—thereby preserving the real value of the endowment forever. Indeed, one suggestion for helping an endowment to calibrate its time preference is to ask the trustees how much they would spend if their only investment option were a risk-free asset paying a 0% real return each year. Any spending in this case would run down the endowment value, and the choice of the pace would calibrate the endowment's time preference.[5]

The US federal government recommends that cost-benefit analyses of social programs should use a real "social rate of time preference" of 1.7%.[6] Another data point that garnered much attention was the UK's Stern report on the economics of climate change (2006), which more controversially used a rate of time preference of 0.1% for weighing costs and benefits occurring over many years. We will use a rate of time preference of 2%, and CRRA risk-aversion of 2 consistent with risk and return numbers in Table 10.1 for the Base-Case analysis that follows.

Comparing Spending Policies

An endowment should prefer one spending policy over another if it generates higher discounted Expected Lifetime Utility of spending. In

Table 10.2 Comparing Spending Rules: Size of Endowment Needed to Generate Equal Welfare Over 100 Years Under Different Spending Policies

Rule 1: Spend $5.40 per annum	Rule 2: Spend 5.4% per annum	Rule 3: Spend 4.1% per annum
$172	$152	$100

Table 10.2, we compare the three spending rules we've already discussed against each other using this metric, in a 100-year simulation based on the assumptions laid out in Table 10.1. What we show for each rule is how many dollars the endowment would need to start with so that it would generate the same amount of Expected Utility under each spending rule over a 100-year horizon. Notice that the endowment would need considerably more assets to start with under Rules 1 and 2 to generate the same expected welfare as under Rule 3. The endowment's choice of spending policy matters a lot.[†]

The Optimal Spending Policy for the Very Long Term

If we can compare the Expected Utility for different spending policies we propose, it begs the question of what is the optimal spending rule? We already have encountered an optimal spending rule for individuals in Chapter 9 under some pretty stringent assumptions. In case the rule isn't indelibly imprinted in your memory, *yet*, here it is for an infinite horizon:

$$\hat{c}_\infty = r_{ra} - \frac{r_{ra} - r_{tp}}{\gamma}$$

where

$\hat{c}_\infty$ is the long (infinite) horizon optimal spending rate,[‡]
r_{ra} is the Risk-adjusted Return of the portfolio,
r_{tp} is the investor's rate of time preference, and
γ is the investor's level of constant relative risk-aversion.

[†]These results are sensitive to choice of time preference, but robust within a reasonable range of choices.
[‡]For $\hat{c}_\infty > 0$.

The optimal fraction to spend is a function of three inputs:

1. The Risk-adjusted Return, r_{ra}, of the total portfolio when invested at the optimal risk level. Higher r_{ra} allows for higher spending rates, but not on a one-for-one basis for investors who are not infinitely risk-averse.
2. The rate of time preference, r_{tp}. Higher r_{tp} increases the optimal spending rate.
3. The endowment's level of risk-aversion, γ. If the portfolio's expected Risk-adjusted Return is higher than the endowment's time preference (as it is under our Base Case), then higher risk-aversion increases the optimal spending rate.

Putting Theory into Practice

Knowing the optimal rule to follow is great, but does it deliver much real improvement over Rule 3, the "sustainable spending" policy? Staying with the same set of assumptions, Merton's optimal spending policy would be to spend 2.4% of the value of the endowment each year. An endowment following the sustainable spending policy 3 for 100 years, spending 4.1% per year, would need about 15% more in starting assets in order to deliver the same Expected Lifetime Utility as by following the Merton-optimal rule—and the gap widens as we look at longer horizons. The simplicity of the sustainable spending rule is attractive, and it's a better starting point than most other policies, but it does not directly take account of the endowment's risk-aversion or time preference—so, in general, it will lead to suboptimal spending decisions, sometimes significantly so.

Exhibit 10.4 shows the median spending under the two spending policies (sustainable and optimal). While the optimal policy may look better at first glance since it represents 60% more median spending over the whole period, it's difficult to decide which spending policy is truly more attractive without having a comprehensive metric that takes account of the main contours of the endowment's preferences over uncertainty and time.

The Sustainable Spending rule is quite close to Merton's optimal spending rule for some sets of preferences, but it's even further away than the Base Case we examine for others. In our example from Table 10.1, if the endowment exhibited time preference equal to 5.5% per year,

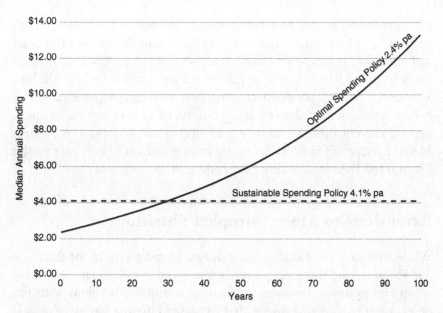

Exhibit 10.4   Median Spending Under Optimal and Sustainable Spending Policies

then Merton's optimal spending policy would be to spend 4.1% per year, the same as the sustainable spending policy. On the other hand, if the endowment had zero time preference, the Merton-optimal spending rate would be much lower, at just 1.4%.

Accounting for Assets and Liabilities Beyond the Endowment's Investment Portfolio

Endowments usually expect to receive further donations over time, and this can be integrated into the model for the optimal investment and spending policy.[†] For example, Yale's endowment has received annual donations of 2% to 2.5% of the value of the endowment over the past decade. Many donors want their contributions to have long-term impact and don't expect them to be used for the annual operating budget. Treating future contributions as an asset and modeling the return, risk,

---

[†] Foundations and wealthy families can usually think about spending policies without these complications as they typically are not the recipients of future contributions by third parties.

and correlation of this significant asset to the rest of the endowment's portfolio can have a big impact on portfolio composition, and the optimal spending policy over time.[†] Endowments often have some relatively fixed long-term liabilities too, which also need to be brought into a fuller analysis of portfolio construction and spending policies. The need to account for the assets and liabilities of a university endowment beyond current financial assets was identified and addressed by Robert Merton (surprise!) in 1991 using the same paradigm of maximizing the Discounted Expected Utility of spending of the university.

Extensions to More Complex Situations

While Merton's 1969 analysis gave us two simple formulas for the optimal spending and investing policy, it was under a stylized and restrictive set of assumptions. However, his formulation of the problem with the objective of maximizing discounted Expected Lifetime Utility of spending is versatile and leads to solutions under a wide array of more realistic assumptions, many of which he provided in subsequent papers.

- The original Merton 1969 formulation was for a two-asset case, but later versions explicitly handle multiple assets. The two-asset case can be used where the risky asset can be considered the optimal portfolio of risky assets. The model handles any choice of risk-free asset, from Treasury bills to inflation-indexed bonds.
- The risk-free rate and expected excess return of the risky asset themselves can be modeled as following independent random walks, but the results remain substantially the same.
- For universities, if the cost of higher education is expected to grow more quickly than indicated by broad inflation measures, the appropriately indexed expected Risk-adjusted Return of the endowment will be commensurately lower, which will result in a lower optimal spending policy.
- Numerical solutions can be found for any concave and smooth utility function.[7]

[†] For example, Middlebury College in Vermont had quite a few generous alumni donors who were senior executives at Lehman Brothers. A more comprehensive analysis that included future contributions as an asset would have suggested that the endowment's portfolio should have small, or even negative, allocations to financial service stocks and other investments highly correlated with the success of Lehman Brothers.

- Spending policies, such as "sustainable spending" or smoothed spending, can be exogenously specified and then an optimal investment policy given that spending policy can be solved for.[8]
- Some investors may have smaller allocations to risky assets than those suggested by their excess return expectations, possibly because of an aversion to leverage. We can still use the Merton spending rule as expressed, using the Risk-adjusted Return on the portfolio that reflects the actual level of risk-taking.

Family Wealth

Taxes on income, capital gains, and inheritance result in significantly lower expected returns for private taxable wealth than those of non-taxable endowments or foundations. As a result, optimal spending policies for pools of private capital will be substantially lower than those of tax-exempt entities. Furthermore, for families who derive utility from supporting the consumption of future generations, the optimal spending rate would be lower still to take account of the expected growth *and uncertainty* in the size of the pool of future beneficiaries. Uncertainty over how many descendants one may have can be particularly impactful. For example, the number of grandchildren plus great-grandchildren that parents with three children can expect is about 13, with a standard deviation of roughly seven.

Other Popular Spending Policies

Probably the first long-term spending policy that occurs to most investors is to spend the interest and dividend income they receive on their portfolio, which they hope will leave the earning power of their portfolio constant over time. While the simplicity of this rule is admirable, it is unlikely to be optimal except by coincidence because it does not explicitly take account of risk-aversion or time preference, and its connection with the expected real return of the portfolio is weak as it ignores inflation and changes in company dividend policy. Of course, a dividend-based rule is not much help for investors who allocate heavily to alternative investments that have arbitrary distribution policies.

A variant of this rule uses some form of earnings yield in place of the dividend yield of equities. The problem with this policy is that earnings yield is an estimate of the expected real return of the equity market, and as we've seen already, spending the expected return of the portfolio is unlikely to be optimal. It's an open question whether earnings yield is a better predictor of the expected arithmetic or geometric return of the equity market, but in either case it's likely to be a suboptimal spending rule.

Many endowments apply a percentage spending rule on a smoothed basis. For example, the Yale endowment states:

> Spending in a given year sums to 80% of the previous year's spending and 20% of the targeted long-term spending rate applied to the market value at the start of the prior year. The spending amount determined by the formula is adjusted for inflation and an allowance for taxes, subject to the constraint that the calculated rate is at least 4.0% and not more than 6.5% of the Endowment's inflation-adjusted market value at the start of the prior year.

Smoothed spending policies share the problem of fixed dollar policies, which can result in the endowment running out of money surprisingly quickly.

Connecting the Dots

The Merton model and its extended family of descendants do not appear to play a central role in shaping the investment and spending policies of major endowments, foundations, or other long-lived pools of capital. For example, in David Swensen's already-mentioned endowment bible, there is no mention of Merton or the cohort of researchers who have extended his work. We found several other influential books on endowment and foundation investing equally silent on Merton's solution to the problem.[9] However, we disagree with the argument that the Expected Utility framework is too abstract to be useful in guiding and linking an endowment's investment and spending policies.

Unlike endowments, individuals are afflicted with tedious burdens like taxes, finite and variable longevity, and an uncertain posterity. These factors make finding optimal rules more complex and change the details in various ways, but the core principles stay the same:

- Risk-aversion and time preference matter.
- Risk-taking should be proportional to excess expected returns and inversely proportional to variance.

- Spending should follow a proportional rule and be linked to Risk-adjusted Return.
- Investment risk and spending risk are inseparable.

Much has changed in the 40 years since Swensen arrived at the Yale endowment and in the half century since Merton's original solution to the endowment investing and spending policy problem. The investment environment can change dramatically over the life of any single individual, let alone in the life of an endowment. For stewards of long-term capital, we think the Expected Lifetime Utility framework and its extensions serve as a valuable navigational lodestar.

11

Spending Like You Won't Live Forever

In this chapter we look at a type of investment which gets a lot less attention than it deserves—the lifetime annuity. In modern times, annuities are typically offered by insurance companies, and they provide the purchaser a fixed monthly payout for as long as he or she lives. It lets individuals or couples virtually eliminate the risk of outliving their savings by allowing them to pool their longevity risk with others.[†]

[†]"Joint and Survivor Annuities" are also available, which pay as long as one spouse of a married couple is alive.

The Annuity Puzzle

The looming savings crisis in the United States is usually attributed to people not saving enough and making poor investment decisions with their savings.[1] As we'll see, we believe additional culprits are the failure of the annuity industry to provide attractive solutions for pooling and reducing longevity risk and a lack of recognition by consumers of the tremendous potential welfare benefits annuities can offer. Franco Modigliani, father of the life cycle hypothesis of saving, labeled this aspect of the savings problem the "annuity puzzle" in his 1985 Nobel prize acceptance speech:

> *It is a well-known fact that annuity contracts. . .are extremely rare. Why this should be so is a subject of considerable current interest and debate.*[2]

Things haven't changed much since then. According to the 2021 *Investment Company Fact Book*, annuities make up a small fraction of the US retirement market, at less than 8% of total private retirement assets of $35 trillion.[†] This isn't entirely attributable to retirees not recognizing the benefits of annuities, as insurance companies make most of their annuity contracts unnecessarily complex, and load them with fees, creating a significant wedge between the value of a "model" annuity and that of the real investment product available in the marketplace. We suspect that if there was broad-based demand from investors, competitive offerings would likely emerge soon enough.

As we saw in the analysis we did for Sam, in Chapter 9, people faced with uncertainty about how long they will live would want to keep some savings in reserve against long life. But if they convert part of their savings into an annuity with reasonable terms, they should be able to reserve less and spend substantially more, as their longevity risk can be pooled with other people. The mystery is why, given these potential benefits, isn't the annuity market much larger?

[†] The fraction of retirement assets in private annuities is substantially higher in some countries, but overall the annuity puzzle holds across most developed economies.

How Big a Free Lunch Is Being Left on the Table?

Our objective here is not to solve the annuity puzzle—much has been written already that does a good job of that—but rather to show, using Lifetime Expected Utility, just how valuable it can be to shed longevity risk through an annuity.

We'll continue to base our analysis on Sam, our 65-year-old single woman in good health who has $1 million of savings and receives social security income, which takes care of her "subsistence" needs. Sam has risk-aversion of 2, and for simplicity let's say she has zero time preference, and she has no interest in future charitable or family bequests. This is to say that her wealth has no utility to her unless she consumes it in her lifetime. We'll also assume the only available investment is an inflation-indexed bond that pays a 0% real rate of interest after tax. We recognize this is a highly stylized scenario, but it's a good starting point to build on, and we can increase realism later.

Exhibit 11.1 shows her life expectancy, which indicates she expects to live 20 years, with quite a bit of uncertainty around that.[3]

In Exhibit 11.2, we show her optimal planned spending if she manages her savings and life-expectancy risk herself. Next to it we show her consumption if she purchased a fairly-priced annuity, that is, an annuity offered with no profit for the insurance company.

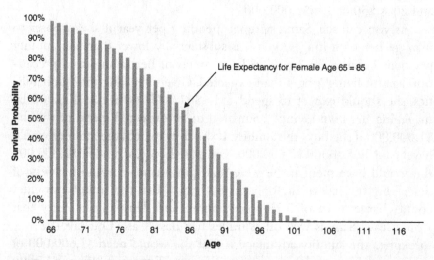

Exhibit 11.1 Longevity Probabilities for 65-year-old Female From US Social Security Mortality Tables (2015)

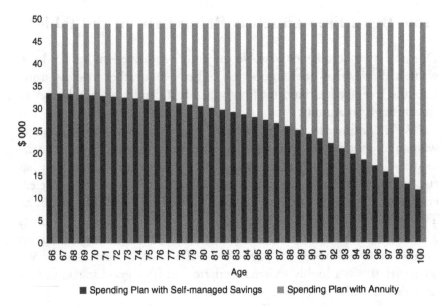

Exhibit 11.2   Comparing Self-Managed Versus Annuity Annual Expenditure for Sam Age 65

The annuity would give her just shy of $50,000 per year of spending. This amount is calculated so that the expected payout to her—given her probability of dying each year—equals $1,000,000. You can see this is roughly the right number, since she is expected to live 20 more years and 20 × $50,000 = $1,000,000.

As you can see, Sam's optimal spending per year if she chooses to manage her own longevity risk is substantially lower than the annuity payment because she needs to keep much of her savings as a precaution against living longer than expected. Given her longevity probabilities, she should expect to spend only $677,000 of her $1,000,000 by managing her own savings, compared to an expected spend of the full $1,000,000 if she buys the annuity. If she lives to 105, the annuity would have paid her about $2,000,000, compared to just under $1,000,000 she would have spent if she were managing it herself. Another way of describing the size of the opportunity gap is that the annuity provider could charge a fee of 3.25% per annum and deliver an annuity that would leave Sam as well off as under her Base Case. Our favorite way to express the annuity advantage is that she would need $1,600,000 of starting wealth in order to generate the same Expected Lifetime Utility she gets from annuitizing.

This analysis may underestimate the benefit of an annuity since many people would find the prospect of spending less and less with each passing year, as called for by the "optimal" spending policy, downright depressing. In the self-managed case, if they opted to spend a lower but constant amount each year, perhaps equal to the income generated by their portfolio, the annuity would be superior by an even larger margin.

Annuities and End-of-Life Bequests

Of course, many people are not like the highly-stylized 65-year-old we've described. For example, if a person highly values making end-of-life bequests that are large relative to lifetime consumption, then the benefit of purchasing an annuity will be lower, and possibly insignificant.[†]

As we assumed in Chapter 9, let's say that if Sam knew for sure she'd live exactly 20 more years, she'd want to spend two-thirds of her wealth on herself, and leave one-third as a gift to her family. Also as discussed in Chapter 9, from this we can infer Sam's preferences for spending versus bequeathing. When we reintroduce longevity risk, we find that she would need $1,150,000 of starting wealth in order to generate, without annuitizing, the same Expected Lifetime Utility as from buying an annuity with two-thirds of her wealth and leaving the other one-third to her family.

If she chose not to buy the annuity and manage things for herself, the expected size of her bequest would be $440,000, much larger than the gift of $333,333 she'd ideally like to make. But in the self-managed case, she can't shoot for a lower expected bequest without taking serious spending risk in her later years. The bequest would be extremely variable too, ranging from almost $1,000,000 if she dies in one year, to almost 0 if she lives to 105.

The gap of $150,000 between managing longevity risk herself versus buying an annuity and gifting the rest is in this case still significant, although much smaller than the $600,000 gap in the Base Case we analyzed with Sam having no desire for a bequest. Increasing the realism of the assessment by accounting for the fees charged by the insurance

---

[†] It has also been argued that full annuitization of wealth can lead to children paying less attention to their parents than otherwise, although at least in fiction, the attention of a child in a hurry to receive an inheritance may be worse than being ignored!

company selling the annuity, the tax treatment of the annuity and the benefit from owning equities directly outside of the annuity can easily result in the conclusion that buying the annuity does not make sense for Sam, given her strong desire to leave capital to her family.

Annuities and Equities

In our starting point analysis, we assumed that if Sam didn't buy an annuity, the only investment she could make was in an inflation-protected bond offering a 0% real rate of return. What if we relax this assumption and recognize that Sam can also invest in the equity market? In this case, we'll find that higher expected equity returns would cause Sam to optimally invest more in equities and annuitize less.

Insurance companies do offer equity-linked annuities, known as variable annuities, but they tend to be complex, with convoluted embedded options and generally higher costs than plain vanilla fixed payment structures. A simple, cost-efficient equity-linked annuity might be a valuable addition to the annuity product menu for many investors. We hope that financial innovation, together with the necessary evolution of insurance regulation, will lead to high quality equity-linked annuities delivered through mutualized structures.

Mutualized annuity pools could be run very cost-efficiently, with a Vanguard-like administrator competently managing the investment, payouts, and pool membership for a low fee. Annuitants subscribing to a mutualized pool would be able to mitigate their longevity uncertainty, while sharing equity returns in a simple formulaic manner. The mutualized structure is a key feature of the solution because it allows investors to trust they are getting the longevity risk sharing and equity exposure they want, without worrying about the frictions and credit risk involved in being on the other side of a transaction with a profit-seeking insurance company.

Annuities Versus Bonds

Some annuity experts make the argument that investors should always prefer a fixed annuity over buying fixed rate bonds in their retirement accounts. This argument has merit. However, it ignores the fact that bonds are liquid and can be easily reallocated into other investments, while annuities by design need to be illiquid—otherwise every annuity holder would seek to redeem or sell when death becomes imminent.

Some of the shortcomings of standard annuities are addressed by deferred income annuities, which involve a smaller upfront payment because they provide income starting at a future date. Sadly, as of the writing of this book, inflation-protected annuities are not currently available in the United States, so if you want inflation protection, you'll need to buy inflation-protected bonds in the form of TIPS or Series I Savings bonds.[†]

We haven't examined the tax treatment of annuities versus other investments, which historically has been a relative negative for annuities. However, recent tax law changes allowing investors to place annuities in their tax advantaged retirement accounts has made annuities relatively more attractive after tax. Expected utility is up to the task of figuring out whether these multiple inter-related practical considerations render the purchase of an annuity worthwhile in each individual's particular circumstances.

Connecting the Dots

The annuity puzzle has received much attention over the years. Despite understanding the reasons why annuities still represent such a small fraction of retirement assets, little progress has been made in unlocking their potential to improve individual welfare. What makes this lack of progress even more vexing is that, unlike taking typical market risks, bearing one's own longevity risk does not offer compensation in the form of a risk premium. For many people, longevity risk can be more consequential than the risk they bear in their investment portfolio. We hope that investors will use the metric of Expected Lifetime Utility to decide whether buying an annuity with some or all of their savings is right for them.

So why might annuities have such a low take-up given the significant risk and dollars-and-cents benefits for a large class of investors? Some possible explanations include existing products that are complex and opaque, high visible and hidden fees, investor aversion to giving up control of their savings, investors worrying about the credit risk of the provider, or underwriters being too conservative in pricing longevity risk.[4] Some wealthier investors may feel they don't need an annuity as long as they can get by on the income from their investment portfolio without eating into capital—a posture that generally results in lower

---

[†]Buying Series I savings bonds is not easy and is limited to $15,000 per purchaser per annum.

consumption than that suggested by maximizing Lifetime Expected Utility. Or if some investors just haven't given enough thought to the reserve they should be holding against their own longevity risk, there could be a benefit from more financial education. An annuity offering with greater transparency, simplicity, efficiency, and security would very likely help. Indeed, in the early 1700s, the British government funded itself through the sale of lifetime annuities, and various mutualized schemes and instruments have seen success in the past. It may be just this kind of bold creative solution that is needed to capture the potential gain from bridging the present disconnect between financial theory and practice.

III

Where the Rubber Meets the Road

12

Measuring the Fabric of Felicity

". . .for there is nothing either good or bad, but thinking makes it so."
—William Shakespeare, *Hamlet,* Act 2, Scene 2

Utility is a measure of the welfare or felicity[†] we derive from using our wealth. Researchers generally presume that an investor knows their own "utility function," which is to say the relationship between their spending

---

[†] Felicity: the quality or state of being happy.

and utility.[†] However, surprisingly little has been written about how an individual can calibrate their personal utility function. And though the study of the lifetime consumption and portfolio choice problem has delivered novel and valuable insights, we haven't seen meaningful adoption by the financial planning or wealth management industries. Financial planners may worry that these relatively stylized academic models of utility don't adequately represent investor preferences in the real world, and fear their clients will be confused by an unfamiliar conceptual framework.

Are these reservations justified? In 2018, we created a short survey to test whether a group of financially sophisticated investors could comfortably communicate their preferences in a way that we could then translate into utility terms and whether these preferences were reasonably consistent with core utility concepts. If so, then we'd have reason to believe that putting the academic research findings into practice could have a big payoff. So, over the course of six weeks, we gave the survey to a group of 31 financially sophisticated friends, clients, and former colleagues from the finance industry. All were reasonably affluent, stating that their current wealth was significantly in excess of what would be needed to support their basic consumption needs. We make no claims that results from this selective sample are directly applicable to broader groups, but we thought it would be a good starting point to see if there's at least a kernel of people who would be comfortable thinking within this framework.

Here is the survey.[1] As we've done before in our research, we framed the survey questions using coin-flipping thought experiments. A utility-based framework is built into the structure of the questions, but you'll see we don't actually use the word "utility" anywhere in the questions, as we hoped to bring as few preconceptions into the survey as possible.[‡]

[†]The expression "fabric of felicity" is attributed to utilitarian Jeremy Bentham: "Nature has placed mankind under the governance of two sovereign masters, pain and pleasure. . . .The principle of Utility recognizes this subjection, and assumes it for the foundation of that system, the object of which is to rear the *fabric of felicity* by the hands of reason and of law." *Introduction to the Principles of Morals and Legislation* (1789).

[‡]Harvard Professor John Campbell introduces his students to CRRA risk-aversion with a simple, memorable thought experiment. Imagine a demon enters your life and insists you gamble 20% of your wealth on the flip of a fair coin. If it lands on heads your wealth increases by 20% and if it lands on tails your wealth is reduced by 20%. What is the *largest* percentage of your wealth you would be willing to pay the demon to make him go away and not make you take that gamble? Your level of CRRA risk-aversion (γ) is roughly equal to that percentage divided by 2. So, if you would pay 4% of your wealth to avoid the gamble, you have CRRA risk-aversion of 2.

game, and the lower risk-aversion of some individuals can have positive side effects—"externalities" in economic-speak—on other members of society through their more aggressive risk-taking in developing new technologies.

It is also believed that dispersion in individual risk-aversion can lead to greater market instability. When the prices of risky assets go down, the most risk-tolerant investors see their wealth decline more sharply than for everyone else. As a result, the wealth-weighted average risk-aversion of the market increases, just when more risk-capital may be needed to stabilize the market.

How Wealth Delivers Utility

One of the benefits of using a utility-centric framework is that it provides some structure for thinking about the big-picture questions of how to use one's wealth, which are often difficult to tackle otherwise. Many people we've talked with haven't thought through these important questions in a serious way—not because they wouldn't like to, but because it's difficult to know how to get started. It's challenging to think clearly about wealth and spending in the absence of knowing how your investments will perform, how much they will be taxed, and when you will die.

Most uses of wealth can be assigned to the following categories:

- Personal Consumption
  - Subsistence
  - Discretionary
- Lifetime Gifts
  - Intergenerational
  - Philanthropic
- Legacy (After-Death) Bequests
  - Intergenerational
  - Philanthropic
- Taxes

Thinking clearly about the change in utility you will derive from spending on these categories is critical to your lifetime financial decision-making. An individual or couple who put low value on unspent wealth at death should be attracted to annuitization, early gifting, and higher levels of personal consumption. Others feel they'll get significant utility from their legacy bequests and may be relying on the current regime not to tax unrealized capital gains or to continue a certain level of estate exclusion. The Expected Utility framework can model a broad range of preferences, and risks, regarding the utility derived from each type of spending and can summarize the attractiveness of different courses of action accordingly.

Intergenerational Bequests

I want to give my children "just enough so they would feel that they could do anything, but not so much that they would feel like doing nothing."
—Warren Buffett

For many people, helping their children and other family members can be a source of personal utility. It's often the case that parents think of such gifts as a residual that's left over after they have lived their lives and consumed whatever amount of their own wealth seemed appropriate. But this is not equivalent to saying that a person gets no utility from leaving a bequest to future generations. Thinking about balancing spending money on one's personal consumption versus funding the future consumption of other family members is time well-spent in making the best decisions under the multiple uncertainties we face. The optimal investment policy can be thought of as a weighted-average blend of risk-taking that is appropriate for the parents and that which would make sense for the children and beyond.

Taxation of gifts, in the United States in particular, is another important consideration that lends itself to Expected Utility analysis. In general, it is more tax-efficient to give gifts to future generations sooner rather than later, but multiple risks also come with accelerated gift giving. We touch on these trade-offs in Chapter 17 in our exploration of how taxes can affect our decisions.

Philanthropy

Thinking about the utility we get from spending our wealth on philanthropic projects is somewhat more challenging than when thinking only about ourselves and our family. We face all the same issues involved in thinking about intergenerational giving, such as the benefit of giving early, in terms of both helping to improve the welfare of our fellow man as soon as possible and tax-efficiency, versus the risk of having given away too much. However, beyond those questions are others that are even more confounding. If we decide to make our gift as early as possible and use a family charitable foundation to hold some of the gift to be donated over time, how should the foundation manage the capital in its care? Should it try to estimate the utility functions of the future recipients of those funds? Should that include contingent recipients who would only benefit from those resources if they grew larger? Or should the foundation simply follow guidelines established by the donor? And when giving resources to projects presently, how should individuals think about the risk inherent in how those charitable projects perform in improving the welfare of those they are trying to help? Should an assessment of the risk of the charitable projects themselves come into play? When Cornelius Vanderbilt made his million dollar gift to found Vanderbilt University, would he have gotten more Expected Utility if he thought it was likely to turn into such a successful investment?

This topic warrants much greater examination than we are giving it here, although it's likely that some of the big questions involved will not have a single answer that satisfies all readers. In practice, we favor a simple approach that treats giving during one's life as part of normal discretionary consumption, and treats family foundations as separate pools of capital to be managed independently.

Subsistence Spending and Wealth

Most people feel that reducing spending below some level they think of as their basic needs is different from cutting back on higher levels of spending that seem more discretionary. The basic needs level of spending is often referred to as "subsistence" spending. One way to include this in one's utility function is to "split" it into two segments: above the subsistence level with your usual risk-aversion and below subsistence where there's a significantly higher level of risk-aversion. In Exhibit 12.2, we show what such a kinked utility function would look like.

Accounting for subsistence with such a kinked utility curve will result in typical investors exhibiting more relative risk-aversion as their wealth decreases, thus reducing the likelihood of spending falling below the subsistence level. Accordingly, investment policies that could lead to outcomes in the subsistence range will be penalized much more heavily than those that don't. For investments that have virtually no possibility of

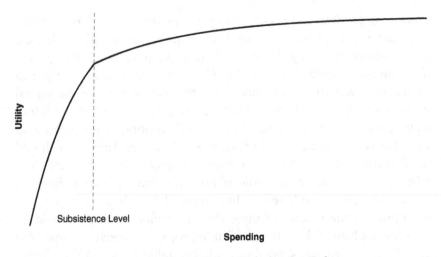

Exhibit 12.2   Utility Curve With Higher Risk-aversion Below
Subsistence Level

causing wealth to fall below the subsistence level, the individual's optimal sizing decisions will be unaffected by the kink.

A common technique in academia is to use a standard utility function, but to "shift" it so that spending the subsistence amount or below is infinitely bad, as spending going to zero would normally be. This generally leads to somewhat smaller optimal sizing than the "kink" method and also tends to be easier to analyze mathematically, hence the popularity. However, because in practice it's typically very difficult or impossible to absolutely guarantee that spending won't fall below any given level, this technique tends to be problematic when applied to real-world scenarios.

The Misguided Strategy Behind Black Monday

On October 19, 1987, the US stock market fell by 22%, the largest one day percentage drop in history. The US government's official investigation of the event, known as the Brady Commission Report, concluded that "Portfolio Insurance" was the proximate cause of the stock market decline. The Portfolio Insurance the Commission had in mind was a dynamic asset allocation strategy called Constant Proportion Portfolio Insurance (CPPI), promoted by investment management firm LOR, founded in 1981 by two prominent finance academics with a quant in between: Leland, O'Brien, and Rubinstein.

The strategy was pretty simple, despite being a closely guarded trade secret at the time. The investor would choose a fraction of his initial investment, say 40%, that he wanted to be invested effectively risk-free, the "insured amount," with the remainder of the investment, referred to as the "cushion," to be allocated to the stock market with a chosen, constant amount of leverage, say three-times. So at the start of a program with those two parameters, an investment with LOR of $100 would have $40 in safe assets and $180 in stocks, since $180 = 3(100 − 40). As the stock market goes up and down, LOR would manage the portfolio to maintain an investment in equities equal to three times the current value of the cushion. If stocks went up by 1% one day at the start of the program when the cushion was $60, then LOR would need to buy another $3.60 of equities (3 × 180 × 1% − 180 × 1% = $3.60). Of course, this works in the other direction too, requiring LOR to sell $3.60 of equities when the equity market goes down by 1%.

Well, it's easy to see how this need to sell equities when the market goes down could, if market liquidity were not adequate, result in a downward spiraling, self-reinforcing feedback loop. That's exactly what the Brady Commission concluded, estimating that Portfolio Insurance programs managed primarily by LOR had to sell $10 billion to $15 billion of equities as the market declined on Black Monday, which probably had the same price impact of someone needing to sell 20 times that amount in today's larger markets.

The LOR strategy was clearly problematic ex post, but why do we say it was "misguided"? The answer comes from thinking about the utility function that investors would need for the product to make sense.[3] The best fit would be a CRRA utility function that starts at the desired risk-free insured amount, much as we described as the second way of treating subsistence wealth. For wealth in excess of the insured amount, the investor would exhibit a very low degree of risk-aversion and, hence, would want to have a highly leveraged exposure to equities with the cushion. This strikes us as a very odd, though not impossible, set of preferences, going from completely risk-averse for wealth below a certain level, to exceptionally risk-tolerant with regard to wealth above it. With hindsight, it's likely that investors bought into the dynamic Portfolio Insurance programs not because it expressed their fundamental utility preferences, but rather in the hope that they'd capture more than 100% of the upside of equities, with solid protection on the downside. The experience of Black Monday was one of the periodic reminders the markets give us to stay clear of promises of financial alchemy.

For individuals whose spending is far above their subsistence spending level, it is not easy to imagine what their preferences will be if they see their wealth decline by say 90%. Will they become much more risk-averse after suffering such a loss or even infinitely risk-averse? Recognizing that this may not be representative of most individuals, your authors both suffered dramatic reductions in our wealth, which before it happened, we'd have thought would bring us close to our personal subsistence levels. When we got there, we both became more risk-averse, but neither of us became dramatically more risk-averse. It may be that we were relatively young when we had this experience, and felt that our human capital (more on that in Chapter 13) was still quite significant, and so our loss of financial wealth wasn't as dramatic. But in any case, it is a firsthand experience, and we've also witnessed a few friends and colleagues who exhibited similar behavior.

Plumbing the Depths of Despair

The CRRA utility function in its pure form has a feature that we often see fit to modify when using it in numerical simulations: as wealth or spending go to zero, utility goes to negative infinity. This can be difficult to handle computationally and also isn't totally realistic. In practice there's no difference between losing 99.9% and 99.99% of your wealth, but pure CRRA utility will suggest you're dramatically worse off. When making standard calculations, such as using the Merton share, this unrealistic characteristic is tolerable, and changing it wouldn't materially affect the results. But it can become an issue when making Lifetime Expected Utility calculations over very long time horizons and with highly volatile assets. So what we tend to do is impose a limitation on the rate of utility decline as wealth approaches zero. This doesn't have much impact at all on normal cases we look at, but it helps in simulations and also moves them in the direction of slightly higher realism.

Imposing this kind of floor also squares with the reality that we're always living in the presence of very low probability events that would have catastrophic consequences, yet these possible outcomes don't swamp our normal decision-making. Fully examining this idea and all its ramifications could easily fill another book.

Risk-Seeking at Low Wealth: Friedman-Savage Utility

One twist on the general shape of utility curves was proposed in a 1948 article by the influential Chicago economists Milton Friedman and Jimmie Savage.[4] They suggested that the shape of a utility curve should not only explain the risk-aversion of middle and high-income individuals, which has been our focus so far, but that it should also be consistent with the propensity of lower wealth individuals to buy both insurance and lottery tickets. Exhibit 12.3 illustrates such a utility curve, which includes a convex, risk-seeking segment in between the more typical segments of risk-aversion resulting from the marginally decreasing utility of wealth. Being "risk-seeking" in this sense doesn't just mean having a high risk tolerance, but instead the much more extreme position of being *willing to pay* to take a risk with no expected gain.

We include this brief mention of Friedman-Savage utility more to provide an understanding of the utility-related arguments and history you may come across, and not because we think it should be used in financial decision-making. In this book we use utility primarily as a

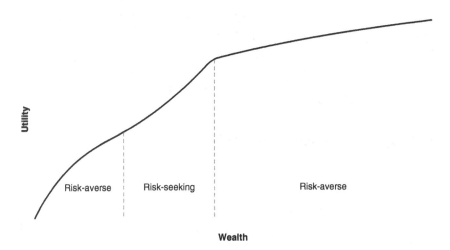

Exhibit 12.3   Friedman-Savage Utility Curve Incorporating Intermediate Range of Risk-seeking

tool for helping to make good decisions, not just as a description of the various, possibly inconsistent decisions we make when left to our own devices. Truly risk-seeking individuals would be expected to lose most of their wealth in short order, paying for the "pleasure" of taking negative edge gambles. Common sense is all that's needed to conclude this can't be consistent with what most people would think of as "good" decision-making.

Predictable Changes in Preferences: Habit Formation

The assumption that the utility enjoyed in each period is independent of that enjoyed at other times can be relaxed, taking account of habit formation with regard to prospective, predictable changes in preferences. This is perhaps the most significant departure from the original Merton assumptions, and much research has been devoted to this topic in the 1980s and 1990s.[5] Most people would agree that spending a given sum of money feels a lot better—i.e., generates more utility—when it's an increase rather than a decrease relative to real spending in previous years. There are a number of ways of modeling this standard-of-living effect, the simplest of which is to require spending in a given year to be partially based on past years' spending levels. In general, recognizing this aspect of individual preferences will make the individual take less investment risk and experience less variability in spending over time.

Utility from Wealth, in and of Itself

We suspect that, in most cases, individuals who claim that the utility they get from their wealth is separate and distinct from what they will spend it on may not have devoted enough time thinking about the uses to which they will put their wealth. In the same vein, we are skeptical of the "score-keeping" story we've heard from a few high-net-worth individuals, wherein they claim to view most of their wealth as "play money." While it's true that wealth is tied to status, wealthy families who do not spend, gift, or donate their wealth can hardly claim to be maximizing their status. In any case, the utility maximization construct can handle most of these alternative objective functions based on wealth as a number rather than what wealth can be used for.

A conventional Expected Utility model would not assign utility to the investment activity itself, only to the returns that flow from it. However, adjustments can be made for individuals who derive utility directly from the investing process or from control positions in investments.[†] Social-impact investing can also be incorporated into the model, for those who effectively mix philanthropic activity and investing decisions.

Time Preference

The general human inclination for enjoyment in the present rather than in the future has long been observed and assumed by economists and philosophers, resulting in an extensive literature in economics, philosophy, and psychology on time preference. In "Personal Identity" (1971), British philosopher Derek Parfit makes the case for positive time preference:

> We care less about our further future. . .because we know that less of what we are now—less, say, of our present hopes or plans, loves or ideas—will survive into the further future. . .[if] what matters holds to a lesser degree, it cannot be irrational to care less.

However, the Harvard psychologist Daniel Gilbert puts forward the case for negative time preference by citing experiments that find people like to defer pleasurable experiences so that they get the double benefit of enjoying the anticipation and then enjoying the experience itself. Another finding that suggests negative time preference is that individuals often state that they would prefer to see their earnings rise year to year rather than to earn the same or an even higher aggregate amount in a steady or declining stream. With positive real interest rates, the steady or declining earnings stream can be turned into a larger rising earnings stream by saving and investing some of the early payments. Various

---

[†]The Bloomberg commentator Matt Levine mused about the utility function of John Paulson, the hedge fund manager who made billions betting against subprime mortgages in the 2008 financial crisis: *I don't know. It seems like if he (Paulson) had quit in 2010, not only would he have had more free time over the last decade, but he'd also be richer. But once you have $9 billion, presumably you are optimizing for something other than increasing, or even maintaining, wealth. For myself, I would be optimizing for leisure and consumption, but that is (part of) why I am not a billionaire hedge fund manager. Presumably reputation, wanting one last big score, etc., were important factors for Paulson during the bad years, and spending a few billion dollars on losing bets was acceptable. Plus he clearly enjoyed getting the fees.*

justifications are put forward for this behavior, such as it helps the individual control spending or the person expects he can get a better-paying subsequent job if his current job finishes at a higher pay level.

Research by behavioral economists, including some experiments involving colonoscopies, has found that individuals have a tendency to rate an experience with a heavy weight on the final moments of it. This desire for a so-called "happy ending" pushes in the opposite direction of the tendency for individuals to be impatient.

Just as we see images that are far from us in less detail, so too do we imagine the future in less detail when it's remote. This is why we habitually agree to do unpleasant things that are far in the future that we wouldn't agree to do tomorrow. This mental perspective can result in what is known as hyperbolic time preference. Surveys of generally young and not very wealthy individuals have found a preference for $19 today versus $20 tomorrow (a 14,000,000,000% annualized rate of time preference!), and at the same time a strong preference for twenty dollars 365 days from today versus nineteen dollars 364 days forward.

Of course, it doesn't take a logician to see that a very profitable business can be built to take advantage of these preferences, borrowing from people in the future and lending to the same people when the future arrives. While hyperbolic discounting is a very interesting and real phenomenon (for very small amounts of money), we think it is not representative of the time preferences of high-net-worth, financially sophisticated individuals and families.

All these different behavioral phenomena make it difficult to pinpoint an individual's personal level of time preference, which we've already touched on in our discussion in the previous chapter on endowment spending. Further thickening the plot is the relationship between average time preference of all individuals in aggregate and the level of interest rates in the economy. Most macroeconomic models hold that the average time preference impacts, but does not by itself determine, the level of interest rates, and so we cannot look to real interest rates for a precise estimate of average or typical time preference for individuals. We have more to say on this topic in Chapter 20.

We believe that affluent individuals and families will tend to settle on rates of time preference in the range of 0% to 4%. The good news is that time preference in this range of values has virtually no impact on optimal investment policy and a relatively small impact on optimal spending policies over 10–20 year horizons, though it does have a material impact over substantially longer time frames, as we discussed in Chapter 10.

Connecting the Dots

The Expected Utility framework won't tell you how to balance personal consumption, intergenerational giving, and philanthropy because your relative preferences are an *input* into the framework. What it will do is provide a good rule for how to spend and invest in light of these preferences and all the different sources of complexity and uncertainty we throw into the mix—taxes, inflation, volatile asset returns, uncertain longevity, uncertain family dynamics, to name some of the most prominent ones. The framework can also help quantify the rational implications of our preferences, which can then feed back into the preferences themselves.

One way to calibrate the preferences we need as inputs, which can be a very useful and illuminating exercise in and of itself, is to think about how you'd spend and invest if you find yourself in a world with no uncertainty at all. Imagine that investment returns, labor income, longevity, procreation, inflation, and taxation, etc. are all completely known. When we've asked people to go through this thought experiment, the biggest stumbling block we see is a resistance to thinking about our own mortality as being fixed. But hopefully it's possible to get beyond this and write down how you'd like to dispose of your current wealth over the rest of your life, and then do the same imagining that you have more or less wealth than you currently possess. If you do this by putting dollar figures into cells of a spreadsheet, then you'll know you're done when you can't move $1 from one cell to another without making yourself less happy. An economist would say you've "equalized the marginal utility of $1 across all possible spending choices." All that remains is to be able to identify a few risky gambles that you would be indifferent to taking, such as stating that you'd just barely accept a 50/50 chance of having your wealth increase by 33% or decrease by 20%. If you can do all this, then you pretty much have everything you need to describe your personal utility function.

This may seem a daunting task, and it's not trivial, but people regularly spend as much or more time and effort researching a new TV to buy. For a matter so consequential, it's by no means an insurmountable challenge, as we've witnessed individuals and families being able to do it. The process is made easier by the fact that others have done it, and their preferences help to set reasonable ranges to narrow down individual preferences. We have seen people find the process of working through the basic questions to be transformational in bringing focus to important trade-offs that many families do not systematically address, even without taking the next step to bring uncertainty into the picture.

Then there is all the extra value to be had by using the Expected Utility framework to figure out the decisions you should make in the real and messy world where all the main variables are uncertain, inter-related, and often non-normal and nonlinear. The list of the decisions it can help with is long. It can help you decide how much investment risk to take for a given level of expected return and risk, how taxes and tax changes will affect how you split up your spending, how longevity and procreation uncertainty impact investment, spending, and gifting deci-sions, when to make intergenerational transfers, when to realize capital gains, whether to purchase annuities, and much more.

13

Human Capital

What Is Human Capital?

Human capital refers to the lifetime earnings of individuals from their labor, usually thought of after-tax and in excess of basic, subsistence living expenses. While it is impossible to put a precise value on an individual's human capital, many economists believe that in developed economies its aggregate value across all members of society is greater than the value of the entire stock market.[†]

[†]For example, there are 130 million households in the United States with a median income of about $70,000 per annum. Assuming $15,000 on average is income in excess of basic expenses, the value of 25 years of such excess would be $50 trillion, roughly the same as the US stock market capitalization.

For young people, it is typical that their human capital far outweighs their financial capital. For most young people, it makes sense to put a lot of thought into career decisions because it is one of the biggest financial decisions they will make, even allowing for the possibility of course changes through life. The Expected Utility concept is valuable in weighing the pros and cons of different career paths, by focusing attention on the risk-adjusted value of human capital. Different vocations will vary dramatically in terms of the uncertainty of outcomes, from those with high expected values but with payoffs similar to those of a lottery ticket to others that resemble the payouts of an inflation-indexed government bond.

Over time, as remaining working years decline, financial capital, including social security and pension income, will come to dominate an individual's balance sheet. It has been mostly for simplicity that we've assumed an individual close to or in retirement as the subject of our case studies so far.

Human Capital and Lifetime Spending Decisions

Exhibit 13.1 shows a stylized representation of the relationship between earned income and spending over a lifetime. In early years, a desire for smooth and constant lifetime spending suggests spending in excess of earnings. This means that when young, it can theoretically make sense to borrow against future earnings, in effect adopting a negative savings rate. In practice though, we think that it will usually make sense for young people to adopt a positive savings rate (excluding the financing of a home purchase), to develop a valuable lifetime habit, to avoid the usually exorbitantly high cost of consumer borrowing and as a safeguard against the risk of financial misfortunes and misadventures.

Even if you knew exactly how much income you'd earn over time, figuring out your precise optimal spending policy would still be very challenging. It requires balancing a desire for smooth and stable spending against the opportunity to earn a positive return on income saved for the future, while taking account of your time preference, that is, your partiality to "now you" versus "future you." The problem becomes more challenging, but can still be usefully addressed with the Expected Utility framework, when you incorporate uncertainty in your earning stream,

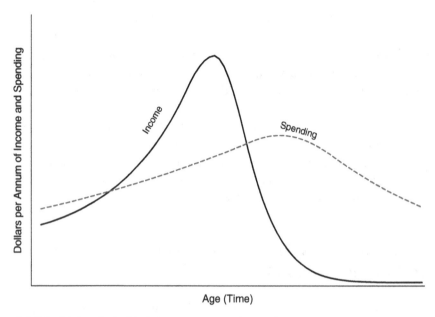

Exhibit 13.1 Typical Lifetime Earning and Spending Pattern

in investment returns and in your personal circumstances including your longevity and bequest desires.

Are You a Stock or a Bond?

Ignoring human capital is not a valid assumption for younger people. In addition to having an idea of the size of one's human capital, it is important to have a sense for how its value varies with the ups and downs of the stock market and the general economy. The economist Moshe Milevsky wrote a book, *Are You a Stock or a Bond?*, that focused precisely on this question. The more your earnings rely on the economy being strong—think high-level executives in banks or industrial companies—the more your human capital is like a stock. In contrast, the more your job is insulated from economic fluctuations—think doctors or tenured professors—the more your human capital is like a bond.

Knowing the character of your human capital is critical in determining an appropriate investment policy. If your human capital is equity-like, you may want your investment portfolio to have less equity risk.

You may also bias your investments in the stock market away from the type of equity risk that is most salient in your human capital. For example, if you work for Citigroup in a role that exposes your human capital to the ups and downs in Citigroup stock, you will not want to hold any more Citigroup stock than required, and you may want to underweight financial companies in your portfolio.

The Expected Utility framework can also be used to help a company assess the potentially very significant cost they impose on employees by compensating them with restricted company stock. They can then compare that to the value ascribed to positive incentive and alignment effects of having employees as shareholders.

Young Investors: High on Human Capital, Low on Financial Capital

Under the Base-Case assumptions we've been using, it is generally optimal for an investor to keep a constant proportional allocation to equities. This result will usually not hold when you include your human capital in wealth, as Yale economists Barry Nalebuff and Ian Ayres describe in their book, *Lifecycle Investing: A New, Safe, and Audacious Way to Improve the Performance of Your Retirement Portfolio*. They argue that younger investors without much savings should have a high or even leveraged allocation to stocks if they have high earnings potential with low correlation to the market. Their optimal allocation to stocks would then drift down over time as their ratio of human capital to financial capital decreases with age.

As an illustration, consider a 35-year-old doctor who has $500,000 in savings but expects to have $500,000 per year of income in excess of subsistence over the next 30 years of practicing medicine. We'd say his human capital is about $15 million, assuming all figures are inflation adjusted and after-tax. We also assume the doctor has no student debt. A traditional financial advisor might recommend that the doctor gradually build up his equities portfolio, keeping the allocation to stocks in his brokerage account constant at 60% through time. An advisor who includes human capital in wealth, on the other hand, would consider the net present value of the young doctor's future $15 million of human capital as if it were already "in the bank" and a part of his current asset pool, which will be used to calculate his optimal equity allocation.

So practical considerations aside, if the young doctor's optimal allocation is 60% in stocks, he should borrow against future earnings and buy about $9 million of equities right now, leveraging his current savings 18-fold!

Nalebuff and Ayres follow this logic to a recommendation that the doctor should buy call options on the stock market. While this may make sense in theory, realistically many young investors will find it difficult to consistently assess and manage an options portfolio efficiently over time to fully implement such a strategy. Nalebuff and Ayres advise capping leverage at about two to one, both for practical reasons and to reduce the risk of human capital assumptions not panning out.

Just how much can this aggressive approach improve investor welfare? We ran a Monte Carlo simulation, assuming a leverage cap of 200% implemented with options, our usual assumptions for equity market expected return and risk, and investor risk preferences. We found that by the end of his career, the doctor can achieve a 12% higher Certainty-equivalent Wealth by taking the more aggressive investment approach, compared to a strategy that ignores the value of human capital. This is a significant uplift, in the sense that the doctor could retire a few years earlier, but it is small enough that much of it could be eroded through trading costs or if the options are rich to fair value.

Also, if we capped his equity exposure at 100%, i.e., using no leverage at all, he could get about one third of the total improvement available. In any case, before implementing such a strategy, an investor should decide just how correlated his human capital is with major asset classes, especially the stock market, and work through the cost of leverage implied by the options, transaction costs, additional taxes, and other risks.[†] In particular, the investor should also take account of the uncertainty, including large negative tail risks, to the value of his human capital, separate from its potential correlation with the economy and stock market returns.

A novel approach that might be available in the future is to implicitly sell some of your human capital through an instrument called an "income share agreement," or ISA. The ISA allows individuals to receive an upfront sum in exchange for paying a fraction of their future earned income subject to various restrictions. ISAs are already being used to

---

[†]There are also some interesting possible use cases for call options as a cheaper alternative to a home mortgage, particularly in cases where home mortgages are recourse to the borrower.

help young people fund trade school and technical training courses. Income-based products provide valuable risk-sharing and signaling features, which may help them to grow in popularity as a way for individuals to unlock their human capital without taking on debt.

Protecting Your Human Capital: The Case for Life Insurance

Life insurance can be thought of as insuring the human capital of a family member who is contributing to the family's financial well-being.[†] As with the case of home insurance, the excess in the premiums charged versus fair value are typically modest because life insurance companies are able to spread their risks over many lives. An Expected Utility analysis will often indicate that the purchase of life insurance can improve the welfare of dependents, even when priced with probabilities of death modestly above their statistically fair values.

When Can I Retire?

For many people, this is one of the most important questions they face. In principle, it can be answered by finding the time to retire that maximizes your Expected Lifetime Utility, but it is different from all the other applications of the framework we've discussed in that it requires an assessment of the utility (for most people, the negative utility) of work. It may be one of those questions that doesn't lend itself to precise quantitative analysis, but even so, we think that the Expected Utility paradigm can help frame the question in a way that's easier to answer.

For example, it may be more helpful in deciding when to retire to see what certainty-equivalent lifetime spending patterns, rather than expected lump-sum wealth, would result from choosing to retire at different ages. Using the Expected Utility framework as an aid in making this decision allows investment risk and longevity risk to be more quantitatively brought into the decision. In the end though, how you weigh work against leisure will be a critical consideration.

[†]Disability and medical insurance can be thought of in the same framework we discuss here.

The framework can also be used to better understand the benefit and impact of flexibility in work and retirement. In practice, you can accelerate or postpone your retirement date as you approach it, and also you can choose how hard you work. This flexibility generally should allow you to take more risk in your investments. You can retire earlier in scenarios where your investments did particularly well, expected investment returns are more attractive than anticipated, or you earned more from your labor than you expected. These effects have been studied and written about broadly in the household finance literature.[†]

Connecting the Dots

Assessing your human capital is a lot more difficult than adding up the value of your financial assets as listed on your brokerage and bank accounts, but in many cases it's well worth the effort. For investors who are in the middle years of their career, when they have built up significant financial capital and still have a large amount of human capital, evaluating the value and character of your human capital can have a material impact on your optimal investing and spending policies. For young investors, they should devote their attention to making the risk-adjusted value of their human capital as high as possible, subject to considerations of career satisfaction of course. They should also pay attention to their investment decisions, since long-term compounding can have a material impact on their success in achieving financial independence.

[†] For example, see Merton, R. (1971), Campbell, J. (2006), Lachance, M. (2004).

14

Into the Weeds: Characteristics of Major Asset Classes

The key issue in investments is estimating expected return.

—Fischer Black

The quality of the investing and spending decisions you make to maximize your Expected Lifetime Utility depends heavily on your ability to estimate the joint distribution of possible outcomes of the investments available to you. Investment risk isn't the only uncertainty that will impact your decisions, but it's an important one. We've seen in many of our case studies that it can be important to think beyond just the expected return and standard deviation of an investment. Ideally, we'd also consider whether the investment has an asymmetric return pattern and to what extent extreme outcomes are more or less likely than suggested by its ordinary variability. In addition, to figure out the right mix of assets to hold, we'll need to understand how the returns of each investment are correlated with the returns of all other investments we're thinking about, and with our human capital, if appropriate. This sounds like a tall order, but this chapter is all about helping you cut it down to size.

Coming up with precise estimates of the joint return distributions for all investments available to an individual investor is effectively impossible. A solution to this conundrum that we are attracted to is suggested by a joke that Victor's father was fond of, about a foolish Sufi wise man named Mullah Nasruddin. The mullah is feverishly searching the kitchen for his wallet. His wife offers to help and asks where he last remembers having it. "In the barn," he replies. "Why are you searching for it in the kitchen?" she asks, to which he replies, "It's too dark in the barn. I'll never find it there!"[†]

We too should look for answers where there is enough light. This means limiting the range of potential investments to those where prospective return distributions are more readily estimated. In general, investment returns that are based on identifiable, inflation-protected cash flows are the easiest to estimate. These are investments whose future return distributions we would feel comfortable estimating even if we had no idea how they did historically. Next are investments with cash flows that are difficult to pin down with precision, but with an aggregate risk so big, so undiversifiable, and so correlated with the performance of the economy at large that we conclude they should offer a risk premium. Hardest to estimate are the returns of investments or strategies whose performance is driven by market inefficiencies, whether they arise from frictions and segmentations or from investor foibles. Our estimates for these investments will necessarily rely heavily on historical performance,

---

[†]There's even a Wikipedia entry on this phenomenon, known as the Streetlight Effect.

which is a cause for concern. Estimating the return distributions for these investments will rely on the challenging task of forecasting changes in market microstructures, investor behavior, and the amount of risk-capital that will be attracted to these opportunities, each of which can change rapidly and unpredictably.

To help cut through all this complexity, we find ourselves always coming back to these three related hypotheses:

- *The efficient markets hypothesis:* The markets, especially large and liquid ones, are fairly efficient.
- *The cost matters hypothesis:* Costs matter.
- *The average investor hypothesis:* The market portfolio is the only investment that everybody can own at the same time.

We'll see that these guiding principles are very effective in narrowing down the plausible return distributions we can expect from the different types of investments we'll discuss. For instance, the belief that markets are at least somewhat efficient suggests you can't do much better than the rate offered by government bonds for a very safe investment, and you can't do much better than the expected return on equities for risk assets whose returns are related to the health of the economy. It also follows that we can't expect to outperform the market using information that everyone knows already, which includes past performance. Given these beliefs, the headline message is that individual investors should avail themselves of the low hanging fruit of high diversification, low fees, and tax efficiency. Such an approach will generally preclude concentrated, high-fee, tax-inefficient investments in hedge funds, structured products, and other complex alternative investments. It is also usually the case that we can get more clarity by thinking about long time horizons, which is a natural fit for the lifetime investment and spending decisions we need to make.

What follows is a discussion of how you could go about approximating the return distributions and other relevant characteristics of the main types of investments available to an affluent investor, ranked in order of the quality of estimation we believe is possible. Unless otherwise stated, we will be focused on pretax characteristics. We devote Chapter 17 to bringing taxes into the Portfolio Choice process.

Long-term Inflation-linked Government Bonds

The US government issues Treasury Inflation-Protected Securities (TIPS). Many other countries issue similar bonds. For all these bonds, the real yield quote is pretty much the real return an investor should expect to earn. For horizons similar to the bond's maturity, the bonds can be treated as risk-free, or as the minimal-risk asset, as they're the closest an investor can get to locking in a forward amount of real consumption. For horizons considerably shorter than the bond's maturity, a normal distribution of returns with historically implied volatilities does a pretty good job describing the potential price fluctuations. These bonds do, in theory, carry the risk of default or restructuring by the issuing government, a highly consequential risk but sufficiently low probability that we view it as simply being part of the large set of background risks—nuclear apocalypse, global economic meltdown, market infrastructure collapse, etc. —that all investors must tolerate.

Nominal Government Bills and Bonds

Most government-issued obligations are not indexed to inflation and promise to pay a nominal interest rate plus principal. In order to estimate the expected real return of nominal bonds, as distinct from the real return on TIPS, we need to have an independent estimate of the future rate of inflation. Various sources of inflation forecasts are generated by economists, consumers, and businesses, but unfortunately, it is generally agreed that forecasting inflation is very difficult and these estimates are fairly coarse. The imprecision of these forecasts is compounded by not knowing the exact points in time when respondents are providing their inflation forecast estimates, making it difficult to consistently apply the forecasts to ever-changing nominal interest rates.

Unfortunately, it does not help to use the difference in yields between nominal bonds and the same maturity inflation-indexed bonds to estimate inflation, because by construction that estimate of inflation would tell us that the nominal bond has a real yield equal to that of the corresponding inflation-indexed bond.[†] So we're stuck

---

[†] We are looking for $\text{Yield}_{nominal} - \text{Inflation}_{Expected}$, but if we set $\text{Inflation}_{Expected} = \text{Yield}_{nominal} - \text{Yield}_{TIPS}$, then we just get $\text{Yield}_{nominal} - (\text{Yield}_{nominal} - \text{Yield}_{TIPS}) = \text{Yield}_{TIPS}$, which doesn't tell us anything about the real return of nominal bonds that's useful.

with the human-generated forecasts. The challenge with these forecasts is that if nominal bonds offered a real return in excess of the real return of inflation-protected bonds, it is generally believed that it should be quite small, something on the order of 0.5% per annum. But few market observers believe that survey-based inflation forecasts are accurate enough to be able to discern a risk premium of that small magnitude.

Estimating the risk of nominal government bonds requires bringing judgment to bear on weighing all the different sources of information on bond variability. When viewed to a long-term horizon, even US T-bills have considerable real return risk. A particularly painful period for investors in US T-bills was from 1941 to 1948, when T-bills lost more than 40% of their inflation-adjusted value. More recently, investors in T-bills from 2009 to the end of 2022 have lost 24% of the real value of their investment.

Stock Markets

As we discussed in Chapter 5, a stock market's cyclically adjusted earnings yield is a decent, though imperfect, estimate of the long-term real return of the stock market. There are a number of variations on this metric, such as those that use dividends and stock-buybacks plus broad economic growth, which are about as effective and logically sound as earnings yield, and investors may reasonably choose one metric over another or average them together. We caution that the assumptions that we think are reasonable for estimating the expected long-term real return of broad stock markets are not appropriate for estimating expected returns of individual stocks, or even industry sectors, where forecasts of growth at the company or industry level are critical inputs.

Compound Versus Average Annual Return

A somewhat technical, but important, question regarding this estimate of the return of the stock market is whether it is best thought of as an estimate of the prospective annualized compound return to a long-term horizon, or of the average annual returns of the stock market, taken one at a time. The first is referred to as a geometric return estimate and the second as the arithmetic return estimate. For example,

(Continued)

over the past 50 years, the geometric annualized return of the US stock market was 10.3%, while the average annual arithmetic return was 12.0%. The difference between the two is the volatility drag we've previously discussed, which is a function of the variability of returns.[†]

Researchers are not of one mind whether the stock market's earnings yield is better viewed as an estimate of the one or the other type of return. We believe the answer is somewhere in between, but we generally make the more conservative choice and use earnings yield as an estimate of the expected arithmetic return. All else equal, an investor who estimates the stock market's prospective return at 5% geometric will want a larger allocation to equities than one who sees the 5% as the expected arithmetic return, and the difference can be quite large.[‡]

A common—but we believe misguided—approach to estimating the prospective return of the stock market is to base it on historical returns. To see why we don't like this method, let's think for a moment about a 10-year bond with no credit risk (e.g., issued by the US government) that's yielding 10%. Then over the next few years, yields decline to 1%. Historical bond returns will look fantastic, but they won't provide any clue that the forward-looking expected return from these bonds is now actually only 1%, which plainly it is. Broad equity markets are obviously not completely bond-like, but they're more similar to bonds than one might think. Earnings yield provides a decent predictor of future long-term returns because corporate earnings look somewhat bond-like when viewed across an entire large economy. Accordingly, you can view the earnings you're getting divided by the price you're paying as a good, though imperfect, estimate for the return you should expect. In contrast, short-term or even long-term history just doesn't provide much forward-looking information.

[†]The volatility of stock market returns over this period was about 18%, leading us to estimate the difference between geometric and arithmetic returns of $\frac{1}{2}\sigma^2 = 1.6\%$, which matches, within rounding error, the observed difference between 12.0% and 10.3%.
[‡]For example, assuming stock market volatility of 20% per annum, the 5% geometric expected return would equate to an arithmetic return of 7% = (5% + ½ x 0.2²), and hence the optimal allocation to equities, using the Merton share, would be two-fifths higher than if the investor believed the arithmetic expected return of the stock market was 5% (assuming a risk-free rate of 0%). See Haghani & White, 2017.

Estimating the risk of the stock market to a long-term horizon is best done taking account of as many different sources of information as possible. Implied volatility of long-term options is a useful, albeit noisy signal, as it is hard to precisely know how much of the pricing represents a risk premium that buyers or sellers of those options are requiring. We also must concern ourselves with the skew and tails of the stock market return distribution, although a focus on long horizons somewhat mitigates these effects.

Much of modern academic finance describes risk using concepts such as continuous time random walks, bell-shaped normal distributions and risk-neutral distributions implied by options markets. Calculating the historical volatility of the market would give us an excellent estimate if it were the case that volatility was constant through time and prices moved continuously. Alas, neither assumption is borne out by historical experience, but we still see historical realized volatility as a useful input to the estimate of stock market risk.

Analyzing stock market crashes is another valuable source for estimating risk. The most dramatic was the near 90% drop in the US market from 1929 to 1932. Not as commonly known is that there were six other episodes in which investors lost 40% to 50%, two occurring since the turn of millennium. While these were painful market busts, we need to keep in mind that the US stock market has been a star performer on the world stage, and so focusing on US performance is likely to lead us to underestimate risk, an effect known as survivorship bias. We need to bear in mind that some markets didn't survive at all, such as those in Russia and China in the first half of the twentieth century.

Stock returns exhibit fat tails, which arise partly from changes in market volatility through time. Markets are made of people, and people can get pretty carried away on occasion. Financial markets do not behave like atoms in a gas, which is the origin of the classical equations financial economists use to describe the behavior of market returns. Financial markets exhibit feedback loops, which can make the whole system prone to instability. No matter how much hurricane coverage insurance companies sell, the probability of a hurricane ripping up the Florida coast is the same, whereas if enough market participants engage in dynamic Portfolio Insurance strategies, that can increase the probability of just the event they were trying to protect themselves against, as illustrated by the October 1987 stock market crash.

What if we don't know much about history or options prices? From first principles, what can we say about how much stock markets can go up or down? The present value of an equity investment depends on two things: the expected cash flow stream—earnings or dividends—and the expected rate of return or discount rate—used for present-valuing those cash flows. Since equity cash flows go far out into the future, small changes in cash flows and discount rates have a big impact on prices. For instance, if companies on average suffer a long-term reduction in earnings of 40% (assuming a steady real earnings stream) and at the same time investors demand a 3% higher expected return (e.g., a discount rate increase from 3% to 6%), stock prices would fall by 70%, which suggests that the 1929 stock market crash was not a one-in-a-million fluke.

There's no clearly "right" way to blend these different estimates of risk together. However, we've tended to estimate long-horizon stock market risk by taking an average of long-term and short-term realized volatility, long-dated option implied volatility across a range of strike prices, and adding in a little extra to capture the low but real possibility of drops of 50% or more in the market. Our goal is to estimate the distribution of future returns of the stock market, recognizing that in reality returns are not normally distributed and prices often jump from one level to the next, without allowing investors a chance to trade at an intermediate price. However, as we'll see in Chapter 18 on parameter uncertainty, the investment policy that maximizes Expected Utility will mainly be a function of the stock market's expected return and standard deviation and is not terribly sensitive to the overall shape of the return distribution for a fairly broad range of plausible inputs.

The larger and more diversified the stock market we are focused on, and the longer the horizon we are evaluating, the better the just discussed techniques for estimating the distribution of possible outcomes should work. We should be able to do a better job estimating the characteristics of the global stock market than the US or Japanese stock market. In the other direction, these methods will work considerably less well when applied to a single industry or an individual stock.

In the next chapter we will return to the question of stock market risk, adopting the perspective of an investor who is primarily concerned with the long-term real purchasing power of his wealth. We will see that for such an investor, the stock market is significantly less risky than for an investor focused on current asset values.

Foreign Equity Markets

Many investors, particularly in high-income economies, view foreign markets as having significantly higher risk, and perhaps lower return, than their own home equity market. This seems a little bit like all parents believing their child is above average.

There are a number of arguments for and against home bias in global equity investing. Investors may view foreign markets as having extra risk in terms of foreign currency fluctuations and possibly lower returns due to frictions in recovering foreign withholding tax on dividends. Some investors may also view their home equity market as being something of a hedge against their future consumption basket of high-end luxury items, such as expensive homes, art, and travel. Warren Buffett and John Bogle have argued that US investors should only invest in US equities because it gives them plenty of international diversification through the foreign operations of US companies.

We are more swayed by the arguments that foreign markets do provide diversification benefits. Even the foreign currency argument can be turned on its head, as exposure to other currencies can be a valuable risk-mitigation against the debasement of one's home currency. Dynamic asset allocation based on changing excess return and risk will generally do better when investors can change their allocation to several large, broad equity markets rather than just one. There is also a strong argument that foreign markets will be less correlated with your human capital, which will tend to be more tied to your domestic economy. In general, the basic approach we've already discussed for estimating the expected return and risk of a broad equity market can be applied equally to domestic and foreign markets.

Whether justified or not, many investors exhibit a significant "home bias" in their global stock market allocations. For example, US investors in aggregate allocate about 85% of their equity holdings to US equities, while the share of US equities in global market capitalization indices at the end of 2022 was a bit under 60%. Investors in other countries also tend to exhibit home bias in their equity allocations. Unfortunately, it is unlikely that the home bias exhibited across markets would naturally balance out without having an impact on pricing.

A simple thought experiment shows how pervasive home bias can impact expected returns in different markets. Imagine we start with global equity market capitalizations and equity investor assets being distributed unevenly, with one big market representing 50% of the global total and 10 small markets representing 5% each. Let's say investors in the big market want to keep 85% of their equity investments in their home market. Let's further assume that in each small market, investors want to keep 50% of their equity investments in their home market, exhibiting an even stronger home bias relative to their 5% market capitalization weight.

With these assumptions, we'll find that supply and demand won't naturally balance out. There won't be enough of the big market to satisfy all the demand, and there won't be enough demand for all the small markets to absorb the supply. The natural first mechanism to achieve balance is for prices to move. We were surprised at just how big those adjustments might need to be. In our toy example, the big market would have to appreciate by 140% relative to the small markets for things to equilibrate, assuming all investors stick to their home bias.[†] However, as prices move, long-term prospective returns would also move. This should mitigate the size of the price move needed, if investors in the big market opportunistically reduce their home bias, and if investors in the small markets reduce their demand for the big market.[1]

Index Funds

Index funds have enjoyed tremendous growth and popularity. However, they are regularly criticized by parts of the investment management industry. Table 14.1 presents some of the claims that have been made and our analysis of the strength of the arguments.

[†] If the big market value appreciated by 140% to represent 71% of total global market capitalization, then everything would balance out, with the big market investors having 85% of their wealth in their home market, and all the small market investors having 50% of their wealth in their individual home markets.

Table 14.1

Criticism	Response
Index funds are a "giant momentum machine" since they have to buy more of a stock as its price goes up.	Not accurate, since once an index fund buys the correct number of shares of a constituent, it does not buy or sell shares as prices move.
They are "fundamentally flawed" in that they will always be overweight in overvalued companies and underweight undervalued companies.	If an investor does not know which companies or types of companies are over- or undervalued, then it is impossible to say that the index fund is flawed in this way. If the investor knows which companies are overvalued, then he should concentrate on being a successful stock picker. For those who don't know which stocks are overvalued, the index fund will be best.
They are too concentrated in the biggest companies.	At the end of 2022, the largest company in the world, Apple, represents 3% of the global stock market index, and the top 10 stocks make up just under 15% of the index. We calculate that the extra return these large stocks need to offer to compensate for their size and concentration is on the order of 0.1% per annum.
A portfolio of 25 stocks gives almost as much diversification as owning the market portfolio.	While it is possible to carefully build a portfolio of 25 stocks that has a standard deviation of returns very close to the full market portfolio, such a concentrated portfolio will still have substantial non-compensated idiosyncratic risk.[2] Economic logic says it should therefore have a lower ratio of expected return to risk. Even a 5% lower ratio of return to risk is a substantial lost opportunity in long-run expected welfare. When greater diversification is being offered for free, why not take it?

(Continued)

Table 14.1   (Continued)

Criticism	Response
Stocks that are about to be added to an index outperform the market just before inclusion (and vice versa for stocks being removed from indexes) resulting in every index systematically underperforming a more inclusive version of itself.	This index "inclusion/exclusion" friction is a real cost, but it is quite small for well-designed indexes with broad market coverage. Unfortunately, the S&P 500 index, which is among the most tracked of all stock market indexes, is not as broad as other stock market indexes.
If everyone invests in index funds, no one will set appropriate prices for individual stocks.	Index fund market ownership is nowhere near a level at which we need worry about this, and even if it grew to be a much higher fraction of the market, there will always be pools of capital that will be attracted to excess returns offered by successful stock picking. Even if index funds owned 100% of the market, active investors could set prices by running leveraged long-short stock portfolios.
The concentration of voting power in the hands of the biggest index fund managers is anti-competitive and will hurt consumers.	There is some validity to this argument from a societal perspective, but it is not a financial reason for individual investors to not buy index funds. In fact, what hurts consumers might help investors! Direct indexing, where an investor actually owns the market portfolio in a separately managed brokerage account rather than via an index fund or ETF, may be a partial solution, allowing each individual investor to exercise his voting rights.

Corporate Bonds and Other Risky Lending

Here we have all the challenges in estimating the risk and return of government bonds, plus the added task of assessing relatively small probabilities of default and the attendant magnitude of loss. The number and severity of defaults by different individual issuers tend to bunch together in times of economic crisis, which of course is the same time that we expect the stock market to be doing poorly. Absent highly specialized and issuer-specific knowledge, it may be difficult to characterize the distribution of outcomes to get a meaningful result in terms of asset allocation to investment grade bonds. It may be that estimating the return distributions of high-yield bonds or other more equity-like debt investments is more tractable, but here too is an area that rewards specialized knowledge and lacks a high quality, general framework for thinking about risk and returns.

For taxable investors, it is generally significantly more tax-efficient to earn the equity risk premium through owning equities directly. In most tax regimes, equities enjoy preferential capital gains treatment and the possibility of tax deferral. Trying to earn the equity risk premium through the credit spread is usually less tax efficient, as income from corporate bonds is typically taxed when earned and at higher ordinary income tax rates.[†] US Treasury bonds are also generally more tax efficient than corporate bonds. Municipal bonds in the United States are generally exempt from federal income tax, but their tax benefits should be expected to be reflected in their pricing. The same challenges of estimating low probabilities of high consequence outcomes holds with these bonds as with investment grade corporate bonds.

One aspect of credit investing that requires extra alertness is that typically the most likely outcome is to have a given bond mature with no losses, thus earning the credit spread. This can encourage investors to focus primarily on the "upside" of credit instruments without a thorough consideration of the risks involved, which for a single corporate bond tends to be highly nonlinear. Overly concentrated credit risk, and too much of it, are often the result, and can explain a good part of what waylaid history's would-be billionaires.

Real Estate

Estimating the expected real return and risk of broadly diversified holdings of commercial, industrial, agricultural, and residential real estate tends to be easier than for the stock market. Instead of using the earnings yield of the equity market as our estimate, we can use the rental yield, cyclically adjusted and adjusted for maintenance capital expenditure, of a

---

[†] Perhaps it is an extreme perspective, but Yale's David Swensen argued that corporate bonds simply do not warrant an allocation in the portfolios of individual taxable investors.

diversified portfolio of real estate. However, for more concentrated port-folios, and for undeveloped land, it generally requires assessing current and future local market conditions.

It seems reasonable that home prices should outpace inflation over long horizons, especially in markets where building new dwellings is restricted. This ex-ante view is consistent with the long-term historical experience in the United States. Over the past 100 years, home prices, excluding net rental income, have grown about 1% faster than inflation, with very roughly half the annual variability of the stock market.[3] These figures mask large variations between different localities but provide a good starting point for thinking about the expected real return and risk of a home.

For many people their home is their biggest actual or potential investment, and nearly everyone of some affluence is faced with a com-plex set of decisions regarding housing. You need to decide whether to buy or rent and, in each case, how much house you can afford. If you buy, then you need to decide whether, how much, and in what form to borrow, and how to invest any excess borrowed proceeds. The decisions are made more complex by housing needs changing over time, driven by lifestyle and family situation.

Housing-related decisions ultimately involve choosing a set of finan-cial policies amidst various future uncertainties, so they fit right into the Expected Utility framework. In general we feel that nonresidential real estate should be treated like any other asset, just an investment with a given return distribution. For residential real estate, there are other reasonable options, and a common one is to simply exclude the house you live in from your net worth and instead focus on your "investable" wealth. While this seems attractive at first, we tend to think it's not the best solution—your house can be an important part of your bequest or store of wealth for future spending, and the various decisions involved are too important to simply sweep under the rug. Instead, we like to think of residential real estate as an investment asset that you're renting out, but to yourself. It has a return distribution like any investment asset (includ-ing its rental income), but also a spending component where owning it causes you to spend the house's fair-market rental rate. This framing has several advantages: it allows decisions about affordability to be made within the lifetime consumption and portfolio choice framework, ena-bles comparisons of rent-versus-buy decisions, allows comparisons of different levels of borrowing, and captures the tax-efficiency of owning and consuming your own real estate.

The following two recommendations are pretty general and don't depend much on specific circumstances or an individual's risk-aversion:

1. Don't keep a mortgage outstanding while simultaneously holding significant low-risk fixed income assets.
2. Avoid owning excess residential real estate—that is, a bigger house than wanted or needed—purely for financial reasons. Such exposure is usually dominated by diversified equities.

Actively Managed Mutual Funds

We find it useful to bear in mind that every divergence from the market portfolio is an active bet, which requires someone else to be on the other side. To the extent that one views all investors who diverge from the market portfolio as "stock pickers" then we get the result that stock pickers in aggregate will earn the market return, less whatever fees and costs are associated with their activities. This is known as "Sharpe's arithmetic," in honor of Bill Sharpe who popularized the idea. The same idea was expressed by John Bogle in his cost matters hypothesis (CMH):

The overarching reality is simple: Gross returns in the financial markets minus the costs of financial intermediation equal the net returns actually delivered to investors. Although truly staggering amounts of investment literature have been devoted to the widely understood EMH (the efficient market hypothesis), precious little has been devoted to what I call the CMH (the cost matters hypothesis). To explain the dire odds that investors face in their quest to beat the market, however, we don't need the EMH; we need only the CMH. No matter how efficient or inefficient markets may be, the returns earned by investors as a group must fall short of the market returns by precisely the amount of the aggregate costs they incur. It is the central fact of investing.[4]

A corollary of Sharpe's arithmetic and Bogle's CMH is that the average active stock picker will have a portfolio of stocks that we'd expect to be riskier than the market portfolio, since all active stock investors will have less diversified portfolios than the market portfolio. Hence, in order for a stock picker to deliver a better Risk-adjusted Return than the market portfolio, he needs to overcome two sources of performance drag: higher fees and higher risk.

After a deep evaluation, you may feel a particular strategy stands up to these hurdles: perhaps it's a good story, has performed well, or it's a strategy based on some sort of idiosyncratic market anomaly. In practice it is not that difficult to construct stories that make a wide range of investment strategies sound plausible, especially when explained by a charismatic manager. When combined with a positive track record, it is easy to understand why so many investors choose to have their savings actively managed, despite higher fees, less diversification, and often much higher tax costs than from more diversified asset class investing.

Estimating the risk of actively managed investment strategies is usually more challenging than assessing the risk of diversified portfolios of equities or real estate. Active strategies are by design more concentrated and the strategies themselves can drift over time.

The Not-so-curious Case of Investor Returns Being Substantially Lower Than Fund Returns

Supportive, but indirect, evidence for the notion that return-chasing behavior hurts investor returns is the finding that mutual fund investors have earned 1.5% to 3% per annum lower returns than the returns of the funds they invested in.[5] The effect probably comes from a combination of poor market timing and poor dynamic selection of funds themselves, putting money into funds that are hot and redeeming from those that are not. This is separate from the effect of fees on investor returns, which gets so much coverage in the financial press; rather, it has to do with the timing of investor flows. That dollar-weighted investor returns have been lower than fund returns historically has not attracted as much attention perhaps because it's a story wherein the perpetrator and the victim are the same party: the investor.

To illustrate, let's take the example of the flagship ETF, ticker symbol ARKK, managed by Cathy Wood's ARK investment management. One dollar invested in the ARKK ETF at its inception on October 31, 2014, would have grown to $1.69 at the end of December 2022, for a compound annual return of 6.6%—quite nice! However,

investors in the ETF in aggregate fared far less well. If we look at the
dollars invested and redeemed, together with dividends and the value
of investors' investment at the end of the period, we find that investors
taken all together experienced an annualized internal rate of return
(IRR) of −37%, a full 43% lower than the fund return. The reason is
that investors put a lot of money into the ARKK ETF after it experienced very high returns, and they took money out after periods
when its returns were poor. While this is an extreme instance of the
damage return chasing can cause to investor wealth, it is by no means
an isolated example.

Factor Investing[†]

Factor investing has spawned hundreds of academic articles and trillions
of dollars in assets under management, much of it invested through long-
only "Smart Beta" strategies. At its core is a high-stakes unresolved ten-
sion spanning the industry and academia: is the stock market essentially
efficient in terms of risk and reward, or are there major inefficiencies
from which large groups of investors can systematically profit?

The story begins with Nobel Laureate Eugene Fama and his 1965
PhD thesis, in which he proposed that the stock market is efficient and
therefore very hard to beat.[6] Decades later, Fama and his colleague Kenneth French noticed that stocks of companies that were either relatively
small or cheaply valued had higher returns than predicted by the most
popular stock market model of the day, the capital asset pricing model
(CAPM). This didn't dissuade Fama from his belief that markets were
efficient; rather, he and French concluded that the CAPM wasn't the
right model. They proposed that two more risk factors were needed in
addition to market beta,[‡] which they termed the size and value factors.
But two of Fama's PhD students, David Booth and Cliff Asness, took the

---

[†]We discussed this in more detail in an article published in the *Journal of Portfolio Management*,
"Smart Beta: The Good, the Bad and the Muddy" in 2018.
[‡]The beta (β or beta coefficient) of an investment is a measure of the systematic risk arising
from exposure to general market movements as opposed to risk that is idiosyncratic to that
individual investment.

same data and reached the opposite conclusion: that factor returns represented a market inefficiency and thus also an investment opportunity. Booth, Asness, and several more of Fama's students went on to become billionaires, building businesses premised on their view that investors would flock to a new factor-focused style of investing.

Investors, voting with trillions of their assets, seem to agree that Booth and Asness are right. But many experts, including the Nobel Prize Committee, think that Fama and the efficient market hypothesis are right too. How can they all be right? We'll try to fairly present the case for factor investing and also some reasons for skepticism, with the hope that readers will be left well-equipped to decide whether and how to incorporate factor investing into their own portfolios.

The central idea behind factor investing is that the best way to explain individual expected stock returns is with multiple systematic drivers, called factors. A multi-factor framework was put forward in an elegant bit of reasoning called arbitrage pricing theory (APT)[7] and caught on quickly because the single-factor capital asset pricing model[8] wasn't doing a very good job explaining the return structure of individual equities.[9] In a seminal 1992 paper, Fama and French proposed the three-factor model, which became the foundational tool in the multi-factor framework. They argued that the CAPM, based on a single "total market" factor, can be significantly improved by adding two additional factors:

1. Value—the differential return between low price/book stocks and high price/book stocks
2. Size—the differential return between small market-cap stocks and large market-cap stocks

They found that exposure to both the value and size factors had historically earned a positive risk premium and that their three-factor model did a much better job than the single-factor CAPM of explaining individual stock returns. Over time, the number of factors that attract investor attention has grown dramatically. These are the most popular choices of factors expected to enhance the quality of portfolio return as suggested by the number and size of funds set up to focus on them:

1. Value—stocks with low price/book ratios
2. Size—small company stocks

3. Dividend yield—stocks with high dividend yield, or high dividend growth
4. Quality—stocks with high profitability and/or conservative investment
5. Momentum—stocks that have outperformed the market over the past year
6. Low volatility—stocks with low historical volatility or low beta

We believe the prime reason investors seek factor exposure is to earn higher Risk-adjusted Returns than the market-cap-weighted index. This isn't unreasonable, since over significant historical periods that's exactly what's happened. Proponents of factor investing argue that not only has the historical record looked great for these factors, but also that sound underlying reasons explain why this should be the case and should continue into the future. These explanations fall into two broad categories: risk-based and behavioral.

Risk-based explanations suggest that exposure to factors involves bearing systematic risk that cannot be fully diversified away, so investors earn a structural positive risk premium to compensate for bearing that extra risk. Value, size, and the rest are called "factors" precisely because they were originally conceived as being "risk factors" explaining expected stock returns in an efficient market. Indeed, the vocabulary of factor investing, with labels like "factor premia," "style premia," and "Smart Beta," is an artifact of its origins in the academic efficient-markets camp.

So what does a risk-based story look like? Taking the size and value factors for example, one plausible conjecture is that a very deep economic crisis will wash away the smallest companies and the companies with lowest relative valuations. As the risk of catastrophic economic depression is a background risk that doesn't show itself in routine equity price movements, it is not picked up in the conventional measurement of market beta and therefore isn't compensated through the market beta risk premium.[†] Instead, the risk is compensated through the size and value factor premia.[10]

[†] This is merely a conjecture because there are not enough actual catastrophic economic events to test it robustly.

Many of the factors—in particular low volatility, quality, momentum and dividend yield—are difficult to explain with a plausible risk-based story. These factors rely more on behavioral explanations that posit that factor returns represent market inefficiencies. In this view, factor investing is a systematic way to profit from deep-seated cognitive investing mistakes of others or from constraints and frictions that give rise to inefficiencies.

Turning now to reasons for skepticism, let's start with risk-based justifications for factor investing, which hold that factor premia are primarily risk-based and efficiently priced. In this case, an investor would want a portfolio with exposure to a given style factor only if she specifically believes she's more or less sensitive to that factor than the average investor. A fundamental fact of market arithmetic is that the sum of all individual portfolios must equal the market portfolio. So for every investor who is less sensitive to the risk of a given factor and wants to earn the factor premium, there must be an investor who is more sensitive and wants to avoid its risk by paying the factor premium.

While this is theoretically possible, for most factors it seems a stretch to think the market functions this way. For one thing, the risk scenarios involved in many of the factors aren't sufficiently clear or well-known for investors to have a strong view about them. And also, if factors really do arise from this sort of risk explanation, where are the funds pitched to investors who want to avoid some factor and earn a return below that of the broad market? For example, we strongly suspect that investors in *both* value and growth funds expect to earn above-market returns, not that growth-fund investors perceive themselves as earning below-market returns in exchange for avoiding the risk of the value factor.

While risk-based explanations are consistent with efficient markets, behavioral explanations explicitly arise from market inefficiencies. The obvious question is: to what extent should we expect these market anomalies to continue? We know many reasons why anomalies tend to dissipate over time. Large pools of opportunistic capital tend to move the market toward greater efficiency, and the composition of market participants changes relative to the historical period during which past returns were observed. The question of anomaly persistence has been addressed in a number of research papers, and most, though not all have found that as a market inefficiency becomes known through published research, it provides smaller excess returns over time.[11]

The correct explanation for some proposed factor premia may be *neither* risk-based nor behavioral. Not all statistical results are *true* in that they accurately reflect an underlying structural reality. The literature of factor results principally depends on statistical regressions, and typically factor "discoveries" have been reported in journals when there's less than a 2% chance the regression result is the product of random noise. That's a good start, but not as rock solid as it might seem.[†] If researchers run enough regressions, eventually the data will oblige with an interesting finding. There are many ways that careful researchers can and do correct for this problem, such as inspecting out-of-sample data from other time periods or other markets for the existence of the phenomenon. And indeed, data for several of the most popular factors stand up to these more rigorous standards, particularly value, momentum, and low beta.

However, "mining" for factors makes statistical limitations a very real concern with factor research more broadly. Financial data are a harsh taskmaster, and many of the available tools of statistical inference have limited power when applied to financial datasets. Since the publication of the Fama-French three-factor model, researchers have searched for and discovered a large number of other factors with positive historical risk premia, decent levels of apparent statistical significance, and improved explanatory power with respect to individual stock historical returns. This proliferation of factors, now in the hundreds, has given birth to the term "factor zoo" in reference to the overall literature.[12] The same phenomenon magnified 10-fold is seen in the explosion in the number of ETFs and indexes on which they are based.[13] Adding to the doubt and confusion over the factor zoo's quickly expanding size is the well-publicized "replication crisis" in social science research, referring to the realization that many academic papers in economics and other social sciences report findings that other researchers are unable to reproduce.[14][‡]

While data mining concerns cast doubt on the authenticity of the factor zoo's exotic members more than on the core factors, another data issue impacts all the factors. Nearly all financial data are subject to complex relationships and periodic regime changes, and moreover, there is rarely enough of it.[15] Adding multiple markets and multiple historical periods doesn't add as much useful information as it could because markets are often affected by common large-scale drivers that spill over

---

[†]If the rate of statistical discoveries being true real-world phenomena is 1%, then with a 2% reporting threshold there's only a 50% chance the statistical discovery is real. The confusion between the 2% prior probability and the 50% posterior probability of a false positive is an example of one form of the *base-rate fallacy*.

[‡]In most cases, outright fraud is ruled out as the primary reason for non-reproducibility.

across markets and time periods. Simply put, it's very hard to use the data to clearly determine what's causing what. It may be that the value factor, for example, has a valid risk explanation, but the feared scenarios have not yet shown up in the data. But it's also possible that the value factor's returns across many markets have historically resulted from a common hidden driver affecting equities everywhere, such as long-term technological shifts or globalization. Investors would probably want more of the value factor if the first explanation were the correct one, but there isn't enough data to know. Researchers and investors are good at finding stories that seem to fit the data, but the data itself is much more close-mouthed about which story is right and, consequently, what to expect in the future.

Why Past Returns Are Usually Not Indicative of Future Returns

It is notoriously difficult to estimate future returns from past performance. Perhaps the mother of all investing sins is "return chasing," making investment decisions based on an extrapolation of recent past performance.[16] This tendency seems to be a deeply ingrained behavioral foible, as documented in a wide range of academic studies. We took a look at this behavior ourselves through a survey we conducted in 2017 in which we asked 702 individuals to guess how many flips they'd want to see in order to be able to discern, with 95% confidence, a fair coin from a coin biased 60% toward heads.[17] You may wish to take a moment to reflect on this question yourself before reading on.

About 50% of our respondents guessed 30 flips or less, and the most common guess was around 10 flips. The correct answer is that 143 flips are needed. We gave the survey to our research subscribers, who we believe are a pretty mathematical bunch, many of whom would have gotten close if they'd taken their time to calculate an answer rather than giving a quick guess as we requested. But the point of the exercise was to illustrate how when we are thinking fast or intuitively, we tend to put too much weight on small samples: a full 30% of respondents thought 10 flips or less was sufficient. This built-in tendency to overweight small samples can easily lead us to excessively rely on past performance. This thought experiment reminds us that it takes a really long time to analyze an investment with this kind of risk/reward by track record alone, even with the assumption that the investment opportunity has not changed over that time.

Even if we accept that both risk-based and behavior-based factors are expected to deliver excess returns in the future, we worry that transactions costs and frictions involved in harvesting them render the net excess return too meager in most cases to warrant holding portfolios with large factor tilts. Factor-focused portfolios require more active rebalancing than market-cap-weighted portfolios, leading to higher turnover, transaction costs, and tax inefficiency. A detailed study by researchers at the investment manager AQR[18] using nearly $1 trillion of actual transaction data estimated that the cost of trading was equal to about 40% of the gross historical extra factor return. Constructing these portfolios also requires considerable care and skill, leading to higher investment management fees.

Factor investing is not as simple or transparent as some of its proponents claim. There are numerous ways to structure a portfolio exposed to any one factor. The various style factors aren't naturally independent of one another, so should a portfolio focused on one given factor ignore its other possible factor exposures, or should it be designed to have zero exposure to all the other factors? In fact, for factor strategies that do not allow shorting, it is usually impossible to construct a portfolio with exposure to just one factor because many of them are correlated with each other.

Finally, we also worry that the *risks* of factor investing will be more extreme than history suggests. We believe that the large flow of funds into factor investing strategies has primarily been driven by investors chasing attractive historical returns and only secondarily by the theoretical models behind them. Periods of poor relative performance can lead to a broad disenchantment with factor investing, with resultant outflows causing losses in individual factors much larger than suggested by the historical record.

Factor analysis is undoubtedly useful in decomposing and understanding past returns, and in understanding what kinds of risks and "bets" are embedded in a given portfolio. With the proliferation of potential factors to invest in, it is critical for investors to understand the fundamental reasons, if any, that a factor has delivered attractive returns in the past and assess the likelihood that they will persist. This is a very daunting task when armed only with historical returns in markets where the players and the rules of the game have been constantly changing. Even for the subset of factors with the most solid risk and behavioral underpinnings, we suspect their expected returns, net of the costs of harvesting them, are considerably lower than their past returns, and that their risks are likely to be substantially higher than historical data suggest.

ESG Investing

ESG investors try to build their portfolios from companies that they view as being the most sensitive and active in safeguarding the **E**nvironment, promoting **S**ocial responsibility and diversity, and fostering good **G**overnance in the workplace. Many institutional and individual investors have brought this constraint to their portfolio construction process, with an estimated $50 trillion of assets being managed with some concern for ESG by 2025, according to Bloomberg Intelligence.

Many ESG investors feel that their approach to investing makes the world a better place and also will result in an improved expected Risk-adjusted Return on their capital. In the short run, it's possible that the flow of funds into assets that have high ESG ratings pushes up their prices, generating excess returns, and also that ESG corporate policies may improve earnings. However, in the long run, recognizing the highly competitive nature of the global marketplace, we wonder if either of these claims can hold.

We suspect that ESG investors will have little real and lasting impact on corporate behavior and will suffer subpar Risk-adjusted Returns due to less diversification and higher fees. Indeed, a 2022 study by Bradford Cornell of UCLA and Aswath Damodaran of NYU reviewed shareholder value created by firms with high and low ESG ratings—scores provided by professional rating agencies. Their conclusion: "Telling firms that being socially responsible will deliver higher growth, profits, and value is false advertising."[19]

Individual Stocks

Assessing the expected return and risk of individual companies is at best very difficult and in some cases probably impossible. Some investors convince themselves that relatively simple accounting ratios can be a good predictor of a single stock's expected return, but if that were reliably the case, stock-picking would be quite easy, contrary to extensive empirical evidence that it's not. Perhaps even more difficult than estimating the expected return of an individual stock is estimating its correlation to other stocks and assets being considered.

This is why returning to our guiding principle of large-scale market efficiency helps simplify our analysis. We know that the expected return on an individual stock should represent compensation for that part of the stock's risk that cannot be diversified away by holding it in combination with all other stocks in the market portfolio. This insight won't help us identify stocks that are over- or undervalued, but it does give us a starting point when considering investing in concentrated single stock positions, or when we wind up with large single stock positions through founding, working for, or having invested early in a very successful company.

The risk of individual companies tends to be substantially higher than the risk of a broad, market capitalization-weighted portfolio of many stocks. For the most part, we can bring the same ideas to estimating the risk of a single stock as we bring to estimating the risk of the broad market. In general, single stocks have annual volatilities that can be as low as that of the broad stock market or as high as five or more times the volatility of the broad market, especially for short periods. A high level of volatility generally implies that the asset price has positively asymmetric outcomes: it can go up a lot, but it can only go down to zero.

To get a more concrete idea of how big an effect this can be, in Exhibit 14.1 we show the probability distribution to a 5-year horizon for a stock that is highly volatile but also has a high return.[20] We can see that even though the stock has an expected return of 10% per annum, due to the high standard deviation of 75%, there is a 50% chance that its price finishes the holding period down more than 60%, and a 70% probability that it will finish below its starting price. And yet, the expected return is 10% because there is a 20% probability that its price finishes at a very high level, well above the 1.61 expected price.

One way to explain what's happening here is provided by the effect of volatility drag. While the stock is expected to rise 10% per year, the volatility drag at 75% volatility is pulling it down by 28% per year, resulting in a net downward trajectory of the median price of 18% per year, and hence the 50% chance that it is below 40% of its starting price. Concentrated portfolios of individual stocks can sometimes deliver tremendous returns, but their high volatility of returns and consequent high volatility drag is the very reason why the majority of US stocks have not beaten the return of T-bills over the past 100 years of stellar US stock market performance.[21]

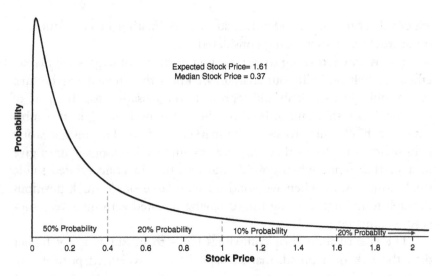

Exhibit 14.1   Stock Price Probability Distribution: 10% per Annum Expected Excess Return, 75% Annual Standard Deviation, 5-year Horizon

Case Study: Revisiting the All-in Tesla Investor

For the two years up to the end of 2021, the historic volatility of Tesla stock was 75% per annum. If you were close to 100% invested in Tesla for the long term because you believed Tesla had twice the expected excess return of the stock market, the probability that you would have more money than you started with would be only 22% to a 10-year horizon. Alternatively, if you kept a constant 10% of your total wealth in Tesla, which is about the optimal amount given our Base-Case degree of risk-aversion, then there's a 65% chance of your total wealth finishing with a gain over 10 years. Even if you believe Tesla has a 30% expected return, if you're all-in there's still just barely a 50% chance of being in the black to any horizon.

Of course, Tesla is by no means alone in being a highly volatile asset. Many other single stocks show similar or even higher variability, and many crypto assets are even more volatile than the most volatile stocks. Even with very high expected returns, being all-in with any one or a small collection of these super-high volatility assets implies accepting a pretty unpleasant distribution of potential outcomes.

Options

In Chapter 16 we discuss in some detail the difficulty in estimating fair value for listed equity options. Options specialists devote considerable resources to evaluating options prices, and competition among specialists should help to make the market fairly efficient. The zero-sum nature of the options market suggests it should not be viewed as an asset class (if it were an asset class, which side would be expected to generate the risk premium?) and is a further hint that individual investors should be skeptical of generating excess returns in this domain.

Special Situations and Near-risk-free "Arbitrage" Investments

Investors sometimes come across special investments that offer much higher quality returns than the big public market asset classes. It is useful to separate these opportunities into those that are non-scalable and those in which you could invest as much of your capital as you'd like to.

On a number of occasions, inflation-protected savings bonds issued by the US government, known as I-Bonds, have offered terms much more favorable than their liquid cousins, TIPS. However, the US Treasury limits how many I-Bonds purchasers can buy each year to $15,000 as of 2022.

A lesser known but fascinating example of a non-scalable special opportunity is referred to as the "odd lot" trade, which involves buying 99 shares or less of a company that is doing a tender offer at a price well above the recent market price, to buy back some of their outstanding shares. In general, the company honors in full all tenders by shareholders who own fewer than 100 shares, but for all other shareholders, the amount of shares accepted is prorated according to total demand for tender. This generally results in a very low-risk profit opportunity for anyone buying 99 shares of the company's stock before completion of the tender. However, for most wealthy investors, this opportunity won't move the needle on their portfolio.

Other examples of non-scalable but attractive investment opportunities have included buying stock in companies that permit dividends to be reinvested at a discount and making deposits in small mutually owned banks that are anticipated to convert to public ownership, allowing depositors to purchase equity on attractive terms. Another characteristic of these types of investment opportunities is that they are fairly labor-intensive and, hence, don't look nearly as attractive after some allowance is made for the investor's time in identifying, executing, and managing the trade.

Special situation trades that are scalable typically exhibit an attractive central case return, a relatively low normal risk level, a high cost of getting into and particularly out of the trade, and negative tail risk that is big and hard to quantify. Often the investments that seem like a sure thing have Base-Case returns that are high relative to normal volatility but low in absolute terms, and so investors feel they need to add leverage to get a high enough return on capital to make the trade worthwhile, which gives the negative tail risk all the more bite.

These sorts of opportunities usually arise at times of peak market turmoil, when the liquid and diversified public market investments are offering very attractive expected returns, without all the "hair." For example, in the darkest depths of the Global Financial Crisis, it was possible to buy investment grade corporate bonds and at the same time insure those bonds by entering into credit default swaps that would effectively make the package risk-free, as long as your bank counterparty did not default or renege on the transaction, which seemed like a relatively small risk at the time for banks like JP Morgan or Bank of America. This near-risk-free package was priced to generate a return of about 5% above T-Bills for a maximum of 5 years, or a shorter time if the corporate bond actually defaulted. This seemed like a tremendously attractive return to risk. But so did owning the global stock market at that time, and if an investor was near-fully invested, it would have made more sense to own equities than to be invested in this illiquid, complex, but very attractive investment earning a near-risk-free 5% extra return per year.

In general these investments have expected returns that are easy to estimate, but much attention needs to be paid to assessing the negative tail risk inherent in most of these situations. If something is mispriced, what stops it from being more mispriced? When it comes to relative value trades, it's hard to know, because when something is super attractive, it shouldn't exist to begin with. When a market situation shouldn't exist, trying to think about its risk is difficult. Once something is already somewhere it shouldn't be, then why can't it go anywhere else that it also shouldn't be? Once you've recognized that it's outside its rational boundaries, then anything is possible. It's very difficult to analyze the risk, especially the risk of leveraged trades involving short positions, where potential losses can be, in principle, unlimited.

Alternative Investments: Private Equity, Venture Capital, Hedge Funds, and Private Real Estate

Without relying on historical performance, it is difficult to estimate the expected return and risk of these investment products. That "past returns are not indicative of future results" makes us very cautious about a potential investment when the only way to assess it is to rely on historical performance.

For high marginal tax rate investors, one important consideration in evaluating these investments is that they tend to be highly tax inefficient, as in many cases management fees and other expenses cannot be deducted from income, they often generate short-term capital gains, and in general will not provide long-term deferral of capital gains. For example, a high income, New York City tax resident[†] would need to earn roughly a 17% pretax, pre-fee return on a hedge fund investment— with standard nondeductible management fees and expenses—to wind up with the same after-tax return as an investment in a broad stock market ETF with a 6% pretax return. Moving from New York City to a state with a zero income tax rate helps, but not much, reducing the 11% difference in required pretax, pre-fee returns by only 3%. It's a high hurdle for an investor, and that's just to break even with the low-fee, tax-efficient stock market investment.[22]

The financial press frequently reminds us of alternative investment managers who have delivered consistently stellar returns on a pretax basis. Perhaps they should be viewed more as the "exception that proves the rule." And that exceptionalism usually means that very few of these recognized star managers are open for investment to individual investors, even very high-net-worth ones.

Turning to the question of estimating risk, your authors can personally attest that some of these active, alternative strategies involve significant amounts of leverage, which logically should result in return distributions with fatter tails than generated by more diversified, long-only,

---

[†]Admittedly an increasingly rare category of investor.

unleveraged strategies. Proponents of alternative investments usually claim that they provide diversification benefits, but many alternatives, such as private equity and venture capital, are still basically equity investments. Some strategies, such as macro-funds and managed futures funds, have a stronger claim of having a low correlation with the overall performance of capital markets, but that should not be expected from the vast majority of assets in this space. Some observers, particularly researchers at AQR, have argued that the apparent lower risk of private, illiquid investments that result from "smoothed" periodic mark-to-market is actually a feature of these investments that some investors value, resulting in a low or even negative liquidity premium.[23]

Do You Know the Significance of 3.9 Purrrcent?

It was the summer of 1993, and I was sitting with two of my partners at LTCM in the lobby of the Helmsley Palace Hotel, discussing a sizable investment in our fund with a billionaire from Abu Dhabi. We had just explained to him that we thought the fund would have an annual expected return of 15%–20% with 15% volatility. There was a long silence, and then he asked ". . .do you know the significance of 3.9 purrrcent?" We looked at each other, stumped, and then he filled us in on his investing secret:

"Earn 3.9 purrrcent each month, and every 5 years, add another zero to your wealth! If you can earn 1% a month, why not earn 3.9%?"

Most billionaires get to where they are from enjoying a period of very high returns on their capital, such as the 60% annual rate of return that results from earning 3.9% per month. But finding an expected return of 60% per annum that doesn't involve taking a commensurate amount of risk through concentration or leverage, and which can bear a large amount of capital, is about as rare as finding pineapple on pizza in Italy. For every one billionaire who gets there from growing his or her capital at 3.9% per month with the typical ratio of return to risk available in the market, many more had their wealth absorbed by the high risk associated with reaching for those returns.

Commodities, Art, Collectibles, and Crypto

We are now squarely in the category of investments that do not generate significant positive cash flows that can be used to estimate their expected real returns (although some do have negative cash flows in the form of storage, insurance, and other holding costs). In the case of commodities such as oil or natural gas, where some entities must hold a vast amount of wealth in the form of reserves in the ground, there is an argument that they will want to sell future production at a discount to the expected price to reduce the risk they bear. This type of argument can be used to estimate a risk premium, but it's highly uncertain.

For other cases where the supply of a desirable asset is limited or fixed, such as gold, collectibles, or some cryptocurrencies, a case may be made that the price will track per capita income of the people who want to own it. We think per capita income growth in developed economies is likely to be 1% to 2% above inflation in the long run.

It certainly seems plausible that holding future oil should offer investors a risk premium, and that owning gold, art, or cryptocurrencies will generate a return that tracks per capita income growth of some segment of the population, or even more. But unfortunately, it is not possible to actually observe and quantify the cash flows associated with this expected return.

Building Your Multi-asset Portfolio

Premature optimization is the root of all evil.
　　　　　　—Donald Knuth, computer scientist, winner of the Turing Award,
　　　　　　　　　　　　and the father of the analysis of algorithms

All our discussion so far has been framed within the context of a two-asset world, with the main decision being how much of your savings to allocate to the risky asset—usually the broad equity market—with the residual invested in the safe asset, usually T-bills or TIPS. In practice, investors form their portfolios with far more than just one risky and one safe asset. In classical portfolio theory with well-behaved asset prices and the kind of utility preferences we've been assuming, we can use what's known as Tobin's separation theorem—a result that helped popularize index investing—to simplify the problem of choosing an optimal portfolio by *separating* the task into two easier-to-handle pieces:

1. Find the portfolio of risky assets with the highest Sharpe ratio (ratio of excess return to risk).
2. Find the optimal amount of that risky portfolio to own, based on your attitude toward risk, and keep the rest in the safe asset (or borrow if the optimum amount is greater than 100%).

The theorem implies that for any two investors with CRRA utility, their optimal mix of risky assets will be the same—they'll simply hold differing amounts of whatever risky portfolio has the highest Sharpe ratio. This insight, along with important contributions by Markowitz, Sharpe, Mossin, Treynor, and Lintner, paved the way to the CAPM, which we've already briefly discussed. Tobin summarized this "important and beautiful result" as "Don't put all your eggs in one basket," while Willem Buiter, in a review of Tobin's contributions added: ". . .and you will only need two baskets for all your eggs."[24]

Finding the risk-return optimal portfolio of all risky assets would be very challenging if we had to estimate the return distributions and correlations among all the thousands of individual public companies and other risky potential investments. But if we believe the market is fairly efficient, we can short-circuit making a direct calculation. In an efficient market, the capitalization-weighted portfolio of all risky assets is itself the best estimate of the risk-return optimal portfolio. Even though this result may not hold precisely for large major markets like global equities, there's good reason to believe it comes pretty close. It is very hard to create portfolios that are indisputably better than the market portfolio, and it's very difficult for active equity managers to consistently outperform. The concept of the market portfolio being the only one that all investors can hold at the same time is a very good framework for thinking about investing.

In cases where the assets in a portfolio are not well described as having a normal return distribution or you have a non-standard utility function or a strong aversion to leverage or shorting, the assumptions of the Tobin separation theorem will not apply, and the two problems of composition and sizing need to be solved together to find the portfolio weights that maximize your Expected Utility. Such analysis requires the use of portfolio optimization tools, which often face a few common problems:

- The input distributions and parameters are difficult to estimate.
- Results are often not very robust to parameter uncertainty. Small changes in inputs can cause large changes in the optimal portfolio.
- Results can take the form of corner solutions, which are extreme and unrealistic.

Fortunately, there has been a lot of progress in developing better-behaved optimization techniques that can mitigate these issues. The optimal portfolios suggested by these enhanced optimizers tend to be less susceptible to negative selection bias and parameter estimation errors. As we've discussed already, Expected Utility is usually quite flat in the vicinity of optimality, which means a small sacrifice in Risk-adjusted Return can give us a portfolio that is more balanced and robust than the unconstrained, theoretically optimal portfolio. Of course, the garbage-in/garbage-out principle still applies, and even when using sophisticated optimization techniques, the onus is still fully on the user to provide sensible inputs.

Taking the problem to the full multi-period, intertemporal setting of the integrated lifetime consumption and portfolio choice framework that we described in Chapter 9 becomes computationally complex, but feasible with a few well-chosen simplifying assumptions.

Connecting the Dots: The "Smell Test"

In early 2016, we asked 60 friends and colleagues from the finance industry, most of whom were high-net-worth taxable US investors, the following question:

What risk-free, inflation-protected, after-tax return would you be willing to accept on the totality of your wealth for the rest of your life in order to completely and forever forgo any other investment opportunity?

The answers we received were almost entirely within a range of 1%–4% per annum, with the lowest required return at 0%, and the highest, which was quite an outlier, at 8%. The average was about 2.5%.

At the time of the survey, 30-year US TIPS offered a pretax real yield of about 1%.[†] We would expect the answers to such a survey to vary over time, as safe and risky returns offered by available assets fluctuate, but we think this survey offers a useful data point to evaluate the assumptions you make in building your best portfolio and estimating its risk-adjusted, after-tax return.

[†]In the early days of the TIPS market in 1999, when they offered a yield of around 4%, Warren Buffett's Berkshire Hathaway was one of the largest buyers, and he reportedly said that he'd be willing to replace his entire portfolio of risky assets with these long-term US Treasury bonds with a guaranteed return of 4% above inflation. At the time, the TIPS market was not big and liquid enough for him to act on this view, and yields on TIPS dropped sharply by the end of 2000.

15

No Place to Hide: Investing in a World with No Safe Asset

Your Personalized Standard of Living Index

In discussing how to estimate the return and risk of various potential investments in the previous chapter, we focused on *real returns*, which means returns relative to a broad measure of inflation such as US Consumer Price Inflation (CPI). In a perfect world, each of us would have our own personalized inflation index based on our own individual spending pattern. A good way to think about this is that if your spending was constant over time when measured in terms of this index, then your standard of living would also remain constant.

Many people feel that if their spending just kept up with the CPI index, their standard of living would actually be falling over time. You might feel this way for a number of good reasons. Most obviously, the CPI index may not reflect the things that you spend your money on. It also may be a biased estimator if your spending patterns don't change in line with the way the basket of goods and services is revised over time. Some people feel that the quality adjustments built into CPI, technically known as "hedonic adjustments," are too large and result in inflation being underestimated. Finally, many people have a gut feeling that if their spending isn't growing comparably to those around them, their standard of living is falling.

Over long periods, it becomes clear that if your spending just kept up with CPI, you would probably feel a dramatic decrease in your welfare. For example, if an adult spending the average amount in the United States in 1900 kept spending the same amount *adjusted for CPI inflation* each year, then in 2022 that (very old) person would be spending just $5,000 per year in 2022 dollars. She would undoubtedly conclude that her standard of living had declined over this long period, given average US per-capita spending is more than 10 times higher, at $55,000.[1]

Calculating your personalized, backward-looking inflation rate can be a valuable exercise in giving a sense for the relationship between the inflation in your personal "basket" relative to broader measures such as CPI. Less personalized, but easier to come by, is a standard of living index of families of your income bracket.[2] The expected mix and timing of your spending—personal, intergenerational, or philanthropic—might suggest a blend of different standard of living indexes, which may also reflect the currency mix of all forms of your expected spending.

From Personalized Standard of Living to Personalized Risk-free Asset

We can now define an asset as being "risk-free" if it has a guaranteed, fixed real return relative to your personalized standard of living index.

Investing in such an asset, or portfolio of such assets depending on their cash flow structure, allows you to turn your current wealth into a risk-free, constant stream of payments that will let you maintain the same standard of living over time. Let's call that risk-free, constant stream of payments a Constant Standard of Living annuity, which we'll refer to as a CSL annuity. Economists would say that this CSL annuity is your *"numéraire,"* the benchmark relative to which you should measure the performance of all other assets. Using the CSL annuity as our numéraire has another benefit. Rather than denominating our wealth in dollars, we can think of it as an annuity equivalent, which is to say how much annual payment we'd get if we put our wealth into the annuity.

For the discussion that follows, we'll keep things relatively simple by assuming your standard of living index is equal to CPI plus 1.5% per annum. So the CSL annuity indexed to CPI + 1.5% is our pro forma risk-free asset, but we can see that TIPS will look pretty risk-free too (setting aside tax issues). The expected return of TIPS is conventionally stated as a real yield, which is the return relative to CPI if you own the bond to maturity. Let's say that TIPS are trading at a real yield of 1.5%. Since your standard of living index is CPI + 1.5%, we can simply restate the real yield of TIPS as paying your standard of living index + 0%. The cash flows of a single TIPS issue won't look exactly like an annuity, but a portfolio of TIPS can. Their market price may be bouncing around by 1% or more each day, but in terms of the metric we really care about, they are (nearly) risk-free.

How Safe Are T-Bills, Really?

While it's true that the nominal value of T-bills doesn't go up or down much day to day, they are dramatically more risky once you focus on their performance relative to the risk-free CSL annuity. Let's say you had $1 million of wealth in 1997, equivalent to a $50,000 per annum 30-year CSL annuity at then prevailing rates. Exhibit 15.1 looks at how your annuity-equivalent wealth evolved over time had you invested solely in T-bills.

Exhibit 15.1   US T-bills Are Far from Risk-free: Constant Standard of Living
30-year Annuity in 1997 Dollars (1997–2022)

It's clear that in these terms, T-bills are far from risk-free. The sharp
downward trajectory in annuity-equivalent wealth results from a combination of real yields falling from just under 4% to about 1.5% over the
period, and also of T-bill returns falling way behind your standard of
living index. If you were invested in T-bills over the whole period, the
standard of living your wealth could support was cut by more than half.
Ouch! And rubbing salt in the wound, you experienced volatility of 12%
per annum, about three-quarters that of the US stock market. This loss
of value was a genuine and significant erosion of the standard of living
your wealth would have been able to support.

Prior to the inception of the TIPS market in 1997, the notion of
a CSL annuity would have been purely hypothetical. Following their
introduction, numerous articles from experts in household finance have
asserted that long-term investors should adopt the CSL annuity perspective to reach sound personal financial decisions.[3] These articles suggest
that investors should adopt TIPS as their minimum risk asset in lieu of
T-bills and other cash-like investments. It is interesting to note that if
investors were to embrace this shift in perspective more broadly, the
long-term TIPS market would have to vastly expand from its current
size of $500 billion, which is less than 2% of the total United States
Treasury and investment grade bond market.

Equities: A Sheep in Wolf's Clothing?

We normally think about the expected return of the stock market as a real return, expressed relative to CPI. As we've discussed many times already, we like using the cyclically adjusted earnings yield of the stock market as our forecast for its long-term real return. Restating that expected return in terms of your standard of living index is as simple as it was for TIPS—just subtract 1.5% from the real return relative to CPI. So if we see global equities offering an expected real return of CPI + 5%, we can restate that as an expected return 3.5% above your standard of living index.

When we measure the long-term realized volatility of the stock market, we get estimates for the annualized standard deviation of returns in the 16%–20% range for most broad markets in major currencies over long horizons, as we discussed in Chapter 14. But what if we thought about investing in the stock market from the perspective of maintaining a constant standard of living, i.e., using our CSL annuity as our numéraire? How much would that change our assessment of stock market risk?

It's hard to know the exact inflation-adjusted payments you should expect from a long-term stock market investment. But one estimate you could use is the cyclically adjusted earnings yield, which suggests that the long-term CSL spending that can be supported by the stock market is directly connected to the average earnings you expect your stocks to generate over time. With this in mind, we calculated changes in US stock market earnings, measured as average, inflation-adjusted earnings over each decade, and compared those changes in earnings to 10-year real stock market returns for the past 140 years.[4] What we found is that earnings have been about one-third as volatile as stock prices: 7% annual volatility for earnings and 20% for market prices. This means that were we to invest in equities, our CSL annuity-equivalent wealth certainly wouldn't look risk-free, but would be much less volatile than equities conventionally appear to be. Note that this difference in perspective is distinct from having a short-term versus long-term investment horizon. When we compare changes in earnings versus changes in stock prices, in both cases we are looking at a relatively long 10-year horizon.

The recognition that stock prices are much more volatile than long-term earnings is not new. It was presented in 1980 by Robert Shiller in his seminal paper, "Do Stock Prices Move Too Much to be Justified by Subsequent Changes in Dividends?," and it is also at the heart of the long-debated "equity risk premium puzzle" that we discuss in Chapter 20.[5] These days, most market observers believe that stock market volatility arises as much (or possibly more) from changes in how people value future earnings, as from changes in the expected future earnings themselves.[6]

It's easy to read too much into this historical analysis, but one interpretation is that equities are intrinsically a bit like the CSL annuity we've been discussing: they provide an indefinite stream of earnings, which naturally adjust, at least somewhat, to CPI inflation. Thus, if you're focused on your long-term spending power and view a risk-free CSL annuity as your benchmark, you may also find equities considerably less risky than their price volatility would suggest.

Recall from Chapter 6 in our discussion of Risk-adjusted Returns that a good rule of thumb is that going half-way to your optimal allocation gives you about three-quarters of the maximum Risk-adjusted Return. This means that even if you don't increase your allocation to equities as much as suggested by the most sanguine assessment of their riskiness, you may still be getting much of the benefit of equities being less risky when assessed against your CSL benchmark.

Before closing this discussion of equity risk, we want to acknowledge the very severe limitations of using US experience in predicting the future. It is just one path that history could have taken, and in the above analysis it only provides us with 14 observations of 10-year average earnings.[†] Taking a long-term view, we must recognize that any given stock market is always in some danger of a total wipe-out in both price and earnings, as experienced by investors in Russian and Chinese stock markets in the twentieth century. The best protections against this important, existential risk are global diversification, the avoidance of leverage, and the sensible sizing of your global stock market risk against your personal benchmark.

What If There's No Perfectly Safe Asset?

Worries of unsustainable public policies leading to debasement or default—through inflation, taxation or repudiation—have sapped confidence in the traditional safe assets of debt issued by the United States and other large, rich countries.[‡] Beyond these issues, even US government-backed TIPS are not risk-free for investors whose personal standard of living index is different from CPI, nor for taxable investors who are subject to a tax wedge that varies with the level of inflation. But fear not—we'll see that you can still use the Expected Utility framework to construct your portfolio in a way that acknowledges the absence of a truly risk-free asset you can buy.

Instead of the common practice of trying to construct an ersatz risk-free asset from a set of available assets that don't really fit the bill—such as equities, real estate, commodities, possibly cryptocurrency—you can instead simply treat the opportunity set as consisting entirely of risky

---

[†]The 95% confidence interval on the sample standard deviation measured from a sample size of 14 observations is about +/-40% of the sample standard deviation. If we believed that we were drawing from a stationary distribution (which we don't), the 95% confidence interval on our estimates of the volatility of earnings and stock prices would be roughly 4%–10%, and 12%–28%, respectively.

[‡]Matt Levine's excellent description of systemic risks in safe assets: "Safe assets are much riskier than risky ones. This is, I think the deep lesson of the 2008 financial crisis. . . . Systemic risks live in safe assets. Equity-like assets— tech stocks, Luna, Bitcoin—are risky, and everyone knows they're risky, and everyone accepts the risk. . . . And so most people arrange their lives in such a way that, if their stocks or Bitcoin go down by 20%, they are not ruined. . . . On the other hand safe assets—AAA mortgage securities, bank deposits, stable coins—are not supposed to be risky, and people rely on them being worth what they say they're worth, and when people lose even a little bit of confidence in them they crack completely" (Money Stuff, 2022).

assets and optimize the real Risk-adjusted Return of the risky portfolio, using your personalized spending index as the deflator. In practice, this approach to portfolio construction in the absence of a truly risk-free asset is flexible enough to handle an arbitrarily large number of different assets and a broad range of assumptions about possible outcomes in asset prices, including discontinuous jumps as well as changing risk and correlation patterns over time.

The impact of this change in perspective will depend largely on the starting point of your asset allocation. If you have low to moderate risk-aversion with a high allocation to equities and other patently risky assets, treating the safest assets as being risky—but still the least risky of the available options—is likely to have a modest impact on optimal portfolio weights. But if you have a high level of risk-aversion and are mostly allocated to the safest assets to begin with, explicitly accounting for their risk can have a significant impact.

How Your Personal Standard of Living Index Impacts Your Optimal Spending

Let's say that before reading this chapter, you had been thinking about the expected Risk-adjusted Return of your portfolio relative to inflation measured by CPI, but now you've decided that your personalized standard of living index is CPI + 1.5%. To keep things simple, we'll make the assumption that this change does not alter your portfolio composition much, and so the expected Risk-adjusted Return on your portfolio expressed relative to your personalized index is now 1.5% lower. Using the optimal spending policy we introduced in Chapter 9, we can see that if you're spending "like you'll live forever," your optimal spending rate will decrease by $1.5\% - \dfrac{1.5\%}{\gamma}$, and if your spending horizon is shorter, the rate at which you'll be annuitizing your wealth will decrease by that same amount. As usual, γ represents your level of risk-aversion, which we've been assuming is 2.

Connecting the Dots

Our approach to saving is all wrong: We need to think about monthly income, not net worth.

—Robert C. Merton, *Harvard Business Review* (2014)

Choosing the right objective can profoundly impact the decisions we make and the outcomes we get. We've seen that T-bills and similar cash-like assets are significantly more risky in terms of a CSL annuity than they appear when viewed in plain dollars. Given their generally low expected real return, this makes cash-like assets look pretty unappealing to hold in excess of amounts needed to cover near-term expenses and contingencies. In contrast, equities may be more attractive if we believe the long-term expected earnings stream they generate makes them somewhat like a long-term, real annuity.

In the nineteenth century and earlier, when wealth was harder to value and less liquid than it is today, it was more common to think about wealth as an annual flow rather than an upfront value. While today it is more straightforward to measure your investment portfolio as a current lump sum, a significant fraction of most peoples' financial resources— their human capital, future social security and pension benefits—are much more readily thought of as long-term real annuities. If you see your wealth as a reservoir for long-term future consumption, we think it's well worth the extra mental effort to think about all your financial resources and decisions with the CSL annuity perspective in mind.

16

What About Options?

Options trading volume grew 20-fold over the two decades to the end of 2022 and doubled in just the last few years of that period.[†] For the first time, the volume of options trading in individual stocks and stock index futures—about $1.25 trillion per day—has matched the volume of trading in the actual stocks and stock index futures on which they are based.[1] Some observers have gone so far as to suggest that, in this brave new world, options are the primary trading venue and stocks should be viewed as derivatives of the options market.

[†] In this chapter, we draw heavily on an article we coauthored with Vladimir Ragulin, published in *The Journal of Derivatives*, 2022, and we thank the *Journal* for their permission to do so.

Judging by this explosive growth in individual investor use of stock options, particularly since the advent of commission-free trading for retail brokerage accounts, it seems that many investors have concluded that options are a valuable addition to, or even warrant a central role in, their investment portfolios. While hundreds of books proffer instruction on how to make money trading options, many books on personal finance do not contain any mention of options, including those written by such well-regarded experts as Jack Bogle, Charles Ellis, and Burton Malkiel.[2] In this chapter, we try to bridge this gap by addressing the question of whether the most popular options strategies make sense for individual investors, assessing them through a framework that accounts for both return *and* risk.

In contrast to investing in the broad stock market, an example of a positive-sum game, every buy or sell of an option has someone on the other side. And so there can be no net wealth creation from options; like individual stock-picking (discussed in Chapter 14), options trading is a zero-sum activity. In fact, taking account of trading costs, most observers see these as negative-sum activities in aggregate, where individual investors have an edge only if there is someone on the other side willing to leave money on the table. More realistically, any value for individual investors in trading options is likely to be found in a different dimension—that of reshaping their investment risk.

Of course, one perspective on whether all this options trading makes sense for individual investors is to argue that anything people do voluntarily must be in accord with their preferences and therefore is just fine. We take a less reductive approach, and start by defining what it means for options to "make sense." Options can have a complex impact on an investor's portfolio, transforming the expected return, risk, and shape of the distributions of outcomes. As we do with all decisions involving uncertain outcomes, we'll say that a particular options strategy warrants a place in your portfolio if it increases your Expected Utility.

Economists were doing a lot of thinking about options right around the time of the birth of the modern stock-options markets in the early 1970s. The best known of the theoretical breakthroughs is the Black-Scholes-Merton model of options pricing, published in 1973 and honored with the Nobel prize in 1997. There were also developments on the higher-level questions of what role options should and would play in improving the welfare of society. There was general agreement that the existence and trading of options would in theory make everyone better off by providing more and higher quality information—through the wisdom of crowds—which would increase economic efficiency through an improved allocation of resources. Options were thought to make markets more "complete," which is a state of optimal sharing of risks among all members of society. It was thought that options would improve the welfare of individuals by allowing them to construct custom-tailored portfolios that gave them just the payoffs they wanted in all different states of the world.

In this chapter, we'll see that when options are used to transform investment outcomes into a pattern that better fits your personal preferences, they can merit a place in your portfolio. However, we find that the benefit of such transformation is highly sensitive to risk-tolerance and tends to be most material for highly-leveraged investors. For investors with more typical risk preferences, any improvement in welfare is quite modest.

We'll start with a focus on individual investor portfolios and how we can use Expected Utility to evaluate and compare strategies. We'll begin with the continuous-time setting of Black-Scholes-Merton, wherein options can be perfectly replicated and, therefore, do not add any value other than as a tactical tool. Once the classical assumptions are relaxed, options become useful. But the story gets complicated, since each investor's desired allocation now depends on the individual's risk preferences and on the option market price relative to fair value. We'll work through several case studies and evaluate the most popular option-based strategies available to individual investors.

Until the final section, our analysis focuses on stock options, as this is the area of primary relevance to retail investors. However, much of what we say about the appropriate decision framework holds equally for options within other asset classes, such as fixed income, foreign exchange, and commodities.

Using Expected Utility to Measure Whether Options Are Making Us Better Off

Expected Utility is a particularly useful paradigm to apply to assessing options, as their inherently nonlinear payoffs make the use of simpler metrics like the Sharpe ratio misleading. We'll say that a particular use of options makes an investor better off if it increases Expected

Utility relative to the best alternative without options. We will calculate Expected Utility by simulating the outcomes of each strategy across all possible scenarios, converting the investor's terminal wealth to utility, and weighing each scenario by the probability of it occurring. We'll continue to assume Base-Case risk-aversion for our illustrations, but we'll also explore how other risk preferences can change our conclusions.

Two-asset Case with Continuous Rebalancing: Fair Options Don't Improve Investor Welfare

Let's start with the simplest set of assumptions in a world where there are only two investment options: a safe asset (e.g., TIPS) and a risky asset (e.g., stocks). We'll begin by assuming the stock market follows a random walk without any jumps and that its expected risk and return are constant.[3] With our usual assumptions as displayed in Table 16.1, you would optimally allocate about 60% of your wealth to the risky asset in order to maximize your Expected Utility.[†]

It's also the case—and this is very important—that with these assumptions, you will want to keep that same 60% of wealth invested in the risky asset as the value of your portfolio goes up and down, which is a product of having CRRA utility plus the constant expected risk and return of the stock market.

In this framework, fairly priced options can be perfectly replicated by continuous trading.[4] Hence, they don't add value for investors who can achieve the same outcome by continuously (or frequently) rebalancing their portfolio. In the case of wanting to maintain 60% of wealth in the risky asset, when its price goes down, you'll need to buy more of it to maintain the 60% allocation and vice versa when the asset goes up.

Table 16.1 Base-Case Investor Assumptions

Equities Expected Arithmetic Return	5%
Equities Annual Volatility	20%
Safe Asset Return	0%
Investor CRRA Risk-Aversion	2

[†]62.5% to be precise.

You could sell a small amount of out-of-the-money puts and calls to take care of the rebalancing automatically, but the amounts would be small—and it's hard to see how that adds much or any value, unless rebalancing costs are otherwise very high or the options are overpriced (a topic we'll return to later). For investors who want to hold more than 100% of their wealth in the risky asset, the same reasoning applies—except that in this case, to keep their allocation to equities constant, they will need to sell equities when they go down in price and buy more when they go up. Options can be used to automate the rebalancing process. There are two important takeaways from this analysis:

1. You can pursue many strategies that involve trading in stocks and options, but adding options to the list of instruments does not expand the possible set of final payoffs, since options can be replicated by dynamic trading.
2. If you have CRRA utility such that your optimal allocation to equities is less than 100% of wealth—and you want to maintain this optimal allocation—then you would need to sell equities after a rally and buy them after a sell-off. It is possible to approximate this behavior with options, but in this case you would be a small *seller* of options, not a buyer. This result is counter to the natural intuition of many investors, who feel that protecting their downside is something inherently worth doing, especially if protection can be purchased at a fair price. We will discuss portfolio protection strategies later in the chapter. Of course, this result requires some pretty stringent and relatively unrealistic assumptions (that we'll relax in a moment), but it's a very useful jumping off point.

No Dynamic Rebalancing: Fair Options Can Add Value, but Not Much

In practice, investors don't rebalance their portfolios continuously or even that frequently. Easing up on the assumption of continuous rebalancing kills two birds with one stone, as it also allows us to explore the impact of jumps in asset prices. We know from experience that financial assets can effectively gap up or down by 5%, 10%, or even 20% over the course of a few days, not to mention the 22% drop in the US stock market on October 19, 1987.

Let's assume that you can rebalance your portfolio only once each year. Now you would find it optimal to include options in your portfolio, so that their nonlinear payoffs approximate the portfolio rebalancing that you are no longer doing. We'll consider two cases: Base-Case risk-aversion, with a 60% optimal equity allocation, and a quite risk-tolerant case using leverage to hold 125% of wealth in equities.[5]

We assume fairly priced 1-year put options struck 10% out-of-the-money, and no transactions costs or taxes.[6] If you optimally want 60% in equities, the optimal allocation to options is negative, in that you would want to sell options in order to get closer to replicating the constant allocation to equities that you want to maintain. It's the opposite way around for the levered case, where you want to buy options to help keep exposure to equities as close to 125% of wealth as you can.[7] The total amount of options used is relatively small in both cases, which is a hint that they're not generating significant value in either case.

We can quantify the contribution of the options to each investor's welfare by comparing Expected Utility, which we'll express as Risk-adjusted Return, with and without options. Exhibit 16.1 shows the increase in portfolio Risk-adjusted Returns from having access to the options markets, plotted against the desired allocation to equities in the absence of options. We've highlighted the 60% and 125% allocations, which are the two cases on which we've been focused.

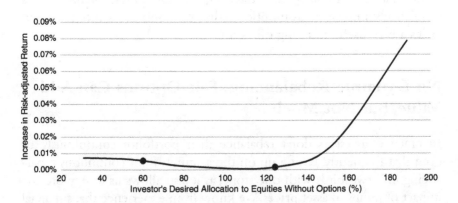

Exhibit 16.1 Contribution of Puts Versus Portfolio Leverage: Increase in Risk-adjusted Return for Optimal Portfolios With Versus Without Put Options

The improvement is small over the range of risk-preferences and optimal allocations we consider. With 60% in equities, the RAR increase is just 0.01% per annum. Notice that the value added by options goes to zero at 100% desired allocation. This is because if you want to maintain a 100% allocation you don't need to rebalance, and hence there's no benefit from options. Even if you wanted to have 200% of wealth in equities, the contribution of options to Risk-adjusted Return is on the order of 0.1% per annum. However, despite the small pickup in RAR, call options may warrant a place in a leverage-seeking investor's portfolio if they are the most cost-effective source of leverage (see Chapter 13 on human capital for more discussion).

Options as Portfolio Insurance

It's accepted wisdom that buying insurance on one's home makes sense for most families, even though the insurance is priced well above the insurance company's expected payout. The insurance company has to cover costs and a profit margin, so if the probability of your house being destroyed by fire or some other cause is 0.1% per annum, the insurance company will charge you, say, 0.2% (or more) of the value of your home. Indeed, the conventional wisdom is consistent with an Expected Utility analysis using Base-Case risk-aversion. You should choose to buy home insurance, even if priced at two times fair value, as long as the value of your home represents 50% or more of your total wealth.[†]

Then why are we finding that, even with fairly priced options, if you want to have 60% of wealth in equities then not only do you not want to buy Portfolio Insurance, but on the contrary, you want to be a *seller* of options? The answer lies primarily in our assumptions for stock market behavior.[‡] If stock market returns are normally distributed with

---

[†] For individuals with a mortgage obligation, the lender will usually require the borrower to take out insurance on the home. There are probably quite a few wealthy families who should be self-insuring their homes, as rebuilding them after a total loss would represent well under 50% of total wealth. It has been widely reported elsewhere that for almost everyone, buying insurance on home appliances and the like doesn't make sense, i.e., it decreases one's Expected Utility.

[‡] The shape of the investor's utility function can also change the conclusion from our Base Case, but we think the more likely explanation lies in assumptions of stock market dynamics.

no jumps, then selling options is a convenient substitute for the dynamic rebalancing you expect to do as the market goes up and down. However, if you believe that, like your home, the stock market can "burn down," and if insurance against that is available and priced at a similar mark-up to home insurance, then you will want to buy that insurance.[†] Let's examine these two "ifs" more closely.

The first "if" concerns whether the stock market can "burn down." History suggests the answer is yes: the US market dropped almost 90% in the 3 years from June 30, 1932. Stock markets in other countries have experienced declines of greater than 90%, and some—such as the Russian and Chinese stock markets—effectively burned all the way down to the ground. This represents a realistic departure from our earlier assumption that "the stock market follows a geometric random walk without any jumps and its expected risk and return are constant."

The second "if" is harder to answer in the affirmative. Home insurance pays out when an event—such as a fire—destroys the value of a home, but it doesn't pay out when the value of a home declines due to changes in market pricing. It is not practical with standard, liquid put options to buy protection on one's stock portfolio against a 90% or greater decline without also effectively paying for protection against much smaller and more likely declines. As we've already seen, with Base-Case risk-aversion, if anything, you would want to sell a small amount of protection against the normal variability in the stock market.

You could, in principle, buy put options struck, say, 70% out-of-the-money, feeling that those options would only pay out in the scenario you want to protect against. However, in practice, such options are not actively traded, and it is very difficult to know how much extra you are paying for this insurance compared to the price at the true odds. With home insurance, it is possible to get an idea of the fair price by looking at statistics on what fraction of homes burn down each year, or looking at the accounts of property and casualty insurance companies. No such parallel exists when evaluating insurance on a stock portfolio. Further-more, the insurance company can diversify the risk of individual houses,

---

[†]Two other important differences are (1) a home is both an investment and a consumption good, and for many families, there's very little flexibility in terms of the amount of housing they need to consume, and (2) it's generally not possible for an individual to sell a part of their family home if they feel their allocation to residential real estate is too high. Whereas they can easily sell a fraction of their stock portfolio at any time and at a low cost.

so its cost of bearing the risk is lower than that of an individual. For the stock market, such cross-sectional diversification of hazards by those offering the "insurance" is not possible.[†]

But let's imagine that you could buy insurance on your stock portfolio, structured like home insurance, that would cover your full losses only if the decline were greater than 70%, and let's say the probability of such a decline is 1% per annum. If such insurance were fairly priced, and if you had Base-Case risk-aversion, you would want to buy it, as it would increase your Expected Utility. Even if it were priced at 1.75 times the chance of occurrence, you would still want to buy the insurance—although the improvement to expected welfare would be modest, at an increase in RAR of about 0.05% per annum. However, if it were priced at three times the fair odds, you would have higher Expected Utility by not buying it. The key assumption is the one-in-a-hundred chance of a 70% or greater decline in the market, which represents a fat, but hard to say if fat enough, tail to the distribution.

Buying Options Helps If Equities Become Less Attractive After a Drop

Insuring one's stock portfolio against a near-total decline in value isn't the only way in which buying put options can increase Expected Utility. If owning equities is expected to be less attractive after a decline, and you do not want to frequently rebalance your portfolio, buying put options can increase welfare. There are three ways in which equities can become less attractive conditional on a price drop: if their riskiness goes up,[‡] if their expected return goes down, or if your risk-aversion goes up.[8] It is reasonable to expect one or more of these three to occur when equities go down, and it's possible to model and quantify the value of buying options to automate the reduction in equity exposure that you'd naturally desire, but in most cases, we don't see options adding much value for most investors.

[†]Buying very far out-of-the-money put options as Portfolio Insurance has the further problem that when you "win" there has been a disaster, and you should rightly worry about whether you'll be paid on your insurance.

[‡]One simple model that suggests this behavior assumes that constant volatility of corporate assets feeds through to higher equity volatility at lower total asset levels through the effect of leverage.

Many investors, including value investors like Warren Buffett, believe that normally when the market declines, its long-term expected return goes up. This is consistent with the idea that when the market goes down, it is partly due to bad news about future corporate earnings and dividends and partly due to investors demanding a higher expected return to own equities. To the extent that investors believe this is the primary way in which the expected return of the stock market evolves over time, *selling* options on their stock portfolios will make sense, expressing this view by either selling put options struck below market (to increase their equity allocation on dips), or by selling call options struck above market (to reduce their equity allocation in "bubbles"). But again, using options to simply automate portfolio rebalancing that you can do yourself does not usually represent a significant source of welfare improvement.

How Can We Tell If Options Are Fairly Priced?

We've so far mostly assumed that options are fairly priced, and under that assumption, we haven't found a lot of reasons for investors to make much use of options. By fairly priced, we mean that the price of the option is such that an option-specialist trader expects to break even by taking a position in the option and dynamically hedging that option to expiration, assuming zero trading frictions along the way.

So, how can you figure out whether options are fairly priced?

First, let's consider the supply and demand of options that provide Portfolio Insurance. As we've just seen, most investors will want to buy these options, if they are not too expensive relative to their fair price. Given this natural demand, it is likely that option specialists will be net sellers of these options, hoping to make a profit by dynamically hedging them until they expire. These options traders have costs they need to cover and profit they want to make for risking their capital, just like insurance companies. But, unlike with home insurance, these traders can't diversify their risk through selling insurance on many distinct houses. Nor are the data they have on what the market might do as stable and predictive as the data insurance companies have on the risk of fire, hurricanes, and floods. It therefore is logical to expect options specialists to offer stock market disaster insurance at a pretty large premium to its fair price.

The second perspective we can take is historical. For options, the record is relatively short—and for financial markets in general, the past is not necessarily indicative of the future. But such as it is, history does support the hypothesis that options on the stock market are generally expensive, which suggests that out-of-the-money puts are expensive as well. For example, over the 10 years to the end of 2021, the average value of the VIX index of stock option implied volatility has been 3.6% higher than the relevant realized volatility.[9] Our simple backtest also agrees with the majority view among academics that, over a long-term cycle, options are priced somewhat rich to fair value.[10]

There has been much heated debate about whether it is possible to buy stock market insurance at a fair or even cheap price. There are a number of purveyors of "tail hedging" investment strategies who contend that they do provide Portfolio Insurance at a discount to its fair value.[11] But other experts argue it's more likely that stock market insurance is priced at a premium to fair value.[12] Also, for investors who care more about the risk of long-term underperformance than of short-term gap moves, evidence suggests that trend-following strategies have been able to provide effective stock portfolio protection at much lower cost.[†]

A limited backtest over the 30 years from 1991 to the end of 2021 comparing a strategy of being 100% invested in the US stock market plus owning 2% out-of-the-money one-month puts versus a simpler strategy of keeping 50% in the stock market and 50% in T-bills found the strategy with puts generates a lower return over the period, with higher risk and a lower Sharpe ratio.[‡] There are some periods over which the strategy with puts would have generated a smaller drawdown, but the maximum drawdown for the two strategies was almost the same. Overall, the historical record isn't positive for the put-buying strategy, which is not surprising given our discussion so far.

Putting all this together, we are somewhat skeptical that buying stock market insurance through out-of-the-money put options is likely to materially improve the welfare of Base-Case investors who want to

---

[†] In fact, it is possibly at a negative cost, in that trend-following strategies may offer a positive expected return and portfolio protection at the same time. Of course, this would be an example of the proverbial free lunch, which should be very rare and fleeting, if it exists at all. See Ilmanen et al. (2021).

[‡] We chose 50% in stocks as that is roughly (48% was the exact figure) the average exposure to the market from a portfolio of long 100% stocks plus long 100% 2% out-of-the-money one month put options.

have the majority (but not all) of their savings invested in equities. However, for investors who are attracted to larger, leveraged allocations to the stock market—due either to being less risk-averse or more bullish on the expected attractiveness of stocks—buying options, even at quite a large premium to fair value, can improve their Expected Utility.

If They're Expensive, Why Not a Seller Be?

Many popular financial products and strategies enhance portfolio yields through selling call or put options.[13] Examples include covered-call writing strategies, reverse convertibles, dual-currency deposits, range accrual notes, and US mortgage-backed securities. The colorful bond investor Bill Gross actively employed selling interest rate options in his PIMCO Total Return Fund. Warren Buffet sold large amounts of long-dated equity index puts in the midst of the 2008 Global Financial Crisis. Does the Expected Utility framework support such investing for individual investors, or is it at best only suitable for large and sophisticated financial institutions?

A good starting point is to recall that when you don't want to buy something, it does not automatically follow that you should want to take the opposite position and short it. Risk, trading costs, and asymmetric information are three reasons why there should naturally be a range of prices for an asset over which you want to be neither a buyer nor a seller.

If you believe that the expected return on equities tends to go up when equities fall in price, you may want to sell puts on the market to automate your rebalancing intentions. If options are expensive to fair value, then this can provide an improvement in welfare. However, if you believe that a combination of cyclically adjusted earnings yield, momentum, and similar metrics are useful indicators of market attractiveness, vanilla options are unlikely to be a good match for a dynamic approach based on these signals. Direct portfolio rebalancing gives you full control over your asset allocation decisions, whereas trying to approximate a sensible dynamic asset allocation strategy with options leaves market exposure over time at the mercy of particular strikes and expiry dates.

A strategy of selling put options delivers less time diversification compared to a constant and comparable exposure to equities without options. For example, a portfolio that has a 100% allocation to stocks for 6 months of the year and 0% allocation for the other 6 months has about 40% more risk than a portfolio with a constant 50% in stocks for the entire year. Over the course of a year, the risk from the market exposure generated from selling short-dated, near-at-the-money put options is about 25% higher than the risk from a constant allocation to equities with the same average exposure. This is a significant hurdle for this strategy to overcome to deliver a higher Risk-adjusted Return than a constant allocation to equities.

As a useful benchmark for a put-selling strategy, we can look at the historical performance of the CBOE PUTY Index, which tracks performance of a passive strategy of writing 2% out-of-the-money puts on a monthly basis while keeping premium proceeds and the collateral invested in T-bills. This is the same index that we used (although in the opposite direction) in the backtest we discussed earlier that looked at the performance of being long the stock market protected with these one month, 2% out-of-the-money put options.

The comparable strategy without options would be to keep 50% (roughly the time average beta of the put-selling strategy in our sample) of wealth in the S&P 500 and the rest in T-bills, since this gives approximately the same average expected exposure as investors get from selling puts on 100% of their wealth.

Over the same period as our other backtest, we found that the returns of the option-selling strategy are about the same as for the simpler strategy of keeping 50% in the stock market. This is a little surprising since we noted earlier that implied volatility of at-the-money options was higher than realized volatility over this period. The attentive reader may be saying, *"Not so fast, this result is more than 'a little surprising,' considering you just showed us that the opposite strategy, of buying the same put options versus a long position in the S&P 500, lost money versus the simpler strategy without using put options!"*

It's rare, because we generally just focus on one side of an investment, but it's quite possible that a strategy and its opposite can both lose money. For example, going back to our trusty coin flipping example, let's say one strategy is to bet 100% of your wealth on heads on 10 flips in a row of a 60/40 biased coin. That certainly seems like a bad strategy, but just as bad (well, even worse) is betting 100% of your wealth on tails on 10 flips of the same heads-biased coin.[†] We're going to discuss losing

---

[†]You'd also lose money betting 50% of wealth on heads or tails consistently on 10 coin flips that resulted in six heads and four tails, although you'd lose 82% betting on tails every time versus "just" 29% betting on heads each time.

money on both sides of the same trade, what we call the "George Costanza trade," in more detail in Chapter 23 in our Puzzles section.

Moreover, once we take risk into account explicitly, the 50% in S&P 500 strategy becomes far superior to put-selling: it has lower risk measured both in terms of standard deviation of returns and large drawdowns. The risk of the put-selling strategy versus the fractional long S&P 500 strategy was 20% higher in daily standard deviation, and 100%, 50%, and 50% higher in terms of the largest daily, monthly, and quarterly drawdowns. Furthermore, we are naturally short equity volatility when we own equities, because the more volatile they are, the smaller the Expected Utility gain we get from owning them. Finally, while it did not occur during the 30-year sample, the PUTY trade explicitly exposes investors to the risk of losing all their money if the stock market goes down 100%, whereas such a decline in the stock market wouldn't be as catastrophic for investors who allocated 50% to stocks.[†] This is all to say that the Risk-adjusted Return of the 50% in the S&P 500 strategy was significantly higher than that of the put-selling strategy.

Of course, 30 years is a short sample, and we do not suggest that an investor make a decision solely on the basis of this limited backtest. But if your prior belief is that put-selling doesn't make sense for individual investors, this backtest should give you moderately greater confidence in it. It may be that a small dose of short volatility strategies would improve investor welfare, but not significantly, especially after accounting for taxes and the transaction, monitoring, and management costs involved in the put-selling strategy.

Investors also may consider a pure play on selling equity market volatility. They can do this in a number of ways. The simplest but least cost-efficient approach is to buy an ETF or structured note that has a payoff inversely tied to market realized or implied volatility. These are the structures that were at the center of events known as "Volmageddon." On February 5, 2018, implied stock market volatility more than doubled, and a number of ETFs and structured products tied to the inverse of the VIX index experienced near-total losses. One vehicle sponsored by Credit Suisse, with the playful ticker XIV, dropped from $1.9 billion in value to $63 million over the course of the day.

[†] It is possible (but highly unlikely) that an investor who is determined to keep 50% in stocks at all times could, through extremely frequent rebalancing, experience a near-total loss of wealth.

A more direct path, but with similar hazards, is for investors to sell listed options on the stock market and then dynamically hedge the market exposure generated by the options as the market moves around. This requires having an option pricing model to suggest the necessary hedging trades, or they could just sell the options and let them expire with no hedging at all.[†]

While selling options may provide a positive expected return, it is likely that profits and losses will be significantly correlated with the performance of the stock market itself. In other words, a strategy of shorting equity volatility likely carries a positive beta to the stock market. Monthly changes in the VIX volatility index versus monthly changes in the S&P 500 index over the 10 years to the end of 2021 exhibit a correlation of −0.7, which suggests that the strategy of selling options because they are priced expensively to expected realized stock market volatility has a very high equity beta.[‡]

That selling stock market volatility has a positive beta to the stock market does not mean it is not worthwhile to do it. But it does make the evaluation more complex. In addition to estimating how expensive options are to fair value, the investor must additionally estimate the beta of the strategy in order to determine that the strategy is not dominated by simply investing in the stock market. These variables are very difficult to estimate, especially in contrast to estimating the long-term expected real return of the stock market, which can look to future corporate earnings and dividends as the main determinants.

Can the "volatility-premium-harvesting" strategy be improved by only selling protective puts when implied volatility is high? While much depends on implementation choices, several studies, including our own analysis, did not find this signal to be particularly helpful, at least for major equity indexes. History does not show a strong relationship between the price of the options and the risk/reward of the subsequent outcomes. In other words, high implied volatility in options prices generally is reflected in high subsequent realized market volatility. So investors who wish to harvest the volatility premium should either do it across all market conditions as a matter of faith or build much better predictive models to improve their odds of success.

[†]Investors should note that being short call options on the market creates the possibility of virtually unlimited losses.

[‡]The equity Beta would be $3.5 = \rho \sigma_{strat} / \sigma_{market}$. Selling longer dated options likely would have a lower beta.

Taking all these considerations into account, we are skeptical that options selling strategies warrant a place in the portfolios of individual investors. Our view of individual investors running systematic short volatility strategies echoes Fred Schwed's observation in his classic 1940 book *Where Are the Customers' Yachts?*:

> Options are infinitely attractive to dream about. (. . .) But when a man stops dreaming about these transactions and tries doing them, something different always seems to happen. . . .

Options and Life Cycle Investing

As we discussed in some detail in Chapter 13, it may make sense for young investors who expect significant income growth over time, and whose income is not highly exposed to the stock market, to hold a leveraged long exposure to stocks. Long-dated call options can be the most practical way to hold and manage this exposure. We found that it is possible for call options used in this way to improve an investor's Expected Lifetime Utility, but that such a conclusion is quite sensitive to assumptions made about the pricing and trading costs of such options, and the riskiness and correlation with equity markets of the individual's human capital. The improvement in expected welfare was significant but not as compelling as advocates suggest.

Options on Single Stocks: Two Times Zero Is Still Zero

Until now, our discussion has focused on whether, and by how much, options on broad stock market indexes, such as the S&P 500, improve investors' welfare—and we have found that the answers are "sometimes" and "not much." But what about options on individual stocks? Do they merit a significant role in individuals' collections of assets?

Judging by trading volumes, investors have given their answer to this question, and it's a resounding "yes." It is remarkable that the notional dollar volume of daily trading in options on single stocks, running at close to $400 billion per day in early 2022, is close to—and sometimes higher than—the daily volume of trading in the underlying shares themselves. However, we are skeptical that, from a purely financial perspective, ignoring the potential "YOLO" (You Only Live Once!) value of speculation, this activity improves individual investors' welfare. When investors trade in options on a single stock, they are likely engaging in two zero-sum games at once—or more likely two *negative-sum* games after trading costs, uncompensated risk, and information asymmetries.[†]

Options markets are perhaps more markedly zero-sum in that every buyer of an option must find a counterparty willing to short that option contract. This likely requires stronger conviction than convincing a counterparty to underweight a particular stock versus its index weight. Taken together, this seems like a pretty strong indictment of individuals buying or selling single stock options. As William Bernstein, champion of DIY investors, says in his book *The Investor's Manifesto*:

> It is often said that the small investor is at an unfair disadvantage to the professional, because of the latter's superior information and trading ability. This is certainly true in individual stocks. It is even more true in the trading of futures and options, where more than 80% of small investors lose money, mainly to the brokerage firms and market makers.

Options as Lottery Tickets

Online discussion groups, such as Wall Street Bets, suggest that buying far out-of-the-money call options on individual stocks is better than purchasing conventional lottery tickets. Indeed, individuals trading options on single stocks often use language that seems more relevant to lotteries and casino games than to investing. For example, this is from a 2021 *Wall Street Journal* article: *"I'm hooked on the options,"* said Britt Keeler, a 40-year-old individual investor based in Winter Park, Florida. *"You could lose it all really quick, but you could hustle and kinda hit the jackpot."*

The purchase of lottery tickets sets a pretty low bar for assessing whether buying out-of-the-money options on a single stock is a good thing to do. Even in the unusual cases where the odds are in the favor of the lottery participant, such as when a pot balloons following a run with no winners, participation in the lottery will hardly increase the individual's expected welfare. This is because the utility-optimal amount to "invest" in the lottery ticket will tend to be less than the price of a single ticket, for most individuals.[‡]

[†] Of course, sometimes it does make sense for an investor to hold a portfolio that differs from the market portfolio, such as when the investor is trying to avoid certain risks he or she already has too much of.

[‡] More on this topic in Chapter 19.

What about buying far out-of-the-money call options on a single stock? Trading in short-dated options on Tesla stock has, on some days, represented more than a quarter of all single stock option trading. Let's use this stock for our example. Say an investor buys a 1-week call option on Tesla, struck 30% out-of-the-money. On December 3, 2021, the option closed at a price of 0.1% of the spot price. But let's assume that Tesla stock options are cheap to fair value, and that the expected value of the option is equal to double the premium, due to exceptionally good forecasts of return and volatility by our investor. We can compute the optimal amount to invest in the option on Tesla and the certainty-equivalent increase in wealth by buying these options.

With $1 million of wealth and Base-Case risk-aversion, you optimally would want to spend $4,000, or 0.4% of wealth on the Tesla calls. The allocation is relatively small,[†] despite the option being available at half the fair price, because Expected Utility puts a higher weight on the highly likely loss of $4,000 versus the much less likely huge gain. And the gain in Certainty-equivalent Wealth is about $1,600, a bit less than half the expected dollar profit from buying this option.[14] Of course, in practice, we doubt that individual investors can systematically find options on single stocks that are this cheap, particularly after they pay the bid-offer spreads involved—but we think it's interesting to note that even if one did find such options, the optimal allocation would be modest.

We are not saying that you should not play the lottery or buy options when the odds are in your favor. Just don't get too big. For example, allocating more than 2.5 times the optimal amount actually reduces utility, leaving you worse off than doing nothing. If you insist on trying your luck, we suspect that spending a couple of dollars a week on the lottery will cause less harm than buying call options on a single stock—because if you are prone to overinvesting in single stock options, the potential overallocation would likely hurt more than sinking $104 a year into the lottery.

Beyond Vanilla Listed Stock Options

Similar logic applies to other asset classes with active options markets, such as fixed income, commodities, or foreign exchange. For most

---

[†]Although not so small in terms of the $4 million notional value of the call option, which is four times your wealth!

individual investors, these asset classes account for a minor part of portfolio returns, in part because many profitable strategies in this space require an institutional set-up or significant leverage. However, options can be useful here to achieve leveraged exposure with limited liability. For example, options can be useful for investors who want to move closer to a Risk-Parity portfolio. For those willing to invest time and resources, the niche of "special situations" can provide a fertile hunting ground to find cheap options in convertible bonds or warrants, thrown off by mergers or other corporate reorganizations.

We have not discussed exotic options, which usually carry much higher transaction costs than vanilla options listed on exchanges. Such products may benefit a few investors faced with idiosyncratic regulatory, tax, or corporate finance issues. However, the majority of individual investors can often achieve a more cost-effective solution with vanilla options or without any options at all. The popular Bloomberg analyst Matt Levine hardly exaggerates when he wrote: *"There are occasional high-finance uses for binary options* [a type of exotic option]*, but they are kind of crude and weird instruments, and in modern usage 'binary option' mainly refers to a product that is used to rip off retail traders."*

Other calls for caution in the use of options include "Sharpening Sharpe Ratios," in which the authors show how option selling strategies can be optimized to artificially inflate portfolio performance statistics.[15] It is not surprising that options played a role in the Ponzi scheme operated by Bernard Madoff, who claimed to be pursuing a "split strike conversion" options strategy.

Hedging the Options You're Stuck With

Throughout our discussion so far, we've evaluated the proactive use of options to create return patterns that might be more attractive to individual investors than what they could achieve through simpler means. Before closing the discussion, it is worth noting that sometimes an investor is effectively forced to hold an option or option-like payoff that he would like to sell but cannot. For example, an employee may hold a vested stock option in her company that she is forced to hold for a few more years and should not exercise early as the option is more valuable alive than dead. In such a case, it may make sense to sell options on that stock to hedge the vested options she has to hold. Even a case like this is not clear cut, as there are cash-flow, tax, and transactions costs considerations that might suggest that only a partial hedge, or no hedge at all, makes the most sense. Naturally, as this is a question involving a return versus risk trade-off, the Expected Utility framework can be gainfully employed.

Connecting the Dots

We have found that, under the right conditions and with due care, options can modestly increase investor welfare as a substitute for portfolio rebalancing, as portfolio protection, or as a source of limited liability leverage. The benefits tend to be greatest for investors who are some combination of risk tolerant, optimistic, or young. But we have also seen that a number of popular options strategies, such as buying out-of-the-money options to speculate on individual stocks, or shorting equity market volatility, are more likely to harm an investor's welfare.

Investors should leave no stone unturned in their search for the best expected Risk-adjusted Return on their savings. Unfortunately, options do not provide any magical "get-out-of-jail-free" card. This is not surprising, given that the options market is a zero-sum game at best, and so whatever benefits investors can get from options are likely to come in the form of reshaping the risks they take to better fit their personal preferences. In the final analysis, the use of options is unlikely to make individual investors materially better off than the more robust and easier-to-stick-with alternative of a diversified, cost-efficient, multi-asset portfolio, with a significant and dynamic allocation to equities.

17

Tax Matters

The hardest thing in the world to understand is the income tax.

—Albert Einstein

It is only your after-tax wealth that you are able to spend or give away, so it's proper to be focused on after-tax outcomes.[†] Tax rules are complex, and so for tax-related decisions, it is common practice to focus on optimizing after-tax wealth in a single central case. However for most

---

[†] In this chapter we provide a framework for thinking about tax-related investment decisions, particularly with reference to US investors. Nothing in this book should be construed as tax advice pertaining to any individual's specific circumstances. We are not tax experts. We have simplified the problems we discuss considerably, ignoring many important details in the interest of a clearer exploration.

tax decisions, risk is an integral part of the problem, and so a static analysis involving a comparison of after-tax wealth under a "most likely" scenario may not lead to the correct decision.

For a good illustration of the risk-return trade-off inherent in most tax decisions, imagine you put a small fraction of wealth into a stock that subsequently went up a lot. It now represents a large fraction of your total wealth, but you don't have a strong opinion about its pricing. At this stage you're probably taking too much total risk and are also insufficiently diversified. In thinking about how much to sell, you need to weigh the cost of paying capital gains tax upon reducing the position versus the benefit of moving closer to a more desirable level of risk and diversification. To reach the best trade-off between expected return and risk, you can find the amount to sell which maximizes your after-tax Expected Utility.

To Realize or Not to Realize

There are three main motivations to realize and pay tax on a capital gain today versus deferring that action to the future:

1. The desire to reallocate investment from the appreciated asset to other assets that will produce a more attractive portfolio
2. The need to fund spending
3. The risk of higher effective tax rates in the future

Considering the first motivation, let's say that some years ago you found it optimal to invest half your portfolio in the stock market and the other half in safe assets. Since then, the stock market tripled in value and now represents three-quarters of your portfolio. Naturally you welcome this increase in wealth, but these much higher equity valuations also mean lower expected excess returns, based on which you would now hold an optimal equity exposure of just one-third of your portfolio. So you're considerably overweight stocks but would have to pay significant capital gains tax to remedy the situation. Should you hold on to this extra-risky portfolio to enjoy the benefit of tax deferral, or should you sell some equities and realize some gains to get closer to an optimal allocation?

If you simply calculate how much after-tax wealth you'll have in 10 or 20 years under a Base-Case assumption of equities outperforming safe assets, you'll find that you should never realize gains because having more equities, and paying less taxes, will always lead to more wealth. But that analysis completely ignores risk. We hope you'll agree that the better analysis is to calculate your Expected Utility for different reductions in equity holdings and choose the amount of reduction, and resultant realization, that gives the highest result. We've put the main assumptions needed for this analysis in Table 17.1 (expected returns are in nominal terms).

In Exhibit 17.1, we can see that reducing the equity exposure from 75% to 59% is the optimal decision. The optimal Merton share allocation

Table 17.1 Assumptions for Capital Gains Tax Realization Decision

Current Equity Allocation	75%	Horizon (years)	20
Unrealized Gains % of Portfolio	50%	Risk-free Rate	3%
Capital Gains Tax Rate Today	30%	Stock Market Expected Return	6%
Capital Gains Tax Rate at Horizon	30%	Stock Market Risk	20%
Tax on Equity Dividends	30%	Stock Market Dividend Rate	2%
Tax on Interest	50%	Investor Risk-Aversion (CRRA)	2
Future Value of Capital Losses*	0		

*If a capital loss arises at the horizon, for simplicity we assume the investor derives no future value from this loss as a carryforward.

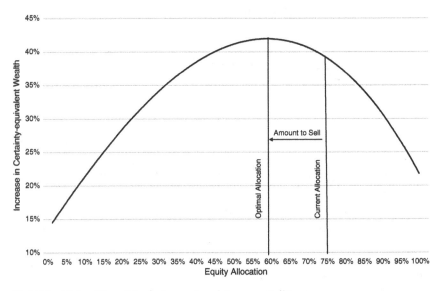

Exhibit 17.1 How Much Appreciated Asset to Sell?

to equities with the same assumptions, but ignoring taxes, would be 37.5%, quite a bit lower than the 59% in this case involving an appreciated asset. The optimal decision results in 3% more Certainty-equivalent Wealth at the horizon than not realizing any gains at all.

Some investors are attracted to the possibility that the basis of their appreciated asset can get "stepped-up" to the current market price on death. To the extent this tax provision remains in effect, it is possible that you can experience a 0% tax rate on capital gains held until death. However, even in this case, running the same analysis as we did before, but with a future capital gains tax rate of 0%, we find that you should reduce your equity exposure from 75% to 62%. This gives you a gain in expected welfare of about 2%, which is roughly equal to a 0.1% per annum improvement in the Risk-adjusted Return of your portfolio earned over 20 years. We can also use the framework to decide to what extent it makes sense to realize gains today and reestablish investments if you expect higher tax rates in the future.

This style of analysis applies equally well to a situation where you have a single stock that is highly appreciated. Your assumption of the expected return of the single stock will be a critical input, but in most cases we've analyzed with a realistic single stock return assumption, the Expected Utility analysis has been pretty consistent in its recommendation to reduce appreciated but highly concentrated holdings. This is because lower risk tends to outweigh lower expected wealth from paying taxes sooner on realized gains.[†]

How Much Should the Tax Tail Wag the Asset Allocation Dog?

How does the prospect of paying capital gains taxes impact an investor's optimal allocation to equities? There's a long history of economists studying the effect of capital gains taxation on risk-taking.[1] In principle, if the government taxed gains and losses symmetrically, then investors shouldn't care about the tax rate at all; they would simply respond to increases in tax rates by increasing their exposure to risky assets so as to keep the post-tax expected return constant.[2] Unfortunately, we don't live in a world of

---

[†]You can find a calculator which suggests the optimal amount of gains to realize in the Tools tab of www.ElmWealth.com.

symmetric taxation, and it's unlikely we'll wake up in that world any time soon. Instead, we're taxed on realized gains, with realized losses creating a tax-loss carry-forward credit that can only be used against future realized gains.[3] But understanding how things would work in the symmetric case is a good starting point for investors with very long horizons or those who hold assets that are highly appreciated versus their cost basis.

To explore how taxes impact risk-taking, let's examine a case using all of the assumptions from Table 17.1 that we used for our first example in this chapter, except we'll assume you are *starting with a fresh portfolio with no unrealized gains*, and the expected return of the stock market is 8%. In a zero-tax world, the Merton share would suggest you allocate 63% of your portfolio to equities. For any investment horizon, we can find the optimal allocation to equities that results in the highest Expected Utility, which we show in Exhibit 17.2.

The dotted line represents the optimal allocation to equities with no taxes at all. When we introduce taxation, we see that for horizons under 3 years, we get a lower optimal equity allocation, represented by the solid line, than in a tax-free world. To see why this is the case, we can think of capital gains tax as being a call option sold for free by the investor to the government. For short horizons, the value of the call option takes a big chunk out of the expected return offered by equities, so owning less is optimal.[†]

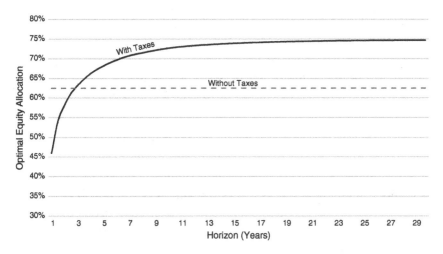

Exhibit 17.2 Optimal Equity Allocation With and Without Taxes for Different Horizons

---

[†]This is an odd sort of option contract, whereby the seller determines the expiration date of the option, and under current rules, the option goes away at death.

As the horizon lengthens, the optionality of the capital gains tax liability decreases as a per annum cost, and the benefit of deferring the tax
payment increases. This, combined with equities typically being taxed at
a lower rate than bonds, results in an increasing optimal equity allocation
as horizon gets longer. Figuring out exactly what is optimal for your
particular circumstances will depend significantly on how you value the
potential tax-loss carryforward that may arise from a realized loss. In this
example, we have assumed for simplicity that it has no value.

Buy-Borrow-Die

One tax-related idea that has received much attention in recent
years involves borrowing money against an appreciated portfolio,
often referred to as the "buy-borrow-die" approach. The basic idea
is to avoid realizing taxable gains by funding spending with borrowing rather than by selling down assets. One reason we think this may
be less sensible than it appears is that, from a risk perspective, funding spending through borrowing is riskier than doing so through
asset sales. Selling assets allows you to keep a desired target risk level
as you spend, while borrowing forces you into taking more and
more risk as a fraction of wealth, because your risky portfolio is staying constant while your wealth is going down. In extreme cases in
which you're spending a significant fraction of total wealth, this can
become highly undesirable. On the other hand, if you're not spending much of your wealth, then you're also likely not realizing much
in gains, so borrowing may add some value but won't make a meaningful difference either way. Whatever your circumstances, Expected
Utility can help you find the right amount of borrowing, if any.

Optimal Equity Allocation with Unrealized Gains

In the example we just discussed, we found that the optimal allocation
to equities accounting for taxes, and assuming your portfolio had no
unrealized gains to start with, was 75% to a 20-year horizon. What if
your starting portfolio has unrealized gains in it? How does that change
the optimal equity allocation?

If your equity portfolio has unrealized gains equal to 50% of its value,
then we'd find the optimal allocation is 78%, only a bit higher than the

75% optimal for a freshly purchased portfolio with no unrealized capital gains. However, the optimal allocation is 88% of your portfolio value *net of its tax liability*. As you'd expect, the divergence between these two ways of measuring your allocation grows with the size of the unrealized gain in the starting portfolio. This gives us a useful rule of thumb: to a long horizon, your optimal allocation won't be significantly impacted by unrealized gains, as long as you think about your portfolio value *without* subtracting the tax liability.

Tax Loss Harvesting

Tax loss harvesting involves selling securities that have decreased in value in order to realize a capital loss. The capital loss can then be used to offset capital gains from the sale of other securities, reducing the overall tax liability. US tax rules require that any sale that generates a capital loss not be preceded or followed within 30 days by a purchase of the same, or nearly identical, security. Tax loss harvesting can significantly improve the after-tax return on your investments, but whether it does so is highly dependent on your personal circumstances. For investors with highly diversified portfolios, tax loss harvesting may not significantly increase the risk of your portfolio and so mostly is a question of weighing the costs and benefits in terms of after-tax expected return, without requiring an Expected Utility analysis. These days, most wealth managers serving taxable US investors offer tax loss harvesting as part of their overall portfolio services.

The Bane of King Lear

It is generally the case that the tax code encourages giving away wealth philanthropically or intergenerationally sooner rather than later. For instance, in the case of giving money philanthropically, accelerated giving is advantageous because a charity can enjoy investment returns tax-free, the tax benefit the donor enjoys from making the donation is more valuable the earlier it is taken, and hopefully making the world better sooner is a good thing and may pay larger dividends in future general welfare. However, there is a risk associated with giving away one's wealth too aggressively, as illustrated in the tragedy of King Lear.

You don't need to be betrayed by your loved ones and cast into the wilderness, as was old Lear, to regret giving away too much of your wealth too hastily. All it takes is some combination of poor investment returns, unexpectedly high expenses, and living a longer and more active life than expected, and you might regret giving away too much too soon.

The Expected Utility framework can help you figure out the optimal amount and timing of gift giving. The challenge is to specify your utility as a function of both personal consumption and gifting. One way to calibrate this more complex utility function is to remove investment risk, longevity risk, and tax uncertainty from the problem. You can then specify how you would like to allot your wealth assuming different levels of initial resources. Combining the information provided by this exercise with questions targeted directly at risk-aversion, the required multi-variable utility function can be inferred, and then used to answer these complex and important questions using the same lifetime portfolio choice framework we explored throughout Section II.

Extensions

The previous examples are meant to give a sense for how to approach tax-related financial decisions using the Expected Utility maximization paradigm. In practice, individual circumstances and tax rules tend to be much more complex than our characterizations. The Expected Utility framework is flexible enough to take into account many real-world tax-planning decisions and circumstances such as the following:

- Multiple horizons over which investors expect to liquidate assets to fund spending
- Assets with different cost bases
- Situations involving short-term and long-term capital gains
- Funding and conversion between different forms of tax-advantaged IRA and 401k accounts
- 1031 exchanges
- Exchange funds
- Other estate planning structures, such as installment sales, Grantor Retained Asset Trusts (GRATs), and Charitable Lead Trusts (CLTs)
- Private Placement Life Insurance (PPLI)

- The ability to get a market value deduction, and avoid realizing a taxable capital gain, from the donation of appreciated assets to recognized charities
- Correlations between tax rates, asset prices, inflation, and interest rates

Connecting the Dots

In the idealized world of Finance 101, with only a risk-free and a risky asset to choose from, no taxation, no transactions costs, and asset prices that follow random walks, your optimal allocation to the risky asset is a function of just three variables: the risky asset's excess expected return, its risk, and your level of risk-aversion. When we bring taxes into the mix, the optimal asset allocation depends on many other variables, and the investment horizon in particular becomes a critical input. However making good decisions with a focus on after-tax outcomes will still almost always involve assessing the cost of bearing risk, which is why Expected Utility is just the tool needed.

18

Risk Versus Uncertainty

*The importance of probability can only be derived from the judgment that it is **rational** to be guided by it in action.*

—John M. Keynes, *A Treatise on Probability* (1921)

Introduction

There is a rich literature on the distinction between risk and uncertainty. We tend to think the distinction is not especially sharp in practice, but "risk" is often taken to refer to random outcomes derived from a known probability distribution, such as whether a fair coin lands on heads or tails. "Uncertainty," more precisely called "Knightian" or "epistemic" uncertainty, is used to describe phenomena that cannot be measured and therefore are beyond the limits of knowledge—the "unknown-unknowns" as famously described by Donald Rumsfeld. Many real-world dynamics don't fall clearly into one camp or the other but are somewhere in the middle. Pure Knightian uncertainty poses challenges to any decision framework, but thankfully most of the variables involved in personal financial decision-making—from the expected real return and risk of the stock market to our own longevity—have distributions that, if we cannot know them precisely, are also not beyond the "limits of knowledge." In general, the kind of parameter uncertainty we are likely to encounter results in the Expected Utility framework suggesting a reduction in the optimal allocation to risky assets.

Investing would be pretty straightforward if we knew the true joint probability distribution[†] of all possible return outcomes for all available assets. Unfortunately, this will always be a dream because (1) financial asset return distributions change over time; (2) the distributions for most financial assets are complex and not normally distributed, characterized by some amount of skew, fat tails, jumps and autocorrelation; (3) return distributions are impacted by capital flows which are responsive to past returns; and (4) given these complexities, we don't have enough historical data to accurately infer the distributions from which actual outcomes are drawn.

It is notoriously difficult to estimate expected returns from historical data.[1] For example, even if we made the heroic assumption that stock returns came from a stationary process, then over the past 100 years with 18% annual standard deviation of returns, our estimate of the mean return would still have a standard deviation of 1.8%. Alas, market-based signals, such as options prices, are of little help in estimating expected returns, but a strong Bayesian prior[‡] would help reduce the noise around an expected return estimate.

[†]A joint probability distribution is a probability distribution that describes the simultaneous occurrence of two or more random variables. It gives the probability of different combinations of values for the random variables.

[‡]In Bayesian statistics, a "prior" belief is a probability distribution that reflects your beliefs about the probability of a certain event occurring before any new data is collected.

Throughout this chapter, we will use the term "parameter uncertainty" to refer to not knowing the true joint distribution of possible gains and losses across potential investments.

The Two Envelopes Paradox: We're All Bayesians Now

Imagine you are presented with two envelopes. You are told one envelope contains twice as much money as the other. You choose one envelope and see how much money it contains. You are given the chance to switch envelopes. Should you?

Much has been written about this puzzle, and its variants such as the less interesting but still amusing necktie paradox,[†] and a number of solutions have been proposed by statisticians, game theorists, and economists. The solution that is the most intuitively resonant and relevant to this chapter relies on the idea that in financial matters, there will always be a bound on the amount of uncertainty that is possible. No reasonable player of this game would have a prior belief that all dollar amounts are equally likely to be found in the envelope. If you were given the opportunity to play this game, you'd have some idea of how much is likely to be in the two envelopes, and you'd surely believe it's a lot more likely that together they contain $50 than $5 billion! In reality, the game would be offered to you in some context, such as some researchers in decision-making running an experiment. With some idea of a plausible budget for such research, if you saw there was $1 in the envelope you chose, you'd probably switch, and if you found $100, you'd probably not switch.

The Bayesian answer to this puzzle is a good illustration of the limits of true uncertainty in financial decisions, and that even though we do not know exactly what the distribution of outcomes is for an investment,

---

[†]Two people, each wearing a necktie, argue over who has the cheaper one. They agree to a bet wherein the person with the more expensive necktie must give it to the other person. The first person reasons that if he loses, he loses the value of his necktie, but if he wins, then he wins more than the value of his necktie. If the chance of winning is 50%, the wager seems to be to his advantage. The second person thinks about it the same way. The paradox is that it seems that both persons are making a bet to their advantage.

Two Envelope Money Machine?

The puzzle has some similarity to the St. Petersburg paradox, as most people would intuitively know just what to do if presented with this opportunity. However, we did hear of the amusing case of a Salomon bond trader in London who offered a variant of the game to some of his colleagues with a surprising result. He put a 50 pound note in one envelope, and a 10 pound note in the other. He then rounded up 10 colleagues to play the game, one after the other, and made sure they didn't communicate with each other after playing. Our friend explained to his colleagues that one envelope had five times more money in it than the other one. He then instructed each player to choose one envelope, take a look inside, and either keep that amount, or for a payment of 120% of that amount, the player could switch envelopes. In the end, every player chose to make the payment to switch envelopes, and our friend walked away with a net profit of 60 pounds! The players who found 50 pounds in their envelope were happy to pay 60 pounds to switch and take the gamble that the other envelope contained 250 pounds, and the players who found 10 pounds inside were happy to pay 12 pounds for the switch. Luckily for our friend, an equal number of players chose the envelope with 50 pounds in it as chose the one with 10 pounds inside.

we can usually put some bounds on the possibilities. Not surprisingly another tool to solve this puzzle is Expected Utility, which for typical levels of risk-aversion will tell you to not switch when the risk of the switch has a very large impact on your total wealth.

Learning

With time, we might find that uncertainty resolves into risk as we learn more about the distributions that are generating what we experience. For assets with relatively low signal-to-noise ratios, such as the global equity market, learning from realized returns will happen quite slowly over time—in general, too slowly to be useful, especially in the presence of regime shifts. But in other cases modeling learning into risk-taking decisions can be useful. One interesting result is that, if we update expected returns in a pro-cyclical way, raising return estimates after positive returns, then we should optimally take less risk than we would otherwise. This is because scenarios where losses of wealth are further compounded by lower expected returns are especially unattractive to risk-averse investors.

The Ellsberg Puzzle

An experiment, known as the Ellsberg puzzle,[†] suggests that most people require extra compensation to bear uncertainty versus risk. The experiment involves two urns each containing 100 balls. The participant is told that Urn A contains 50 red and 50 black, but Urn B contains 100 balls in an unknown mix of red and black, with every mix ratio being equally likely. The participant must draw one ball and will receive a prize if a red ball is chosen. It was found that when given a choice, people had a strong preference to pick from Urn A, despite there being an identical likelihood of pulling a red ball from each urn.

Ellsberg coined the term "ambiguity aversion" to describe this preference, which was viewed as irrational in the context of the experiment. However, only a tiny tweak to the setup is needed to make the ambiguity aversion rational: if we allow the participant to repeat the game more than once, replacing the chosen ball each time and requiring commitment to the same urn throughout, then a rational person would prefer to draw from Urn A as it's known to be 50/50. If the participant is allowed to repeat the game 100 times and win $100 each time a red ball is picked, they should expect to make $5,000 whichever urn they choose to pick from, but they're taking a lot less risk picking from Urn A rather than from Urn B , as illustrated in Exhibit 18.1.[‡]

[†] Historical trivia: Daniel Ellsberg, besides being a renowned economist, was a political activist who released the Pentagon Papers in 1971 and was ultimately acquitted of the charge of treason. Ellsberg, D. (1961). "Risk, Ambiguity, and the Savage Axioms." The Quarterly Journal of Economics, Vol. 75, No. 4. pp. 643-669.

[‡] The peaks in probability for the cases of getting either 100 or 0 red balls can be understood by realizing that there is a 0.99% probability of choosing the urn with 100 red balls, in which case you will pull out 100 red balls, but there's also a 0.99% chance of getting the urn with 99 red balls, in which case you have a 37% chance of pulling out 100 red balls, and so on, resulting in a 1.6% probability of getting 100 red balls.

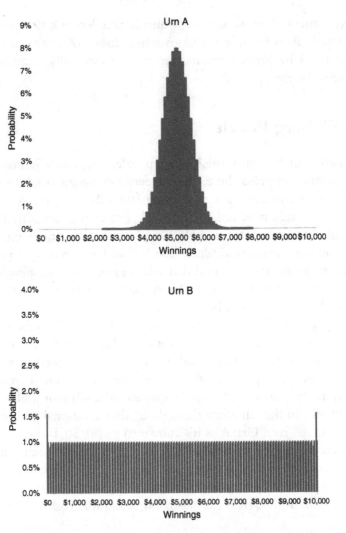

Exhibit 18.1 Multi-Round Ellsberg Experiment: $100 Prize for Choosing Red Ball, Choosing 100 Rounds from Urn A or from Urn B, Urn A: 50 Red and 50 Black Balls, Urn B: 100 Balls, Uniformly Likely Combinations of 0—100 Red and Rest Black

So we see that in this stylized but useful thought experiment, ambiguity aversion is hard to justify over a single iteration, but it is consistent with risk-aversion over multiple iterations—and the "wedge" between the risk of the certain distribution (Urn A) and uncertain distribution (Urn B) increases as the number of iterations increases.

When we run simulations of investing in a risky asset, we find a very direct parallel. If we're investing in an asset with uncertain expected returns over a single period, the uncertainty does not change our optimal allocation relative to the case of a certain expected return. However, over multiple periods we would optimally allocate less in the case of the uncertain expected return, with how much less increasing as time horizon lengthens.[2]

In Table 18.1, we consider a risky Asset A with known 5% expected return and Asset B, which has a 50/50 likelihood of either having an expected return of 3% or 7%. Both assets have 20% volatility. We assumed our typically risk-averse Base-Case investor.

We can see that the uncertainty in expected return is having two effects: increasing realized volatility and increasing the asset's expected price at the horizon.[†] For normal levels of risk-aversion, the increased volatility dominates the higher expected price, and allocations are reduced as uncertainty increases and as time increases.[3]

Table 18.1

Horizon	Asset A				Asset B			
	Opt Alloc	Return of Exp Price	Exp Comp Return	Vol	Opt Alloc	Return of Exp Price	Exp Comp Return	Vol
1y	62.5%	5.0%	3.0%	20.0%	62.2%	5.0%	3.0%	20.1%
5y	62.5%	5.0%	3.0%	20.0%	60.9%	5.1%	3.0%	20.5%
10y	62.5%	5.0%	3.0%	20.0%	59.5%	5.2%	3.0%	21.0%
30y	62.5%	5.0%	3.0%	20.0%	54.5%	5.6%	3.0%	22.8%
100y	62.5%	5.0%	3.0%	20.0%	44.5%	6.3%	3.0%	28.2%

[†]Compounding at 5% results in a lower price than the average of the prices you get from compounding at 3% and 7%, i.e. $1.05^n < \frac{1}{2}(1.03^n + 1.07^n)$, for $n > 1$.

Parameter uncertainty has a larger impact on risk-taking for more risk-averse investors. For a full Kelly bettor,[†] the parameter uncertainty modeled in this case would have no impact on the optimal allocation to equities. This result is actually somewhat surprising, as advocates of Kelly betting often suggest investors use half-Kelly to account for uncertainty in expected returns, but this example suggests that may not be an entirely consistent response to this kind of uncertainty.

The Shape of Uncertainty

Uncertainty about the return distribution of financial assets goes well beyond not knowing the expected return and expected standard deviation. We will often be uncertain regarding the distribution's general shape and character—for example whether the distribution is skewed, fat-tailed, or involves large jumps in price. As we saw in Chapter 16 in discussing options, the shape of the distribution can have a big impact on whether or not options will increase an investor's Expected Utility. However, in some important cases—such as deciding how much to invest in equities in typical market conditions—the shape of the distribution can have surprisingly little effect on the optimal decision. For example, Exhibit 18.2 shows four very differently shaped distributions for equity returns, all of which have the same expected return and standard deviation of returns. It is comforting to note that the equity allocations that maximize Expected Utility are roughly the same (within 1% of the 62.5% recommended by the Merton share) under each of these differently shaped distributions.

Parameter Uncertainty with Multiple Risky Assets

In the discussion so far, we've focused on parameter uncertainty in the context of a single risky asset, though that asset may itself be a portfolio that we're simply treating as one asset. Parameter uncertainty becomes an even bigger challenge when we're building a portfolio of multiple

---

[†]Reminder: the objective of the Kelly bettor is to maximize the rate of growth of his wealth, which is equivalent to saying he is an Expected Utility maximizer whose utility is equal to the natural logarithm of wealth.

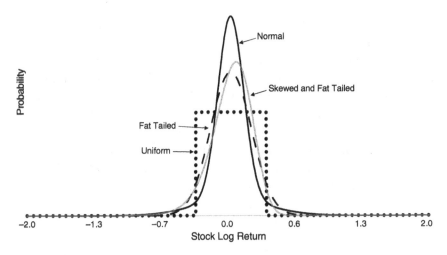

Exhibit 18.2 Less than 1% Difference in Optimal Allocation to Equities Under These Four Different Probability Distributions of Stock Price Returns, All with the Same Expected Return (5%) and Risk (20%) for Investor with Risk-aversion of 2

assets, whose relative returns and covariances are also subject to uncertainty. Standard mean-variance optimization is particularly sensitive to uncertainty in expected returns. For example, in "The Effect of Errors in Means, Variances, and Covariances on Optimal Portfolio Choice" by Vijay Chopra and William Ziemba (1993), the authors find errors in estimating expected returns are 10 times more impactful than errors in estimating variability and correlations. It also makes sense that an error in estimating the probability of a rare but highly consequential event is more impactful on your Expected Utility than making an equal absolute size mis-estimation of an event that is more like a 50/50 coin toss. Academics and practitioners have suggested many ways to make this kind of portfolio construction more robust to uncertainty in the main inputs. Most of the solutions involve putting constraints on the optimization that impose more diversification on the optimal portfolio than would naturally come out of a standard, unconstrained optimization.

Connecting the Dots

In this chapter, we've explored the effect of uncertainty on investment decisions. We used a very simple two-asset case where the only uncertainty is in the expected return of the risky asset. We've neglected many other inputs to the investment process from an uncertainty perspective, including volatility, skew, kurtosis, crisis characterizations, and risk-aversion level. Further, if we parameterize the possible distribution of any given input, we could find ourselves exploring the uncertainty of these uncertainty parameters, and so on *ad infinitum*. What stops us from falling down this rabbit hole is that there's a pretty quick decrease in impact beyond first order uncertainty in the most important inputs. Indeed, uncertainty about expected returns is usually significantly more important than for any other type of parameter, and we've seen that even uncertainty in expected returns (in the stylized case we explored) is ultimately not especially impactful for one of the most important situations we care about.

IV

Puzzles

19

How Can a Great Lottery Be a Bad Bet?

One of the great unsolved mysteries in financial economics is the huge aggregate sums of money spent on legal lottery tickets worldwide. In the United States alone, roughly $100 billion is spent each year, which comes to about $300 per annum for every adult in the country. The average spend for people who buy at least two lottery tickets each year is likely above $1,000 per annum! In general, the expected value of a lottery ticket for a big prize is well under half of the price paid for the lottery ticket and even lower after taking taxes into account.

But what about massively undervalued lottery tickets? Yes, sometimes they do exist, and it's very interesting to think about what to do when they're available. In November 2022, there was a lot of press coverage of a lottery called "Powerball" that had an eye-catching jackpot of $2.04 billion, or a lump sum cash value of $998 million (both figures are pretax). When a pot gets this big, and if you choose your tickets to avoid popular numbers and patterns that too many people crowd around, some experts assert that the lottery ticket becomes *undervalued*, and you are presented with the opportunity to play the lottery with a positive edge.[1] What should you do then?

Well, it depends. Specifically, it depends on how much the odds are in your favor, how much the ticket costs relative to your wealth, and the shape of your personal utility function. Let's assume you have $100,000 of wealth and you are quite risk tolerant, with risk-aversion of 1. We'll assume that a $2 ticket gives you a 1 in 10 million chance of winning the $2 billion jackpot. In other words, you're paying just $2 for a ticket "worth" $200.

You know you've got a great deal based on expected value, but what about Expected Utility? Well, despite the expected value of the ticket being 100 times its face amount, the Expected Utility of buying the ticket is negative—in fact, really negative. You'd be the equivalent of about $1.90 worse off by buying the lottery ticket for $2. Put differently, you would need to pay less than $0.10 to have a good investment from an Expected Utility perspective, ignoring its fantasy-fun value. Even if you had $1 million of wealth instead of $100,000, you'd still find buying the ticket for $2 to be a negative Expected Utility proposition.

Is this something we should pay attention to, or is there a problem with utility theory here? We assure you—we're paying attention! Expected Utility puts weights on the almost-certain loss versus the almost-impossibly huge gain in a way that is both intuitively appealing (to your authors at least) and theoretically sound. With $1 million of savings, let's say you kept being offered the chance to play a series of lotteries this attractive as many times as you wanted to and you were willing to spend all your savings trying to win. So, you play the lottery 500,000 times, or until you win. Unfortunately, the probability of losing all your money is 95%, which gives some intuition for the finding from the Expected Utility calculation. We don't think many people would want to take a 95% chance of losing all their money for a 5% chance of winning $2 billion.

The utility-based decision rule isn't saying that you shouldn't play the lottery when the odds are in your favor; it's just saying that $2 is too big of a bet relative to $100,000 or even $1,000,000 of wealth. Your optimal bet size, with those great odds and $1,000,000 of wealth, would be to buy only one-twentieth of a ticket.

We agree with friends who tell us we shouldn't overthink what we do with $2 for a lottery ticket. After all, as Bloomberg journalist Matt Levine wrote, "Ten bucks won't even get you into a movie, and isn't this more fun to think about?" Yes, people do weird things with small sums. So, someone with $100,000 of wealth might turn down a fair coin flip that would win $110 versus lose $100, even though that's a far better deal than a normally risk-averse investor should need. It's fascinating that people tend to play the lottery when it's clearly unfavorable but then refuse symmetric but small favorable bets when they should take them.

Connecting the Dots

Lots of investments out there can look like lottery tickets, with positive expected value arising from a small probability of a big payout and a high probability of a relatively small loss. Viewed through the lens of expected value, we might be tempted to commit some serious dough to these lottery-ticket style investments. That's when we need to coolly pull out our Expected Utility tool kit to get a clearer picture of an investment's attractiveness and how much of it to take on board.

So What About *Selling* an Overvalued Lottery Ticket?

It was a quiet Friday afternoon on the Salomon trading floor in early January 1987. The markets had closed, the day's trades were confirmed, and we were sitting around discussing weekend plans. In walked 6 1/2 feet of the most enthusiastic and well-liked of all the Salomon managing directors, a man who believed nothing was impossible. He went by just two letters, OG, and he was an Original!

How about that stock market! Up every day this year so far—6 days in a row! I think it's going to be up every day this year. What odds would you guys give me on $1,000 that I'm right?

We perked up. Another 245 trading days were left in the year, and even if we assigned an 80% chance to the market being up each day, the odds that it would be up the next 245 in a row were about a trillion trillion to one.[†] But then again, maybe thinking of it as a series of biased coin flips wasn't the way to think about it. After all, for one thing, the market might close for the rest of the year due to some emergency, and the odds of that were certainly much higher than one in a trillion trillion. What if we thought the odds of him winning were 1 in 10,000? Then maybe we should have offered him 1,000 to 1 odds on $1,000, exposing us to a million dollar loss, which would have represented a reasonably low percentage of our collective personal capital. Expected Utility could help us think about this at a higher level, recognizing that selling such a crazy low-probability-high-consequence risk was never going to be something that made a lot of sense. But it was also about trying to figure out the odds of the event happening and figuring out the lowest odds he'd accept on $1,000.

We agreed to syndicate the risk among five of us, and we offered him odds at 1,000:1, but only on $50, for a total downside to us of $50,000. He scoffed, muttered a few expletives under his breath, and walked away dissatisfied—no bet. Then, as if to show us that anything remotely possible might just happen, we watched the Dow go up each of the next 7 days, an 11% rally altogether, until the streak finally ended on the 14th day. That turned out to be quite an unusual year. Even more unlikely than the stock market's 13-day winning streak at the start of 1987 was Monday October 19 later that same year, when the stock market fell by more than 20% in one day! Good thing he didn't ask us to give him odds on that one!

[†]And it took a good few seconds for our HP 12C to do that calculation.

20

The Equity Risk Premium Puzzle

What level of interest rates and equity returns can we reasonably expect from the economy? This is the animating question of the Equity Risk Premium puzzle (ERP), which has been keenly studied and debated since the 1980s. The heart of the "puzzle" is that the long-term realized returns of stocks and bonds simply don't agree very well with the equilibrium predictions from the most commonly used economic models. Viewed narrowly, there need not be any puzzle here—in the natural sciences, if a model fails when brought into contact with experimental evidence, the general procedure is to discard the model, not proclaim the real world puzzling for failing to match the chalkboard.[†] But a more generous understanding might see the "puzzle" as encompassing a broad range of questions concerning how best to think about the natural level of expected returns and what we should make of the historical experience relative to expectations.

The formulation of the ERP was crystalized in a 1985 paper by Mehra and Prescott.[1] They posit an "endowment" economy, in which perishable consumption goods—fish, for example—are periodically harvested, with some variability in amount but also with a known average growth rate. The members of the economy are risk averse, and they all start out with an equal share of the providential harvest. If they start to trade with each other, they can quickly get packages of trades that look like bonds and stocks, and either by simulation or through some financial math, you can work out the equilibrium level of interest rates and equity returns. The trouble is that when Mehra and Prescott input levels of harvest growth and volatility based on the US economy with what seemed like a reasonable level of risk-aversion, the equilibrium level of interest rates was quite high and the implied risk premium was very low. This is the opposite of the historical high realized equity market risk premia relative to safe bonds and the relatively low real rates on safe bonds. An unrealistically high level of risk-aversion, amongst other inputs, was needed to get the model in the ballpark of historical market returns. One of this book's central topics has been risk-aversion, and it turns out that risk-aversion, and the marginal decreasing utility of consumption that underlies it, is at the very heart of how we think about markets.

The story of interest rates often begins with time preference, the idea that consumption tomorrow is worth less than consumption today. But this is only part of the story. Even in a world with no time preference and no inflation, nonzero interest rates can still make sense. To see why, let's say you're one of these fishermen, and life is pretty good, but you're thinking about how you could make it even better. One thing you've noticed is that the harvest, on average, gets bigger over time. Instead of having 10 fish now and an expected 12 fish next harvest, you'd rather just have 11 fish both times. This makes sense without any theory,

---

[†]We are reminded of a cartoon, perhaps in the *New Yorker*, of two professors in front of a chalkboard dense with equations with the caption: "It works in practice, but will it work in theory?"

but we've also seen in Section II how evening out consumption tends to improve Expected Lifetime Utility. So how do you go about evening out your expected consumption? Essentially you sell a fish bond. You go to your friend Sven and offer to give him an extra fish next harvest, guaranteed, if he gives you a fish now. The bond market is born!

The trouble is, Sven and everyone else are all making exactly the same calculation: they all want to sell a bond too. So far, our market has only sellers and no buyers, not a very promising start—thus, interest rates. To entice Sven into becoming a bond buyer, you offer to give him back the fish you borrowed, plus throw in some extra fish roe by way of interest. The aromatic roe does the trick, and the first bond trade clears with a positive interest rate. We can clearly see that the more growth you expect from the harvest, the more interest you'll be willing to pay, and Sven will need to receive, to make the trade happen.

So now you're really sitting pretty, having used the bond market to pull forward some of the expected future harvest growth to increase your fish consumption today. But you're still not satisfied; you think with some clever trading perhaps you can do even better. One thing you're worried about is that even though the harvest increases over time *on average,* it's still pretty variable, and there can be some skimpy dinners indeed. To mitigate this, you go back to friend Sven and make him a proposition: if the harvest is really bad, he'll give you an extra few fish, and if it's really good, you'll give him an extra few fish. Economists would call this "trading state claims," meaning you're agreeing to a package of future payoffs that depend on the future state of the economy. But essentially you're trying to sell some of your stock in the harvest to make your exposure a bit more bond-like.

But again, the trouble is that Sven and everyone else are making the exact same calculation. For everyone, the utility from having some extra fish in the bad times is dramatically higher than the utility from having extra fish when times are already good. So to make the trade workable, you propose getting two extra fish in a bad harvest, but in a good harvest, you'll provide Sven three fish by way of compensation. Sven accepts, and now the stock market is born too. And just as we saw with the "bond" trade, higher expected economic growth will make you willing to pay more, and Sven will need to receive more in the way of compensation. But in the case of this stock trade, the form of compensation is a little different than it was with the bond. Bond compensation took the form of interest, a guaranteed payment made at a fixed time. But the stock compensation comes in the form of expected return, where Sven expects to receive more from the trade than he gives out *on average* rather than at any one single harvest. This is a core quality of real stock markets as well.

In these trades, we've seen that expected economic growth is a key driver, but so is risk-aversion. If you had no marginal decreasing utility of consumption, you wouldn't place any value on smoothing it out, all that would matter is total lifetime consumption, so there's no need for bond trading. And similarly, without risk-aversion, you wouldn't value extra consumption differently in harvests small or large, so there's no need for stock trading. The marginal decreasing utility of consumption, and the risk-aversion it engenders, is at the very heart of what makes markets tick.

If trades like the bond and stock trades with Sven are allowed to happen in a market, then under the assumptions of our endowment economy, both interest rates and stock expected returns will eventually converge around an equilibrium level. Under the stylized endowment economy we've been talking about, the equilibria for interest rates, r_{bond}, equity returns, r_{stock}, and the equity risk premium are as follows:

$$r_{bond} = \delta + \gamma \left(\mu - (1+\gamma)\frac{\sigma^2}{2} \right)$$

$$r_{stock} = \delta + \gamma \left(\mu - (\gamma - 1)\frac{\sigma^2}{2} \right)$$

$$\textit{Equity Risk Premium} = r_{stock} - r_{bond} = \gamma\sigma^2$$

μ is the expected growth of the economy, σ is the variability in that growth, γ is the coefficient of risk-aversion, and δ is the time preference of the representative individual.

These equations are highly attractive and elegant to those of a certain mind, but unfortunately, they don't agree with real-world returns especially well. Let's treat the "fish harvest" as being represented by total corporate earnings (public and private businesses). If we assume real earnings growth of 1.5% per annum with volatility of 6%, and we assume individual risk-aversion of 2 and time preference of 2%, the model yields real interest rates of about 4% and equity risk premium of less than 1%. In contrast, historical real interest rates have been lower (less than 1% for

T-bills) and equity risk premia much higher (5%–7%). This is the heart of the Equity Risk Premium puzzle.

What could be going on here? One thing that jumps out right away is that real corporate earnings might have a volatility of 6% per annum, but equities sure don't—more like 16%–20%. But if we put 18% volatility into the model, keeping the other inputs the same, we get a risk premium of 7%, which is more in line with history, but a real interest rate of −5%, quite far from average historical real interest rates.

We've seen in Chapter 15 that Shiller and others have shown that equities are much more volatile than can be explained by the volatility of earnings, and our endowment economy hasn't accounted for that. So one possible lesson from this puzzle is that equities have exhibited excess volatility, which has led to them carrying an overly generous risk premium, and that excess volatility may also have reduced the returns available from safe assets.

There are many other lines of thought on how to resolve the puzzle. Here are a few of the major ones:

- The theory makes predictions about expected returns in equilibrium. But neither expected returns nor equilibrium levels are directly observable; we can only observe realized returns along one path of the world, which may not be representative either of expected or equilibrium levels.
- The experience of the US equity market in the twentieth century may be an anomaly and not representative of general long-term expected returns. It may be biased by an artificially high amount of survivorship bias, not to mention a doubling of the price-earnings ratio over the period. A broader international survey of equity market excess returns finds the US equity market to have been among the best performing global stock markets.[2]
- The large observed equity risk premium may be fair compensation for rare, unobserved, time-varying, and largely unrealized disaster risks. John Campbell referred to this as "dark matter for economists" since we cannot directly observe the probability or magnitude of these rare events, but only infer their existence through the historically large equity risk premium.[3] While we cannot observe the true probability of disaster risks, through survey data we can measure the likelihood investors attach to them. For example, Shiller has conducted a survey since 1989 asking a sample of financially sophisticated individual and

institutional investors the probability they attach to a 1 day decline in the US stock market of more than 13% sometime in the next 6 months. The average response has generally been between 15% and 20%, an order of magnitude greater than the historical experience. It seems investors fear severe stock market crashes quite a bit.[4]

- The theory may be failing to incorporate important features of real-world markets, such as transaction costs (particularly for the first half of the twentieth century), subsistence consumption levels, habit formation,[5] heterogeneous and uninsurable idiosyncratic shocks,[6] separation between risk-aversion and intertemporal substitution,[7] market segmentation, and information asymmetry.

Connecting the Dots

The ERP puzzle remains an unresolved question in economics, and research is actively underway exploring each one of these potential explanations. It's one of our favorite economics puzzles because of how it makes the connections among risk-aversion, interest rates, and equity risk premia and also because—possibly—it helps explain why the equity markets play such an important role in modern economies.

21

The Perpetuity Paradox and Negative Interest Rates

We are actively competing with nations who openly cut interest rates so that now many are actually getting paid when they pay off their loan, known as negative interest. Who ever heard of such a thing? Give me some of that. GIVE ME SOME OF THAT MONEY. I WANT SOME OF THAT MONEY.

—Donald J. Trump (Economic Club of New York, 2019)

In Chapter 20, we just described a framework, with utility and risk-aversion at its core, that allows for the possibility of negative equilibrium real interest rates even in a world where everyone has positive time preference favoring present versus future spending. However, while economists have long recognized the theoretical possibility of negative long-term interest rates, most didn't think they'd ever become reality.

It's hard to describe how far-out the idea of negative interest rates has been to economists and market participants throughout history. What would Sidney Homer, coauthor of the 4,000-year survey *A History of Interest Rates* and Salomon Brothers' first director of bond market research, have made of UK investors locking in a 65% loss of purchasing power? Yet they did exactly that by buying 50-year inflation-linked bonds at a yield of −2% per annum, the prevailing rate for much of 2018 through 2021.[†] Influential economists and philosophers, including Marshall, Fisher, von Mises, Hicks, Hayek, Knight, Keynes, and Friedman, all wrote books and articles proposing differing theories of interest rates. One common thread was that none of them envisioned negative interest rates as a realistic phenomenon they needed to seriously consider.

In contrast, in the decade following the 2008 Great Financial Crisis, acceptance has been growing that negative interest rates may be a feature of the "new normal" environment, particularly with respect to real interest rates. For example, US, European, British, and Japanese inflation-protected bonds offered negative real interest rates over the entirety of 2020 and 2021. There's still wide-ranging disagreement on the long-term impact of these negative rates, be it good, bad, or neutral.[‡]

Negative Rates and Ultra-long-term Bonds

For Wall Street's bond-pricing models, negative interest rates have mostly been no big deal; the same code, in some cases with relatively minor modifications, works just fine when yields are negative instead of

---

[†] Very roughly, assuming the bond has a 0% coupon (it actually has a 0.125% coupon), the calculation is $1 - (1 - 2\%)^{50} = 0.64$.

[‡] We'll use the term "interest rates" to refer to both nominal and real, inflation-adjusted interest rates, except where we think it's useful to make a distinction. We'll also use "yield" and "yield to maturity" to refer to the internal rate of return (IRR), which discounts a set of bond cash-flows to a given price.

positive. Negative interest rates do imply an arbitrage for investors who can keep cash under the mattress, but this generally doesn't apply to institutional investors.[†] Interest rate derivative models have also required only minor modifications to allow for negative interest rates.

There is at least one exception, a bond type that cannot abide a negative yield: a "consolidated annuity," or consol bond for short. Even though governments don't issue them anymore, they're one of the simplest and oldest of all bond types. Also known as perpetuities, these bonds provide the holder with a fixed interest payment each year in perpetuity. They were issued and reissued by governments such as the United Kingdom, France, and the United States and were often the market's largest and most actively traded issues. The United Kindom retired its last consol bonds in 2015, and today virtually no government-issued perpetual bonds are outstanding. However, investors can buy plenty of other perpetual or near-perpetual cash flow streams (e.g., the stock market), and recently issued sovereign bonds with maturities of 50 to 100 years may feel like near-perpetual offerings to many investors.

The basic formula for the price of a perpetual is simple:

$$p = \frac{c}{y}, \text{ with the symbols representing } \mathbf{p}\text{rice, } \mathbf{c}\text{oupon, and } \mathbf{y}\text{ield, for } y > 0.$$

The formula has two noteworthy aspects: (1) for any positive coupon and positive finite price, the perpetuity cannot have a negative yield, and (2) price approaches infinity as the yield of the perpetuity approaches zero.

Exhibit 21.1 illustrates the relationship between the price and yield of a perpetuity and annuities with tenors of 100 and 1,000 years. Notice how extremely convex these curves become at very low interest rates. This kind of convexity is generally an attractive characteristic for buyers of such investments and a terrifying one for short sellers. It wasn't until the late 1970s that economists started to directly embed uncertainty and randomness into interest rate models, thereby taking account of the convexity central to the perpetuity paradox we'll discuss.[1]

To avoid having to deal directly with infinity—clearly a price that no one would be willing or able to pay—we'll consider a 1,000-year

---

[†]An even stronger arbitrage bound, which doesn't require stuffing cash into your mattress, is that 1-year interest rates need to be greater than −100%, or else borrowing money would be an arbitrage—you would get paid today to receive $1 in the future.

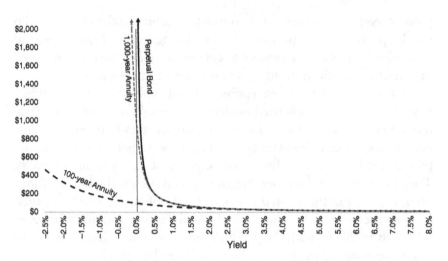

Exhibit 21.1   Price of 100-year, 1,000-year and Perpetual Annuities: Present Value of $1 per Year

annuity paying $1 per year, rather than a true perpetuity. If we know interest rates are fixed for the next 1,000 years, we can easily calculate and see the annuity's price in Exhibit 21.1, but what's a reasonable fair price given some uncertainty in interest rates?

Let's estimate this value by imagining 1,000 different interest-rate scenarios. Let's say that, in 999 scenarios, interest rates will equal 2%. But in just one scenario, we'll assume rates will instead average −1%, in the spirit of the "new-normal" for interest rates and the possibility that interest rates can be negative for sustained periods in the future. The expected value of the annuity is the probability-weighted average of the values of the annuity that result from those scenarios, producing a result that is pretty remarkable:

99.9% probability of 2% rates; annuity value of $50
0.1% probability of −1% rates; annuity value of $2,316,257
Expected value of the annuity is $2,366, which is a yield of −0.15%

The Perpetuity Paradox Finds Expected Utility in St. Petersburg

What we're calling the "perpetuity paradox" is the conundrum facing a person who simultaneously believes there's a small chance that negative interest rates can persist for long periods but would not pay a price anywhere close to the $2,366 expected value of the annuity. One solution to this potential paradox is suggested by the resolution to the St. Petersburg paradox, which we've discussed in Chapter 6. The common thread in both the perpetuity paradox and the St. Petersburg paradox is that the amount someone should be willing to pay is, in the absence of riskless arbitrage, better determined by the Expected Utility rather than the expected value of the outcomes. We find that even at a price of just $51 for the annuity, a typical investor would optimally invest only 0.10% of his or her wealth, even though the price represents a 98% discount to expected value. Buying this annuity is a lot like buying an undervalued lottery ticket, which we explored in Chapter 19.

Much closer to the expected value of $2,366, a price of $2,100 merits an optimal investment of only 0.005% of wealth. Thus, we can see the Expected Utility line of reasoning presents one resolution to the "paradox": even though the small possibility of negative rates makes the "gamble" on the annuity highly valuable, you wouldn't invest more than a tiny fraction of your wealth in it anywhere near its expected value. Sadly, the UK government can forget about issuing a single 1-pound-per-year inflation-indexed perpetuity to pay off the entire national debt!

Connecting the Dots

We can't say if negative interest rates will be a regular feature of financial markets, but it seems difficult to dismiss negative rates as just a fleeting phenomenon. That means it's worth seriously thinking through the issues involved in valuing and investing in long-lived cash-flow streams near or even below the zero interest rate bound.

22

When Less Is More

We might define an efficient market as one in which price is within a factor of 2 of value, i.e., the price is more than half of value and less than twice value. . . . By this definition, I think almost all markets are efficient almost all of the time. . . .
——Fischer Black, 1986 presidential address to the American Finance Association titled "Noise"

In general, the more optimistic we are on the prospects of an investment, the more of it we'll want to own. However, at extreme levels of bullishness, the normal relationship can be turned on its head, and it can make sense to own less of an asset the more we like it. It's hard to think of everyday examples that work like this, so this puzzle is perhaps unfamiliar. It's a problem that gets little attention in mainstream finance because we rarely witness high enough forecasts of investment quality to observe this effect in the wild. However there actually may be one asset class where forecasts are high enough. We can thank the digital-asset revolution and its band of optimistic crypto-enthusiasts for bringing this problem into focus, which also gives us some valuable insights that apply in other domains of financial decision-making.

Crypto Risk and Return

It is hard to know how to accurately model the price behavior of digital assets, but most would agree their returns are far from being well-described by the standard normal distribution. Even more so than their vanilla financial cousins, digital assets experience price jumps and fat tails, and their variability and expected returns are difficult to estimate and can change dramatically over time. Additionally in the case of digital assets, many investors recognize some risk of losing their investment through hacking, hard forks, loss of private keys, etc.—more like seeing one's house burn down than experiencing a bad run in the market. To cut through all the uncertainty of crypto return distributions, we're going to radically simplify and assume that to some chosen horizon there's a 50% chance the asset goes to 0, and a 50% chance it goes up by a factor of P, the "payoff ratio."

Exhibit 22.1 shows the optimal amount you should allocate to this crypto asset given a range of payoff ratios and assuming you fit the profile of our Base-Case investor. We're also assuming this is the only investment opportunity available. As we increase the payoff ratio from 1:1 to 2,048:1, the expected return and risk of the asset go up—and crucially, the ratio of return to risk, the Sharpe ratio, also goes up. That's what we mean when we say that the *quality* of the investment is getting better and better. The optimal allocation $\hat{k}$ is what maximizes your Expected Utility.

When the expected payoff ratio is between 4:1 and 8:1, the optimal allocation reaches its peak at about 17%. Then—and this is the whole point —at *higher* payoff ratios, the optimal bet size *declines*. For very optimistic investors, an allocation well under 10% may be optimal.

Explaining the Hump

An intuitive explanation for this hump is the following:

- It starts at zero: At the 1:1 ratio at the far left of the chart in Exhibit 22.1, since the upside and downside are equally likely and equal in size, the optimal allocation starts at zero since you shouldn't take risk without some expected reward.

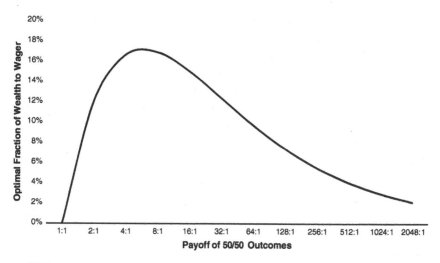

Exhibit 22.1 How Much to Wager on a Digital Asset as Payout Becomes More Favorable: Investor with CRRA Utility Risk-aversion 2

- Then it goes up: As we increase the payoff ratio by moving to the right, the investment opportunity warrants some allocation of capital, initially rising almost linearly with the payoff multiple.
- Then it eventually goes back down to zero again: At some point (rarely seen in practice), when an asset is sufficiently attractive, holding even a small amount of it will make you fabulously rich in the good outcome—so there's no reason to hold a ton of it and risk the bad outcome on a large fraction of wealth. This effect takes the optimal allocation back down again toward zero, giving us the hump shape.

While the circumstances that give us this result are something of an oddity, a closer look at what's going on gives us insights about wealth and risk that are more broadly applicable.

A Different Perspective on Wealth and Risk

Normally, we think of our financial wealth as the sum of the current market values of the assets we own. Investors in private, illiquid assets often value them at their cost basis, or somewhere between cost and an estimate of fair market value. This works well enough in most circumstances, but when you feel you've come across an outstanding gem of an investment, using the market price rather than a value that reflects the higher intrinsic risk-adjusted value can lead to suboptimal decision-making. Encountering an asset that you believe has a 50/50 chance of delivering a 100:1 payoff ratio makes you effectively wealthier than a standard mark-to-market accounting treatment would indicate. If you really believe in the attractiveness of the investment, you would need a substantial compensating payment to forego investing in it. As we've seen before, your Certainty-equivalent Wealth is the level of wealth that you would be equally happy to possess with absolute certainty instead of your current wealth plus the opportunity to invest in the highly attractive asset.

To illustrate, say you decide to invest 17% of your wealth in a crypto-asset that has a 50/50 chance of going up eightfold or down to zero. The expected return of the asset is 300%, and your expected wealth is 51% higher than your starting wealth. But your Certainty-equivalent Wealth is that level of wealth that delivers the same Expected Utility as being able to invest in the risky asset. In this case we calculate that your Certainty-equivalent Wealth is about 25% higher than your starting wealth.

We now turn to the question of risk: how much risk are you taking in the previous illustration? Normally, one might say that your downside is losing 17% of starting wealth, and that's your downside risk—but that ignores that your "true" wealth, your Certainty-equivalent Wealth, is 125% of nominal starting wealth because you bought this great investment. If that's your relevant starting wealth, now we see that the downside is much higher, at 34% (the loss from wealth going from 1.25 to 0.83) if the asset's downside case is realized. Just as we'd expect, as the investment gets more attractive you are indeed taking more downside risk, measured against Certainty-equivalent Wealth. What we see from this example is that we need to think about risk more broadly than just how much we can lose from our initial investment. A better evaluation of risk measures the variability of outcomes from a starting point that includes the embedded value of your opportunity set.

Is It Still "Risk" If You Can't Lose Money?

It's 1964, and you're trying to decide between investing your savings for the long run in a diversified stock portfolio or choosing an active manager. If you decide you want to go with an active manager, you are shown two doors. You are told that behind one of them is an investor named Warren Buffett, who will beat the stock market by 10% a year for the next 58 years, while behind the other door is an average stock-picking mutual fund manager, who will underperform the market by 2% a year after fees. All the different investment options come with the same investment risk and no taxes.

Would you choose to index or to take a chance on the two-door gamble, with a 50% chance of investing with Warren Buffett and turning $100,000 of investment into $3.8 billion? From 1964 to the end of 2022, Warren Buffett's Berkshire Hathaway stock is up 38,000x, while the S&P 500 is up about 250x, representing a 20% and a 10% compound return, respectively. We've assumed the actively managed mutual fund had an 8% return over that period, for an 85x total return. Notice that in the worst case, you'd still make 85x your initial investment if you took the gamble and got the mutual fund manager rather than Buffett to shepherd your savings.

In expected value terms, the 50/50 Buffett versus mediocre-manager bet is worth about 19,000x, much more than the 250x you'd get from investing in the S&P 500 index fund.

However, in Expected Utility terms, with our usual risk-aversion assumption, you would choose the low cost index fund option, and by a decent margin.[1] This can be seen from realizing that the actively managed mutual fund performance would represent a reduction in your end wealth of about 65% relative to the S&P 500 investment, a risk of loss too big for most investors to accept on a 50/50 coin flip.

Connecting the Dots

The assumptions we've made in this analysis have been chosen for simplicity and illustration. In particular, we recognize that modeling outcomes of digital assets in a binary manner is not realistic, though it does capture a certain kind of view that digital assets will either go to the moon or fade away. But the general effect we describe, that the optimal holding of an asset at some point goes *down* as its attractiveness goes *up*, holds over a pretty broad range of assumptions about distributions of outcomes and investor risk preferences. But not all whales are of the humpback variety. This effect may not hold in two notable cases: (1) if the asset follows a continuous random walk and the investor can rebalance his portfolio continuously without frictions or (2) if an investor has a risk-tolerance equal to or greater than a full Kelly bettor.

The insight that we should view our base wealth as inclusive of the value provided by attractive investment opportunities isn't analytically anything new since the Expected Utility framework we've been discussing throughout implicitly incorporates this viewpoint. But it can be an interesting and important perspective when we're thinking heuristically about our wealth. For example, a hedge fund or private equity manager might be prone to overinvest in the fund he manages if he underestimates the value and risk associated with his ownership interest in his fund management business.

23

The Costanza Trade

Seinfeld Season 10: The ETF Episode

Here's the puzzle, set as a fanciful dialogue between the Seinfeld characters George and Kramer in "The ETF Episode":

Sometime in late 2018. . .

George: *How about this stock market? Down 14% in three months. It's killing me. Day after day and all I see are big red numbers next to every single one of my investments. Everything I buy goes straight down—I can't take it!*

Kramer: *Ooooooweee, buying stocks is no good.*

George: *No good?*

Kramer: *Here's a can't-lose strategy for you: invest half your money in SPXL and the other half in SPXS.*

George:	*I never heard of these stocks before. What are they?*
Kramer:	*They're not stocks, they're ETFs—exchange traded funds, and they're TURRRRBO-charged! SPXL is a 3x leveraged long S&P 500 ETF and SPXS is a 3x leveraged short S&P 500 ETF. There's no limit to how much they can go up, and you can't lose more than you put into them. One or the other is gonna make you rich. Kaching!*
George:	*It's gotta be better than what I'm doing now. What could possibly go wrong?*
	15 Months Later. . .
George:	*KRAMER!! What'd you do to me?!!? I should never have listened to you.*
Kramer:	*What are you talking about? What's the problem?*
George:	*It's those two leveraged ETFs you told me about. The stock market is up 6% since our little chat, but SPXL and SPXS are both down big —one is down 20% and the other one is down almost 50%!*
Kramer:	*Hmmm. . .doesn't seem possible. I've got another idea: from now on, just do the opposite of whatever you think is a good idea?*
George:	*I tried that already, and I'd rather not talk about it.*[1]

Leveraged ETF Returns: Not What George Was Expecting

George's surprise at losing on both SPXL and SPXS is understandable; they sound like direct opposites of each other. Given the 3x leverage and the stock market up 6%, he probably expected SPXL to be up about 18% and SPXS to be down about 18%.[†] Instead, both underperformed the "anticipated" result by more than 30%. The ETFs were not poorly managed, and the relatively high fees (about 1%) don't come close to explaining the performance gap. In understanding this particular puzzle, we won't need Expected Utility, but we will see an outstanding illustration of one of the central themes of this book, which is that choosing the right investment sizing can often be more important than choosing the right investment.

[†]By 3x leverage we mean Total Assets/Capital = 3.

These highly leveraged long and short ETFs provide a perfect example of how overly aggressive investment sizing can turn a good trade into a losing one. When you borrow money to take a leveraged position in an asset, you'll need to keep trading the asset if you want to maintain a constant leverage ratio as the asset price fluctuates. For example, 3x leveraged ETFs are structured and labeled as being managed so that they are 3x leveraged at the end of each day. For a 3x long ETF, that means the ETF needs to buy every day the market goes up and sell when it goes down. This creates a nasty surprise: if the S&P 500 starts at 2,500, goes up to 3,000 one day, then back to 2,500, the 3x-long ETF has to buy at 3,000 and then sell at 2,500, locking in a loss over the 2 days even though the market is flat. We've met this phenomenon of "volatility drag" all the way back in Chapter 3 and several more times since. It is the loss that comes from trading to maintain constant leverage. On any single day, the 3x leveraged ETF return is equal to 3x the daily return, but over multiple days, because of this daily trading, the 3x leveraged return will differ from 3x the compound return. The more volatile the market, the greater will be the volatility drag on the compound return.

What if you just decide not to rebalance to a constant leverage ratio? In that case, the volatility drag is transformed from a relatively stable cost through time into a path-dependent, one-off risk of total wipe-out, without changing the overall expected outcome. For example, if the two ETFs George had invested in started at 3x leverage and then did no rebalancing, the result would have been that SPXL would have returned about 12%, but SPXS would have lost 100% in mid-February 2020, when the S&P 500 had gained more than 33.3% since the start of George's investment. So, with no rebalancing, George's combined ETF investment would have lost 44% rather than 35% on the daily rebalanced ETFs. Of course, this was just one path, but it's a good illustration of how the rebalancing frequency introduces both path dependency and knockout risk.

High leverage combined with high realized volatility can have a powerfully negative impact on returns, enough to explain George's realized return of −20% for SPXL and −50% for SPXS relative to the market return of 6%. In Exhibit 23.1, we simulate how George's 3x-leveraged long ETF would have done over a range of returns for the S&P 500, given the 28% realized volatility of the stock market over his holding period.[2] For SPXL to have outperformed an unleveraged investment, the

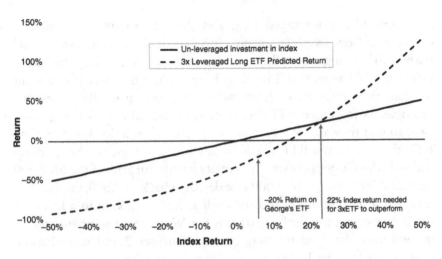

Exhibit 23.1   3x Leveraged Long ETF Predicted Return Versus Unleveraged Index Return: George's 1.25-year horizon. S&P 500 Volatility = 28%

market needed to go up by more than 22% to overcome the leverage-induced volatility drag.

Market Impact of Leveraged ETFs: 1987 Portfolio Insurance Sequel?

Even though George hadn't heard about these leveraged ETFs, they've been around since 2006, and they've grown to be more than a sideshow in the marketplace. Leveraged ETFs had assets of close to $50 billion at the end of March 2023, and that's just tallying up the US-listed structures that are publicly registered—there's likely considerably more in privately structured products and non-US vehicles.[3]

To gauge the potential market impact of these leveraged long and short ETFs, let's take a closer look at what trades SPXL and SPXS would have to execute after a 10% market rise.

We can see that after a 10% market rise, SPXL would be under-levered and SPXS would be overlevered. To return to 3x-long and 3x-short, *both* ETFs need to buy more S&P 500. Assuming both ETFs start with $100 of assets per share, SPXL needs to buy $60 of the

S&P 500 and SPXS needs to buy $120. If the market falls instead, the numbers are the same, but the ETFs will need to sell. As you can imagine, the turnover within these levered funds can be enormous. For a 3x leveraged-long ETF assuming 1% daily moves (16% annualized), annual turnover would be 1,500%, and 3,000% for a 3x leveraged-short ETF.

In terms of the potential market impact of the trades these ETFs need to make each day, we estimate that their managers need to buy or sell about $10 billion of equities when the stock market goes up or down by 5%, and most of that trading has to happen near the closing bell each day. Of course, many market participants are aware of these and other similarly predictable flows coming from options-hedging and leveraged investment strategies, such as Risk Parity and volatility targeting funds. In trying to profit from them, opportunists smooth them out and make them harder to pinpoint, but we doubt the impact of these forecastable flows completely disappears.

Sizing Your Stock Market Exposure for the Long Term

Choosing your equity allocation should be a forward-looking exercise, driven by your assessment of future return and risk and your own circumstances and personal level of risk-aversion. That said, it's still interesting and instructive to review the past, and so let's take a look at how different levels of stock market exposure—including leveraged exposure—would have performed over the long term.

From 1927 to the end of 2022 (the longest period over which we can easily get daily stock market data), the annualized total return on the S&P 500 was 9.8%, which would have turned a $1 million investment into $7 billion today—not too shabby. Average stock market volatility was just about 19%, T-bills returned 3.6%, and inflation in the United States over the period was 3.0%. If you were around in 1927 and had a crystal ball, wouldn't you have been tempted to invest in equities on margin and really make a killing for your lucky descendants? After all, if investing 100% of your savings in equities for the long term was sure to be great, why not invest 200% or 300% of your savings?

Table 23.1 works through this thought experiment, showing how things would have turned out if you had taken on different amounts of leverage over those nearly 100 years. Notice that 2x leverage leaves you with the most money at the end, but at some point, you'd have experienced a drawdown of 98.5%. You might have initially guessed that, at 2x leverage, your return would be equal to the unleveraged return of equities plus the excess return of equities over the borrow rate (we assume 1% above T-bills or 4.6%). This works out to a return of 15.0%, but *your return would have been just 11.1%.* The shortfall of 3.9% is the result of volatility drag.

Above 2x leverage, compound returns actually go down, as volatility drag outweighs the extra return you'd get from owning equities returning 9.8% funded with a 4.6% borrowing rate. At 4x leverage, after suffering more than a 99.999% drawdown, you'd eventually be left with about $5, barely above the $1 you started with (just $0.28 inflation-adjusted), and at 5x leverage you'd have been fully wiped out on October 19, 1987.

If you were standing in 1927 with a crystal ball, what level of exposure would you have chosen?

Table 23.1

Leverage Ratio	Compound Return per Annum (nominal)	Risk per Annum	End Value of $1	Maximum Peak-to-Trough Drawdown
0.50	7.1%	9.5%	$682	−55%
0.75	8.6%	14.2%	$2,437	−73%
1.00	**9.8%**	**19.0%**	**$7,059**	**−84%**
1.50	11.0%	28.5%	$19,503	−95%
2.00	11.1%	38.1%	$22,882	−98.5%
3.00	8.5%	57.7%	$2,233	−99.9%
4.00	1.7%	78.4%	$4.79	−99.999%
5.00	−infinity	170.7%	$0.00	−100.000%

The table assumes daily rebalancing, no transaction costs, no fees, no market impact, borrowing at 3-month T-bill rates +1%. Attentive readers will notice the maximum loss of 84% in the case of the 1.0 leverage ratio, which is smaller than the near 90% loss we have referred to previously. The difference is that here we are measuring total returns including dividends, while the near 90% loss is exclusive of dividends.

Opposite George?

What if George followed Kramer's advice and did the opposite of whatever he thought was a good idea—so instead of buying these two leveraged ETFs, he shorted them? As we explained in Chapter 16 in the context of buying or selling put options, being short is not the opposite of being long. In fact, if we assume that George wants to keep the value of his short equal to his capital in the trade, then being *short* the 3x leveraged long ETF looks exactly the same as being *long* the 3x leveraged short ETF, and vice versa, so the total outcome is identical from the long side and the short side.

The closest thing to achieving the opposite of the leveraged ETFs' volatility drag would be to invest in a balanced portfolio, such as 50% equities and 50% T-bills. Maintaining the 50/50 weight over time would require buying equities when they go down and selling when they go up, creating a volatility "lift" instead of a "drag" from the portfolio rebalancing. Unfortunately, this lift is naturally limited in scale: you can create as much drag as you want by using large leverage, but you get the maximum lift by maintaining a position size at 50% of total capital.

Get Shorty

Victor recalls a puzzle posed by one of the senior bond traders at Salomon Brothers sometime in 1987. There was a high-flying stock called Home Shopping Network (HSN) that investors had bid up to the moon. The trader was thinking about shorting the stock in his personal account (as Wall Street compliance departments allowed back in the 1980s). He asked: what is the right strategy for shorting a stock that you're sure will go to zero, eventually, but in the meantime is so volatile, and the market is so crazy, that it can go up to almost any imaginable price?

In case that trader picked up this book and is still reading, here's a tentative, belated answer. We'll assume this stock has a daily standard deviation of about 6%, its expected return is −20% per year, and its returns are normally distributed. With these characteristics, the probability that the price of the stock would have dropped by more than 95% over the next 10 years is about 90%, and there's a 50% chance that the stock would have dropped by more than 99.9%!

(Continued)

That seems to capture the view that the price is almost definitely going to zero, while allowing for some small probability that the stock would become unborrowable or the company would be bought by a larger company at a price way above zero.

The strategy that maximizes Expected Utility (ignoring other possible investments) would be to short an amount of the stock equal to 10% of your wealth and to continually rebalance the position to maintain that 10% sizing. Following such a strategy (and ignoring commissions, bid-offer trading spreads, and stock borrow fees) would result in a roughly one-third chance of losing money on the trade, and an expected Risk-adjusted Return on wealth of 1% per annum.[†]

It might come as a surprise that you'd expect to record a profit only if the stock drops by more than 99% over the 10 years! In the very unlikely event (about a 1% chance) that HSN finished the 10 years at the same price at which it started, you'd expect to lose about 40% of wealth.

When the dust settled, the short position in HSN resulted in a profit for the Salomon bond trader, but only after a very wild ride with an unrealized loss at some point of triple his initial position size. As it happens, he didn't rebalance the trade at all once he initiated it, and we're not suggesting that in this case he should have rebalanced to keep a constant fraction of his wealth exposed to it as the stock price fluctuated. But it is interesting to note that if he had followed that approach, he probably would have lost money on the trade even though the stock price went down about 75% when he finally exited it. Altogether a relatively happy ending, which provided some valuable and cautionary lessons with regard to shorting highly overvalued, highly volatile assets.[‡]

Connecting the Dots

A big problem with holding leveraged long and short ETFs for more than 1 day is that most investors are likely to think they are making a decision based on a view of where the market is going: up or down. As we've explained though, that can often be far from the full picture of

---

[†]And yes, we considered the use of options to express this trade, but with our assumptions that wouldn't materially alter the conclusion.

[‡]Don't do it!

what to expect. Rather, the return on a leveraged long or short ETF held over time will incur a drag that increases dramatically with both leverage and realized volatility. As George's experience attests, you can have the right call on market direction while the investment outcome is overwhelmed by the impact of high realized volatility.

The exchange between George and Kramer is fictional, but the disappointing returns on George's two leveraged ETFs are sadly quite real. The lesson from George's misadventure isn't only for those thinking about investing in highly leveraged ETFs. For all investments, as position size increases, there's a point beyond which you'll be more likely to wind up with losses than with gains, and further still, an amount of exposure at which you'll be almost assured of losing all your money. Much of the art of investment sizing lies in appreciating and choosing where on the expected return versus risk curve is right for you.

24

Conclusion: U and Your Wealth

Say not I have found the truth, but I have found a truth.
—Kahlil Gibran, *The Prophet* (1923)

We started our discussion of financial decision-making by examining a random coin flip as a simple model of uncertainty. From the starting point of that one small coin flip, we were able to discover some intuitive and useful rules of thumb, from constant fractional betting to a simple formula tying together expected return, risk, and individual risk-aversion. From these building blocks we get the result that for optimally sized bets, the Risk-adjusted Return will generally equal half of the raw expected return, which follows from the insight that the amount of compensation you should demand for bearing risk goes up with the square of the risk. In an example we took from the opening pages of Michael Lewis' *Liar's Poker*, we saw that the cost of risk in a 50/50 gamble for $10 million should be 100 times the cost of risk in a 50/50 gamble for $1 million.

We introduced the concept of utility to take us beyond coin flips, and the core of the utility-based framework is that good decisions are those that maximize Expected Utility. The utility framework is a more flexible tool than thinking about decisions as made up of coin flips and the binomial distributions that arise from them. It allows us to assess more realistic situations that involve asymmetric and fat-tailed distributions, helping us to focus on the low-probability, high-impact events—like depressions, pandemics, and wars—that can be even more important than the quotidian risks that buffet our financial lives in normal times.

Making decisions guided by Expected Utility is not a new idea, but it also is not currently a popular one, and we've discussed at length the major criticisms of this approach. By far the most common criticism is that Expected Utility doesn't do a good job of describing how most people actually make decisions. We agree with that, but we don't see it as a reason to look elsewhere. This book is meant to help improve the financial lives of our readers, helping them to make *better* decisions, not just to help them understand or replicate all the various biases and inconsistencies of human decision-making. As such we primarily care that our framework does a good job of pointing to sensible, consistent, welfare-enhancing decisions.

We discussed how risk-aversion is normal among affluent individuals, and it is a direct consequence of the decreasing marginal utility of wealth. For risk-averse individuals, there is an answer to the question of "how much of a good investment opportunity is best?" Too little or too much of a good thing are both suboptimal. In particular, in numerous examples, we saw how making sizing decisions with the objective of maximizing expected wealth, rather than Expected Utility, can be absolutely ruinous! It is a matter of your personal degree of risk-aversion, but we have found that in practice, there's a relatively narrow range of risk-aversion that seems to span the preferences of affluent investors.

We then moved on to consider the ways in which spending our wealth increases our welfare. This took us from a single period to a multi-period analysis, and we came across important new sources of uncertainty beyond investment risk that we needed to build into our decision framework. The most important new risk was uncertain lifespan. We found that Expected Utility was well suited to helping us think about this more realistic intertemporal framing of the problem we all face.

Two important concepts emerged from moving to a lifetime perspective on how we spend our wealth. First, investment risk and spending risk are inextricably linked. If we cannot stand to reduce spending when we experience bad investment outcomes, then it is not sensible to take risk in our investment portfolio. We were able to go further, finding an optimal spending policy that reflected not only personal preferences, but also the effects of investment and longevity risk. Second, adopting the lifetime perspective suggests we should be measuring our wealth as was customary in bygone times, as the real annual spending it can support, rather than the value of our net assets today. This change in view brings with it the idea that the most appropriate safe assets for long-term investors are inflation-protected bonds, like TIPS, rather than cash in the bank, T-bills, or fixed rate nominal bonds.

If we lived in a world where there was no uncertainty in our financial future, we would not need the concept of Expected Utility to weigh the different possible outcomes. If all investments produced risk-free returns, if we knew how much we'd earn in our jobs and for how long, if we knew exactly how long we and our loved ones would live (and how many of them we'd be loving), if income and estate tax policy were immutably fixed, then we could just fill in the cells of a spreadsheet for how we'd like to spend our financial and human capital for the rest of our lives.

Alas, there is tremendous uncertainty in all these important aspects of our financial lives, and we cannot arrive at good decisions from focusing solely on the most likely outcome or Base Case. Incorporating uncertainty into our decisions is why we need the framework we've laid out in this book. The framework is not there to tell us what our preferences *should be*; its job is to tell us the decisions that are best in light of the unknown future, given what our core personal preferences *are*. Alternative frameworks exist, but as we've seen when comparing them to Expected Utility in numerous case studies, they all come up short.

We've shown how to apply the Expected Utility framework in a range of case studies, but there are far more situations where Expected Utility can help us make better decisions than the ones we've covered. At the risk of appearing like men with a hammer who see every problem as a nail, here are a few further examples:

- Should you rent or buy your home? If you buy, how should you finance it? What should be your overall portfolio construction with or without the house? We also need to recognize that home ownership is not a purely financial decision, as it can impact your family dynamics and your relationship to a community.
- How much should you invest, or keep invested, in your own business?
- How much should you pay to diversify away from a highly appreciated, concentrated risk asset?
- Should you pay to insure death, disability, longevity, and long-term care?
- How much and when should you make intergenerational and philanthropic gifts?
- What's the best way to manage vested employee stock options?
- When's the best time to start taking social security benefits?
- When should you retire?

We believe the ideas we've presented are simple and intuitive. But then why do so many of us stumble badly in the big financial decisions in our lives? Why are there so many "missing billionaires"? Just because something is simple, doesn't mean it's easy, as Warren Buffett is fond of saying. Temptation and trepidation goad us to alternate between too much risk and high living, and selling out of our investments at the exact wrong time and staying underinvested in equities for too long. And all these woes are exacerbated by a financial system that wants a piece, as big a piece as possible, charging us fees and getting us to play games with the odds stacked against us. These are the challenges we face and to which many earlier travelers on our road succumbed, but there are many encouraging signs that individuals currently are doing much better with their financial decisions than previous generations.

It took a long time for individual investors to help themselves to the free lunch of diversification extolled by Harry Markowitz in 1952, but investors today are finally enjoying the bountiful harvest germinated by ideas of financial economists a half a century ago. Individuals benefit to the tune of hundreds of billions of dollars a year from the lower cost and increased diversification offered by stock and bond index funds and ETFs, effectively free banking and brokerage services, and tax incentives and other nudges to help individuals make sound long-term investing and saving decisions. There's excellent financial advice available too, if one knows where to look for it. While much of the research and writing of finance academics is written in what appears to outsiders as their own private language, plenty of books and articles from these thinkers are written expressly for nonspecialists, and they tend to present a consistent message. You don't need to read a dozen of these books to know what most of them say.

However, both the good and the not-so-good financial advice available to nonspecialists is almost exclusively focused on choosing what to invest in rather than the equally critical question of how much investment is the right amount. The press needs to tell a new story every day, so they'll prognosticate on whether the stock market or interest rates are going up or down, which stocks or sectors to buy, where the economy is headed, and what that means for what you should own. They'll speculate on the merits of investing in hedge funds, private equity, tech startups, New York City luxury apartments, or index funds. Many of these stories will be fascinating but not so useful for figuring out the future, as they are primarily telling you what's already in the past.

Assuming you can sift through all this information and figure how to put your portfolio of good investments together from the myriad choices available, you're still only halfway there. You still need to decide how much of that portfolio you should own and how much to keep in safe assets or to borrow so you can own even more. On this question, the press and personal investing books provide almost no guidance at all. As we've seen, the "how much" question goes beyond investing decisions, to just about every important financial decision we'll encounter: how much to spend now and over time, how much to give to others, how much capital gains to realize, and how much to work. There is a large academic literature addressing these questions, but not enough has been written in a nontechnical form. We hope that this book will go some way to filling that gap.

We cannot ignore the market excitement of 2021 over meme stocks, extreme growth stocks, single stock options, SPACS, and cryptocurrencies. Whatever the final value of these investments turns out to be, it is fair to say that many investors have likely been too concentrated in their portfolios and taken too much risk, relative to a reasonable set of beliefs about expected returns, risks, and risk-aversion. We hope and expect that this most recent movement of retail investors making concentrated "all-in" investments with a commitment to hold them forever, "HODL with diamond hands" in the vernacular of the day, will be a hiccup on the continued path towards better individual financial decision-making.

Some observers suggest that the best way, perhaps the only way, to learn sound financial decision-making is through trial and error and learning from our mistakes.[1] Unfortunately, as we've discussed already, it takes a lot of data, often more than a lifetime's worth, to be able to learn sound financial decision-making from the data and one's personal choices alone. As Victor's father was fond of saying: "A person needs two lives: the first to gain experience, and the second to put that experience to use."[†] We hope that for some readers, this book will be at least a partial substitute for learning things the hard way.

Our focus has been on the individual or family unit, and not on society at large. Indeed, some readers may feel that it's good that so many fortunes, such as the Vanderbilts, have come to woe, as wealth inequality would be greater than it is today if the tens of thousands of missing billionaires were not missing. It's impossible to know for sure, but our feeling is that sound financial decision-making one person at a time would aggregate to an overall wealthier society, one with much less inequality. Yes, there might be more billionaires, but there would be many more affluent families too. However, it's also possible that sound financial decision-making might result in fewer individuals with fortunes of many billions of dollars, since many of those fortunes arose from highly concentrated and successful investments that should likely have been diversified sooner, or from fees or trading profits on "other people's money," which would be harder to come by if more people were making better financial decisions.

In "Mind the Gap: Inequality and Diversification,"[2] we discussed how the level of wealth inequality existing in the United States today could be explained by households holding concentrated portfolios of individual equities. From the 1950s through the 1980s, before the growth of index funds, the median number of stocks held in individual brokerage accounts was just two.[3] The mechanism of overly concentrated investment portfolios leading to dramatic wealth inequality provides an alternative to the explanation proposed by Thomas Piketty in *Capital in the 21st Century*. Piketty assumes that equity returns are high and constant, and so once a household gets rich enough to have significant investable wealth, they're going to get richer and richer.[4]

[†] We suspect this is an old Persian proverb, but it might also be related to the counsel from Confucius: "We have two lives, and the second begins when we realize we only have one."

Instead, pervasive suboptimal financial decision-making predicts the frequently observed downward mobility of the undiversified wealthy and gives us a simple and concise answer to the puzzle of the "missing billionaires." It also points the way to a more level distribution of wealth in the future, due to the growth over the past 20 years of index funds and other diversified mutual funds.[5] It shines a bright and hopeful light on one possible path to less wealth inequality in the future, which is for investors to think more carefully about diversification and investment-sizing, thus improving their chances of participating in the long-term expected wealth creation opportunities offered by public markets.

Returning to the case of the individual, we appreciate that most of the decisions we need to make on a daily basis are of low consequence and don't merit a slow and deliberate evaluation of the Expected Utility of different potential decisions. In other words, don't sweat the small stuff—you can safely leave those decisions to your gut and intuition. But for the big decisions, we hope you'll slow down your thinking, and reach for the Expected Utility toolkit to answer the particular flavor of the "how much" question you're facing. In the long run, the expected improvement in your financial welfare can be very substantial.

We know there's more to a full and happy life than making financial decisions that maximize your Expected Utility, but making sound financial decisions is doable and sure can help with the rest. As the comedian Milton Berle said:

Money can't buy you happiness, but it helps you look for it in a lot more places.

Bonus Chapter: Liar's Poker and Learning to Bet Smart

We thought an inside, detailed account of Liar's Poker as it was played at Salomon Brothers in the late 1980s might be of interest, as it's become part of Wall Street lore, and it's a fun game to play among friends to see who's going to pick up the dinner tab! It also nicely illustrates the importance of thinking in probabilities which is a key to making good decisions under uncertainty.

Here's Victor's account:

We played Liar's Poker a lot in the days that Michael Lewis wrote about in his book named after our game. Michael wrote *Liar's Poker* thinking it would be taken as a warning to future generations to stay clear of Wall Street, but it seems to have had the exact opposite effect, attracting promising young minds to the Street like bees to honey or, in his view, like moths to a flame.

Despite the title, the book devotes just a few pages to the actual game of Liar's Poker, which we've already touched on in Chapter 4. We used the game as an illustration of the idea that the compensation we should require for risk-taking should go up with the square of the risk being taken. For example, the compensation needed to take a 50/50 gamble to win or lose $200,000 is four times the compensation required to take a 50/50 gamble to make or lose $100,000.

The rules of Liar's Poker, or LP as we called it, are simple. It's played with the eight-digit serial number on a US bill. Each player takes a bill and keeps the serial number hidden from the other players. The player with the lowest letters flanking the numbers starts, making an opening bid of how many occurrences of a particular digit he believes there are across everyone's bills. The player holding the bid wins if, when challenged by everyone, the total number of the digits on all the players' bills, including the bidder's, is at least equal to the bid. Let's illustrate with an actual game.

"Five 8s."

Pete's bid had been challenged by all the other players and had come all the way around to me. The bidding goes clockwise, and I was sitting just to Pete's right, making me the last player who could either challenge his bid or make a higher bid of my own. I was the final line of defense, and I was holding two 8s on my bill. I remember feeling pretty lonely in the middle of the giant Salomon trading floor. It was 1986, and I was 24, the most junior trader on Salomon's government arb desk. It wasn't the best time in my career to mess up. If I didn't up Pete's five 8s bid and he decided to count them, Pete would win his bid of five 8s if there were five or more 8s that appeared across everyone's bills, including his own.

The game was open to anyone who wanted to play, a reflection of how flat Wall Street firms were then. The houses that were succeeding in those days of rapid change mixed street smarts with geeky smarts and that was definitely on display as I looked around the circle. To my left was Pete, a younger, and better looking version of Jack Nicholson, with a wicked sense of humor. He loved to bluff and tended to get away with it. Next was Wilkie, a slow talking, fast thinking former Otis elevator repairman from Alabama who became the firm's top interest rate swap trader. Then there was Moz, a US national math champion and on everyone's shortlist for the smartest guy at the firm. He knew a lot about game theory but was a bit mechanical in his LP play. And then there was Eric, a former Harvard Business School professor and excellent poker player. He knew the odds but, better than that, seemed able to read the rest of us like an open book. These were just four of the dozen or so regulars, and then there were the drifters who'd float in and out, often exiting the game a little lighter in the wallet.

I can't exactly say what made LP so addictive. Maybe it was the deceptive simplicity of the game, or maybe it was how it combined elements of luck and skill, much as backgammon does compared to chess, and so gives hope to the beginner and a reminder to the expert that skill isn't always enough. Anyone could win a big hand, and when combined with our natural human tendency to see ourselves as above average, that made it hard to know which side of the fleecing operation you were on. Although we played for money, no one ever mentioned it. We talked about playing for units. LP was a game of wits, maybe even of character, and talking about money didn't feel right.

At the end of a hand, no one was ever asked to show their bill either, you just held up your fingers to show how many of the bid digit you had, or a clenched fist if you had none. Remember, this was at a time when most bond trades were taking place over the phone, sometimes in hundred million dollar clips, without voice recordings, and mostly without problems.

The "sheet" was the running tally of all players' credits and debits, kept by the most meticulous of the group. It was an honor to be trusted with the sheet. Generally the sheet was settled monthly. It was not expected that the sheet-keeper would calculate or share statistics with players beyond the past month's tally. On one occasion, the sheet-keeper gave a life-to-date tally to one of the players, who then dropped out of the game forever, much to the vexation of the rest of the players. The sheet-keeper was usually also responsible for printing out "strips" with randomly generated eight-digit numbers on them, which we eventually switched to as our appetite for fresh bills to play with seemed to be outpacing the Fed's attempts to grow the money supply.

As I glanced down at my bill to see if those two 8s were still there, and they were, I ran through the choices in my head. I could either challenge or raise Pete's bid, with a bid such as five 9s or six 3s, which then would become the prevailing bid. By the way, we treated 0s, or "10s" as we called them, as the highest digit, which you'll need to know if you plan on playing the game with your friends. If my bid was challenged by everyone, then I'd have an option to either count them, or I'd have one chance to raise my own bid. If I got challenged all the way around on my second raised bid, that was it, and I'd have to ask for the count.

The key was to be unpredictable, to disguise what you had by randomly bluffing. Another tactic that required strong nerves was to challenge even though you had several of that digit, in the hope that someone else would go up, and that you could slip in a higher bid later. That was the infamous "snake-in-the-grass" strategy, and when it backfired, and you were caught red-handed challenging with lots of the number bid in your hand, taking all the other players down, all hell would break loose.

The banter and theatrics made the game. A few players who tended to be timid and challenged a lot, like me, were sometimes accused of lacking a pulse. As the eyes turned to me, Pete said: "So what's the play from the coffin corner, young Vic?"

You're probably getting the idea that going to work, if you could call it that, was a blast, and it was. But despite the fun, or maybe because of it, Salomon was leading the revolution taking place in the newly deregulated bond market, in terms of both innovation and making money. We loved to trade: bonds during the day, and after the markets closed, we'd move right on to LP. You'd often find a few stragglers, especially the unmarried ones like me, playing at midnight, despite each successive hand being proclaimed the "final-final-no-tears."

Back to those five 8s staring me down. I was pretty sure that if I challenged, Pete would ask for the count, and win, as I figured he had two or three, and with my two 8s he'd only need to get one from the other three players even if he only had two 8s himself. It occurred to me that I had bid four 8s earlier in the hand, so Pete might have bid 8s to goad me into going up. But then again, if I challenged, and there were five (or more) 8s, I'd be responsible for the other three players in the game, and me, losing the hand to Pete.

What would you do? . . . Well, this is what I did—I raised Pete's bid and went up to six 8s. My heart sank as it got challenged all the way around in a flash. I had nowhere else to go, so I called for the count. Eric had none, but Moz and Wilkie each had one, so I was feeling pretty good, just needing two from Pete and I'd be home. Then Pete held up his hand and slowly curled his fingers into a fist, showing us he had none. He had been bluffing, betting I'd take the bait. Now I felt not only dumb but 4 units poorer too, losing 1 unit to each of the other players.

As they say, experience is what you get when things don't turn out the way you want. I learned two lessons from that hand: first, it's always better to take a small, near certain loss, than to roll the dice on a gamble with a bigger expected loss in the hope of avoiding a loss altogether. Sounds obvious, but it's not easy because of the little gremlin in our heads that hates taking losses. This is exactly what Kahneman and Tversky found that led them to their prospect theory of decision-making under uncertainty. As we discussed in Chapter 7, they found that many people would rather take an 80% chance of losing $4,000 and a 20% chance of not losing anything, than to take a for-sure loss of $3,000. That is about as close to provable irrationality as you can get. The emotional challenge involved in crystalizing losses is so big that it probably accounts for why traders who follow a tight stop-loss approach tend to be both rare and successful.

LP also probably sharpened our trading skills. To win at LP, as to win in investing, you have to approach the game dispassionately, with a thick skin, and not worry about how you're going to be viewed by others.[†] It's about betting and playing smart to get the best expected outcome; it's not about minimizing regret. Learning to appreciate and play according to the probabilities was a valuable skill when it came to thinking about larger risks.

A rookie mistake was to bid too aggressively, not factoring in that bidding carries a winner's curse, that you tend to get challenged when the other players don't have the number you're bidding. In the example of a six-man game, you'd expect four of each digit from the other five players in the field, but conditional on people only challenging if they have zero or one of the digit bid, the expected number of each digit is only 2.5. To give a greater incentive to bid, and to spice things up, the bidder would win bonus units if he won with an extra high bid, or with a bid of 6s.

It was a zero-sum game, and so you had to keep asking yourself what mistakes might these other smart players be making. Often I worried that the best I could hope for was to break even. If you played enough, you could see a number of decision-making biases of the Kahneman-Tversky variety in action—sadly, I hadn't heard of them at the time—including confirmation bias, anchoring, herding, and the fallacy of sunk costs, driving some players to double down and bid more aggressively to try to dig themselves out of a hole. Bidding sometimes seemed aimed at minimizing regret rather than maximizing gains. Above all, people tend to be overconfident, as exemplified by the well-known finding that 90% of automobile drivers believe themselves to be above average drivers. Most players didn't like to see themselves as passive and so didn't like to follow a strategy heavy on challenging, which made the more passive approach a good one and had the added benefit of allowing you to be a pretty dangerous snake in the grass on occasion. Sometimes a challenging strategy would come into vogue, and then it would be time to become a more active bidder.

I can't recall my first hand of LP at Salomon, but I'll never forget the last one I played the day I left the firm in 1993. I think it was the

---

[†]At the time of writing, our friends Richard Dewey and Jeff Rosenbluth have been working with researchers at Google DeepMind to develop a computer program to play Liar's Poker at a level at or above the best human players of the game. We wish them luck and hope their efforts will introduce more people to this most excellent game of skill and luck.

biggest hand I ever won. You're probably wondering just how big, but it wouldn't really be in the spirit of the game to say! No one can recall why, but once our merry band left Salomon and started LTCM, we stopped playing Liar's Poker. I'm not superstitious, but who knows, maybe things would have turned out differently if we'd carried on playing. One thing's for sure, having fun in the workplace is an underrated and essential ingredient in successful organizations.

Cheat Sheet

1. **Getting risk right is very important**. It's nearly impossible to go broke by picking bad investments if you get the sizing right, but it's easy to go bust by taking too much risk, even if you choose great investments! Taking twice the optimal amount of risk completely wipes out the risk-adjusted benefit of a good investment and taking more risk than that makes you exponentially worse off than doing nothing at all. Too much exposure, even to really good investments, can end in total wipeout. The Merton share is a useful rule of thumb and starting point for determining the right exposure to take. Optimal investment size is a function of personal risk-aversion, and goes up in proportion to expected excess return and down in proportion to risk measured as variance (σ^2).

2. **Markets are highly competitive**. A good working assumption is that *you cannot get more return without taking more risk*. However, it is easy to get more risk without getting more return. For example, you probably won't get compensated for bearing stock-specific, idiosyncratic risk that can be eliminated through diversification. Maximize diversification across all asset classes, including international markets, and avoid zero-sum activities where you do not have an edge. Steer clear of leverage, shorting, concentration, and complexity. Accept that it is unlikely you can beat the market with public information. When considering stock-picking, bear in mind that the majority of individual US stocks have returned less than T-bills.

3. **Decide how to measure your financial well-being**. If it's your capacity to spend on your needs, wants, and gifts to others over your lifetime, then it's the *real, after-tax income stream* that your capital can generate and that you can spend over time that matters, not the

lump-sum present value of your wealth. This perspective on financial well-being makes inflation-protected bonds (TIPS) and equities
less risky than they appear on a present value basis and T-bills and
fixed rate bonds riskier.

4. More income is better than less, but each additional unit of "more"
generates a decreasing marginal unit of "better." This decreasing
marginal utility of income and spending is what makes us *risk-averse*
and makes us require compensation to bear risk. **Making your
investing, saving, and spending decisions to *maximize* your
Expected Lifetime Utility of spending can improve your expected
lifetime welfare by 25%–50%** relative to following simpler
heuristics such as the "4% rule" for spending, the "hundred minus
age rule," or the "maximize the probability of reaching a goal" for
asset allocation. Maximizing expected wealth is perhaps the most
dangerous of all possible objectives.

5. **You need to know the Risk-adjusted Return (RAR) of your
investment portfolio to decide how much to spend and save
over time.** The RAR of an investment is its expected return minus
the cost of bearing its risk.

6. **To make good financial decisions, you'll need estimates of
the distribution of returns of the investments you're considering** and the correlation between them, assessed on a *real, after-tax
basis*. It is usually easier to do this to a long-term horizon for assets
with returns that are naturally thought of in real terms and for those
that generate cash flows. TIPS, equities, and real estate meet these
criteria. Assets that are more difficult to evaluate are nominal bonds;
assets whose returns depend mostly on what someone will pay for
them in the future, such as collectibles, commodities, and crypto;
and assets whose expected returns depend on extrapolating from
past performance or expecting a reversion to historical averages,
which is the case for most active investment strategies.

7. **Take explicit account of your human capital**, especially if you
are young. How big is it? How uncertain is it? Are you more like a
stock or a bond? Consider reducing exposure to investments that are
correlated with your human capital, such as equity of the company
where you work. The more flexibility you have to affect its size, the
more investment risk you can take. Make your asset allocation and

spending and saving decisions based on your total wealth, which is the sum of your financial savings and your human capital.

8. **The long-term expected return and risk of assets vary over time, and you should dynamically update your asset allocation and spending and savings decisions accordingly.** Lower expected returns or higher risk relative to safe assets should lead to a lower exposure to risky assets and to lower spending and higher saving. Lower returns offered by safe assets, holding the excess return and risk of risky assets constant, should not lead to a change in asset allocation but will call for lower spending and higher saving.

9. **Dynamic asset allocation can improve lifetime expected welfare significantly.** You can do it yourself or hire someone to do it for you for a low fee. The next best option is to stick to a static asset allocation comprised of a low-cost *global* equity index fund with most of the rest invested in long-term TIPS, with weights that make sense under typical market conditions, given your personal level of risk-aversion and taking the size and nature of your human capital into account.

10. **Saving and spending should be regulated toward generating a smooth spending stream over time**, while recognizing that they need to be updated in response to changes in the value of your total capital, including your human capital, and in the Risk-adjusted Return you expect to earn.

11. **Most big financial decisions require putting a cost on risk** and cannot be answered by only considering the most likely outcome.

12. **Try to make your decisions as early as practical**, to make the most of the power of compounding and the structure of many tax benefits.

13. **Control what you can by being attentive to fees, taxes, and efficiency in expenditures.** Financial products are often an exception to the rule that the more you pay for a service, the better its quality.

14. **Strive to be disciplined**, rules-based, and algorithmic in your investing in order to keep your behavioral foibles at bay. Know thine enemy—it is primarily yourself, but don't forget that many others will be trying to get a slice of your financial pie too.

15. **No plan is perfect, but it is better to stick to an imperfect but sensible plan than to keep changing the plan**, which can often give a backdoor entrance to harmful practices, such as return chasing. Decisions that are in the general vicinity of optimality will give you nearly all the benefits of going all the way to the hypothetically perfect spot.

16. **There's more to life than your financial well-being, but getting that right will help with everything else**.

A Few Rules of Thumb

Constant relative risk-aversion (CRRA) utility

$$U(W) = \frac{1 - W^{1-\gamma}}{\gamma - 1} \text{ for } \gamma \neq 1$$

$$U(W) = ln(W) \text{ for } \gamma = 1$$

Merton share for asset allocation, risk-taking, and bet-sizing

$$\hat{k} = \frac{\mu}{\gamma \sigma^2}$$

$\gamma = 1$ is equivalent to the Kelly criterion

Risk-adjusted Return (r_{ra}), a.k.a., Certainty-equivalent Return

$$r_{ra} = r_{rf} + \frac{\hat{k}\mu}{2} \text{ for optimal } \hat{k}, \text{ or more generally}$$

$$r_{ra} = r_{rf} + k\left(\mu - \frac{k\gamma\sigma^2}{2}\right)$$

$$\text{Cost of Risk} = \frac{\gamma(k\sigma)^2}{2}$$

Optimal spending

$$\hat{c}_\infty = r_{ra} - \frac{r_{ra} - r_{tp}}{\gamma} \text{ for infinite life and}$$

$$\hat{c}_t = \frac{\hat{c}_\infty}{1 - (1 + \hat{c}_\infty)^{-T}} \text{ for finite life } T, \text{ i.e., wealth annuitized over}$$

T at rate $\hat{c}_\infty$. For $\hat{c}_\infty = 0$, $\hat{c}_t = \frac{1}{T}$.

Symbols and assumptions
- W is wealth
- c is consumption as a fraction of wealth per unit time
- k is the fraction of wealth allocated to the risky asset
- $\hat{k}$ is the optimal allocation
- γ is coefficient of risk-aversion in CRRA utility (for wealthy investors above subsistence typically 2–3, the higher the more risk-averse)
- r_{rf} is safe asset return (for long-term US investors, real yield of long-term TIPS)
- r_{tp} is the investor's rate of time preference (typical values 0%–4%)
- μ is expected excess return of risky asset above safe asset return (for broad equity markets typically 3%–6%, expressed as arithmetic expected return)
- σ is the variability of risky asset expressed as standard deviation of returns (for broad equity markets typically 15%–20%)

Endnotes

Preface

1. For example, Back, 2017; Campbell, 2017; Cochrane, 2005; Huang & Litzenberger, 1988; Ingersoll, 1987; Skiadas, 2009.
2. Ranked first and second on the list of personal finance books on website Goodreads.com December 2022. [https://www.goodreads.com/shelf/show/personal-finance]. See James Choi (2022), *Popular personal financial advice versus the professors*, National Bureau of Economic Research.

Chapter 1

1. Dichev, 2007; Hsu et al., 2016; Dalbar , 2021; Morningstar "Mind the Gap" reports.
2. Fellowes et al., 2019.
3. Choi, 2022.
4. Manually produced yield tables were being printed as early as the 1920s, but they were inexact and cumbersome to use.

Chapter 2

1. In this chapter we draw heavily on an article Victor coauthored with Richard Dewey, published in the *Journal of Portfolio Management,* 2017, and we thank the *Journal* for their permission to do so.
2. Haghani et al., 2017.
3. Powdthavee and Riyanto, 2012.

Chapter 3

1. Two such bets of 10% of wealth each year represents risk of about 14% and expected return of 4%, both of which are a bit lower than the historical risk and return in excess of T-bills of the US stock market, but not miles away.
2. Merton, 1969. Paul Samuelson, Merton's mentor, is also credited for his contribution to the development of this formula.
3. Kelly, 1956.

Chapter 4

1. Difference in arithmetic mean returns. Using data from Robert Shiller. US bonds are 10-year fixed rate bonds.
2. This is the basic insight of the capital asset pricing model (CAPM). The development of the CAPM is attributed to Jack Treynor, William Sharpe, John Lintner and Jan Mossin, building on the earlier work of Harry Markowitz and James Tobin. Sharpe, Markowitz and Merton Miller received the 1990 Nobel Prize in Economics for their work on CAPM.
3. Assuming 20% stock market volatility, a 24-hour trading day and 256 trading days in a year.
4. Reported by G. Zuckermann, *The Man Who Invented Money*.

Chapter 5

1. A variety of simple structural corporate-growth models can produce the result that real equity returns will be centered around the earnings yield. One basic condition under which real returns will equal the earnings yield would be if earnings can grow with inflation, with all earnings paid out currently to shareholders. While these models are all caricatures of the real world in a variety of ways, they nonetheless provide a solid starting point for making sense of long-term historical data. For another perspective on CAPE as a predictor of real equity returns (particularly assessed in non-US equity markets) see "Predicting Stock Market Returns Using Shiller CAPE" by Norbert Keimling and Peter Huber (2016). They conclude: "Existing research indicates that the cyclically adjusted Shiller CAPE has

predicted long-term returns in the S&P 500 since 1881 fairly reliably for periods of more than 10 years. Furthermore, the results of this paper find that this was also the case for 16 other international equity markets in the period from 1979 to 2015, admittedly a relatively short historical experience from which to draw a strong conclusion."

There is also debate on the question of whether the CAEY should be considered a predictor of the arithmetic or geometric real return of equities. We discuss this in "What Our Market Return Forecasts Really Mean: Equity Convexity and Investment Sizing" (2017), and also you can find a discussion in Campbell (2008), slide 28. If you think CAEY should be viewed as a predictor of the expected geometric real return of equities, you will generally be drawn to higher equity allocations in your portfolio.

2. For a deeper dive, see our 2017 article "Market Multiple Mean-Reversion: Red Light or Red Herring?"

3. The dividend yield in 1965 and 1985 was respectively 2.8% and 4.3%.

4. For example, comparing earnings yield to the yield on T-bills would not be consistent, as earnings yield is a real return estimate while the yield on T-bills is a nominal return estimate. A dynamic asset allocation rule based solely on the earnings yield of the stock market would make sense if the expected real return of T-bills was constant through time, but we know this is not the case.

5. This statement ignores taxes, which generally favors holding equities for taxable US investors. There are other reasons an investor may want to own some equities under these circumstances, such as to avoid putting 100% faith in the earnings yield metric, as a form of hedging demand as described in Merton (1971), or as a hedge of an affluent investor's consumption basket.

6. You can see a chart of our estimation of US stock market riskiness in Chart 7 of our 2022 note on www.elmwealth.com, "Man Doth Not Invest by Earnings Yield Alone: A Fresh Look at Earnings Yield and Dynamic Asset Allocation."

7. This is the idea behind generalized autoregressive conditional heteroskedasticity (GARCH) models, which have become industry standard tools for predicting future asset price volatility.

8. The earnings yield of the US equity market was below 3%, while US 10-year TIPS yields were almost entirely above 3.5%.

9. Note that we bound the equity allocation between 0% and 100%, as we do not allow shorting or leveraged holdings of equities.

10. In calculating the Sharpe ratio, we are adding ½ σ^2 to the geometric realized return to convert to an arithmetic return to use in the numerator of the ratio.

11. For all the details, please see our 2022 research note, "Man Doth Not Invest by Earnings Yield Alone: A Fresh Look at Earnings Yield and Dynamic Asset Allocation" on the Elm Wealth website. Of particular note is the decade following WWII during which we estimate 10-year TIPS would have traded at an average yield of −1.5%. During this period, the 10-year nominal Treasury bond yield averaged 2.5% and inflation ran at about 5%, touching 20% in the years directly following the end of the war.

12. You can find all the details in Haghani and White (February 2022), "Man Doth Not Invest by Earnings Yield Alone: A Fresh Look at Earnings Yield and Dynamic Asset Allocation" on ElmWealth.com.

13. Assumptions: $\gamma = 2$, $\sigma = 20\%$, annual rebalancing.

14. A long-term investor may choose to measure risk in terms of the long-term real annuity value of his wealth—for example, using a long-term inflation-protected bond portfolio as his numéraire. See Appendix of "Man Doth Not Invest by Earnings Yield Alone: A Fresh Look at Earnings Yield and Dynamic Asset Allocation" (2022) on Elm Wealth.

15. When momentum is positive, the strategy increases its allocation to equities by 30% (assuming it has not hit the zero leverage constraint), and reduces the allocation by 30% when momentum is negative.

16. See John Cochrane's "Portfolios for Long-Term Investors" (2021), pp. 19–20 for a deeper discussion of the average investor theorem and the look-in-the-mirror test.

17. Campbell & Sigalov, 2020.

Chapter 6

1. This is a nontechnical description of the axioms. For a mathematically precise description, see von Neumann and Morgenstern, *Theory of Games and Economic Behavior* (1944).

2. See our note "What's the Best Way to Get Invested in the Market" (2017) for more.

3. See Phillips, 1995.

4. See Kahneman, 2011.

5. From Zuckerman, 2013.

6. Landsburg, 2009, 2018.
7. Ross, 1999.
8. In searching for the optimal goal-based strategy, we made the additional assumption that the investor would never be willing to bet more than 40% of his wealth on any flip of the coin. The strategy without this assumption is even more suboptimal in Expected Utility. For a more comprehensive treatment, see "Bold Betting Strategies" in Dubins and Savage (2014) for an example.
9. Samuelson, 1963.

Chapter 7

1. Bhattacharya, 2022.
2. Rabin & Thaler, 2001.
3. Example taken from Luce & Raiffa, 1957.
4. From Klarman's book *Margin of Safety* (1991). Copies in good condition sell for thousands of dollars, making it one of the most expensive modern books on investing.

Chapter 8

1. While we don't have a figure for the total profitability of the proprietary trading activities run by Meriwether over the entire 20-year period, we do know from a 1993 Salomon public disclosure, that in just the 4 years to 1993, its proprietary trading activities had generated $3.42 billion in income, representing more than 100% of its pretax income in 1990–1992, and a substantial fraction of its net income in 1993. To put this further into context, Salomon Brothers had an average amount of book equity over these years of $4.3 billion, which was only partially allocated to these proprietary trading activities. Source: Salomon Inc. 1993 Annual Report.
2. This assumes that it was not possible to do nonrecourse borrowing to invest more in the Fund. Borrowing recourse money to invest more in the Fund would violate my requirement to not wind up with less than my minimum acceptable wealth in a disaster scenario, because with recourse borrowing, I'd be on the hook if the value of the Fund fell below the value of the loan.

3. In a letter of October 1994, the partners explained to LTCM fund investors that fund returns would be fat-tailed relative to a normal distribution, and in particular, that a 20% monthly loss could be expected at least once every 50 years.
4. The analysis was done for a 5-year horizon, and then annualized.
5. Warren Buffett, speech to students at Florida School of Business, October 1998.

Chapter 9

1. See Markowitz, 1952.
2. The discipline is often called lifetime portfolio choice and consumption. Many consider Robert Merton's Lifetime portfolio selection under uncertainty: The continuous-time case, *Review of Economics and Statistics*, Vol. 51, No. 3 (Aug. 1969) to be the seminal paper. For a brief overview, see John Campbell, Strategic Asset Allocation: Portfolio Choice for Long-Term Investors, NBER (2000). For a more in depth treatment, see: John Campbell and Luis Viceira, Strategic Asset Allocation (2002), John Campbell, Financial Decisions and Markets (2017), Robert C. Merton, Continuous Time Finance (1992), John Cochrane, Asset Pricing (2005).
3. Merton went on to apply stochastic calculus to many other problems, including the general solution of the pricing and production of derivative instruments, including options.
4. A few other assumptions are also made, such as time-separable utility, discounting of utility, ability to trade in continuous time, infinitely divisible units of account, etc.
5. More complex utility functions, such as the Epstein-Zin model (1989), deal separately with an individual's preferences for smooth consumption over time and aversion to bearing investment risk. We believe the added complexity of such models of individual preference outweigh their potentially greater realism.
6. Expected returns are expressed in nominal terms. We assume Sam's mortality probabilities are typical for a woman of her age in the US population. We assume she will not live beyond 110 years of age, which is the maximum age in most mortality tables. Given the current state of medical technology, actuaries believe that the chances of someone who is 65 years old today living beyond 110 years of age is about 2 in 100,000 for a woman, and 1/10th that probability for

a man. No estate tax expected, as Sam's estate would be below the federal estate tax exclusion.

7. Bengen, 1994.
8. Arends, 2020; Bengen, 2020.
9. Although we have not done it in this example, it is easy, and some individuals may find it more attractive, to introduce some smoothing into the spending policy. For example, the spending rule can be applied to the individual's average level of wealth over the most recent 3 years.
10. Ignoring taxes and social security.
11. Assuming 60% allocation to equities, 6.5% equity expected excess return above T-bills, T-bill return of 2%, inflation of 2%, no taxes, and 18% annual volatility of returns for equities, as in the period from 2000 to 2022.

Chapter 10

1. As per the 2020 NACUBO-TIAA Study of Endowment Results (2010-2019 Spending), which covers US College and University Endowments and related foundations. Yale spends about 5.25%, more than the average endowment. Private foundations in the United States are required by law to spend 5% of their assets each year.
2. Tobin, 1974.
3. See Dybvig & Zhenjiang, 2019; Campbell & Sigalov, 2020.
4. Alternatively, for an endowment wishing to decide on an investment policy, there is a very reasonable range of CRRA risk-aversion levels which can serve as a useful starting point without requiring a complicated, idiosyncratic calibration exercise.
5. Time preference is equal to the desired spending rate in the zero-return scenario multiplied by the coefficient of risk-aversion of the endowment, which we've assumed is equal to 2. So if the trustees felt that they would spend 1% of the endowment each year in a zero return environment, this would imply the endowment's time preference would be 2% per annum.
6. Office of Management and Budget Circular A-4, 2020.
7. In a further extension, utility preferences that separate relative risk-aversion from the elasticity of intertemporal substitution of consumption, known as the Epstein-Zin utility, can also be used.

8. One particular spending policy modeled in Campbell and Sigalov (2020) suggests that as expected investment returns fall, the optimal policy is to take more risk—a phenomenon known as "reaching for yield." We do not think this spending policy is a sensible one, for endowments or individuals, but it is an interesting exercise.

9. Such as Foundation and Endowment Investing: Philosophies and Strategies of Top Investors and Institutions; Endowment Asset Management: Investment Strategies in Oxford and Cambridge; The Sustainable Endowment; or The Household Endowment Model: Wealth Planning for Affluent Families.

Chapter 11

1. In 2019, Boston College estimated there was a $7.1 trillion retirement-savings shortfall among American households, with half of them facing a lower standard of living once they stop working. The same general situation holds in many other high-income economies internationally.

2. See Modigliani, 1985.

3. According to data from the Social Security System website. Probability goes to zero at age 115.

4. See Shu et al. (2018) for further discussion. They find product fairness to be the biggest driver of investors' annuity aversion. Insurance companies may be charging an extra risk premium for longevity risk, which is only partially hedge-able with sales of term life insurance.

Chapter 12

1. Another approach would have been to ask people about their investment portfolios and their assumptions of expected return and risk of their portfolios in order to back out an implied degree of risk-aversion from their portfolio choices. We felt that would be considerably more complex and blurred by other considerations that respondents might bring to their decision-making, such as the degree of mean-reversion in equity markets, making it difficult to isolate the characteristics of their utility functions.

2. See Conard (2012), who argues that a society that is less risk-averse is better off.

3. Perold & Sharpe, 1988.

4. Friedman & Savage, 1948.

5. Hindy & Huang, 1989, 1992; Campbell, 2017; Campbell & Cochrane, 1999; Constantinides, 1990.

Chapter 14

1. See Haghani & White, 2019.

2. See Chin & Israelov, 2022.

3. See Shiller, 2015.

4. Bogle, 2005.

5. As noted in Dichev, 2007 Chapter 1; Hsu et al., 2016; Dalbar 2021; and Morningstar "Mind the Gap" reports.

6. While Fama is the financial economist most popularly linked to the efficient market hypothesis, his work built upon that of many predecessors from Louis Bachelier (1900) to Friedrich Hayek (1945) to Paul Samuelson (1965).

7. APT was introduced by Ross (1976), but Robert C. Merton (1973) proposed the first multi-factor, intertemporal extension of CAPM.

8. Treynor, 1961; Sharpe, 1964; Lintner, 1965; and Mossin, 1966.

9. For example, Black, Jensen, and Scholes (1972) found that low beta assets earn more, and high beta assets earn less, than predicted from CAPM.

10. Fama and French (1996) argue similarly that "the value effect might be explained by a high covariance between value stock returns and the value of human capital, if value stocks tend to be financially distressed and the failure of distressed firms is associated with destruction of human capital of the firms' employees." Campbell, 2017. Also see Campbell and Vuolteenaho (2004) for an explanation they call "good beta, bad beta" grounded in the ICAPM.

11. Notably, McLean and Pontiff (2016) and Ilmanen et al. (2019) argue that post-publication decay is more a sign of in-sample overfitting than of informed traders reducing the factor return. Some of the research indicates a reward for early adopters in which returns increased in the period right after publication before decaying away, likely a result of more capital being attracted to the anomaly when it was a freshly discovered trade idea.

12. Cochrane, 2011.

13. Clarke et al., 2012.

14. e.g., Ioannidis et al., 2017.

15. More technically, the data tend to be nonlinear, nonstationary, sparse, and have high co-linearity and low cross-sectionality.
16. The distinction between return chasing (bad) and momentum (good) is that return chasing generally takes place more gradually, over longer horizons, while momentum strategies typically involve binary changes in positioning. See Haghani & McBride, 2016.
17. Haghani et al., 2017.
18. Frazzini et al., 2012.
19. Cornell & Damodaran, 2020.
20. We're also assuming a zero safe asset rate, no inflation, and no dividend on the stock for this example.
21. Bessembinder, 2018.
22. See Haghani & White, 2018.
23. Ilmanen et al., 2019.
24. Buiter, 2003.

Chapter 15

1. Based on data kindly provided by Robert Shiller on http://www.econ.yale.edu/~shiller/data.htm
2. Robert Merton and Arun Muralidhar suggest that governments address population retirement needs by issuing securities indexed to national per capita income growth in their idea of standard-of-living indexed, forward-starting, income-only securities. See Merton & Muralidhar, 2020 .
3. Campbell, & Viceira, 2001; Cochrane, 2021; Bodie & Taqqu, 2011.
4. As usual, using data provided by Professor Robert Shiller.
5. See Mehra & Prescott, 1985; Grossman & Shiller, 1981.
6. See Cochrane (2011) for an excellent, broad survey of the topic.

Chapter 16

1. Reports from Options Clearing Corporation, 2021; CBOE, 2021; CME Group, 2021.
2. Bogle, 2007; Ellis, 2013; Malkiel, 2013.
3. More precisely, it follows a geometric random walk, meaning that the log of the stock price follows a normal random walk.
4. Merton, 1973.

5. In our simulation, we assume no taxes or transaction costs and use puts struck 10% out-of-the-money, but the results are robust to other choices of strike prices.

6. For simplicity, we've limited the analysis to looking at options at just one strike price. Doing this analysis using options with a range of strike prices does not materially change the results.

7. This is a well-known result. For example, see Carr et al. 2001.

8. Campbell & Cochrane, 1999.

9. The VIX is a measure of the weighted average implied volatility of 1-month options on the S&P 500. VIX is usually significantly above the implied volatility of at-the-money options, primarily because it is averaged across different strikes, including significant weights on out-of-the-money puts. Over the same 10-year period, the average implied volatility of at-the-money 1-month options on the S&P 500 was 0.6% higher than realized volatility over the life of each option. There are other possible convexity effects that may result in the average VIX index level being above realized volatility while at the same time the dynamic hedging of options portfolios breaks even. However, the magnitude of those effects is likely well below the 3.6% difference in the average VIX level versus realized volatility over the period cited.

10. Alpstein & Samanci, 2018.

11. Spitznagel, 2021.

12. Israelov & Nielsen, 2015; Israelov, 2019.

13. Villalon et al., 2019.

14. Assuming this was either the only trade investors were doing or that it was uncorrelated with the rest of their existing holdings.

15. Goetzmann et al., 2002.

Chapter 17

1. See Domar & Musgrave, 1944; Stiglitz, 1969; Feldstein, 1969.

2. This also assumes zero risk-free interest rates, that the capital asset has a zero dividend rate (which can be achieved for equity risk by using equity index futures), and that investors are willing and able to borrow to leverage their position in the capital asset at the risk-free rate if required.

3. Under current US rules, taxpayers can allocate $3,000 of capital losses per year to offset earned income, but otherwise can only use losses to offset future gains.

Chapter 18

1. See for example, Merton, 1980.
2. We're assuming relatively realistic return distributions, and also what we view as realistic levels of risk-aversion. For exceptionally low levels of risk-aversion (CRRA coefficient of risk-aversion ≤ 1), the investor may be neutral or even positively disposed to increasing uncertainty, but we view this as an unrealistic case for nearly all investors.
3. Indeed, some observers argue that stocks are riskier in the long run due to uncertainty of the expected return of stocks. See Pastor and Stambaugh (2012). Also see Grinblatt and Linnainmaa (2011).

Chapter 19

1. For a more detailed description of these positive odds opportunities (or, in their words, "fantastic expected rates of return offered by certain lottery drawings") along with a more detailed discussion of the ideas in this chapter, see "Finding Good Bets in the Lottery and Why You Shouldn't Take Them," by Aaron Abrams and Skip Garibaldi, 2010.

Chapter 20

1. Mehra & Prescott, 1985.
2. See Dimson et al., 2001.
3. Campbell, 2008; also referred to as the "peso problem" in Krasker, 1980.
4. Goetzmann et al., 2016.
5. Campbell & Cochrane, 1999.
6. Constantinides & Duffie, 1996.
7. Epstein & Zin, 1989.

Chapter 21

1. Since then, many stochastic interest rate models have been proposed, including those by Vasicek (1977), Cox et al. (1985), Heath-Jarrow-Morton (1989), Black et al. (1990), and Hull & White (1990). The paper "Long Forward and Zero-Coupon Rates Can Never Fall" by Philip Dybvig, Jonathan Ingersoll, and Stephen Ross (1996) discusses the asymptotic behavior of interest rates as time to maturity goes to infinity and makes a case based on no arbitrage for why long-date forward rates cannot continually fall.

Chapter 22

1. In this example, we ignored the riskiness of each of the three alternatives, but if we took that into account, it would have put the S&P 500 index fund even further ahead.

Chapter 23

1. See our note "If George Costanza Were a Hedge Fund Manager" for more of George's mis-adventures in investing. Inspired by *Seinfeld* Season 5, Episode 22, "The Opposite."
2. We assume the ETF finances its leveraged position at 1% above the average T-bill rate, and that it charges a fee of 1% per annum.
3. From ETFDB.com, https://etdfb.com/etfs/leveraged/equity/ downloaded May 6, 2023.

Chapter 24

1. See for example, Aaron Brown's article: "Crypto-Trading Addiction Is the 'Reefer Madness' of 2022," Bloomberg (April 26, 2022).
2. Haghani et al., 2019.
3. See Clarke et al., 2019.
4. See Wood & Hughes, 2015.
5. See Calvet et al. (2007) for how Swedish households at the turn of the twenty-first century were making better investment decisions (with room for material improvement) than Americans were for most of the twentieth century.

Suggested Reading

Books

Bernstein, P. (1996). *Against the gods: The remarkable story of risk*. London: Wiley.

Campbell, J. (2017). *Financial decisions and markets: A course in asset pricing*. Princeton: Princeton University Press.

Campbell, J. and Viceira, L. (2002). *Strategic asset allocation: Portfolio choice for long-term investors*. London: Oxford University Press.

Ilmanen, A. (2011). *Expected returns*. London: Wiley.

Kritzman, M. (2000). *Puzzles of finance*. London: Wiley.

Lewis, M. (1989). *Liar's poker*. New York: W. W. Norton & Company.

Picerno, J. (2010). *Dynamic asset allocation: Modern portfolio theory updated for the smart investor*. Bloomberg Press.

Vanderbilt, A. (1989). *Fortune's children: The fall of the house of Vanderbilt*. New York: William Morrow & Co.

Articles

Asness, C., Moskowitz, T., and Pedersen, L. (2013). Value and momentum everywhere. *Journal of Finance,* 68(3), 929–985.

Bogle, J. (2005). The relentless rules of humble arithmetic. *Financial Analysts Journal,* 61(6), 22–35.

Campbell, J. (2006). Household finance. *The Journal of Finance,* 61(4), 1553–1604.

Choi, J. (2022). *Popular personal financial advice*. Cambridge: National Bureau of Economic Research.

Cochrane, J. (2011). Presidential address: Discount rates. *Journal of Finance,* 66(4), 1047–1108.

Dichev, I. (2007). What are stock investors' actual historical returns? Evidence from dollar-weighted returns. *American Economic Review,* 97(1), 386–401.

Haghani and White articles on Elm Wealth website:

- Man doth not invest by earnings yield alone: A fresh look at earnings yield and dynamic asset allocation
- Measuring the fabric of felicity
- Home biased: A case for more indexing
- Market multiple mean-reversion: red light or red herring?
- What's past is not prologue

Merton, R. (1969). Lifetime portfolio selection under uncertainty: The continuous-time case. *The Review of Economics and Statistics,* 51(3), 247–257.

Perold, A. (2007). Fundamentally flawed indexing. *Financial Analysts Journal,* 63(6), 31–37.

Samuelson, P. (1963). Risk and uncertainty: A fallacy of large numbers. *Scientia,* 57(98), 108–113.

Samuelson, P. (1979). Why we should not make mean log of wealth big though years to act are long. *Journal of Banking & Finance* 3(4), 305–307.

Shiller, R. (1981). Do stock prices move too much to be justified by subsequent changes in dividends? *The American Economic Review* 71(3), 421–436.

Shiller, R. (1996). Price earnings ratios as forecasters of returns: The stock market outlook in 1996.

References

Abrams, A. and Garibaldi, S. (2010). Finding good bets in the lottery, and why you shouldn't take them. *The American Mathematical Monthly,* 117(1), 3–26.

Acharya, S. and Dimson, E. (2007). *Endowment asset management: Investment strategies in Oxford and Cambridge.* London: Oxford University Press.

Akbas, F., Armstrong, W., Sorescu, S., and Subrahmanyam, A. (2015). Smart money, dumb money and capital market anomalies. *Journal of Financial Economics,* 118(2), 355–382.

Alpstein, G. and Samanci, S. (2018). *Portfolio protection strategies: A study on the protective put and its extensions.* KTH Royal Institute of Technology.

Angle, J. (1986). The surplus theory of social stratification and the size distribution of personal wealth. *Social Forces,* 65(2), 293–326.

Annable, V. (2019). *The household endowment model: Wealth planning for affluent families.* Scottsdale: Wealth Strategies Advisory Group.

Archer, S. (1970). Managing educational endowments: Report to the Ford Foundation. *Journal of Finance,* 25(4), 962–963.

Arnott, R., Clements, M., Kalesnik, V., and Linnainmaa, J. (2018). Factor momentum. *SSRN Electronic Journal.*

Arnott, R., Harvey, C., Kalesnik, V., and Linnainmaa, J. (2019). Alice's Adventures in Factorland: Three Blunders That Plague Factor investing. *Journal of Portfolio Management,* 45(4), 18–36.

Arnott, R., Hsu, J., and Moore, P. (2005). Fundamental indexation. *Financial Analysts Journal,* 61(2), 83–99.

Arrow, K. (1951). Alternative approaches to the theory of choice in risk-taking situations. *Econometrica,* 19(4), 404–437.

Arrow, K. (1971). *Essays in the theory of risk-bearing.* Amsterdam: North-Holland Publishing.

Asness, C., Ilmanen, A., and Maloney, T. (2017). Market timing: Sin a little, resolving the valuation timing puzzle. *Journal of Investment Management,* 15(3), 23–40.

Asness, C., Moskowitz, T., and Pedersen, L. (2013). Value and momentum everywhere. *Journal of Finance,* 68(3), 929–985.

Austen, J. (1813). *Pride and prejudice.* London: T. Egerton, Whitehall.

Bachelier, L. (1900). *Theory of speculation.* Princeton: Princeton University Press.

Back, K. (2017). *Asset pricing and portfolio choice theory* (2nd ed.). Oxford University Press.

Balcer, Y. and Judd, K. (1987). Effects of capital gains taxation on life-cycle investment and portfolio management. *Journal of Finance*, 42(3), 743–761.

Barber, B. and Odean, T. (2000). Trading is hazardous to your wealth: The common stock investment performance of individual investors. *Journal of Finance*, 55(2), 773–806.

Baumeister, R., Loewenstein, G., and Read, D. (2003). *Time and decision: Economic and psychological perspectives of intertemporal choice*. New York: Russell Sage Foundation.

Baz, J., Guo, H., and Hakanoglu, E. (2022). *Portfolio selection and asset pricing: Models of financial economics and their applications in investing*. New York: McGraw Hill.

Bengen, W. (1994). Determining withdrawal rates using historical data. *Journal of Financial Planning*, 7(4), 171–184.

Bentham, J. (1789). *Introduction to the principles of morals and legislation*. London: T. Payne.

Benzel, R. and Demmert, J. (2019). *The sustainable endowment*. Los Angeles: New Insights Press.

Bernard, C. and Boyle, P. (2009). *Mr. Madoff's amazing returns: An analysis of the split-strike conversion strategy*. SSRN.

Bernstein, P. (1996). *Against the gods: The remarkable story of risk*. London: Wiley.

Bessembinder, H. (2017). Do stocks outperform Treasury bills? *Journal of Financial Economics*, 129(3), 440–457.

Bessembinder, H. (2017). Do stocks outperform Treasury bills? *Journal of Financial Economics*, 129(3), 440–457.

Bessembinder, H., Chen, T., Choi, G., and John Wei, K.C. (2019). Do global stocks outperform US Treasury bills? *SSRN Electronic Journal*.

Bhattacharya, A. (2022). *The man from the future: The visionary ideas of John von Neumann*. New York: W.W. Norton Publishing.

Black, F. (1976). The investment policy spectrum: Individuals, endowment funds and pension funds. *Financial Analysts Journal*, 32(1), 23–31.

Black, F. (1986). Noise. *Journal of Finance*, 41(3), 528–543.

Black, F. (1993). Estimating expected returns. *Financial Analysts Journal*, 49(5), 36–38.

Black, F., Derman, E., and Toy, W. (1990). A one-factor model of interest rates and its application to Treasury bond options. *Financial Analysts Journal*, 46(1), 33–39.

Black, F., Jensen, M., and Scholes, M. (1972). The capital asset pricing model: Some empirical tests. In: *Studies in the Theory of Capital Markets*. Westport: Praeger Publishers.

Black, F. and Scholes, M. (1973). The pricing of options and corporate liabilities. *Journal of Political Economy*, 81(3), 637–654.

Bodie, Z. and Taqqu, R. (2011). *Risk less and prosper: Your guide to safer investing*. London: Wiley.

Boghosian, B. (2019). Is inequality inevitable? *Scientific American*.

Bogle, J. (2005). The relentless rules of humble arithmetic. *Financial Analysts Journal*, 61(6), 22–35.

Bogle, J. (2007). *The little book of common sense investing: The only way to guarantee your fair share of stock market returns*. New York: Wiley.

Breeden, D. (1979). An intertemporal asset pricing model with stochastic consumption and investment opportunities. *Journal of Financial Economics, 7*(3), 265–296.

Briggs, R. A. (2019). Normative theories of rational choice: Expected utility. *Stanford Encyclopedia of Philosophy.*

Brown, A. (2011). *Red-blooded risk: The secret history of Wall Street.* London: Wiley.

Brown, A. (2022). Crypto-Trading Addiction Is 2022's "Reefer Madness." *Bloomberg Tax.*

Buffet, W. (1998). *Lecture at the University of Florida School of Business* [video]. https://www.youtube.com/watch?v=7Z6x-Ov1smU

Buiter, W. (2003). James Tobin: An appreciation of his contribution to economics. *The Economic Journal, 113*(491), 585–631.

Calvet, L., Campbell, J., and Sodini, P. (2007). Down or out: Assessing the welfare costs of household investment mistakes. *Journal of Political Economy, 115*(5), 707–747.

Campbell, J. (2006). Household finance. *The Journal of Finance, 61*(4), 1553–1604.

Campbell, J. (2008). *Risk and return in stocks and bonds.* Princeton Lectures.

Campbell, J. (2011). Investing and spending: The Twin challenges of university endowment management. *Forum for the Future of Higher Education Symposium.*

Campbell, J. (2017). *Financial decisions and markets: A course in asset pricing.* Princeton: Princeton University Press.

Campbell, J. and Cochrane, J. (1999). By force of habit: A Consumption-based explanation of aggregate stock market behavior. *Journal of Political Economy, 107*(2), 205–251.

Campbell, J., Ramadorai, T., and Ranish, B. (2019). Do the rich get richer in the stock market? Evidence from India. *American Economic Review, 1*(2), 225–240.

Campbell, J. and Shiller, R. (1988). Stock prices, earnings and expected dividends. *Journal of Finance, 43*(3), 661–676.

Campbell, J. and Sigalov, R. (2020). Portfolio choice with sustainable spending: A model of reaching for yield. *Journal of Financial Economics, 143*(1), 188–206.

Campbell, J. and Viceira, L. (2001). Who should buy long-term bonds? *American Economic Review, 91*(1), 99–127.

Campbell, J. and Viceira, L. (2002). *Strategic asset allocation: Portfolio choice for long-term investors.* London: Oxford University Press. (Also available online in downloadable pdf.)

Campbell, J. and Vuolteenaho, T. (2004). Bad beta, good beta. *The American Economic Review, 94*(5), 1249–1275.

Carhart, M. (1997). On Persistence in mutual fund performance. *Journal of Finance, 52*(1), 57–82.

Carr, P. and Madan, D. (2001). Optimal positioning in derivative securities. *Quantitative Finance 1,* 19–37.

Chakraborti, A. (2002). Distributions of money in model markets of economy. *International Journal of Modern Physics, 13*(10), 1315–1321.

Chen, Y. and Israelov, R. (2022). *How many stocks should you own?* https://ndvr.com.

Chicago Board Options Exchange. (2021). *Daily market statistics.* Retrieved January 10, 2023 from https://www.cboe.com/data/market_statistics/

Choi, J. (2022). Popular personal financial advice. Cambridge: National Bureau of Economic Research.

Choi, J., Laibson, D., and Madrian, B. (2010). Why does the law of one price fail? An experiment on index mutual funds. *Review of Financial Studies*, 23(44), 1405–1432.

Clarke, A., Nolan, M., and Sampson, T. (2019). *What is a mutual fund worth?* Vanguard.

CME Group. (2021). Daily equity volume and open interest. CME Group. (2021). Daily equity volume and open interest. January 10, 2023.

Cochrane, J. (1999). *Portfolio advice for a multifactor world* (Working Paper Series 7170). Cambridge: National Bureau of Economic Research.

Cochrane, J. (2005). *Asset pricing*. Princeton: Princeton University Press.

Cochrane, J. (2011). Presidential address: Discount rates. *Journal of Finance*, 66(4), 1047–1108.

Cochrane. J. (2015). A new structure for US federal debt. *SSRN Electronic Journal*.

Cochrane, J. (2019). Why stop at 100? The case for perpetuities. The Grumpy Economist.

Cochrane, J. (2021). Portfolios for long-term investors. *Review of Finance*, 26(1), 1–42.

Congressional Research Service. (2021). *The US income distribution: Trends and issues* .

Constantinides, G. (1990). Habit formation: A resolution of the equity premium puzzle. *Journal of Political Economy*, 98(3), 519–533.

Constantinides, G. and Duffie, D. (1996). Asset pricing with heterogeneous consumers. *Journal of Political Economy*, 104(2), 219–240.

Cooper, A. and Howe, K. (2021). *Vanderbilt: The rise and fall of an American dynasty*. New York: HarperCollins.

Cornell, B. and Damodaran, A. (2020). Valuing ESG: Doing good or sounding good? *The Journal of Impact and ESG Investing*, 1(1), 76–93.

Cox, J. and Huang, C. (1992). A continuous-time portfolio turnpike theorem. *Journal of Economic Dynamics and Control*, 16(3), 491–507.

Cox, J., Ingersoll, J., and Ross, S. (1985). A theory of the term structure of interest rate. *Econometrica*, 53(2), 385–407.

Dalbar, Inc. (2021). *Quantitative analysis of investor behavior* [online].

Dammon, R., Spatt, C., and Zhang, H. (2001). Optimal consumption and investment with capital gains taxes. *Review of Financial Studies*, 14(3), 583–616.

Davies, J., Sandström, S., Shorrocks, A., and Wolff, E. (2009). *The level and distribution of global household wealth* (Working Paper 15508). Cambridge: National Bureau of Economic Research.

Dichev, I. (2007). What are stock investors' actual historical returns? Evidence from dollar-weighted returns. *American Economic Review*, 97(1), 386–401.

Dickson, J., Padmawar, S., and Hammer, S. (2012). Joined at the Hip: ETF and Index Development. *Vanguard*.

Dimson, E., Marsh, P., Staunton, M. (2001). *Triumph of the optimists: 101 years of global investment returns*. Princeton: Princeton University Press.

Domar, E. and Musgrave, R. (1944). Proportional income taxation and risk-taking. *Quarterly Journal of Economics*, 58(3), 388–422.

Dubins, L. and Savage, L. (2014). *How to gamble if you must: Inequalities for stochastic processes.* Dover Books on Mathematics.

Duke, A. (2018). *Thinking in bets: Making Smarter decisions when you don't have all the facts.* London: Portfolio.

Duke, A. (2022). *Quit: The power of knowing when to walk away.* London: Portfolio.

Dybvig, P. (1995). Dusenberry's ratcheting of consumption: Optimal dynamic consumption and investment given intolerance for any decline in standard of living. *Review of Economic Studies,* 62(2), 287–313.

Dybvig, P., Ingersoll, J., and Ross, S. (1996). Long forward and zero-coupon rates can never fall. *Journal of Business,* 69(1), 1–25.

Dybvig, P. and Koo, H.K. (1996). Investment with taxes. *Washington University,* 126: 620–635.

Dybvig, P. and Qin, Z. (2021). How to squander your endowment: Pitfalls and remedies. *SSRN Electronic Journal.*

Dybvig, P. and Zhenjiang, Q. (2019). *How to squander your endowment: Pitfalls and remedies.* Washington University in St. Louis.

Editorial Board. (2019). Schwab leaves San Francisco for Texas. *Wall Street Journal.*

Ehsani, S. and Linnainmaaz, J. (2019). Factor momentum and the momentum factor. *Journal of Finance,* 77(3), 1877–1919.

Ellis, C. and Malkiel, B. (2013). *The elements of investing.* New York: Wiley.

Ellsberg, D. (1961). Risk, ambiguity, and the Savage axioms. *The Quarterly Journal of Economics,* 75(4), 643–669.

Ennis, R. and Williamson, J. (1976). *Spending policy for educational endowments.* New York: Common Fund.

Epstein, L. & Zin, S. (1989). Substitution, risk aversion, and the temporal behavior of consumption and asset returns: A theoretical framework. *Econometrica,* 57(4), 937–969.

Fama, E. and French, K. (1992). The cross-section of expected stock returns. *The Journal of Finance,* 47(2), 427–465.

Fama, E. and French, K. (1996). Multifactor explanations of asset pricing anomalies. *Journal of Finance,* 51(1), 55–84.

Fama, E. and French, K. (2008). Dissecting anomalies. *Journal of Finance,* 63(4), 1653–1678.

Fama, E. and French, K. (2014). A five-factor asset pricing model. *Journal of Financial Economics,* 116(1), 1–22.

Federal Reserve. (2021). *DFA: Distributional financial accounts* [online].

Feldstein, M. (1969). The effects of taxation on risk taking. *Journal of Political Economy,* 77(5), 755–764.

Feldstein, M. (1983). *Capital taxation.* London: Harvard University Press.

Fellowes, M., Fichtner, J., Plews, L., and Whitman, K. (2019). *The retirement solution hiding in plain sight.* United Income White Papers.

Feng, G., Giglio, S., and Xiu, D. (2020). Taming the factor zoo: A test of new factors. *Journal of Finance,* 75(3), 1327–1370.

Fenton-O'Creevy, M., Nicholson, N., Soane, E., and Willman, P. (2003). Trading on illusions: Unrealistic perceptions of control and trading performance. *Journal of Occupational and Organizational Psychology,* 76(1), 53–68.

Franklin, B. (1737). Hints for those that would be rich. In: *Poor Richard's Almanac.* Philadelphia.

Frazzini, A., Israel, R., and Moskowitz, T. (2012). Trading costs of asset pricing anomalies. *SSRN Electronic Journal.*

Frazzini, A. and Pedersen, L. (2013). Betting against beta. *Journal of Financial Economics,* 111(1), 1–25.

Friedland, N., Keinan, G., and Regev, Y. (1992). Controlling the uncontrollable: Effects of stress on illusory perceptions of controllability. *Journal of Personality and Social Psychology,* 63(6), 923–931.

Friedman, M. and Savage, J. (1948). The Utility analysis of choices involving risk. *Journal of Political Economy.* 56(4), 279–304.

Gennotte, G. (1986). Optimal portfolio choice under incomplete information. *Journal of Finance,* 41(3), 733–746.

Gillen, B. (2016). *Subset optimization for asset allocation* (Working Paper 1421). California Institute of Technology.

Gilovich, T., Vallone, R., and Tversky, A. (1985). The hot hand in basketball: On the misperception of random sequences. *Cognitive Psychology,* 17(3), 295–314.

Goetzmann, W., Ingersoll, J., Spiegel, M., and Welch, I. (2002). *Sharpening Sharpe ratios.* Cambridge: National Bureau of Economic Research.

Goetzmann, W., Kim, D., and Shiller, R. (2016). *Crash beliefs from investor surveys.* Cambridge: National Bureau of Economic Research.

Goetzmann, W. and Swensen, D. (2002). *Yale endowment management course description* [online].

Gossen, H. (1854). *The laws of human relations and the rules of human action derived therefrom.* Cambridge: MIT Press.

Graham, B. and Dodd, D. (1934). *Security analysis.* New York: McGraw Hill.

Green, B. and Zwiebel, J. (2018). The hot hand fallacy: Cognitive mistakes or equilibrium adjustments? Evidence from Major League Baseball. *Management Science,* 64(11), 4967–5460.

Grimaldi, M. and De Grauwe, P. (2003). Bubbling and crashing exchange rates. *SSRN Electronic Journal.*

Grinblatt, M. and Linnainmaa, J. (2011). Jensen's inequality, parameter uncertainty, and multi-period investment. *The Review of Asset Pricing Studies.*

Grinold, R., Hopkins, D., and Massy, W. (1978). A model for long-range university budget planning under uncertainty. *Bell Journal of Economics* 9(2), 396–420.

Grossman, S. and Shiller, R. The determinants of the variability of stock market prices. *The American Economic Review,* 71(2), 222–227.

Gupta, T. and Kelly, B. (2019). Factor momentum everywhere. *Journal of Portfolio Management,* 45(3), 13–36.

Haghani, V. (2017). Do index buyers make overvalued stocks more overvalued? *Journal of Portfolio Management,* 43(2), 2–5.

Haghani, V. and Dewey, R. (2017). Rational decision making under uncertainty: Observed betting patterns on a biased coin. *Journal of Portfolio Management.*

Haghani, V., Hilibrand, L., and White, J. (2019). When it pays to pay capital gains. *SSRN Electronic Journal.*

Haghani, V. and McBride, S. (2016). Return chasing and trend following: Superficial similarities mask fundamental differences. *SSRN Electronic Journal, and Elm Wealth.*

Haghani, V. and Morton, A. (2017). Optimal trade sizing in a game with favourable odds: The stock market. *SSRN Electronic Journal.*

Haghani, V., Ragulin, V., and White, J. (2022). Do options belong in the portfolios of individual investors? *Journal of Derivatives.*

Haghani, V., Rosenbluth, J., and White, J. (2017). *What's past is not prologue.* Elm Wealth.

Haghani, V., Rosenbluth, J., and White, J. (2019). *Mind the gap: Inequality and diversification.* Elm Wealth.

Haghani, V. and White, J. (2017). *Market multiple mean-reversion: Red light or red herring?* Elm Wealth.

Haghani, V. and White, J. (2017). *What our market return forecasts really mean: Equity convexity and investment sizing.* Elm Wealth.

Haghani, V. and White, J. (2017). *What's the best way to get invested in the market?* Elm Wealth.

Haghani, V. and White, J. (2018). Measuring the fabric of felicity. *SSRN Electronic Journal.*

Haghani, V. and White, J. (2018). *US tax reform leaves even less of the pie for individual investors in alternatives.* Elm Wealth.

Haghani, V. and White, J. (2019). *Home biased: A case for more indexing.* Elm Wealth.

Haghani, V. and White, J. (2019). *If George Costanza were a hedge fund manager.* Elm Wealth.

Haghani, V. and White, J. (2020). Smart Beta: The good, the bad and the muddy. *Journal of Portfolio Management,* 46(4), 11–21.

Haghani, V. and White, J. (2020). The equity risk premium: A novel perspective on the past fifty years. *SSRN Electronic Journal.*

Haghani, V. and White, J. (2022). *A missing piece of the SBF puzzle.* Elm Wealth.

Haghani, V. and White, J. (2022). *Man doth not invest by earnings yield alone: A fresh look at earnings yield and dynamic asset allocation.* Elm Wealth.

Harvey, C. and Liu, Y. (2019). A census of the factor zoo. *SSRN Electronic Journal.*

Harvey, C., Liu, Y., and Zhu, H. (2016). . . . and the cross-section of expected returns. *Review of Financial Studies,* 29(1), 5–68.

Hayek, F. A. (1945). The use of knowledge in society. *The American Economic Review,* 35(4), 519–530.

Hayes, B. (2002). Follow the money. *American Scientist,* 90(5), 400–405.

Heath, D., Jarrow, R., and Morton, A. (1992). Bond pricing and the term structure of interest rates: A new methodology for contingent claims valuation. *Econometrica,* 60(1), 77–105.

Heldman, J. (1990). How wealthy is Mr. Darcy—really? *Jane Austen Society of North America*, 12:38–49.

Hilibrand, L. (2015). *Expected returns, over-extrapolation and asset pricing*. Working Paper.

Hindy, A. and Huang, C. (1989). *On intertemporal preferences with a continuous time dimension II: The case of uncertainty*. Newark: Palala Press.

Hindy, A. and Huang, C. (1992). Intertemporal preferences for uncertain consumption: A continuous time approach. *Econometrica*, 60(4), 781–801.

Homer, S. and Sylla, R. (1963). *A history of interest rates*. London: Wiley.

Horenstein, A. (2019). The unintended impact of academic research on asset returns: The CAPM alpha. *Management Science*, 67(6), 3321–3984.

Hou, K., Xue, C., and Zhang, L. (2020). Replicating anomalies. *Review of Financial Studies*, 33(5), 2019–2133.

Hsu, J., Myers, B., and Whitby, R. (2016). Timing poorly: A guide to generating poor returns while investing in successful strategies. *The Journal of Portfolio Management*.

Huang, C. and Litzenberger, R. (1988). *Foundations for financial economics*. North-Holland.

Hull, J. and White, A. (1990). Pricing interest-rate derivative securities. *Review of Financial Studies*, 3(4), 573–592.

Hurst, B., Johnson, B., and Hua, Y. (2010). Understanding risk parity. *AQR*.

Ibbotson, R. and Brinson, G. (1992). *Global investing: the professional's guide to the world capital markets*. McGraw-Hill.

Ilmanen, A. (2011). *Expected returns*. London: Wiley.

Ilmanen, A. (2022). *Investing amid low expected returns: Making the most when markets offer the least*. London: Wiley.

Ilmanen, A., Chandra, S., and McQuinn, N. (2020) Demystifying illiquid assets: Expected returns for private equity. *The Journal of Alternative Investments*, 22(3), 8–22.

Ilmanen, A., Israel, R., Moskowitz, T., Thapar, A., and Wang, F. (2019). Factor premia and factor timing: a century of evidence. *SSRN Electronic Journal*.

Ilmanen, A., Thapar, A., Tummala, H., and Villalon, D. (2021). Tail risk hedging: Contrasting put and trend strategies. *Journal of Systematic Investing*, 1(1), 111–121.

Ingersoll, J. (1987). *Theory of financial decision making*. Rowman & Littlefield Publishers.

Investment Company Institute. (2017). *2018 investment company fact book* [online].

Ioannidis, J., Stanley, T. D., and Doucouliagos, H. (2017). The power of bias in economics research. *The Economic Journal*, 127(605), F236–F265.

Israelov, R. (2019). Pathetic protection: The elusive benefits of protective puts. *Journal of Alternative Investments*.

Israelov, R. and Nielsen, N. (2015). Still not cheap: Portfolio protection in calm markets. *Journal of Portfolio Management*.

Jegadeesh, N. and Titman, S. (1993). Returns to buying winners and selling losers: Implications for stock market efficiency. *Journal of Finance*, 48(1), 65–91.

Kahneman, D. (2011). *Thinking fast and slow*. New York: Farrar, Straus and Giroux.

Kahneman, D. and Tversky, A. (1974). Judgment under uncertainty: Heuristics and biases. *Science*, 185(4157), 1124–1131.

Kahneman, D. and Tversky, A. (1979) Prospect theory. *The Econometric Society,* 47(2), 263–292.

Keimling, N. (2016) Predicting stock market returns using the Shiller CAPE—An improvement towards traditional value indicators? *SSRN Electronic Journal.*

Kelly, J. L. (1956). A New interpretation of information rate. *Bell System Technical Journal,* 35(4), 917–926.

Khandani, A. and Lo, A. (2011). What happened to the quants in August 2007: Evidence from factors and transactions data. *Journal of Financial Markets,* 14(1), 1–46.

Klarman, S. (1991). *Margin of safety: Risk-averse value investing strategies for the thoughtful investor.* New York: HarperCollins.

Kochard, L. and Rittereiser, C. (2008). *Foundation and endowment investing: Philosophies and strategies of top investors and institutions.* London: Wiley.

Kochkodin, B. (2019). How negative rates can send bond prices soaring. *Bloomberg.*

Koijen, R., Moskowitz, T., Pedersen, L., and Vrugt, E. (2016). Carry. *Journal of Financial Economics,* 127(2), 197–225.

Konnikova, M. (2020). *The biggest bluff: How I learned to pay attention, master myself, and win.* London: Penguin Press.

Krasker, W. (1980). The 'peso problem' in testing the efficiency of forward exchange markets. *Journal of Monetary Economics,* 6(2), 269–276.

Kraus, A. and Litzenberger, R. (1972). Skewness preference and the valuation of risk assets. *Journal of Finance,* 31(4), 1085–1100.

Kreps, D. (1988) *Notes on the theory of choice (Underground classics in economics).* London: Rutledge.

Kritzman, M. (2000). *Puzzles of finance.* London: Wiley.

Krkoska, E. and Schenk-Hoppé, K. (2019). Herding in smart-beta investment products. *Journal of Risk and Financial Management,* 12(1), 47.

Lachance, M. (2004). *Retirement income insurance: A do-it-yourself approach.* SSRN.

Lakonishok, J., Shleifer, A., and Vishny, R. (1994). Contrarian investment, extrapolation, and risk. *Journal of Finance,* 49(5), 1541–1578.

Landsburg, S. (2009). *The big questions: Tackling the problems of philosophy with ideas from mathematics, economics, and physics.* New York: Free Press.

Landsburg, S. (2018). *Can you outsmart an economist?: 100+ puzzles to train your brain.* New York: Harper Business.

Langer, E. (1975). The illusion of control. *Journal of Personality and Social Psychology,* 32(2), 311–328.

LePan, N. (2019). The history of interest rates over 670 years. *Visual Capitalist.*

Levine, M. (2018). It's OK to get distracted by mega millions. *Bloomberg.*

Levitt, S. (2016). Head or tails: The impact of a coin toss on major life decision and subsequent happiness. *The Review of Economic Studies,* 88(1), 378–405.

Lewis, M. (1989). *Liar's poker.* New York: W. W. Norton & Company.

Li, J., Boghosian, B., and Li, C. (2018). The affine wealth model: An agent-based model of asset exchange that allows for negative-wealth agents and its empirical validation. *arXiv.org.*

Lintner, J. (1965). The valuation of risk assets and the Selection of risky investments in stock portfolios and capital budgets. *The Review of Economics and Statistics,* 47, 13–37.

Lopez de Prado, M. (2019). The 7 reasons most econometric investments fail. *SSRN Electronic Journal.*

Lowenstein, R. (2001). *When genius failed: The rise and fall of long-term capital management.* New York: Random House Publishing.

Luce, R. and Raiffa, H. (1957). *Games and decisions: Introduction and critical survey.* New York: John Wiley & Sons.

MacLean, L., Thorp, E., and Ziemba, W. (2010). Good and bad properties of the Kelly criterion. In: *The Kelly Capital Growth Investment Criterion.* Singapore: World Scientific.

MacLean, L., Thorp, E., and Ziemba, W. (2010). *The Kelly capital growth investment criterion.* Singapore: World Scientific.

Markowitz, H. (1952). Portfolio selection. *The Journal of Finance,* 7(1), 77–91.

Mauboussin, M. (2007). *More than you know: Finding financial wisdom in unconventional places.* New York: Columbia University Press.

McLean, D. and Pontiff, J. (2016). Does academic research destroy stock return predictability? *Journal of Finance,* 71(1), 5–32.

Mehra, R. and Prescott, C. (1985). The equity premium: A puzzle. *Journal of Monetary, Economics* 15(2), 145–161.

Merton, R. (1969). Lifetime portfolio selection under uncertainty: The continuous-time case. *The Review of Economics and Statistics,* 51(3), 247–257.

Merton, R. (1971). Optimum consumption and portfolio rules in a continuous-time model. *Journal of Economic Theory,* 3(4), 373–413.

Merton, R. (1973). An intertemporal capital asset pricing model. *Econometrica,* 41(5), 867–887.

Merton, R. (1980). *On estimating the expected return on the market: an exploratory investigation.* Cambridge: National Bureau of Economic Research.

Merton, R. (1991). Optimal investment strategies for university endowment funds. In: *Studies of supply and demand in higher education.* Chicago: University of Chicago Press.

Merton, R. (1992). *Continuous time finance.* London: Wiley.

Merton, R. (2014). The Crisis in retirement planning. *Harvard Business Review.*

Merton, R. and Muralidhar, A. (2017). Time for retirement 'SeLFIES'? *SSRN Electronic Journal.*

Merton, R. and Muralidhar, A. (2020). SeLFIES: A new pension bond and currency for retirement. *SSRN Electronic Journal.*

Merton, R. and Samuelson, P. (1974). Fallacy of the log-normal approximation to optimal portfolio decision-making over many periods. *Journal of Financial Economics,* 1(1), 67–94.

Miller, J. and Sanjurjo, A. (2014). A cold shower for the hot hand fallacy (Working Papers 518). *IGIER.*

Modigliani, F. (1985). Life cycle, individual thrift and the wealth of nations. *American Economic Review,* 76(3), 297–313.

Moskowitz, T., Ooi, Y., and Pedersen, L. (2012). Time series momentum. *Journal of Financial Economics,* 104(1), 228–250.

Mossin, J. (1966). Equilibrium in a Capital Asset Market. *Econometrica,* 34(4), 768–783.

Mossin, J. (1966). Optimal multiperiod policies. *Journal of Business,* 41(2), 215–229.

Nabuco. (2020). *Public NTSE tables.* https://www.nacubo.org/Research/2020/Public-NTSE-Tables.

Odean, T. (1998). Are investors reluctant to realize their losses? *Journal of Finance,* 53(5), 1775–1798.

Options Clearing Corporation. (2021). *Daily volume.* Retrieved October 4, 2021, from https://www.theocc.com/newsroom/press-releases/2021/10-4-occ-september-2021-total-volume-up-21-8-perce

Orr, L. (2019). David Swensen is great for Yale. Is he horrible for investing? *Institutional Investor.*

Pastor, L. and Stambaugh, R. (2012). *Are stocks really less volatile in the long run?* Cambridge: National Bureau of Economic Research.

Patterson, S. (2011). *The quants: How a new breed of math whizzes conquered Wall Street and nearly destroyed it.* New York: Crown Business Publishing.

Perold, A. (1999). *Long-term capital management.* Connecticut: Harvard Business School.

Perold, A. (2004). The capital asset pricing model. *The Journal of Economic Perspectives,* 18(3), 3–24.

Perold, A. (2007). Fundamentally flawed indexing. *Financial Analysts Journal,* 63(6), 31–37.

Perold, A. and Black, F. (1992). Theory of constant proportion portfolio insurance. *Journal of Economic Dynamics & Control,* 16(3 & 4), 403–426.

Perold, A. and Sharpe, W. (1988). Dynamic strategies for asset allocation. *Financial Analysts Journal,* 44(1), 16–27.

Phillips, D. (1995). *A deal with the devil.* Morningstar Research.

Picerno, J. (2010). *Dynamic asset allocation: Modern portfolio theory updated for the smart investor.* Bloomberg Press.

Piketty, T. (2014). *Capital in the 21st century.* Belknap Press.

Poundstone, W. (1989) *Fortune's formula: The untold story of the scientific betting system that beat the casinos and Wall Street.* New York: Hill and Wang.

Powdthavee, N. and Riyanto, Y. (2012). Why do people pay for useless advice? Implications of gambler's and hot-hand fallacies in false-expert setting. *SSRN Electronic Journal.*

Rabin, M. (2000). Risk aversion and expected-utility theory: A calibration theorem. *Econometrica,* 68: 1281–1292.

Rabin, M. and Thaler, R. (2001). Anomalies: Risk aversion. *Journal of Economic Perspectives,* 15(1), 219–232.

Raiffa, H. (1988). *Decision analysis: Introductory lectures on choices under uncertainty.* New York: Random House.

Raiffa, H. and Schlaifer, R. (1961). *Applied statistical decision theory.* Cambridge: MIT Press.

Read, D., Baumeister, R., and Lowenstein, G. (2003). *Time and decision: Economic and psychological perspectives of intertemporal choice.* New York: Russell Sage Foundation.

Rivas, A. and Gomez, J. (2021). Inflation rate calculator: Customize your own consumer-price index. *Wall Street Journal*.

Ross, S. (1976). The arbitrage theory of capital asset pricing. *Journal of Economic Theory*, 13(1), 341–360.

Ross, S. (1999). Adding risks: Samuelson's fallacy of large numbers revisited. *Journal of Financial and Quantitative Analysis*.

Rotando, L. and Thorp, E. (1992). The Kelly criterion and the stock market. *American Mathematical Monthly*, 99(10), 922–931.

Saeedy, A. (2019). 100 year bonds? Why "ultra-long" bonds have caught on in 14 countries and counting. *Fortune*.

Samuelson, P. (1963). Risk and uncertainty: A fallacy of large numbers *Scientia*, 57(98), 108–113.

Samuelson, P. (1965). Proof that properly anticipated prices fluctuate randomly. *Industrial Management Review* 6, 41–49.

Samuelson, P. (1969). Lifetime portfolio selection by dynamic stochastic programming. *Review of Economics and Statistics*, 51(3), 239–246.

Samuelson, P. (1974). Challenge to judgment. *Journal of Portfolio Management*.

Samuelson, P. (1979). Why we should not make mean log of wealth big though years to act are long. *Journal of Banking & Finance*, 3(4), 305–307.

Samuelson, P. (1989). The judgment of economic science on rational portfolio management: Indexing, timing, and long–horizon effects, *The Journal of Portfolio Management*.

Samuelson, P. (1994). The long-term case for equities. *The Journal of Portfolio Management*.

Schwert, W. (2002). *Anomalies and market efficiency* (Working Paper Series 9277). Cambridge: National Bureau of Economic Research.

Sharpe, W. (1964). Capital asset prices: A Theory of market equilibrium under conditions of risk. *The Journal of Finance*, 19(3), 425–442.

Sharpe, W. (1964). Mutual fund performance. *Journal of Business*, 39(1), 119–138.

Sharpe, W. (1994). The Sharpe ratio. *Journal of Portfolio Management*, 21(1), 49–58.

Sharpe, W. (2006). *Investors and markets: Portfolio choices, asset prices, and investment advice*. Princeton: Princeton University Press.

Shen, W. and Wang, J. (2017). *Portfolio selection via subset resampling*. The Thirty-First AAAI Conference on Artificial Intelligence.

Shiller, R. (1981). Do stock prices move too much to be justified by subsequent changes in dividends? *The American Economic Review*, 71(3), 421–436.

Shiller, R. (1982). Consumption, asset markets, and macroeconomic fluctuations. Cambridge: National Bureau of Economic Research.

Shiller, R. (1996). *Price earnings ratios as forecasters of returns: The stock market outlook in 1996*. http://www.econ.yale.edu//~shiller/data/peratio.html.

Shiller, R. (2015). *Online data*. http://www.econ.yale.edu/~shiller/data.htm.

Shu, S., Zeithammer, R., and Payne, J. (2018). The pivotal role of fairness: Which consumers like annuities? *Financial Planning Review*, 1(3).

Skiadas, C. (2009). Asset pricing theory. Princeton: Princeton University Press.

Social Security Administration. (2019). *Actuarial life table.* https://www.ssa.gov/oact/STATS/table4c6.html

Sommer, J. (2017). The market is high. beware of portfolio drift. *New York Times.*

Spitznagel, M. (2021). *Safe haven: Investing for financial storms.* New York: Wiley.

Stiglitz, J. (1969). The effects of income, wealth, and capital gains taxation on risk-taking. *Quarterly Journal of Economics, 83*(2), 263–283.

Swensen, D. (2000). *Pioneering portfolio management: An unconventional approach to institutional investment.* New York: Free Press.

Taleb, N. (2001). *Fooled by randomness: The hidden role of chance in life and in the markets.* New York: Random House.

Taleb, N. (2016). *The precautionary principle (with application to the genetic modification of organisms)* (Working Paper Series). NYU School of Engineering.

The White House. (2023). *Office of Management and Budget Circular A-4.*

Thorp, E. (1961). *The game of blackjack.* American Mathematical Society.

Thorp, E. (1966). *Beat the dealer.* New York: Random House Publishing.

Thorp, E. (1969). Optimal gambling systems for favorable games. *Review of the International Statistical Institute, 37*(3), 273–293.

Thorp, E. (1975). Portfolio choice and the Kelly criterion. *Stochastic Optimization Models in Finance,* 599–619.

Tobin, J. (1958). Liquidity preference as behavior towards risk. *Review of Economic Studies, 25*(67), 65–86.

Tobin, J. (1974). What is permanent endowment income? *American Economic Review, 2*(64), 427–432.

Tobin, J. (1996). *Essays in economics; national and international.* Cambridge: The MIT Press.

Treynor, J. (1961). Market value, time, and risk. *SSRN Electronic Journal.*

Tuckman, B. and Serrat, A. (2022). *Fixed income securities: Tools for today's markets.* London: Wiley.

U.S. Department of the Treasury. (2021). *Office of Tax Analysis.* https://home.treasury.gov/policy-issues/tax-policy/office-of-tax-analysis

Vanderbilt, A. (1989). *Fortune's children: The fall of the house of Vanderbilt.* New York: William Morrow & Co.

Vasicek, O. (1977). An equilibrium characterization of the term structure. *Journal of Financial Economics, 5*(2), 177–188.

Villalon, D., Brooks, J., and Tsuji, S. (2019). Superstar investors. *Journal of Investing, 28*(1), 124–135.

Von Neumann, J. and Morgenstern, O. (1944). *Theory of games and economic behavior.* Princeton: Princeton University Press.

White, J. and Rosenbluth, J. (2023). *Merton share derivations.* Elm Wealth.

Wikipedia contributors. (2021). *Allais paradox.* https://en.wikipedia.org/wiki/Allais_paradox

Wikipedia contributors. (2021). *Merton's portfolio problem.* https://en.wikipedia.org/wiki/Merton%27s_portfolio_problem

Wikipedia contributors. (2022). *Gini coefficient*. https://en.wikipedia.org/wiki/Gini_coefficient

Wikipedia contributors. (2022). *Isoelastic utility*. https://en.wikipedia.org/wiki/Isoelastic_utility

Wikipedia contributors. (2022). *Kelly criterion*. https://en.wikipedia.org/wiki/Kelly_criterion.

Wikipedia contributors. (2022). *Wealth Inequality in the United States. https://en.wikipedia.org/wiki/Wealth_inequality_in_the_United_States.*

Wood, G. and Hughes, S. (2015). The central contradiction of capitalism? A collection of essays on capital in the twenty-first century. *Policy Exchange.*

Yale Investment Office. (2019). *2019: The Yale endowment.*

Ziemba, W. (2015). Response to Paul A. Samuelson letters and papers on the Kelly capital growth investment strategy. *Journal of Portfolio Management,* 42(1), 153–167.

Zuckerman, G. (2013). *The frackers.* New York: Portfolio Publishing.

Zuckerman, G. (2019). *The man who solved the market.* New York: Penguin Random House.

Zweig, J. (2008). *Your money and your brain: How the new science of neuroeconomics can help make you rich.* New York: Simon and Schuster.

Zweig, J. (2009). *The little book of safe money: How to conquer killer markets, con artists.* New York: Wiley.

Zweig, J. (2018). What investors can learn from gamblers. *Wall Street Journal.*

Index

Page numbers followed by *e*, *n* and *t* refer to exhibits, footnotes/endnotes and tables, respectively.

Actively managed mutual funds, 215–217
Active managers, 306–307
Active trading, 6, 88
Allais' paradox, 104
Alternative investments, 229–230
Ambiguity aversion, 279, 281
Annuities:
  Constant Standard of Living (CSL) annuities, 237–239
  lifetime (*see* Lifetime annuities)
Annuity puzzle, 166
Anomaly persistence, 220
AQR, 223, 230
Arbitrage pricing theory (APT), 218, 351n7
Arbitrage theories, 116
ARKK, 216–217
Art, 231
Asness, Cliff, 217–218
Asset classes, 201–234
  actively managed mutual funds, 215–217
  alternative investments, 229–230
  art and collectibles, 231
  commodities, 231
  corporate bonds, 212–213
  crypto, 231
  ESG investing, 224
  factor investing, 217–224
  foreign equity markets, 209–210
  index funds, 210–212
  individual stocks, 224–226, 226*e*
  long-term inflation-linked government bonds, 204
  nominal government bills/bonds, 204–205
  options, 227
  real estate, 213–215
  special situation trades, 227–229
  stock markets, 205–208
Average annual return, compound vs., 205–206
Average investor hypothesis, 203
Axioms of rational choice, 74

Bachelier, Louis, 351n6
Bacon, Louis, 61
Bankman-Fried, Sam, 106n
Base-rate fallacy, 221n
Bayesian statistics, 276n
Behavioral economics, 104, 190
Bengen, Bill, 142
Bentham, Jeremy, 116, 176n
Bequest function, 138n
Bequests:
  end-of-life, 169–170
  intergenerational, 182
Berkshire Hathaway, 307
Bernoulli, Daniel, 7, 70–72,
  74, 113
Bernstein, William, 261
Beta, 217n, 351n9
Bezos, Jeff, 131
Bias, home, 209–210
Binary options, 263
Black, Fischer, 201, 351n9, 303
Black Monday, see October 1987
  stock market crash
Black-Scholes-Merton model of
  options pricing, 247
Black-Scholes option pricing
  formula, 39
Bloomberg, 189n, 263
Bogle, John ("Jack"), 64, 209,
  215–216, 246
Bonds. See also Treasury
  Inflation-Protected
  Securities (TIPS)
  annuities vs., 170
  consol, 299
  corporate, 212–213, 228
  and interest rates, 293–294
  municipal, 213
  nominal, 204–205

Booth, David, 217–218
Borrowing, funding spending
  through, 270
Bubbles, 254
Buffett, Warren, 125, 131, 182, 209,
  254, 307, 322
"Buy-borrow-die" approach, 270
Buy vs. rent decision, 214

CAEY (cyclically adjusted earnings
  yield), 345n1
Call options, 197n, 262
Campbell, John, 50n, 52, 150, 151,
  295, 350n8
CAPE (cyclically adjusted
  price-to-earnings
  ratio), 50, 344n1
Capital asset pricing model
  (CAPM), 217, 232, 344n2
Capital gains taxes, 9, 45, 161, 182,
  192, 213, 229, 266–272,
  267t, 269e, 323
Capital in the 21st Century
  (Piketty), 324
Certainty-equivalent Return (CER),
  82–83, 108n, 198, 340
Certainty-equivalent Wealth, 100,
  124, 146, 197, 262,
  267, 268, 306
Choi, James, 7, 100
Choice theory, 74–75
CMH (cost matters hypothesis),
  203, 215
Cochrane, John, 52n
Cognitive biases, 8, 77
Coin-flipping experiment, 6,
  11, 13, 15–25
  description, 16–17
  optimal strategy in, 17–19, 18t

results of, 19–22, 21*e*, 29*t*
stock-market investing vs.,
  23–24
Collectibles, 231
Commodities, 231, 262–263
Competitiveness, of markets, 335
Compound return, average annual
  vs., 205–206
Consolidated annuities (consol
  bonds), 299
Constant absolute betting, 18–19
Constant fractional betting,
  18–21, 24, 28
Constant proportional betting, 24
Constant Proportion Portfolio
  Insurance (CPPI), 184
Constant relative risk-aversion
  (CRRA) utility, 75–79, 76*e*,
  87, 89, 90, 107, 108n, 109,
  109*e*, 113, 114, 340
  adjustments to, 186
  with digital assets, 305*e*
  with endowments, 155, 156
  in investment opportunity
    exercise, 177–178
  and mix of risky assets, 232
  with options, 248, 249
  with retirement spending, 134*t*
Constant Standard of Living (CSL)
  annuities, 237–239
Consumer Price Index (CPI),
  235–237, 239–242
Corporate bonds, 212–213, 228
"Costanza" trade, 258, 309–317
Cost basis, 269
Cost matters hypothesis
  (CMH), 203, 215
Covered-call writing strategies, 256

CPI, *see* Consumer Price Index
CPPI (Constant Proportion
  Portfolio Insurance), 184
CRRA utility, *see* Constant relative
  risk-aversion utility
Cryptocurrencies, 231, 304, 305*e*
CSL (Constant Standard of Living)
  annuities, 237–240, 243
Currency fluctuations, 209
Cyclically adjusted earnings yield
  (CAEY), 344n1
Cyclically adjusted price-to-
  earnings ratio (CAPE),
  50–51, 344n1

Decision-making:
  biases in, 332
  criticisms of expected-utility-
    based, 103–116
  rational and consistent,
    as goal, 104
  under uncertainty, 11
Deferred-income annuities, 171
Defined-contribution savings
  plans, 131
Derivatives, 116
Desire, and risk-taking, 68–69
Dewey, Richard, 6, 16, 22,
  60, 61, 343n1
Digital assets, 231, 304–305,
  305*e*, 307
Diminishing marginal utility of
  consumption, 69
Disability insurance, 198n
Discounted Lifetime Utility, 131n
Discount rate, 208
Dividend-based spending rule,
  161

Doubling down betting, 18, 21

Drag, lift vs., 31–33

Dybvig, Philip, 355n1

Dynamic allocation strategy, 54, 54e, 55e, 59, 61e, 63–64, 337

Dynamic programming, 136

Earnings yield, see Cyclically adjusted price-to-earnings ratio (CAPE)

Efficient markets, definition of, 303

Efficient markets hypothesis (EMH), 203, 215

Ellsberg, Daniel, 279n

Ellsberg puzzle, 279, 280e, 281–282

Elm Wealth, 10, 11, 17, 123

EMH (efficient markets hypothesis), 215

End-of-life bequests, 169–170

"Endowment" economy, 292

Endowments, 149–163
    complex situations affecting, 160–161
    definition of, 150
    dividend-based rule with, 161
    earnings-yield policy with, 161–162
    and family wealth, 161
    future contributions to, 159–160
    optimal spending policy with, 157–158
    smoothed spending policies with, 162
    spending policy options with, 151–154, 151t, 152e, 153t, 154e
    and time preference, 155–156

Epistemic uncertainty, 276

Epstein-Zin preferences, 348n5

Equity-linked annuities, 170

Equity Risk Premium (ERP) puzzle, 291–296

ESG investing, 224

ETFs, 212, 216–217, 221, 258, 309–313, 312e

Exotic options, 263

Expected compound return, 154, 154e

Expected excess return, 160

Expected Lifetime Utility, 8, 130–133, 134t, 135, 142, 144, 145, 201
    with annuities, 169–171
    calculation of, 133, 155
    with endowments, 156–157, 160
    importance of maximizing, 336
    with options, 260
    and sequence of returns, 141
    steps in using, 138

Expected rate of return, 208

Expected Utility, 7–9, 122–126, 320–321, 325. See also Expected Lifetime Utility
    alternative theories to, 115–116
    with annuities, 170
    assumptions needed for analysis using, 122–123, 122t
    and certainty-equivalent return, 82
    and choice theory, 74–75, 79–88, 92, 93, 96–100
    criticisms of, 103–116
    with endowments, 155–157
    and housing-related decisions, 213–215
    and human capital, 194–196, 198

for life and death choices, 115
and lotteries, 288–290
with options, 247, 253
and retirement, 131–132, 141
and risk-aversion, 180
and St. Petersburg paradox, 300–301
and taxation, 266–273
and uncertainty, 282
Expected Utility hypothesis (von Neumann), 104
Expected value, 28, 35
Expected wealth, maximizing, 29–30, 29*t*, 33, 33*t*

Factor investing, 217–224
Factor premia, 219–220
Factors, 218
Fallacy of large numbers, 96–97
Fama, Eugene, 217–218, 351n6, 351n10
Fama-French three-factor model, 221
Family wealth, 161
Financial planning, 129–130
Financial well-being, measuring your, 335–336
Foreign currency fluctuations, 209
Foreign equity markets, 209–210, 262–263
401ks, 131, 272
4% rule, 141–142, 152–153, 336
Fractional Kelly strategies, 113
Franklin, Benjamin, 11, 44, 88
French, Kenneth, 217, 218, 351n10
Friedman, Milton, 103, 187, 298
Friedman-Savage utility curve, 187–188, 187*e*

Future outcomes, unknowability of probabilities of, 111–112

Gamblers, professional, 45
"Gambler's Ruin," 19
Gambling, 105–106
Game theory, 74
Geometric average return, 154, 154*e*
Gifts, taxation of, 182
Gilbert, Daniel, 75, 189
Global Financial Crisis (2008), 228, 241n, 256, 298
Global stock market, 208
Goal, investing to reach a, 98–100
Goal-based approach, 100
Gold, 231
"Goldilocks" bet-sizing, 33, 33*t*, 35
Government bills and bonds, nominal, 204–205
Graham, Benjamin, 50n
Grantor Retained Asset Trusts (GRATs), 272
Great Depression, 256
Gross, Bill, 256
Gutfreund, John, 46

Habits, 188
Haghani, Victor, 3, 4, 6, 16, 21, 22, 38, 46, 60, 61, 86, 105, 106, 117–120, 122–126, 179, 202, 315–316, 324, 328
Half-Kelly, 113–114
Happiness curve, 71–73, 71*e*
Harvard Business School, 5, 118n, 125, 329
Hayek, Friedrich, 298, 351n6
Hedge funds, 117–126, 189n

Hedging demand, 62–63, 145
Hedonic adjustments, 236
Historical returns, 206, 207,
    221–224, 229
A History of Interest Rates
    (Homer), 298
Home, as investment, 213–215
Home bias, 209–210
Home insurance, 251, 252
Homer, Sidney, 298
Home Shopping Network
    (HSN), 315–316
Howard, Alan, 61
Human capital, 124, 193–199, 336
    definition of, 193
    and lifetime spending decisions,
        194–195, 195*e*
    protecting, with life
        insurance, 198
    and retirement, 198–199
    and "stock" vs. "bond" investors,
        195–196
    and young investors, 196–198
Hyperbolic time preference, 190

I Bonds, 227
"Inclusion/exclusion" friction
    (index funds), 212
Income share agreements
    (ISAs), 197–198
Independence axiom, 110
Indexes, 221
Index funds, 210–212
Individual stocks, investing in,
    224–226, 226*e*
Inflation-protected annuities, 173
Inheritances, 161, 169n
Initial public offerings
    (IPOs), 93–94

Institutional investors, 299
Insurance, 7
    home, 251, 252
    life, 198, 272
Insurance companies, 165–166
Interest rate options, 256
Interest rates, 297–301
    and endowments, 150–151
    negative, 297–301
    nominal, 204–205
    nonzero, 292–293
    stability of, 75
    and time preference, 189, 190
Intergenerational bequests, 182
International diversification, 61–62
Inter-temporal framework, 130
IPOs (initial public offerings),
    93–94
IRAs, 131, 272
ISAs (income share agreements),
    197–198
iTunes, 22

Japan, 208, 298
Jensen, M., 351n9
Joint and survivor annuities, 165n
Jones, Paul Tudor, 61
JP Morgan, 228

Kahneman, Daniel, 104, 107–110,
    331, 332
Kelly, John, 37
Kelly betting, 282
Kelly criterion, 37–38, 112–115,
    121, 340
Keynes, John M., 111, 275, 298
Klarman, Seth, 116
Knightian uncertainty, 276
Konnikova, Maria, 32–33

Landsburg, Steven, 94–96

Large numbers, fallacy of, 96–97

Learning, 278–279

Lehman Brothers, 160n

Levine, Matt, 189n, 241n, 263

Lewis, Michael, 5, 46, 118, 320, 328

Liar's Poker (game), 327–333

Liar's Poker (Lewis), 5, 46, 320, 328

Life and death choices, expected utility for, 115

Life expectancy (longevity), 140, 144

Life insurance, 198, 272

Lifetime annuities, 165–172

  and annuity puzzle, 166

  deferred income, 171

  and end-of-life bequests, 169–170

  equity-linked, 170

  inflation-protected, 171

  and longevity risk, 167–169, 167*e*, 168*e*

Lifetime Expected Utility, *see* Expected Lifetime Utility

Lift, drag vs., 31–33

Lintner, John, 232, 344n2

Lo, Andy, 32n

Log-utility function, 71

Longevity risk, 167–170, 167*e*, 168*e*

Long-Term Capital Management (LTCM), 4–5, 117–126, 179, 230, 333

Long-term inflation-linked government bonds, 204

Long-term tax deferral, 62

LOR, 184, 185

Loss aversion, 109

Lottery, playing the, 105, 261–262, 287–289

LTCM, *see* Long-Term Capital Management

Macroeconomic models, 190

Madoff, Bernard, 263

Malkiel, Burton, 64, 246

Marginal tax rates, 229

Market timing, 63–64

Markowitz, Harry, 56, 130, 232, 322, 344n2

"Martingale system," 18

Mayweather, Floyd, 82

Median, 30–33, 91, 114, 152–154, 158

Mehra, R., 292

Mercer, Robert, 45

Meriwether, John, 46–47, 118

Merton, Robert C., 8, 37, 62, 87, 121, 132, 135–136, 151, 158, 160, 243, 348nn2–3, 351n7

Merton optimal spending rule, 158–159, 159*e*

Merton-Samuelson lifetime consumption and portfolio choice framework, 132–141

Merton share, 10, 37–39, 41–47, 53, 53*e*, 62–64, 68, 89–92, 136, 186, 206n, 267, 335

"Middle" wealth, maximizing, 30–31, 31*t*

Milevsky, Moshe, 195

Mill, John Stuart, 103, 116

Miller, Merton, 56, 344n2

Modigliani, Franco, 166

Money pump, 96

Monte Carlo simulations, 99, 142, 197

Morgenstern, Oskar, 74–75, 110

Mortgage-backed securities, 256
Mortgages, 215
Morton, Andrew, 86
Mossin, Jan, 232, 344n2
Municipal bonds, 213
Musk, Elon, 43
Mutual funds, 6, 215–217

Nalebuff, Barry, 196–197
Natural gas, 231
Necktie paradox, 277
Negative risk-aversion, 109
Negative savings rate, 194
Negative time preference, 189
1929 stock market crash, 208
Nominal government bills and
     bonds, 204–205
Nonzero interest rates, 292–293

October 1987 stock market crash
     (Black Monday), 184–185,
     207, 249, 290, 313, 315
Odd lot trade, 227
Oil, 231
Options, 197n, 227, 245–264
  alternative classes of, 262–263
  determining fair price
     for, 254–256
  and equity price drops, 253–254
  exotic, 263
  hedging, 263–264
  interest rate, 256
  and life cycle investing, 260
  as lottery tickets, 261–262
  as portfolio insurance, 251–253
  and portfolio rebalancing, 248–
     251, 248t, 250e
  selling, 256–260
  on single stocks, 260–261

trading in, as zero-sum
     activity, 246
trading volume of, vs. stocks, 245
two-asset case with,
     248–249, 248t
using Expected Utility
     with, 247–248
Outlier events, 23
Out-of-the-money call
     options, 262

Parameter uncertainty, with
     multiple risky assets,
     282–283
Parfit, Derek, 189
Paulson, John, 189n
Perold, André, 118n
Perpetuities, 299, 300e
Perpetuity paradox, 309
"Personal Identity" (Parfit), 189
Personal trading, 63
Personal utility function, 9
Philanthropy, 182–183
Piketty, Thomas, 324
Ponzi schemes, 263
Portfolios:
  asset mix in, 231–233
  options and rebalancing of,
     248–251, 248t, 250e
Powerball, 288
Present value, of an equity
     investment, 208
Price of risk, 83–87, 84e
Private Placement Life Insurance
     (PPLI), 272
Professional gamblers, 45
Prospect theory, 109
Put options, 250e, 252,
     253n, 256–257

Rabin's calibration paradox, 105
Ragulin, Vladimir, 245n
RAR, *see* Risk-adjusted return
Rate of growth, optimizing the, 38
Rational choice, axioms of, 74
Real, after-tax income, 335
Real estate, 213–215
Realized gains, 266–268
Real returns, focusing on, 235
Renaissance Technologies, 45
Renting, buying vs., 214
Residential real estate, 213–215
Retirement, 198–199
Return chasing, 222
Reverse convertibles, 256
Reward-to-variability ratio (R/V
    ratio), 56–57
Risk(s):
  and desire, 68–70
  of factor investing, 223
  importance of calculating, 335
  putting a cost on, 337
  risk-adjusted return and price of,
    83–87, 84*e*
  standard deviation as meas-
    ure of, 34–35
  uncertainty vs., 275–284
Risk-adjusted return (RAR), 90,
    91*e*, 240–242
  endowments, 156–158, 160
  ESG investing, 224
  factor investing, 219
  formula for, 340
  importance of knowing, 335
  mutual funds, 216
  options, 250, 250*e*, 257, 258
  and price of risk, 83–87, 84*e*
  and retirement, 135–137
  and taxation, 268

Risk-aversion, 36–38, 41–42, 69,
    75–79, 86–87, 105–107, 108n,
    109, 113, 114, 179–181, 281,
    292, 319, 335. *See also*
    Constant relative risk-
    aversion (CRRA)
Risk-free assets, 236–237
Risk-neutrality, 106n
Risk parity, 92–94
Risk-seeking, 77, 106,
    187–188, 187*e*
Rosenbluth, Jeffrey, 332n
Ross, Stephen, 351n7, 355n1
Rumsfeld, Donald, 276
Russia, 207, 241, 252

"SafeMax" withdrawal rate, 142
St. Petersburg Paradox, 7, 70, 72,
    73*t*, 74, 75, 111, 278, 301
Salomon Brothers, 5, 46, 118–121,
    347n1, 278, 289, 298, 315–316,
    327, 328, 331–333
Samuelson, Paul, 8, 344n2, 96–98,
    100, 103, 113, 132,
    135–136, 351n6
Satisficing, 104n
Savage, Jimmie, 104, 187
Saving:
  negative vs. positive rates of, 194
  regulation of, 337
Savings crisis, 166
Scholes, Myron, 32n, 351n9
Schwager, Jack, 61
Schwed, Fred, Jr., 117, 260
Seinfeld, 309–310
Separation theorem, 231–232
Series I Savings bonds, 171
Sharpe, William, 56,
    215–216, 344n2

Sharpe ratio, 54, 56–60, 62, 82,
    89–92, 177, 232, 247,
    255, 263, 304
Sharpe's arithmetic, 215
Shiller, Robert, 240, 295
Sizing, 4–6
    "Goldlocks" bet-sizing,
        33–34, 33t, 35
    and lift vs. drag, 31–33
    of stock market exposure, for the
        long term, 313–314
Skew, 63
Smart Beta strategies, 217, 219
Smith, Adam, 72
Smoothed spending policies, 162
Social Security, 6
Soros, George, 61
S&P 500, see Standard & Poor's 500
SpaceX, 43
Special situation trades, 227–229
Spending, regulation of, 337
Spreadsheets, using, 10
Standard deviation:
    and "Goldlocks" bet-sizing, 36
    as measure of risk, 34–35
    in Sharpe ratio, 57
Standard & Poor's 500 (S&P 500),
    143t, 257, 258, 260,
    307, 311–313
Stern report, 156
Stock market crashes, 207. See also
    specific crashes
Stock markets, 205–209. See also
    US stock market
Stock pickers (stock picking), 211,
    212, 215–216, 224,
    246, 307, 335
Stocks:
    options on single, 260–261

    trading volume of, vs.
        options, 245
    volatile, 226, 226e
Streetlight Effect, 202n
Stumbling on Happiness (Gilbert), 75
Style premia, 219
Suboptimal betting, 20
Subsistence spending, 140,
    183–186, 184e
Sustainable spending rule, 158–159
Swensen, David, 107, 150, 162

Tail hedging, 255
Tail risk, negative, 228
Taleb, Nassim Nicholas, 23, 118
Target Date funds, 64
Tax deferral, 213
Tax efficiency, 62
Taxes (taxation), 265–273
    capital gains, effect of, 268–269
    and Expected Utility
        framework, 272
    and family wealth, 161
    of gifts, 182
    optimized allocation with unreal-
        ized gains, 270–271
    and realized gains, 266–268
    and risk-return trade-off, 266
Tax-inefficient investments, 229
Tax loss harvesting, 271
T-bills, see US Treasury bills
1031 exchanges, 273
Tesla, 43–44, 226, 262
Thorp, Edward O., 24, 45
Time horizon, in Merton Share
    formula, 45–46
Time preference, 133, 135–137,
    146, 155–159, 349n5,
    189–190, 292, 294–295, 298

"Times Series Momentum"
(Moskowitz et al.), 60
Tobin, James, 154, 155,
231–232, 344n2
Tobin's Q, 59
"Trading Can Be Hazardous to
Your Health" (Barber
and Odean), 6
Trading state claims, 293
Treasury bills, *see* US Treasury bills
Treasury Inflation-Protected
Securities (TIPS), 52–56, 54e,
171, 204, 227, 231, 234, 234n,
237–239, 241, 336
A Treatise on Probability
(Keynes), 275
Treynor, Jack, 232, 344n2
Trump, Donald J., 297
Turnover, and tax efficiency, 62
Tversky, Amos, 104, 107–110,
331, 332
Twitter, 43
Two-asset world model, 43
Two envelopes paradox, 277–278

Uncertainty, risk vs., 275–284
United Kingdom, 156,
298, 299, 301
Unrealized gains, 270–271
US stock market, 4, 23–24, 55e, 294
and expected utility, 85–86
1929 crash, 252
1987 crash, 184–185, 207,
249, 290, 314
probability of 90%
declines in, 123
realized return of, since 1900, 43
return distribution of, 112
US Treasury, 227

US Treasury bills (T-bills), 23, 142,
205, 225, 228, 231, 237–238,
255, 257, 314, 314t, 345n4
US Treasury bonds, 50,
125, 212–213
Utility. *See also* Expected Utility
and certainty-equivalence, 82–83
definition of, 72
usefulness of, as concept, 107
and wealth, 72, 181–182, 188–189
Utility function(s), 7–8
and choice theory, 74–75
suite of, 75–78, 76e

"Value and Momentum
Everywhere" (Asness
et al.), 60
Vanderbilt, Cornelius, 1, 2, 183, 324
Vanguard, 64, 170
Variable annuities, 170
Viceira, Luis, 52
VIX volatility index, 259, 353n9
Volatile stocks, 225, 226e
Volatility drag, 32–33, 153, 206,
225, 311, 312, 314, 315
Volatility-premium-harvesting
strategy, 259
Von Mises, Ludwig, 298
Von Neumann, John,
74–75, 104, 110

Wall Street Bets (online group), 261
Wealth, 319–325
certainty-equivalent, 306
inequality of, 324–325
measures of, 127
and subsistence spending,
183–186, 184e
and utility, 72, 181–182, 188–189

Where Are the Customers' Yachts?
(Schwed), 117, 260
White, James, 5, 69
"Why Do People Pay for
Useless Advice?"
(Powdthavee), 25
Winfrey, Oprah, 127
Wood, Cathy, 216–217

www.elmwealth.com, 10

Yale University, 7, 100, 150,
153–154, 159, 162,
349n1, 196
Yield to maturity, 9, 51, 298n

Ziemba, William, 283